Correctional Counseling and Treatment

Second Edition

Peter C. Kratcoski
Kent State University

WAVELAND
PRESS, INC.

Prospect Heights, Illinois

For information about this book, write or call:
Waveland Press, Inc.
P.O. Box 400
Prospect Heights, Illinois 60070
(708) 634-0081

Table of Contents

10 Correctional Treatment: Past, Present and Future 387

Preface

Correctional Counseling and Treatment, Second Edition, was written with two distinct purposes in mind—to provide the reader with material on a number of treatment techniques currently being used in American corrections and to describe and demonstrate the applicability of these treatment techniques in correctional settings.

No attempt was made to include every counseling and treatment method currently in use. Rather, the author concentrated on the most widely used techniques, and chose to describe and discuss those that can be applied to juveniles and adults in both institutional and community settings.

The scope and purposes of correctional treatment today and methods of evaluating correctional treatment are considered in the opening chapters. A key element in the controversy that has arisen over the comparative effectiveness of various treatment is the fact that the *purpose* of correctional treatment has come to be regarded as prevention of recidivism. Many staff members who administer correctional treatment programs maintain that the goals of correctional treatment must be more broadly defined, and that successful treatment should be measured not only in terms of lack of recidivism, but also by such progress as improved mental health, ability to perform adequately in a work situation, successful adjustment in the community, and appropriate handling of interpersonal relationships. These factors take on increased importance when considered against the background of "self-reported criminal activity" studies, which have repeatedly revealed that a high proportion of the adult population has committed acts that were criminal in nature and could have led to arrest and/or conviction. Court personnel must also be aware of court decisions and innovative proposals in their field.

Chapter 3 is devoted to career opportunities in corrections today and the characteristics and unique problems of those involved in correctional work. The selections included were chosen to reflect the problems and patterns of development of correctional personnel and also to describe new approaches to dealing with the stresses of correctional work.

In Chapter 4, "Classification for Correctional Treatment," the many facets of an offender's case (age, sex, family history, offense record, results of psychological and educational testing, physical health, presentence investigation, and reports by social and correctional workers) that may have a bearing on the type of treatment chosen are explored. Various classification systems developed, implemented and evaluated by experts in the field are described.

Chapters 5, 6, 7, and 8 are devoted to detailed descriptions of various correctional treatment techniques, including crisis intervention, reality therapy and responsibility training, behavior modification, and group counseling. Each chapter includes an introductory section which defines the treatment method considered and explores the key issues related to its use. The first selection in each chapter describes the treatment technique, its theoretical basis, and methods for implementing it. The remaining selections in each chapter were chosen to present applications of the technique to various offender populations or to present the applications in contrasting settings.

Chapter 9 presents the problems and unique situations which arise when counselors are working with retarded or mentally ill offenders, sex offenders, or substance abusers. The selections in this chapter provide many practical suggestions for working with such problem clients and describe programs which have been applied effectively.

Chapter 10 summarizes the successes and problems of correctional treatment and highlights innovations in correctional supervision and administration, including the use of electronic monitors and privatization of correctional services.

No attempt is made here to discuss the relative merits of various counseling and treatment techniques or to compare the effectiveness of community and institutional programs. Instead, the techniques are presented in such a manner that they can be applied in either type of correctional setting, with juvenile or adult offenders, or adapted to deal with the adjustment problems of members of the "normal" (noncriminal) population.

Counseling and treatment techniques cannot be considered without reference to those who apply them. A number of selections in this book report the efforts frustrations, styles, reactions, and learning experiences of correctional personnel engaged in treatment.

Presentation of the wide range of correctional counseling and treatment techniques described here would not have been possible without the cooperation of the many contributing authors and their publishers. In addition, the encouragement and support of Neil Rowe helped make this book a reality.

1 The Scope and Purposes of Correctional Treatment

This book is designed to present and describe some of the counseling and treatment techniques that are available to assist correctional workers toward accomplishing the goals they have established for their work. These goals are broadly defined as (1) to assist the offender to establish a lifestyle that is personally satisfying and conforms to the rules and regulations of society and (2) to protect the community from harmful activity by offenders placed under the correctional workers' supervision. These dual demands of correctional work—to provide assistance, counseling, and treatment and, at the same time, to act in a manner that will minimize the offender's threat to the community—are present for correctional workers who serve as youth counselors, guards, probation officers, juvenile aftercare supervisors, parole officers, social workers, psychologists, or coordinators of educational or employment programs.

In the view of many, correctional counseling and treatment is associated with employment by a government agency (federal, state or local) which has the responsibility to control offenders. While this description is accurate for the majority of individuals who work with delinquent and criminal offenders, there has been a significant trend in recent years toward contracting correctional or counseling services with private agencies or corporations. As a result, many of the professionals who work with offenders have credentials in fields other than criminal justice and corrections, including psychology, rehabilitation counseling, education, sociology, and social work.

Occupations which involve some contact with offenders through counseling or treatment activity also include parole officer, child welfare caseworker, recreation leader, social group worker, academic teacher, vocational instructor, correctional counselor, and psychiatrist.

Traditionally, the correctional worker's role was viewed as one of supportive assistance and surveillance-supervision. The correctional worker had to balance these two facets of the role and decide whether allowing certain behavior to occur was in the best interests of the offender or of the residents of the community. Today, the roles of correctional workers, particularly those who work in community settings, have become more complex. The expertise needed to provide the appropriate types of counseling, therapy, or treatment appropriate for certain offenders may be beyond the scope of a single professional's training. For example, offenders who have problems with alcohol or drug abuse, sexual deviance, mental retardation, or violent behavior may require widely divergent types of counseling and therapy. Thus, a very important function of correctional counseling today is assessment, classification, and referral activity. In many instances, a correctional counselor must be aware of the possibilities for referral and make decisions as to the most appropriate therapy, rather than attempt to personally provide specialized types of counseling to the offenders. The ambiguities and pressures associated with such decision making are documented and discussed by various authors in this book.

Defining Correctional Treatment

When correctional treatment is discussed, terms such as humanitarian reform, corrections, rehabilitation, and treatment are often used interchangeably, creating some confusion as to just what correctional treatment involves. Also at issue is the part played by incarceration and mandatory supervision in the correctional treatment process.

Humanitarian reforms are usually thought of in terms of what directly benefits and affects the physical welfare of the offender. Such initial modifications of the penal system as elimination of long periods of solitary confinement, flogging, or bread-and-water diets obviously fall within this definition, as do more contemporary changes that allow prisoners to wear personal clothing rather than uniforms and provide recreational facilities for inmates. Such liberal practices as allowing attendance at college classes outside the institution, weekend home visits for selected prisoners, or providing opportunities for conjugal visitation within the prisons or social contacts between male and female inmates have caused some critics to observe that humanitarian reforms have gone too far and that the "country club" atmosphere of many institutions has minimized or virtually eliminated the impact of incarceration as punishment. Such thinking ignores or downplays the importance of personal motivation as an important factor in correctional treatment.

As implied in the word itself, "corrections" means to change a condition that is considered to be undesirable or has been a mistake and to bring things back to a state that is considered desirable or appropriate. In the correctional process, measures are taken to change the behavior of the offender to that which conforms with the standards and laws of the society. Corrections involves care, custody, and supervision of convicted offenders who have been sentenced or whose sentences have been suspended. The correctional process can occur in a federal or state correctional institution; as part of parole from such an institution; in a local jail or workhouse; or as part of probation at the federal, state, or local level. With the advent of diversion, pretrial intervention, deferred prosecution, and similar types of programs, it is logical to say that corrections has an opportunity to occur at any stage within the criminal justice process after a contact has been made between the offender and a law enforcement official.

The primary goal of corrections is to change the offensive behavior of the offender to a behavior that is designated appropriate by the laws of society. Before the eighteenth century, punishment was considered the central ingredient of corrections in European countries;

thus, the dispensation of justice involved some form of physical torture or mutilation, banishment, or enslavement in galleys or on work farms. Prisons were used almost exclusively for those awaiting trial and for political prisoners. It was not until the eighteenth century that Cesare Beccaria (1738–1794) proposed the *pleasure-pain principle*—that is, that punishments should only be severe enough to deter offenders from repeating their unacceptable behavior.[1] At the same time, Jeremy Bentham (1748–1832) expounded his theory of *utilitarianism* in England. Both Beccaria and Bentham assumed that, given a free choice, a reasonable person would choose to avoid behavior for which he was sure to be punished. Bentham envisioned the prison as a correctional institution, located within the community, where citizens who had chosen to violate the law would be punished, while others would view it as a daily reminder of the penalties for violation of the law.[2] The idea that the punishment should "fit the crime" became an accepted part of correctional practice and various types of prisons and workhouses were built for the express purpose of being correctional centers or "houses of correction."

In the above context, "correction" did not include rehabilitation as a key component. As time passed it became apparent that punishment alone did not guarantee a reduction in the criminal behavior of offenders, and there was gradual acceptance of the notion that those who would be eventually returned to society must be given some guidance and opportunities that would lead them toward a socially acceptable future life style. Thus, while present-day "corrections" is not synonymous with "rehabilitation," it is very closely linked to it. Rehabilitation activity is set in motion when an individual comes to the attention of the correctional system after conviction. Such rehabilitation is involuntary in the sense that the offender has not actually sought it, but is rather required to undergo certain therapies, engage in counseling, or follow specified courses of action.

According to Francis A. Allen, the theoretical basis of rehabilitation is a complex of ideas that assumes human behavior to be a product of antecedent causes which are in turn part of the physical-social environment. This idea also presupposes that, given knowledge of the causes of human behavior, it is possible to scientifically control human behavior. Measures designed to treat the convicted offender should therefore serve a therapeutic function and should effect changes in his behavior that will be in his own best interests.[3]

The notion of correctional rehabilitation as a return to a point in an individual's development when his behavior was satisfactory has been challenged by those who have observed that many offenders never experience anything in their lives resembling satisfactory adjustment, and that such persons are candidates for "habilitation" rather than *re*habilitation. "Habilitation" here would refer to familiarity with and adjustment to normal society and the holding of values in line with the norms and laws of the community. Correctional work concerned with "habilitation" could well involve attack on the causes of an individual's poor adjustment to society (family problems, unemployment, lack of education) in addition to guidance toward acceptable behavior.

Correctional treatment, then, can be defined as any planned and monitored program of activity that has the goal of rehabilitating or "habilitating" the offender so that he or she will avoid criminal activity in the future.

The Effectiveness of Correctional Treatment

In *Correctional Counseling and Treatment*, we will explore the many ways in which correctional treatment may be attempted, and note points of disagreement, controversy, or even diametric opposition in the approaches advocated.

No individual type of treatment has proved to be a panacea for reducing criminal activity. During the past twenty years, a debate has raged regarding the possibility that correctional treatment may be ineffective in reducing recidivism (additional criminal behavior) by those who receive it. If this is true, should correctional treatment attempts be abandoned, or is lack of recidivism by offenders the only factor to be considered in assessing treatment success? Is partially successful adjustment of the offender to his or her social environment justification for providing correctional treatment, even if some recidivism does occur? We must also consider another question that has gained considerable attention in recent years—is the application of correctional treatment better or more effective in changing offenders' behavior than doing nothing at all? If the answer is negative, should we revert to a punishment-centered correctional philosophy?

Punishment vs. Treatment

In *We Are the Living Proof*, Fogel noted that two camps developed in regard to the advisability of undertaking rehabilitative correctional treatment with all types of offenders. One side, disillusioned by revelations of the inadequacy of policies in criminal justice and corrections, and buttressed in its arguments by high crime rates, citizens' fear of crime, and the apparent ineffectiveness of correctional treatment in preventing recidivism, advocated a very punitive, severe sentencing approach. The opposite camp had not given up on the possibilities of effective correctional rehabilitative treatment, but contended that the failure of correctional policies and programs was linked to inadequate resources, poorly trained personnel, political interference, and the existence of huge, brutalizing and dehumanizing prisons, which were schools for crime. This group was convinced that, with improvements in these areas, attempts at rehabilitative correctional treatment could still be successful.

Between these two points of view, Fogel saw an approach that would place renewed emphasis on an offender's responsibility and accountability for his or her actions, coupled with an emphasis on rehabilitative treatment that is *available* but not *mandatory*. Fogel termed this the "justice model for corrections." In this model, "justice as fairness should be the goal of all attempts at corrections, and all agencies of criminal law should perform their assigned tasks with offenders lawfully."[4] Fogel addressed the area of the offender's responsibility for his actions and noted that restitution might often be substituted for harsh punishment, depending on the nature of the offense. He suggested an alternative to indeterminate sentences (1-3 years, for example). In their place, Fogel advocated a return to "flat time," a set length of time in prison, which could be shortened only by good time (lawful behavior) credit, not by participation in any sort of treatment program.[5]

In applying the justice model to the prison, Fogel noted that time in a prison is an "enforced deprivation of liberty" and that opportunities for self-improvement should be offered but not made a condition of freedom."[6] Those in charge of the prisoners have the obligation to treat them in a lawful and just manner. Being in prison in itself is a form of punishment, and out of humanitarian concerns correctional personnel should avoid adding to the burden of loss of freedom and dignity which the incarcerated person experiences merely by being there.

As Fogel saw the justice model, in order to learn responsibility and be able to accept prison, inmates would be given some degree of self-governance or be part of an inmate-staff governance group. Conflicts within the institution would be resolved through rule of law, and prisoners would be given opportunities for legal aid, while an ombudsman would oversee the activities of both inmates and staff. Counseling and self-help and improvement programs would be available, but not required; and taking part in them would not help determine the inmate's readiness for release. Work programs would involve the inmate being paid for his work in wages that would be commensurate with what he would receive on the outside. In turn, the inmate would be required to compensate the institution for lodging and food, pay taxes, send allotments to his family, and pay restitution to the victims of his crime.[7]

This justice model which emphasizes responsibility under the law, could reasonably be applied in programs outside institutions, including probation, parole, and community residential programs.

In the late 1970s and throughout the 1980s, the obligation to provide offenders with treatment was debated. Some correctional specialists and legal scholars advocated a return to a punishment model, believing that this approach might be the most productive manner of changing the criminal's behavior. Others, while not abandoning the notion of treatment as an essential ingredient in the correctional process, seriously questioned the effectiveness of treatment and counseling approaches which were being used in institutional and community correctional settings.

In the correctional activity, particularly in an institutional setting, certain standards must be met and services provided. This is true for jails, juvenile detention centers, and longer term institutions for juveniles and adults. Thus, such activities as exercise, some recreation, opportunities for attendance at religious services, and provision of adequate diet and medical care are associated with humanitarian reforms, but also tie in directly with the rehabilitation process. Beyond these, the legal mandate to provide treatment is less clear.

For juveniles, the right to treatment was established in *Morales v. Turman*, a Texas case in which two juvenile institutions were ordered closed because of brutal handling of juveniles and lack of documented treatment there.[8] The court ordered that a community based system of treatment be developed in place of the institutions, and held that the "normal needs" of a youth must be met as part of the treatment program. These needs were defined by the court as "a sense of self-respect, warm and understanding adults, a chance to participate in decisions that affect him, adequate diet and recreation, opportunity for adventure and challenge, and legitimate outlets for tension, anger, and anxiety."[9] The court also stated that a juvenile must feel free from physical and psychological abuse, understand what is expected of him, and what the treatment plan hopes to achieve.[10]

For adults, treatment has been closely allied with indeterminate sentencing, with release contingent upon performance in the institution and evidence of rehabilitation. This interdependency has come under fire in recent years, and many states have abandoned indeterminate sentencing in favor of determinate or flat sentencing, which mandates a minimum amount of time to be served and does not make release contingent upon participation in various forms of correctional treatment. Adult prisoners may be "warehoused" for their prescribed sentences, and need not be offered treatment or required to participate in it.

Such proposals as the justice model and flat sentencing seem to indicate that correctional thinking may have come full circle and be about to return to the "pleasure-pain" ideas of Beccaria and Bentham, with emphasis on punishments severe enough to be deterrents to crime so that an individual makes a free choice to be law abiding or a lawbreaker in the light of this knowledge. Correctional treatment, in such a context, may emerge as a "privilege" which is not the offender's right, but which may be accorded to him or requested by him.

In most community or institutional corrections situations, the matter of choosing or rejecting treatment is not so extreme. Juvenile corrections continues to provide a range of counseling, education, vocational development and treatment services. On the adult level, those on probation or parole or placed in community rehabilitation facilities discover that involvement in substance abuse counseling, employment counseling, or family therapy is likely to be required as a condition of placement in this status. Even those serving determinate sentences may elect to take part in correctional counseling or treatment as a matter of choice. Correctional counseling and treatment continue to be vital aspects of correctional work.

Notes

1. Edwin H. Sutherland and Donald R. Cressey, *Criminology* (Philadelphia: Lippincott, 1974), p. 50.

2. Sue Titus Reid, *Crime and Criminology* (Hinsdale, Ill.: Dryden Press, 1976), p. 106.

3. Francis A. Allen, "Legal Values and the Rehabilitative Ideal," in *The Borderland of Criminal Justice* (Chicago: University of Chicago Press, 1964), pp. 25–41.

4. David Fogel, " . . . *We Are the Living Proof* . . . " (Cincinnati: Anderson Publishing, 1975), p. 184.

5. Ibid., p. 247.
6. Ibid., p. 204.
7. Ibid., p. 261.
8. *Morales* v. *Turman*, 364 F. Supp. 166 (1963).
9. Ibid.
10. Ibid.

2 Evaluation of Correctional Treatment

Introduction

In this era of tightening state and federal budgets and emphasis on cost efficiency and fiscal accountability, any treatment program extensive enough to seek state or federal funding must contain some provision for evaluation. Quarterly statistical reports, which concentrate on numbers of clients served, hours worked by staff, estimates of the number of community members affected directly or indirectly by the program, and recidivism rates of the clients are familiar to those involved in correctional treatment. It has become very important to examine whether a certain type of treatment works as well as or better than another type, and whether clients given a specific mode of therapy or supervision adjust in the community or remain offense-free more frequently than those given another type of treatment or no treatment at all.

Producing a meaningful and effective evaluation of any type of treatment program is beset with problems. It is difficult and often impractical to establish control groups with which those receiving treatment can be meaningfully compared, and there is concern about the ethics of giving treatment to some offenders and withholding it from others for the sole purpose of comparative research. The short length of time between the initiation of the program and the first evaluation report frequently makes it difficult to establish comparative experimental and control groups. The ideals of random placement of those treated in experimental or control groups, or even matching of offender populations ac-

11

cording to age, number of prior offenses, or background characteristics must frequently give way to less meaningful comparisons. For example, the current residents of a halfway house that has a new job-training or employment-education program may be compared with those who resided in the house before the program began, with regard to their ability to get and hold jobs. In such an instance, changes in economic conditions within the community between the two time periods may be sharp enough to render the validity of such a comparison questionable.

Evaluation may also be colored by the personal biases or characteristics of the evaluators. Internal evaluations are particularly prone to this type of problem, since those in charge are anxious to show that the program is succeeding and that they are doing a good job. Outside consultants also lean toward showing that the program is successful, since payment for their services in the future obviously hinges upon continuation and refunding of the program. The subjects of a treatment program may also behave in such a way as to color its results. If, for example, subjects are aware that they are involved in a new or experimental program, they may do everything in their power to make sure it appears to succeed—or may sabotage it, if they dislike the demands made upon them.

Another problem in program design is formulation of a definition of "success." The indicator chosen most often to measure the success of correctional treatment is amount or rate of recidivism. Even on this point evaluation cannot be precise, because the recidivism (new offense) statistics are available only for those offenders who have been arrested and do not necessarily include all unlawful behavior that has occurred following correctional treatment. The level of supervision given to those who complete treatment is an important consideration in the amount of recidivism reported, particularly if violations tabulated as "new offenses" are probation or parole violations.

Also, the length of time covered by recidivism measurements has a bearing on the effectiveness evaluation. For example, the Highfields experiment in guided group interaction was declared a success because the recidivism rates one year after its completion were much lower for the experimental group than for a comparison group. After two years had passed, however, the variations in levels of recidivism between the two groups were greatly reduced.

If measures other than recidivism rates are used for purposes of evaluation, the problem of bias by the evaluators increases. Such instruments as personal adjustment checklists and case reports by probation or parole officers, which report the offender's readjustment to the community or degree of effort put forth in working on solutions to his or her problems, are obviously colored by the reporter's reaction to the offender.

Even when a program has been judged to be successful by what appear to be objective evaluators and firm criteria, the reasons for its success may lie in the dedication or ability of the program's directors or workers or in certain ethnic or environmental characteristics of those being treated, and the program's replicability in other settings proves difficult.

The matters of correctional treatment and the possibilities for rehabilitation of offenders came under scrutiny in the 1970s, when Robert Martinson, a sociology professor, wrote a series of articles in *The New Republic* which described and commented on his extensive examination of correctional treatment programs in English speaking countries in the years 1945 through 1967. While the evidence presented in these articles was grounded in empirical research and eventually published in the book, *The Effectiveness of Correctional Treatment* (1975), by Douglas Lipton, Robert Martinson, and Judith Wilks, their conclusion that "with few and isolated exceptions, the rehabilitative efforts that have been reported so far have no appreciable effect on recidivism,"[1] aroused a furor in correctional circles. Those who felt that the criminal justice system had gone too far in terms of protecting the rights and interests of offenders at the expense of the victims of crime seized upon the study's conclusion, simplified it to contend "nothing works" to change the behavior of criminals, and used this contention as the basis for calls for harsher treatment of offenders.

It is true that Martinson painted a gloomy picture of

the possibilities for rehabilitation success. In his article, "What Works?—Questions and Answers About Prison Reform," (1974), he reported the specific types of programs which he had evaluated and found lacking in success in preventing recidivism. The types included academic education, social skill development, vocational education, individual counseling, group counseling, and even milieu therapy, which used every element of the inmate's environment as part of the treatment modality. After reviewing many community treatment programs administered in halfway houses or as part of probation or parole activity, the author stated: "In some, even in the case of treatment programs administered outside penal institutions, we simply cannot say that this treatment in itself has an appreciable effect on offender behavior."[2] On the basis of his examination of more than 200 programs of correctional treatment involving hundreds of thousands of offenders, Martinson stated that, although instances of success or partial success were noted, no pattern emerged to indicate that any method of treatment was effective in reducing recidivism.[3]

There is no doubt that *The Effectiveness of Correctional Treatment*, popularly known as "The Martinson Report," had a strong impact. The trends toward nonintervention, extension of probation to all but the most hardened juvenile offenders, placement of offenders in community residential treatment rather than in institutions, calls for determinate sentences, and shifts in emphasis in many correctional programs to punishment rather than rehabilitation closely followed circulation of the view that "nothing works" or that very little can be done to change the behavior or offense patterns of juveniles or adults who have been involved in offenses serious enough to warrant their formal handling by the justice system.

Stuart Adams, in a review and critique of Martinson's research, observed that academicians as well as administrators and politicians may cloud the real issues and findings with rhetoric. He noted that before *The Effectiveness of Correctional Treatment* (the book which detailed the research) appeared, Martinson's articles in *The New Republic* and his appearance on the television program "60 Minutes" created a good deal of public interest in his findings. Efforts to capsulize them for popular consumption resulted in their simplification into what might be termed the "Nothing Works Doctrine," which became a rallying point for those interested in changing the focus and direction of correctional policy.

When Adams systematically compared the evaluations of specific programs cited in *The Effectiveness of Correctional Treatment* with evaluations of the same programs by other researchers, he found considerable variations in the conclusions reached regarding the effectiveness of the programs. For example, Palmer reported that 40% of the 231 program evaluations in *The Effectiveness of Correctional Treatment* showed at least partial positive results, and termed them "partially or fully successful," while Martinson characterized the same programs as "few and isolated" instances of success. In addition, Adams concluded that the key factor in programs that achieved some success was the change agent—the rare individual who could inspire, goad, coax, frighten, or bully an offender enough to make him or her want to change.[4]

Martinson continued to explore the degree of success of correctional treatment programs. In the article, "New Findings, New Views: A Note of Caution Regarding Sentencing Reform," he reported the results of additional research, which included not only evaluative research studies, which matched control groups with the experimental groups receiving treatment, but also studies that reported on the progress of groups of more than nine sentenced offenders. Believing that the term "recidivism" was a confusing one, Martinson developed the notion of "reprocessing" in his later studies, with "reprocessing" defined as "subjecting an offender to further arrest, conviction, or imprisonment." Based on his new information, from 555 studies, Martinson retreated from his earlier conclusion that "with few and isolated exceptions, the rehabilitative effects that have been reported so far have no appreciable effect on recidivism." Instead, he declared that some programs were beneficial, others were neutral (had no impact), and still others were detrimental. He identified the key factor in the success of treatment programs as the "conditions under which the program is delivered."[5]

In Selection 1, "The 'Effectiveness' Issue Today: An Overview," Ted Palmer reviews the debate sparked by Martinson's findings, and concludes that two quite divergent points of view regarding the effectiveness of correctional treatment emerged in the late 1980s. Those who belong to the "skeptical" camp either have concluded that rehabilitation should be given a minor role because it holds little promise or that the research into its effectiveness or the implementation of rehabilitation programs have been so flawed that we still do not know if it can work. In contrast, Palmer's "sanguine" camp holds that some programs have been shown to work with certain offenders, even though many or most offenders will not be positively affected, or that the specific approach and external conditions are the key factors which dictate whether offenders will respond positively, neutrally, or negatively to treatment programs. He identifies intensive applications of "multiple modality" approaches, which combine various types of counseling or training and distribution of treatment and counseling according to the needs, interest, and limitations of individual offenders rather than to the total offender population, as areas where both camps agree efforts should be concentrated.

While the debate over the effectiveness of correctional treatment has not resulted in the total demise of treatment programs, it has had the positive effect of making those responsible for administering correctional treatment more selective in the types of treatment offered. The faddishness which was associated with earlier choices of treatment, with many techniques used experimentally because they appeared to offer novel approaches, has disappeared. Administrators and program directors now have to reach some degree of conviction that a treatment technique has long term merit before it is instituted.

Notes

1. Robert Martinson, "What Works? Questions and Answers About Prison Reform," *Public Interest* (Spring 1974): 25.

2. Ibid, 50-51.

3. Ibid, 54.

4. Stuart Adams, "Evaluation: A Way Out of Rhetoric," in Robert Martinson, Ted Palmer, and Stuart Adams, *Rehabilitation, Recidivism, and Research,* Washington, D.C., National Council of Crime and Delinquency, 1976, 75-91.

5. Robert Martinson, "New Findings, New Views: A Note of Caution Regarding Sentencing Reform," *Hofstra Law Review,* 7,2 (Winter 1979), 243-58.

The "Effectiveness" Issue Today: An Overview

Ted Palmer

In 1974, a wide-ranging debate regarding the effectiveness of rehabilitation was launched by Robert Martinson's assertion that nothing or almost nothing works. [18] Since then, rebuttals and counter-rebuttals have been exchanged and, in the process, some light has been shed though considerable heat and haze remain. This process has been difficult but necessary; and though "sides" are still sharply drawn, the justice system may soon reap some benefits from the exchange. What, then, is the current status of this debate, and what are its emerging trends?

The overview that follows derives primarily from several major works conducted during 1966-1980. Chief among these are reviews and evaluations by: Adams; Bailey; Empey; Gendreau and Ross; Greenberg; Lipton, Martinson, and Wilks (LMW); Martinson; the National Academy of Sciences Panel; Palmer; Romig; Wilson; Wright and Dixon. [1; 3; 6; 7; 10; 14; 18; 20; 21; 23; 24; 26; 27] These efforts focused on experimental studies of juvenile and adult offenders in institutional as well as community settings. Each such category of offender and setting was well-represented in the studies reviewed, as were the major, traditional, rehabilitation methods (individual and group counseling; vocational and educational training; etc.); other, less common interventions were also included. Most such methods were implemented under non-voluntary conditions and—in the case of institutional programs—in an indeterminate-sentence context. Though the studies which were reviewed related to minor as well as serious or multiple offenders, the present overview will emphasize the implications of those reviews for the latter individuals. Throughout, the central question will be: Does rehabilitation work?

To address this question we will focus on programs that were judged successful or unsuccessful because—whatever else they did or did not

Reprinted by permission from *Federal Probation*, 47 (2) (June 1983): 3-10.

accomplish with their target group—they either did or did not reduce recidivism. Use of recidivism is consistent with our view that the ultimate goal of rehabilitation is increased public protection. *Clearly,* rehabilitation efforts may also produce successful or desirable outcomes with respect to attitude-change, skill development, and various aspects of community adjustment, and these as well as other outcomes often do—but often do not—relate to recidivism. Nevertheless, for present purposes, the central criterion of success or effectiveness will be the reduction of illegal behavior—arrests, convictions, and related actions. This criterion was also used in the reviews mentioned above.

As discussed in this overview, rehabilitation or habilitation includes a wide range of interventions whose principal as well as ultimate goal is the increased protection of society. This, the *socially centered* goal of rehabilitation, is achieved when the offender's behavior is modified so that it conforms to the law. It is promoted but not in itself achieved by modifying given attitudes, by strengthening the offender as an individual, by reducing various external pressures and increasing given supports or opportunities, and/or by helping him or her become more satisfied and self-fulfilled within the context of society's values. Attitude-change, increased coping ability, etc., comprise the secondary or *offender-centered* goal of rehabilitation. Though this goal has absolute value in itself, it is—from the perspective of the overall justice system and this system's function in society—chiefly a "means" to the socially centered "end" of public protection. [20]

Before proceeding, let us briefly indicate what we mean by the phrase "rehabilitation program or approach." The following is not a formal, exhaustive identification of rehabilitation or habilitation; however, for present purposes, it will suffice.

The primary and secondary goals of rehabilitation are achieved by focusing on such factors and conditions as the offender's present adjustment techniques, his interests and skills, his limitations, and/or his life-circumstances, in ways that affect his future behavior and adjustment. Rehabilitation efforts are thus focused on particular factors or conditions and are directed toward particular future events. Insofar as they involve specific components or inputs (e.g., counseling or skill-development) that are organized, interrelated, and otherwise planned so as to generate changes in those factors and conditions (e.g., skills or life-circumstances) that may *in turn* help generate the desired future events, those efforts can be called rehabilitation programs or approaches. Such efforts—"interventions"—may involve what has been called treatment, external control, or both. Under some conditions, what has been called punishment may be considered an adjunct approach to rehabilitation.[1] However, methods such as electroshock treatment, psycho-surgery, etc., are not included under rehabilitation despite the factors or conditions on which they may focus and despite the specific effects—e.g., reduced illegal behavior—they may produce or be designed to produce.[2]

We now turn to the overview of "effectiveness."

Current Status of "Effectiveness"

Martinson's conclusion that "nothing works," which was widely accepted during the middle and later 1970s, is increasingly seen as a faulty synthesis of the findings from 138 recidivism studies previously described by Lipton, Martinson, and Wilks. [14; 18] Palmer's critique of Martinson's method of synthesizing those findings showed that the latter's conclusion was valid only in the following sense: No single, broadly categorized treatment *method*, e.g., group counseling or vocational training (each of which, of course, has many variations[3]), is guaranteed to reduce the recidivism of its target group. [21] The critique ("Martinson Revisited") showed that several group counseling *programs* (in effect, variations or types of group counseling) did reduce recidivism either for the target group as a whole or for various subgroups within the total target group. This was observed in high-quality and acceptable-quality research studies alike. Because of this and subsequent critiques, Martinson, in 1978 and 1979, explicitly repudiated his highly pessimistic conclusion that nothing or almost nothing works. Instead, he recognized the difference between evaluative statements concerning *individual* programs and those relating to *groups* of programs, i.e., broadly categorized methods. [2; 8; 17; 20]

Though extreme pessimism no longer prevails regarding the effectiveness of rehabilitation or habilitation programs, the pendulum is by no means swinging rapidly toward the opposite extreme. Nor is it even approaching the rather optimistic position that *most* treatment efforts (broadly categorized or not) have substantially reduced recidivism with many or perhaps most offenders, even in certain settings only (e.g., institutions). Moreover, what might be considered today's officially sanctioned position—that taken by the National Academy of Sciences in 1979—is very guarded: No single correctional program (and, therefore, no broadly categorized method) has been unequivocally proven to reduce the recidivism of its target group; that is, using very strict standards of evidence, none has been shown to work beyond almost all doubt. At any rate, none can be guaranteed to work. [24]

Despite its extreme scientific caution and stringent methodological standards, the NAS Panel indicated the following (these views were based on what it acknowledged as the "suggestions . . . concerning successful rehabilitative efforts" that were reported by *LMW*, and partly on the above and subsequent critiques):

(1) A few approaches may perhaps be working for some subgroups within the total target group; however, the quality and especially quantity of evidence do not allow for definite conclusions regarding the subgroup-success of these approaches.

(2) Though no specific approaches have been proven to work, neither have they been disproven; instead, it is simply unclear which approaches have and have not been "given a fair trial." [24]

(3) Many programs might have proven effective if they had been better implemented, if they had operated more intensively (i.e., had more treatment-input per client), etc.

In sum, the NAS Panel's position was very guarded and carefully qualified, but contained some glimmers of hope. In 1981, the Panel reaffirmed its position and further discussed these glimmers. [15]

The Panel's marked caution seemed to closely parallel the position taken by Empey in 1978, both as to the "inconclusive" nature of most research studies and the extreme difficulty of scientifically sorting-out precisely what works. [6] (That is, sorting-out is difficult even when good-quality research designs exist and certainly when program operations are only sketchily described.) Yet Empey was less restrictive than the Panel in one respect. He apparently did not believe that the results from all research studies which, methodologically, had been somewhat less than flawless but which were still relatively strong, should be discounted as a basis for correctional policy recommendations. Rather than insist that the results from any given study be demonstrated with almost absolute certainty, e.g., beyond the shadow of a doubt, he seemed to accept what amounted to a preponderance-of-evidence standard in this regard. As a result, he believed that some programs, though probably not many, *had* been adequately shown to be successful with serious offenders; at least, they seemed promising enough to have positive policy implications. Beyond this, Empey—like the NAS Panel after him—believed that some programs might have produced better results if they had been directed, not at the full range of offenders, but at certain subgroups only. This view reflected the already existing "differential intervention" position, summarized below.

Several researchers and scholars—chiefly Palmer and Warren; Romig;

Gendreau and Ross—have expressed a more sanguine view than that offered by the NAS Panel, by Greenberg, and, more recently, by Conrad. [4; 7; 10; 20; 23; 24; 25] To be sure, these individuals, like the Panel and Conrad, believe that *much* criminal justice research has been mediocre and that *most* rehabilitation efforts have probably been unsuccessful thus far, relative to their overall target group. Nevertheless, they believe that many programs, often well-researched programs by *LMW*'s detailed standards and those of others, have been shown to work with specified offenders (subgroups) under specific conditions. Their view—with the partial exception of Romig's—is generally known as the differential intervention (DI) position.[4, 5] This view, which mainly grew from the early efforts of Warren, et al., in California's Community Treatment Project [25] goes beyond another well-known view—that which focuses on "amenability" alone:

In contrast to DI (see below), what might be termed the basic treatment-amenability (BTA) position only minimally distinguishes among types of offenders. The BTA position generally asserts that (1) certain offenders (e.g., the "bright, verbal, and anxious") will respond to many treatment approaches, presumably under most conditions or settings, and (2) most remaining offenders will respond to few if any approaches, again, regardless of conditions or settings. In contrast, the differential intervention view suggests that some offenders (BTA's amenables included) will respond positively to given approaches under certain conditions only, and that these individuals may respond *negatively* to other approaches under very similar conditions; other combinations of offender, approach, setting—and resulting outcome— are also implied. Finally, DI also suggests that many offenders who in the BTA view are generally described as nonamenables may in fact respond positively to certain approaches under particular conditions, e.g., close structuring within institutional settings. [7; 20; 25]

> In short, overly simplified, DI asserts that certain categories of offenders (e.g., the Conflicted) but not others (e.g., the Power Oriented) will respond positively to certain approaches only, at least under specified conditions—and that the opposite may occur in response to other approaches or conditions. There are no all-around amenables and nonamenables, even though some individuals do usually perform better than others.

Thus, compared with BTA, the DI view is both more and less "optimistic" about so-called amenables; it is more optimistic about offenders who are often considered non-amenables, as well.

The "basic treatment amenability" and "differential intervention" positions have both been supported by Glaser, Adams, and others. [1;

8] The *amenability* view has, in addition, recently been supported by Wilson, a long-time critic of rehabilitation who also accepts the NAS Panel's overall caution regarding the validity of research findings to date. [26] All in all, there is increasing agreement among researchers, academicians, and practitioners as to which offenders are most likely to respond positively to standard—and, to a lesser extent, more specialized—rehabilitation approaches. *DI* has further been supported by Jesness, Hunt, Quay and Parsons, Megargee, et al., Wright and Dixon, and others. [11; 12; 13; 19; 22; 27] By 1979, Martinson himself was essentially supporting differential intervention:

> ... no treatment program now used in criminal justice is inherently either substantially helpful or harmful. The critical fact seems to be the *conditions* under which the program is delivered. For example, our results indicate that a widely-used program, such as formal education, is detrimental when given to juvenile sentenced offenders in a group home, but is beneficial (decreases reprocessing rates) when given to juveniles in juvenile prisons. Such startling results are found again and again in our [recent] study, for treatment programs as diverse as individual psychotherapy, group counseling, intensive supervision, and what we have called 'individual/help' (aid, advice, counseling). [17]

Finally, as indicated, both Empey and the Panel believe there may be something to this view.

In sum, both the BTA and DI positions have received moderate but clearly growing support within the justice system community; quantitatively, this applies to their empirical support as well. Nevertheless, as the Panel indicated, this evidence—while suggestive—is neither overwhelming nor entirely consistent.[6] [9; 24]

Whether *many* programs or only a *small percentage* of programs have reduced recidivism is unclear. (Here, it makes little difference whether numbers or percentages are considered. However, by "many" we mean at least 302 of the sample-of-programs reviewed by such authors as *LMW*, Bailey, and Adams, respectively—recognizing that many programs were included in more than one such sample.) The many-programs position is found not just among differential intervention proponents but among reviewers who have questioned the effectiveness of rehabilitation efforts. The small-percentage view—with no specific percentage or percentage-range having been stated—is that implied by the Panel, by Empey, and by Greenberg.[7] Though the truth (objective reality) may well lie between these positions, the available evidence favors the former—assuming that "small" means less than 15 percent. More specifically, direct counts (Bailey's included, e.g., for "experimental studies") suggest that—conservatively—at least 20-25 percent of all experimental programs reviewed have reduced recidivism for their total target groups, while at least an additional 10-15 percent have done so for one or more subgroups only. [1; 3; 20; 21] However, the exact percentages may not be too important. What may matter in the long-run is whether knowledge has been and can be gathered regarding the nature of (1) those programs which work and (2) offenders whom those programs apparently serve best. Such information could make it possible to reproduce, improve, and more efficiently utilize those and similar programs, and to discard whatever approaches seem to accomplish little for the preponderance of their clients. In this way, the percentage of successful programs could increase—whether from today's small or more substantial level.

Long-range considerations aside, percentages—or at least terms such as "most," "many," and "few"—have nevertheless played a large and often confounding role in the effectiveness literature. For instance, DI proponents believe that many individuals who consider rehabilitation programs ineffective consistently overlook or ignore a basic fact, whether or not recidivism is involved as the sole outcome-measure. Although *most* programs have probably not worked well and *most* research was probably not done well, this still leaves numerous programs—i.e., from among the several hundred that were experimentally studied—that did work well or moderately well, that were researched satisfactorily, or both. Moreover, even if only 10 percent of those several hundred were found to work, this would still leave "many."

> In short, proponents feel that, by overlooking this fact, these effectiveness-critics erroneously conclude or at least imply that since most programs—literally hundreds of programs—have not done well, rehabilitation efforts are obviously a failure and claims of effectiveness can be dismissed. Yet, in context, most is far from *all*.

DI proponents also believe that the dozens of programs mentioned above have, collectively, provided not only very strong evidence that *something*, in fact several things, work, but substantial converging evidence as to *what* works for many offenders. Thus, given these numerous positive-outcome programs, they consider it immaterial that the *general* quality of research-to-date, and even program-implementation-to-date, may have been far from satisfactory, or perhaps even lamentable. Meanwhile, however, effectiveness-critics suggest that DI and perhaps BTA proponents greatly exaggerate the importance or implications of what they, the critics, consider the *few* programs that may possibly have worked. In any event, effectiveness critics usually emphasize the atypical—and, by implication, the probably-difficult-toreplicate—nature of these few.[4]

Apart from *how many* programs reduce recidivism, there is the question of how sizable that reduction is. *LMW* indicated that although some programs did indeed work, "corrections has not yet found satisfactory ways to reduce recidivism by significant amounts." [14] They neither defined significant nor presented a percentage-reduction figure. In addition, Martinson, in 1976, suggested that the reduction in question was probably trivial—meaning, 5-to-15 percent.[16] (In 1979, however, he stated: ". . . contrary to my previous position, some treatments *do* have appreciable effect on recidivism." [17] The NAS Panel was silent on this point, and, at present, only one percentage-reduction figure seems to exist: Focusing on all programs reported in *LMW* which reduced recidivism by at least 10 percent.[8] Palmer found an average reduction of 32 percent, the mean follow-up being 19 months; from a public-protection as well as cost perspective, even half this figure might often be considered important.[20] At any rate, since this is the only available figure, it is perhaps best to conclude that little is presently known regarding the average recidivism-reduction of positive-outcome studies—i.e., of *all* such studies (not just *LMW's*), and using varying definitions of success. Nevertheless, we suspect that the average reduction is substantial, e.g., over 20 percent. (The problem of defining successful programs is independent of the fact that *LMW* and Martinson may have made their estimates by combining successful and unsuccessful programs. At any rate, much depends on how success is operationally defined.)

The following question is closely related to the issue of percentage reduction in recidivism. For what percentage of the total target group, i.e., all offenders combined, have programs been "appropriate?" That is—in terms of the presently considered criterion—how often have they reduced recidivism? Here, no specific answer is known, and no average figure exists. Despite this absence of information, certain principles and related implications can be stated: Clearly, if a program and all its offender-subgroups are matched, the percentage reduction that may result will be larger than if unmatched, in this case "inappropriate," subgroups are included. To date, few programs or even major program components have been designed for defined offender subgroups only— more specifically, for only those individuals who would presumably or theoretically be matched to those particular approaches. However, where program/offender matching *has* been used—as in California Youth Authority institutions during the 1960s—it has shown considerable promise. [12] Of course, the ideal program would perhaps be one that is flexible enough or contains enough relevant components to successfully work with *all* major subgroups, even though that program might not quite maximize the percentage reduction in recidivism for all its offenders combined.

Such programs—in effect, near-panaceas—are nowhere on today's horizon; in fact, as indicated, the NAS Panel believes that no approach has been decisively shown to work even for *specific subgroups*. To be sure, the Panel's view with respect to demonstrated subgroup success is shared by neither differential intervention nor treatment-amenability proponents. Yet, despite this disagreement, both sets of individuals agree as to the existence of two major preconditions to effective rehabilitation or habilitation:

    (1) Single-modality approaches may be too narrowly focused to deal with the complex or multiple problems of most serious offenders. Instead, combinations-of-methods, e.g., vocational training *and* individual counseling, may be required.

    (2) Program input may have to be considerably greater ("more intense") than it has typically been—that is, if, as in (1) above, one wishes to generate lasting behavioral or other forms of change in most serious offenders.

These preconditions would apply regardless of the program components or specific input involved, provided, of course, that the latter do bear on the particular offenders' problems. As indicated, the Panel believed that—with improved research designs—many approaches might have been shown to work if they had met preconditions such as these.

This agreement among otherwise differing observers is important, particularly in light of their further agreement regarding the value (or, in the case of the Panel, the directly implied value) of matching offenders with programs. Together, these preconditions/principles suggest that concentrated efforts, and perhaps greater individualization than in the past, are needed in order to affect substantial change in serious offenders. These suggestions may comprise some of the more constructive or at least potentially constructive products of the effectiveness-debate thus far. At any rate, they would have policy implications regardless of *how many* programs have been successful, and exactly *how* successful they have been.

Finally, it should be added that differential intervention proponents largely agree among themselves on two additional points (here, the Panel took no public stand):

    (1) Some offenders probably require, not so much the standard rehabilitation inputs such as counseling, vocational training, etc. They may require—primarily, or perhaps on an equal footing—external controls, heavy structuring, and, with respect

to community programs, considerable surveillance.

(2) Staff characteristics and staff/offender matching are probably major factors in successfully implementing given approaches, at least for many offenders.

Though the evidence for these points is neither overwhelming (quantitatively) nor entirely consistent, it is by no means insubstantial and has grown considerably in the past several years. At any rate, the present author would add a different and perhaps broader point, one that focuses on likely preconditions to effective rehabilitation and applies across the board:

(3) Fairness or fair treatment by the justice system, and humane interactions overall, can help create a tolerable, believable, sometimes supportive atmosphere for involvement and decision-making by offenders, especially but not exclusively in institutions.

Yet the following might be kept in mind. Fair treatment, etc., like just deserts and standardized dispositions by themselves, do not supply the direction, do not arouse the motivation, and do not provide the feedback or personal reward that probably must exist before realistic, satisfying decisions are generated and maintained by those individuals. That is, unlike many rehabilitation efforts, they do not address the specifics or the offenders' future—their concrete needs and opportunities within an often demanding environment. Nor do they address the often complex task of motivating or realistically helping them come to grips with that environment and, in many cases, with themselves. Thus, for many offenders, fairness and humane interactions without programmed assistance can be empty, in a sense blind, and programs without fairness can be futile, even pathetic. [20]

Review and Conclusion

An unsettled atmosphere exists regarding the effectiveness of rehabilitation or habilitation. Neither the global optimism of the 1960s nor the extreme pessimism of the middle and later 1970s seem justified, and neither view in fact prevails. Two slightly more moderate "camps" have replaced them, and a sizable but not entirely unbridged gap exists between these two.

Within the "skeptical" camp, some individuals believe it is clear— based on what they consider enough adequately conducted research— that relatively few rehabilitation programs work; moreover, those which work probably reduce recidivism by fairly small amounts. These individuals feel that rehabilitation, while not a total loss, therefore holds little promise and should be given a minor role. The remaining individuals within this group believe that *very little* is clear: Because of (1) minor or major research flaws in almost all studies, (2) poorly implemented programs, or (3) both, we don't really know whether given approaches do or do not—can or cannot—work, for their target groups as a whole. In this respect, rehabilitation has not been "given a fair trial." Though some approaches may possibly have worked for at least some offenders, the picture is again unclear because the findings are neither ironclad for any one study nor entirely consistent across various studies. These individuals believe that rehabilitation may well have promise—and a major role—but that no specific approaches can be recommended right now, at least not widely.

The more "sanguine" camp agrees that most programs have not been particularly effective thus far, certainly with their overall target groups. However, it believes that many programs and approaches have been shown—with reasonable scientific assurance—to work for specified portions of their target group. Some such proponents believe that certain offenders ("amenables") will respond positively to many approaches under a wide range of conditions and that many or most remaining offenders will probably respond to very few. Other proponents partly accept this view but believe that almost all offenders will respond positively, neutrally, *or* negatively depending on the *specific* approach and the external conditions or setting. The objective evidence, while neither vast in quantity nor flawless in quality, tends to support the latters' position while not negating the formers'. Both groups believe that successful programs often reduce recidivism by substantial amounts; they also feel that various approaches can be recommended right now for some offender-groups, even though these recommendations would reflect knowledge that is still largely "atheoretical" or at least not systematically and explicitly linked to a carefully defined set of underlying mechanisms and principles which have themselves been largely validated or seem quite plausible. Moreover, whether few or many programs have worked thus far (however those terms are defined), those and similar programs can perhaps be built upon and the remaining programs or approaches can eventually be discarded. In addition, whether recidivism reductions are considered moderately large or relatively small within typical programs to date, those reductions—like the percentage of successful programs itself—can probably be increased through program/offender matching, in future rehabilitation efforts.

The differences between the more skeptical and more sanguine individuals are complex and can only partly be traced to technical factors such as differing units of analysis,[9] differing standards of evidence, differing approaches to synthesizing as well as generalizing various findings from within and across studies, etc. They seem to be partly experiential and philosophical as well. For the most part, these differences—especially the latter two—will probably long remain, even though the former (the technically centered) will doubtlessly be narrowed quite a bit. Beyond this, disagreement exists as to when the results from a given study or *group* of studies should be used for various types and levels of policy recommendation, especially if those results are positive. At a more basic yet related level, disagreement has clearly emerged as to what constitutes an adequately or well-researched study, one whose findings—whether positive or negative—can be considered valid and somewhat generalizable.

Given such differences and disagreements, it is significant that certain areas of agreement nonetheless exist: Basically, many "skeptics" and "sanguines" seem to believe that, to be effective with serious or multiple offenders, rehabilitation programs must be broader-based and more intensive than in the past. That is, given the often complex and interrelated problems, limitations, and attitudes of most such offenders, future programs will often have to use "multiple modality" approaches, e.g., simultaneous or successive combinations of vocational training, individual counseling, and perhaps others. Moreover, to achieve substantial rather than minimal impact, such approaches will have to be provided on a more intensive basis. One final area of agreement exists or is at least implied: program/offender matching. Here, a program's resources—multiple or otherwise, intensively provided or not—are organized and distributed according to the needs, interests, and limitations of the offender subgroups that are present; they are not applied to the *total* offender group in an indiscriminate, across-the-board manner. Taken together, these areas of agreement suggest that future programs should be more carefully adapted to the life circumstances and personal/interpersonal characteristics of offenders. This view has policy implications regardless of the exact content of those as well as present programs.

The truth regarding "effectiveness" may lie between the skeptical and more sanguine views—in fact, it probably does. Yet however the effectiveness issue may finally devolve, the future of rehabilitation or habilitation programs will be neither dim nor dull; for one thing, not only direction but considerable room for improvement already exists. In any event, the above areas of agreement may reflect one important part of that truth, and future.

And regarding that future, three last points. First, rehabilitation need not be wedded to a medical model; it can proceed on the assumption that offenders, like nonoffenders, have positive potential which they can, should, and usually wish to use. Offenders need not be viewed as defective; and, like most nonoffenders, the vast majority are quite capable of recognizing the potential relevance to their lives of various forms of assistance, e.g., vocational training. To assume that offenders lack this ability or can seldom exercise or sustain it is to consider them defective or highly indifferent indeed—no less so, perhaps, than in a "medical model" itself. Along a related line, the fact that some or perhaps many offenders often play "treatment games" within or outside institutions does not mean that the majority do so or that they do so most of the time. [20]

Secondly, rehabilitation need not be linked to indeterminate sentencing; it can be implemented for—and by—offenders under conditions of determinate sentencing, with or without written contracts.

Finally, rehabilitation or correctional intervention need not demean its participants or interfere with given reform movements. It can disassociate itself from the more questionable or undesirable practices of the past and can be integrated with numerous justice system concerns and legitimate strivings of the present and future. Correctional intervention can operate in a framework of humane interaction and exchange despite the unavoidable need, outside and inside the system, for some degree of social control. By building on its past *successes*, be these "many" or "few," it can eventually regain its place and recognition (this time on more solid grounds) as one more useful tool— another option for society and offenders alike. [5; 20]

Notes

1. Though punishment—temporary confinement, withdrawal-of privileges, added restrictions, etc.—may well affect future behavior and adjustment, it is not part of a rehabilitation effort if used as an end in itself or as a means to such ends as revenge. However, if used in the context of focused, directed, and organized activities such as the above, e.g., if occasionally used to bolster given components by gaining the individual's attention, it may be considered part of rehabilitation. Nevertheless, the distinguishing features of most rehabilitation programs are those which have been designed to (1) change/modify the offender mainly through positive incentives and rewards, subtle and otherwise, or to (2) change/modify his life-circumstances and social opportunities by various pragmatic means.

2. Perhaps arbitrarily, we are including only those methods whose "humaneness" is not open to serious, certainly widespread, question. At any rate, we are focusing on methods that basically utilize, develop, or redirect the powers and mechanisms of the individual's mind, not reduce, physically traumatize, disorganize, or devastate them, whether or not by mechanical means; the former may be called positive treatment programs (PTP's) the latter, drastic or traumatic rehabilitation approaches (DRA's). We are also excluding various methods—not infrequently used in other times and/or places—such as: mutilation or dismemberment; sterilization or castration; physical stigmatization (e.g., branding); public humiliation (e.g., via stock and pillory).

3. That is, each *individual program* which is categorized as, say, a "group counseling" *method* represents a variation within the method.

4. These individuals believe that the conclusions which were drawn from several hundred studies conducted during 1945-1978 (mainly 1960-1975) were justified either in terms of a preponderance-of-evidence standard or, somewhat more strongly, beyond a reasonable doubt; at least, this applied to the conclusions from numerous studies that yielded positive results. In any event, they regard the latter conclusions as scientifically supportable even though the individual study designs were indeed far from flawless and the conclusions were therefore not justified with almost absolute certainty (as the NAS Panel would have preferred), i.e., virtually beyond the *shadow* of doubt. Moreover, they believe it would be inappropriate and certainly peculiar to dismiss the similar or converging evidence regarding given program approaches and program components that was observed *across* many such positive-outcome studies—studies which they feel had defensible research designs and that involved at least adequate program implementation.

5. Romig, while accepting this view, believes one should go beyond it—to "truly individualized treatment." [23] Thus, he supports but does not identify with DI per se. (It might be noted that individualization is a relative term.)

6. Regarding the question of (1) which offenders are usually more amenable than others? and (2) which approaches seem to work for whom?, BTA and/or DI proponents and supporters generally believe that results from various studies, i.e., *across* studies, are more consistent than inconsistent and show greater convergence than scatter. At any rate, they believe the consistency and convergence is substantial and revealing, and that it—in some respects, an expression of partial replication—partly compensates for less-than-flawless research designs. On this latter point, "the importance of scientific replication does not negate that of unusually impressive [e.g., the virtually flawless] individual studies. However, the latter value can hardly substitute for the former. . ." Thus, for example, one unusually impressive study which, say, "focused on particular treatment inputs and involved specific operating conditions" would not necessarily be seen, by most DI proponents, as outweighing "several acceptable [or perhaps high-quality] studies which, collectively, may have covered a wider range of treatment inputs and operating conditions." [20]

7. The reason for substantially differing estimates is somewhat unclear. At any rate, the many-programs estimates generally range from 30% to 55% and were obtained not just from reviews which did, but from others which did not, include the following among their sample-of-programs: those for which positive results were reported either for the total target group or only for a major subgroup within the total group. When the latter were included, estimates were only slightly higher than when they were not. An explanation for the differing estimates may partly lie in the fact that the various reviewers seldom focused on an identical or even nearly identical set of programs. Beyond that, they used somewhat different definitions of success.

8. Included here was 42% of *LMW's* pool of positive- and negative-outcome studies combined. These 42% comprised four-fifths of all programs which—based on a behavioral, not just a policy-related index such as revocation or discharge—had reduced recidivism by *any* amount, i.e., by 1% or more. (Again, programs that reduced recidivism by less than 10%—viz, by 1-9%—were *not* considered positive-outcome studies in this as well as in most reviews and evaluations; if these programs *had* been included in the present analysis, the 32% recidivism-reduction figure would have dropped to 26%.) Most of the 42% showed a statisically significant difference (0.5 level) between the total target group and its control or comparison group. *LMW* had categorized many studies from within this 42% group as high-quality, not just adequate-quality. [14; 20]

9. For example, an emphasis on either (1) broadly categorized treatment methods only (in effect, treatment-*types* or types of individual programs—as in Martinson, pre-1978), (2) overall programs, i.e., individual programs, viewed as undifferentiated entities, (3) program components within the overall program, or (4) similar program components or common factors that are found *across* numerous overall programs.

References

Adams, S. "Evaluation research in corrections: status and prospects." *Federal Probation, 38(1),* (1974):14-21.

Allinson, R. "Martinson attacks his own earlier work." In: *Criminal Justice Newsletter, 9,* (December, 1978): 4.

Bailey, W. "Correctional outcome: an evaluation of 100 reports." *J. Crime, Law, Criminology, and Police Science. 57,* (1966): 153-160.

Conrad, J."Research and developments in corrections: A thought experiment." *Federal Probation, 46(2),* (1982): 66-69.

Cullen, F. and Gilbert, K. *Reaffirming Rehabilitation.* Cincinnati, Ohio: Anderson Publishing Co. 1982.

Empey, L. *American Delinquency: Its Meaning and Construction.* Homewood, Ill.: Dorsey, 1978.

Gendreau, P. and Ross, R. *Effective Correctional Treatment.* Toronto: Butterworths. 1980.

Glasser, D. "Achieving better questions: A half century's progress in correctional research." *Federal Probation, 39,* (1975): 3-9.

Gottfredson, M., Mitchell-Hersfeld, S. and Flanagan, T. "Another look at the effectiveness of parole supervision." *J. of Research in Crime and Delinquency, 19(2),* (1982): 277-298.

Greenberg, D. "The correctional effects corrections: A survey of evaluations." In: Greenberg, D.(Ed.) *Corrections and Punishment.* Beverly Hills, Calif.: Sage Publications. 1977. 111-148.

Hunt, D. *Matching Models in Education.* Toronto: Ontario Institute for Studies in Education. 1971.

Jesness, C. *The Preston Typology Study: Final Report.* Sacramento: California Youth Authority. 1969.

Johnson. S. "Differential classification and treatment: The case against us." *The Differential View, 11.* (1982): 7-18.

Lipton, D., Martinson, R., and Wilks, J. *The Effectiveness of Correctional Treatment: A Survey of Treatment Evaluation Studies.* New York: Praeger. 1975.

Martin, S., Sechrest, L., and Redner, R. *New Direction in the Rehabiliation of Criminal Offenders.* Washington, D.C.: The National Academy Press, 1981.

Martinson, R., "California research at the crossroads." *Crime and Delinquency, 22,* (1976): 180-191.

_____. "Symposium on sentencing. Part II." *Hofstra Law Review, 7(2),* (Winter, 1979): 243-258.

_____. "What works?—questions and answers about prison reform." *The Public Interest, 35,* (Spring, 1974): 22-54.

Megargee, E., Bohn, M. Jr., Meyer, J. Jr., and Sink, F. *Classifying Criminal Offenders: A New System Based on the MMPI.* Beverly Hills, Calif.: Sage Publishers, Inc. 1979.

Palmer, T. *Correctional Intervention and Research: Current Issues and Future Prospects.* Lexington, Mass.: Lexington Books. 1978.

_____. "Martinson revisited." *J. of Research in Crime and Delinquency, 12,* (1975): 133-152.

Quay, H. and Parsons, L. *The Differential Behavior Classification of the Juvenile Offender.* Morgantown, West Virginia: Robert F. Kennedy Youth Center. 1970.

Romig, D. *Justice for Our Children.* Lexington, Mass.: Lexington Books. 1978.

Sechrest, L., White, S., and Brown, E. *The Rehabilitation of Criminal Offenders: Problems and Prospects.* Washington, D.C.: The National Academy of Sciences. 1979.

Warren, M. "Classification of offenders as an aid to efficient management and effective treatment." *J. Crime, Law, Criminology, and Police Science, 62* (1971): 239-258.

Wilson, J. " 'What works?' revisited: New findings on criminal rehabilitation." *The Public Interest, 61,* (Fall, 1980): 3-17.

Wright, W., and Dixon, M. "Juvenile delinquency prevention: A review of evaluation studies." *J. of Research in Crime and Delinquency, 14(1),* (1977): 35-67.

3 Correctional Personnel

Introduction

Correctional personnel form three broad categories—administrators, treatment or supervisory personnel, and correctional officers (guards). In all of these categories males and whites predominate by wide margins, but otherwise there are wide variations both in the characteristics of personnel involved in the three types of positions and in the duties they perform.

Administrators tend to have the longest terms of employment in the corrections field. They may have obtained their present positions by political appointment, civil service examination, or advancement through the ranks. The managerial style of an administrator may be the result of personal experience or philosophy; acquaintance with styles of administration now in apparently successful use elsewhere; or pressures to adopt current emphases or fads in correctional organization and/or treatment in vogue on federal, state, or local levels. As the range of activity covered by corrections has expanded, administrators have been called upon to demonstrate management skills in institutional management, prerelease and work release program planning, residential community-based treatment, juvenile institutional and residential treatment, innovative pretrial diversion programs, probation, parole, juvenile aftercare, and various types of adult and juvenile diversion activity. And they must be prepared to deal with prisoner rights issues, disturbances within institutions, and close monitoring of institutional activity by civil libertarians and other interest groups.

Correctional treatment or supervisory staff occupy the next step in the descending hierarchy of correctional personnel. The majority hold baccalaureate degrees, and many have pursued graduate study. The vast majority of personnel on this level work outside institutions, in probation, parole, juvenile aftercare, furlough or work release programs, educational program supervision, or residential correctional treatment. Those within institutions serve as psychiatrists or psychologists, social workers, instructors in educational programs, or treatment personnel.

At the lowest level of the correctional personnel ladder, in terms of prestige, education, and salary, are the correctional officers (guards). They make up the vast majority (approximately two-thirds) of prison employees. From 1979 to 1988, the number of full-time prison staff increased by nearly 45 percent, and custodial staff accounted for approximately 82 percent of this increase.[1] The chief responsibility of correctional officers is maintaining the security of the institution, although in some instances they are regarded as part of the "treatment team" and asked to participate in rehabilitation efforts. This is most often true in juvenile corrections. Corrections officers have the highest levels of direct interaction with offenders, and bear chief responsibility for the orderly operation of the institution. Their operational styles vary, but there is frequently a sense of "accommodation" between successful correctional officers and inmates, which benefits both.

Both in numbers and in funding used for them, state correctional workers hold the leading position. In 1985, 61 percent of the individuals employed full time in corrections were working at the state level, while 35 percent held positions at the local level, and 4 percent worked in federal correctional activities. In the same year, 61 percent of the expenditures for corrections were made at the state level, 34 percent at the local level, and 5 percent at the federal level.[2]

The number of positions available in corrections has shown a steady increase. In 1987, more than 217,000 persons were employed by state and federal correctional agencies, and an additional 33,000 were employed by state juvenile agencies.[3] Per capita spending for corrections by state and local governments increased 42 percent from 1980 to 1988, and is expected to continue to increase.[4]

The rapidly expanding field of corrections has suffered severe manpower problems, including shortages of specialized professional personnel, poor working conditions, and underrepresentation of women and members of ethnic minorities in the correctional manpower workforce. In 1987, approximately 13 percent of custodial staff in state adult agencies and the federal system were females.[5]

Another severe problem in manpower allocation involves the disproportionate allocation of resources. Approximately 2.2 million adult offenders, were under community supervision (probation and parole) in 1987, supervised by approximately 35,000 probation or parole officers, while 523,000 inmates of state and federal prisons were supervised by approximately 111,000 custodial staff members.[6] Thus, although less than one-fourth of all correctional workers were involved in community-based corrections in 1987, 81 percent of the offenders under supervision in that year were in community-based programs.

One of the most troublesome problems involved in recruitment of corrections personnel is the low status of corrections work in the public mind. Those involved in corrections work, particularly correctional officers, have rarely chosen this profession, but have entered it by chance after service in the military or because of the need for a secure job. The location of large institutions in rural areas has allowed the entry into correctional work of poorly trained and poorly motivated personnel, chiefly because better qualified individuals were not available. Media exposés of prison corruption and brutality have done little to enhance the public image of correctional work.

Manpower shortages in corrections are related to the emerging roles of private firms and individuals as providers of correctional services. Although such involvement has been in place for many years in such areas as food service and prison industries, and professionals such as medical doctors or psychologists have been associated with correctional work as providers or specialized services, in recent years financing of prison construction by private firms, who then lease the buildings to the government, or operation of the institutions themselves by firms which provide total correctional services have emerged as options. Involvement of the private sector in correctional activity provides another area of correctional employment and presents the possibility of many more corrections related positions. The chief appeal of private sector involvement is the perceived cost efficiency and reduced expense to taxpayers of such operations. However, a number of legal and ethical issues also emerge, as noted in the *Report to the Nation on Crime and Justice* (1988). These include:

> Can the government delegate its powers to incarcerate persons to a private firm?
>
> Can a private firm deprive persons of their liberty and exercise coercive authority, perhaps through use of deadly force?
>
> Who would be legally liable in the event of lawsuits?
>
> Who would be responsible for maintaining the prison if the private employees go on strike?
>
> Would a private company have the right to refuse to accept certain types of inmates, for example, those with AIDS?
>
> If a private firm went bankrupt, who would be responsible for the inmates and the facility?
>
> Could a private company reduce staff salaries or hire nonunion members as a way of reducing costs?
>
> Would the "profit motive" operate to the detriment of the government or the inmates, either by keeping inmates in prison who should be released or by reducing services to a point at which inmates, guards, and the public were endangered?
>
> What options would a government with no facility of its own have if it became dissatisfied with the performance of the private firm?

Is it appropriate for the government to circumvent the public's right to vote to increase debt ceilings?[7]

Because of ever increasing prison populations and overcrowding, these legal and ethical issues are likely to receive increased attention, if state and local governments are pressured by circumstances to turn to private sector involvement as a solution to their problems.

The first selection in this chapter, "Career Opportunities in the Corrections Field," describes the range of employment opportunities and the higher education preparation regarded as appropriate for corrections positions. A survey of the types of degrees held by administrative and treatment personnel working in corrections today would reveal backgrounds of higher education in such fields as political science, public administration, social work, history, education, psychology, and sociology. Entrants to the field in the past ten years may have more specialized degrees in criminal justice or corrections, but it is typical for personnel working in corrections to have been educated for work in a general "helping" occupation rather than to have specifically prepared for a career in corrections. The selection presents specifics on salary ranges and advancement opportunities, and also describes research and teaching opportunities related to corrections.

In the second selection, "A Novice Correctional Worker Reflects on the Vagaries of Correctional Treatment," Karen Amy discusses her discovery that the inmates have a great deal to do with the type or style of treatment successfully used, and noted changes in her own approaches and attitudes during the time she spent as an intern in an institution.

The third selection in this chapter, "Burnout: Avoiding the Consequences of On-The-Job Stress," by Richard M. Morris, describes the stressful features of correctional work which also occur in other occupations and those which are specifically tied to the identity of "correctional officer." Stress management strategies for the correctional worker and his or her family are described.

Notes

1. Bureau of Justice Statistics, *Report to the Nation on Crime and Justice,* 2d ed. (Washington, D.C.: U.S. Department of Justice, 1988), 120.

2. Bureau of Justice Statistics, *Sourcebook of Criminal Justice Statistics-1986* Washington, D.C.: U.S. Department of Justice, 1987). 6.

3. George M. and Camille Graham Camp, *The Corrections Yearbook 1987* (South Salem, New York: Criminal Justice Institute, 1987), 43,63.

4. Bureau of Justice Statistics, *Report to the Nation on Crime and Justice,* 120.

5. George M. and Camille Graham Camp, *The Corrections Yearbook 1987,* 44.

6. Ibid., p. 1., 38, 43, 77, 81.

7. Bureau of Justice Statistics, *Report to the Nation on Crime and Justice,* 119.

Career Opportunities in the Corrections Field

Peter C. Kratcoski

The field of corrections offers a wide range of career opportunities including administrative and supervisory positions in institutions or agencies, work as a practitioner or activity in program development, evaluation, research, and teaching. Corrections includes the care, custody, and supervision of convicted offenders who have been sentenced or whose sentences have been suspended. On the juvenile level, it involves supervision and counseling of adjudicated delinquents in institutions or in the community, and also such activities as employment preparation and work in alternative schools and youth service bureaus. Thus individuals who are broadly defined as being in the field of corrections can range from prison wardens, psychologists, and custodial personnel, to administrators or counselors in a program designed to assist the families of convicted offenders or victims of crime.

Employment Opportunities in Corrections Today

It is estimated that there are one and a quarter million positions in the criminal justice field today, and of these, approximately 250,000 are specifically related to corrections. When tangential positions, such as work in group homes, diversion, or chemical abuse programs, which are not specifically designed as corrections work but are closely related to the field, are included, it is apparent that many additional job opportunities exist in this area.

The patterns of growth in corrections positions and the continuing growth of the correctional inmate population indicate that careers in

Reprinted by permission from *Journal of Applied Sociology* 2 (1975): 23-31.

corrections will continue to be available. Figure 1, below, illustrates the increase in full-time criminal justice employees of federal, state, and local governments form 1971 to 1979. The increase in corrections positions illustrated is a 54 percent increase (U.S. Department of Justice: 15).

During the time period illustrated in Figure 1 (1971-1979), the total number of federal corrections employees increased 71 percent, state correctional employees increased 52 percent, and corrections employees of local governments increased 56 percent (U.S. Department of Justice: 21, 23, 27). Employment opportunities in public juvenile custody facilities also continue to increase. For example, such facilities had more

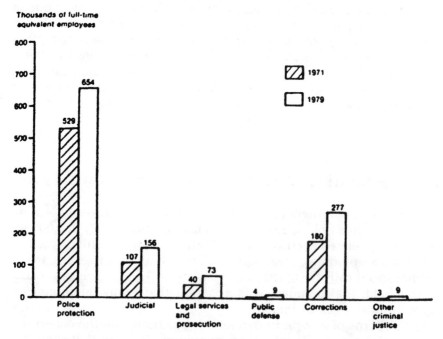

Figure 1
Criminal Justice Full-time Equivalent Employment
By Federal, State, and Local Governments
By Types of Activities: 1971 and 1979

Source: U.S. Department of Justice, *Sourcebook of Criminal Justice Statistics-1983* (Washington, D.C.: U.S. Department of Justice, 1984: 15). Figure provided by the Bureau of Justice Statistics, U.S. Department of Justice.

than 48,000 employees in 1979, a three percent increase over the 1977 figure (U.S. Department of Justice: 120).

Qualifications for Corrections Positions

Although it is still possible to obtain positions in the corrections field without a two-year or four-year college degree, the work is likely to be custodial, and involve duties such as prison guards, houseparents in group homes, or youth leaders in juvenile detention centers. The more professionally oriented positions require a baccalaureate degree in the social sciences, criminal justice, or corrections. In adult corrections, these include jobs as probation or parole officers, or counselor positions in community treatment centers or drug or alcohol rehabilitation centers.

In the juvenile justice area, positions include youth leaders or counselors in institutions, intake or probation officers in the juvenile court, and many types of agency positions involving job or career preparation, counseling, or education. The fact that the adult prison population is currently at an all time high makes institutions an important career placement possibility. Those who wish to move into supervisory positions in agencies or institutions need a master's degree, and experience is generally also required.

Higher Education Preparation for a Corrections Career

Specific academic programs in corrections were not available until the 1960s. Before that time, students drawn to the general area of correctional work were likely to major in sociology, social work, or psychology. There were few textbooks dealing specifically with corrections, and those available took a non-theoretical, technical approach to the subject.

A major factor in the delay in the emergence of corrections as a field of study was the fact that the image of what constitutes corrections was not well defined. In the eyes of the public, corrections was equated with institutional work in prisons or jails. It was not until the 1960s, when increased federal funding created many new programs in law enforcement and corrections, that varied career opportunities in criminal justice appeared.

In the turbulent 1960s, inner city disturbances, campus unrest, public fear of crime, revelations of abuses and primitive conditions in institutions, and demands by prisoners for better conditions and recognition of their rights led to legislation which provided funds for expansion of existing programs in criminal justice and the creation of many new programs. The Law Enforcement Assistance Administration, which provided colleges and universities with curriculum development grants for programs in law enforcement and corrections and gave students training grants and tuition loans, supplied a powerful economic incentive for institutions of higher learning to become involved. Many new programs were hastily formulated to take advantage of the available federal funding. In 1960, only 26 colleges and universities in the United States offered full-time programs in any law enforcement related field. However, by 1970, the Law Enforcement Education Directory listed 292 institutions which offered 340 different programs, and many other colleges and universities offered a specialization in some type of law enforcement related field within their sociology or political science departments, making the actual number of existing programs much higher (Tenney, 1971).

Tenney (1971) developed a model to characterize programs in the criminal justice field, labeling them "training," "social science," and "professional." The training oriented programs are primarily designed to teach the mastery and application of rules, the development of mechanical skills to operate equipment, and the mastery of mechanical skills in the performance of maneuvers. The social science programs, in contrast, approach the field from a general theoretical perspective and do not prepare a student for specific work in the subject area. The professionally oriented program is designed to provide both a theoretical foundation and experiences in the field, but goes beyond job training and gives students opportunities to view their experiences in criminal justice and corrections from a wider perspective through internalization of values and setting of goals.

As new higher education programs in criminal justice and corrections developed, the tendency was to create separate departments of criminal justice or law enforcement rather than develop them as specializations within existing departments of sociology or social science. Since the available sociological solutions called for broad changes in the political and economic systems of the community and the country that would require years of effort to implement, there was a movement to create new departments and programs which emphasized training in social control skills. In addition, many of the social science and sociology programs were not designed or prepared to provide the types of field experience and direct training for employment which were now viewed as important. The new departments and programs that were created tended to rely heavily on part-time faculty members who were employed in the field and could offer the students practical advice and the benefit of their expertise.

Since 1970, many of the hastily designed programs which emphasized training have been eliminated. Most of these were located in community colleges and were two-year programs within large colleges or universities which were heavily dependent upon federal subsidies. When funding for the Law Enforcement Assistance Administration was severely reduced and eventually eliminated, these institutions were unable to attract students for the programs or to continue to support them, and they were eventually dropped. Other programs survived and became part of independent departments of criminal justice. By 1980, 816 institutions of higher education were offering crime related programs. This included 1,209 associate level programs, 589 baccalaureate programs, and 222 graduate programs (Myren, 1980: 23). When members of the American Society of Criminology and the Academy of Criminal Justice Sciences were asked to rank graduate programs in criminology and criminal justice in order of prestige, it was found that the majority of programs ranked high in prestige were the older, established programs, which existed before the creation of the Law Enforcement Education Program, administered by the LEAA, in 1968 (DeZee, Joint Commission on Criminology and Criminal Justice Education and Standards, 1980: 18-20). Many of the faculty members teaching in these programs received their degrees in sociology, political science, or psychology.

The current emphasis on criminal justice education is on the types of programs which Tenney characterized as "professional," which stress a strong interdisciplinary curriculum and frequently include courses in professional ethics and in research methods and statistics.

Salaries and Advancement

The salaries of entry level positions in corrections vary tremendously. Positions in the federal system generally provide higher salaries and more attractive fringe benefits than those on the state or local level. A federal correctional officer may have a beginning salary of $21,000, while a state correctional officer with comparable duties may have a salary ranging from $15,000 to $20,000. Likewise, the salary range for federal probation officers is $16,559 to $38,185, while at the state level it is $16,000 to $22,000. Salaries for supervisors and specialists in the federal system highest range include $63,800 for the U.S. Parole Commissioner, $41,277 to $63,115 for chief district parole officer, and

$34,930 to $53,661 for a federal parole hearing examiner. On the state level, a state director of probation and parole's salary averages between $32,000 and $42,000, and a senior state parole officer's salary is in the $21,000 to $28,000 range (U.S. Department of Justice, 1983: 95).

Most of the individuals who pursue careers in corrections eventually move into administrative and supervisory positions. In the past, those who held such positions were predominantly holders of the Master of Social Work degree, and this degree was considered the highest needed to move into the more responsible and better paying positions. This dominance of the administrative levels of institutions and agencies by social workers has gradually eroded, and those who hold M.A.s in criminal justice, corrections, or applied sociology are now being given equal consideration for administrative positions. For example, the Director of the Ohio Department of Rehabilitation and Correction has a Ph.D. in Sociology and began his career by undertaking an extensive evaluation of the effectiveness of halfway houses in Ohio. An individual with a M.A. in Corrections is the classification director at the Cuyahoga County (Ohio) Correctional Center. Her work entails classification and placement of offenders, compilation of statistics on offenders, and testing of new classification and prediction instruments.

Once an individual reaches an administrative or specialized position, the opportunities to advance or to make a parallel move into another agency increase. The management and supervisory skills needed to be effective in administering the juvenile court system, for example, are quite comparable to those needed to administer a county mental health facility. Once a certain level of administrative expertise is developed, it is quite common for persons to transfer from one correctional or social service agency to another.

Other Opportunities

The job opportunities which require the use of skills of research design, evaluation procedures, and statistics are increasing in the field of corrections. Most of the agencies are required to submit various types of periodic statistical reports and to complete records on their operations. In addition, even the smaller agencies have computerized their records and office procedures. The skills needed to fill these positions do not necessarily have to be obtained in a corrections degree program. Since much of the research and theoretical development in corrections and criminal justice has emanated from sociology, political science, and psychology departments, graduates of a variety of academic programs who have an aptitude for research and some experience with statistics and the use of computers can fit into these positions. However, those with degrees in corrections have an advantage because of their familiarity with the criminal justice process, the terms used in statistical reports, and the legal facets of criminal justice and corrections work. In addition, they are likely to have completed an internship which further familiarizes them with the types of reports involved and the legal and criminal justice terminology used.

Teaching in the corrections area on the college level is another career opportunity. We noted earlier that more than 800 colleges and universities offer programs in criminal justice, law enforcement, or corrections. A large number of these programs are offered out of two year technical schools or community colleges, and part-time teaching opportunities exist for practitioners who wish to pursue them. While full-time teaching positions in colleges and universities are virtually unavailable in many subject areas, they still exist in the criminal justice and corrections areas. A doctorate is the usual entering qualification for those seeking tenured positions. The specific doctorate which the candidate for such a position holds is not as crucial as the emphasis of the coursework and specialization. Since a limited number of universities offer doctorates in criminal justice, the new faculty members in criminal justice and corrections programs are drawn predominantly from applicants with doctorates in sociology, political science, psychology, or law. Advertisements for candidates for such positions generally state the minimum requirements as including a doctorate in criminology, criminal justice, or a closely related field. Thus an applicant with a doctorate in sociology who specialized in deviance, criminology, delinquency, or even complex organizations, and who has a solid background in research methods and statistics would be a very viable candidate.

Summary

The field of corrections is broad enough to allow for a large number of persons with varying educational backgrounds, interests, and skills to carve out satisfying careers. There are opportunities to work in the community and in institutions, and to deal with adults and juveniles through various agencies and widely different types of interaction. While the majority of careers in corrections involve direct contact with offenders in a supervisory or counseling role, there are also positions in administration, training, research, evaluation, and education.

References

DeZee, Matthew R. 1980. "The Productivity of Criminology and Criminal Justice Faculty." Report prepared for the Joint Commission on Criminology and Criminal Justice. Chicago: University of Illinois at Chicago Circle.

Myren, Richard A. 1979, "Criminology and Criminal Justice: Definitions, Trends, and the Future." Pp. 23-38 in Two Views of Criminology and Criminal Justice: Definitions, Trends and the Future. Washington, D.C.: U.S. Department of Justice.

Tenney, Charles W., Jr. 1971. Higher Education Programs in Law Enforcement and Criminal Justice. Washington, D.C.: U.S. Government Printing Office.

U.S. Department of Justice. 1983. Report to the Nation on Crime and Justice. Washington, D.C.: Bureau of Justice Statistics.

U.S. Department of Justice. 1984. Sourcebook of Criminal Justice Statistics - 1983. Washington, D.C.: U.S. Department of Justice.

A Novice Correctional Worker Reflects on the Vagaries of Correctional Treatment

Karen Amy
Peter C. Kratcoski

Editor's Note

This article presents excerpts from the daily journal of a graduate student who was completing an internship at a federal correctional facility as one of the requirements for a M.A. in Corrections. The portions of the journal included here were chosen to illustrate the range of treatment being applied and also to reflect the intern's day-to-day maturation as she was initiated into the system. Karen was assigned to the Women's Unit and required to assist in a wide variety of activities and treatment techniques designed to rehabilitate or correct the residents. She astutely observed that the inmates were frequently as involved in shaping her behavior and attitudes as she was in trying to change theirs.

Introduction

Up until I began my internship, corrections existed only in books, articles, and lectures. It was something that talked about people, scientifically, categorically. My experience at the institution put some life into corrections. It put the personal element into the word. It had something to say about the people who were the clients, and the people who were the staff, and what must be overcome in oneself

"A Novice Correctional Worker Reflects on the Vagaries of Correctional Treatment" by Karen Amy and Peter C. Kratcoski also appeared in *Correctional Counseling and Treatment* by Peter C. Kratcoski, (Monterey, California: Duxbury Press, 1981), 92-106.

before the unique problems of corrections can be solved.

My weekly journal was an endeavor toward a descriptive and interpretive analysis of the internship experience. It became the vehicle by which thoughts and feelings that were a large part of the internship experience could be expressed. It was the "open section" that allowed not only for job description, explanation of institution policies and procedures, and interpretation of events, but also for the more intimate expressions of feelings and emotions that working with people often evokes. . . .

Editor's Note

The classification and review of inmates is a crucial activity of any institution. Appropriate classification upon entrance to the facility may play an important part in the success or failure of the treatment program. The author describes her experiences with classification.

The Journal

Tuesday is classification and review day for one of the unit caseworkers. This is the meeting of the treatment team, where program is discusssed for residents on the caseload. Classification is the initial program meeting, where new residents are informed as to what programs are available for enrollment and what the responsibilities are for those enrolled in the program. Dollar amounts are assigned to the various activities. The resident may earn specified amounts for each step, based on active participation, conscientiousness, and improvement in her program performance. The money is only awarded upon favorable evaluation by staff involved in group, educational or vocational training and work assignment.

By the time of this initial classification meeting, educational testing has been completed so that the team and the resident may decide what kind of education or vocational training is warranted, based on the individual's aptitude. Also, by this time, the counselor has met individually with the resident, and engaged in conversation to determine what problem areas the group will have to work on with the resident.

Monthly reviews are made after the initial classification session. The resident and the team together look at the behavior of the resident during the past month, her performance in any activity for which she is programmed, and at any disciplinary action that may have been taken against her. At this time, changes in the program may be made, if the team decides they are warranted.

Although the resident is supposed to have a choice in her programming, teams often strongly advocate a certain program to the point where residents' wishes are not heard. For example, one woman had the ability, according to testing, to attain her GED (High School Graduate Equivalency Diploma). Although she had no desire to pursue such study, the treatment team, after short discussion with her, programmed GED courses for her. While the resident did not strongly object, one wonders whether she will get anything out of the classes, if she attends, since the decision to attain a GED was not hers. . . .

The psychologist asked me to substitute for him in his admission and orientation group. The group is made up of women just entering the institution and is designed to teach some of the processes to be encountered in group treatment. It also functions to acquaint the women with policies, procedures, and rules of the institution. Each woman is required to attend four sessions that deal with the different areas of feedback, communication, an open session on institution rules, and trust. The session I was to conduct dealt with feedback. The exercise consisted of using cards on which categories were drawn— flower, bird, tree, car, animal, month—from which the women were to choose and then describe themselves in terms of that category. For instance, a woman might choose to describe herself in terms of a flower, a rose, and describe what qualities she had that she felt likened her to a rose. Then the women were asked to describe another person in terms of a specific category. The theory behind the exercise is that each person possesses certain qualities that are often associated with inanimate objects. It forces the women to examine themselves and others in an abstract sense. Most of the women were fairly articulate, although I had to rely on feedback from the other residents as to whether or not the descriptions were accurate, because I was not well enough acquainted with them to know. When asked to describe me, their insight narrowed a bit, as all they could see was my role as a staff person, and therefore, "the police." At times, the ambiguity of my position here is very apparent; I am considered a staff person because I am not a resident, but I am not a very useful staff person to them, since I have no authority to help them with most of their requests, and I have no evaluative input of any consequence. . . .

In another Human Relations Lab exercise in feedback, the group members were asked to name a person each would like to be in the company of in a certain situation, and why. The questions asked included, "Who would you like to take to an important social event?"

"Who would you like to represent you at an adjustment committee meeting?" and similar questions. The exercise is designed to make the residents examine those qualities in people that they value and upon which they place importance.

At the next session, the group was asked to give direct feedback to group members in a special way. Each person, in turn, sat in the middle of the group, while each of the others approached her with a slip of paper that had those qualities written on it that were outstanding characteristics of the person in the center, according to the resident doing the evaluating. Often, appearance was noted, as was friendliness or sensitivity. Two things were very apparent—the residents had no negative feedback for anyone, and their evaluations of staff members were a lot more reserved than those they made of the other residents.

Throughout the group meetings with the Human Relations Lab, I was struck by how receptive and enthusiastic the residents in this group were as compared to the residents in the other groups in which I had participated. They were more willing to volunteer thoughts and feelings, were anxious for each session, and usually stretched its length with questions at the end. At the last session, after the certificates were handed out, the counselors explained that a caseworker would be willing to meet with the residents in a less structured group setting beginning the following week, if the group members felt that the sessions had been productive and wanted to see what they could continue to accomplish. All of the residents agreed that they would like to continue; of course, their actual enthusiasm will be revealed by how many come next week. But there is definitely a difference with this group of residents. Is it their newness at the institution, which has not afforded them the time to acquire a distaste for groups yet? Is it the type of group format, in the sense that a more structured group setting relieves some of the pressure of individual scrutiny and makes the time more fun and seemingly less work? How many residents actually show up at the next group meeting and how they participate should explain some of the questions.

Editor's Note

In this excerpt, the intern relates her first on-the-job experiences with group counseling.

The Journal

I held my first group session in the television studio, where it was taped. I was asked to fill in for one of the counselors who had to take a shopping trip out. Five women were supposed to be in the group; two showed up. The psychologist had us go ahead with the session, nevertheless. The results were very disappointing. The discussion was superficial and I did not pick up the emotion at all; my nervousness was helping me react only to the content. Here, it is very apparent that a different therapy model than the one that I had been trained in would be more effective in this particular setting. My training consisted of nondirective counseling techniques, which are very nonjudgmental and concentrate on feeling. It asks, "How does that make you feel?" "What do you do when you feel that way?" "Is that behavior helpful?" "What would be more helpful?" No active questioning of the rationality of the behavior goes on. It is important, I think, to actively question behavior and values. A nondirective role is ineffective in the type of situation I encountered because the group members were not participating willingly. An active role can help to generate a discussion, whereas it is doubtful that residents will feel unhappy if nothing at all is said in a group session.

There is a tendency to oversympathize with the residents and their preoccupation with the unfairness of it all, their parole dates, and the urgency of all their needs. It is important to remember that they were the "masters of their own fate." There is a balance to be maintained, though, for in the routine of a bureaucratic job, what is an emergency or stress situation for a resident is often just an every-day occurrence for the staff person, and his removed objectivity seems like indifference to the resident.

Editor's Note

In this section, the writer reflects on the feelings of insecurity experienced by an intern who is placed in a decision-making position. She also observes that her own moods, feelings, and state of health inevitably affect her performance and effectiveness as a counselor.

The Journal

During one group session I brought up the topic of how uncomfortable

I felt at being in an authoritarian position. After a period of discussion, two residents decided that they had had enough and asked permission to leave. I had ambiguous feelings. I wanted them to stay and participate, but I wanted their participation to be voluntary. I also did not like the idea of giving a supposed adult permission to come or go. It gave me a feeling of omnipotence with which I was not comfortable. The psychologist explained that in a group situation where I was the group leader I was responsible for the structure of the group, while the content is provided by those participating. I was suffering from guilt feelings over not making the session worthwhile enough for the residents to want to stay. As to the asking permission to leave, since "group" is mandatory, that was a responsibility I had to accept along with the position of being the facilitator. . . .

I had been away over the weekend and left early Monday morning to get back in time for work at 1 P.M. The drive had worn me out, and by evening I was very tired. I had a long interview with a woman in the unit that afternoon. Talking to her was invigorating, but several times during the conversation I felt weariness overcoming me. It was apparent to the woman, also, for she hinted that perhaps I would like to continue the discussion some other time. It occurred to me that the moods of the interviewer and the interviewee play an important part in how successful the interaction is. I noticed that when I was receptive and interested she was encouraged to speak, but when my interest appeared to be lagging she was uncertain about continuing. Perhaps moods can be used in a productive way. To influence a reluctant participant, the interviewer could display enthusiasm and spontaneity to elevate the interviewee's mood. Conversely, if the willingness to participate is not there, a dull and unenthusiastic interviewer will not serve to generate the lacking enthusiasm.

One of the staff had mentioned the subject during an "unwind" session—that the mark of a professional is such that the person is able to carry on in his job and function up to his capacity despite external stress, or when that stress becomes too great he can recognize that he will be unable to function on his job and should not attempt to do so at that time.

I am still struggling with that—trying to find my functioning capacity and maintaining consistency in it. I find myself concentrating too much on the person's reaction to me at any particular time, rather than what response would be most helpful to him. . . .

Editor's Note

Gaining the trust and confidence of others is not an easy job on the outside. In a prison setting it becomes a formidable task. The inmates have developed defenses which are difficult to penetrate. In this excerpt the writer describes a technique used to help inmates learn to place trust and confidence in others.

The Journal

Dave asked me to take his group and participate in the trust exercise with them. The exercise seeks to develop the mutual trust that is essential to a cohesive and productive group encounter. He suggested that I begin with a discussion of the decisions people make daily to take certain risks with other people and to trust them with more of oneself. The exercise involved having a person stand behind another, assuring the first woman, who is facing forward, that she will catch her if she falls backward with a straight body. Whether the first woman trusts her to make the catch is determined by a bent body, a step backwards, or any attempt to catch herself from falling freely.

After each woman had tried both positions, we talked about the different thought processes that occurred during the exercise, particularly what determined one's decision to take the risk and fall into the other's arms. A split second after that decision to fall was acted on, was there a doubt—a questioning of the decision to fall? The women also noted that there was a feeling of relief upon landing safely.

They talked, then, about the things that indicate a person can be trusted, and the kinds of small risks that are taken to test someone's ability to be trusted. This was easily related to the staff, when one woman noted that most of the decisions to allow privileges or grant parole were based on how the staff perceived her trustworthiness. The opposite was also true for the residents, who stated that they based their trust in staff on consistency, fairness, and the nonrevelation of confidences. . . .

Editor's Note

In this excerpt, the intern took part in a transactional analysis group led by an inmate. Transactional analysis is a treatment technique that relies on introspection and analysis of one's behavior as fitting that of models set as "child, parent, or adult." (See Chapter 8 for a detailed description of transactional analysis techniques.) In this instance the therapist was an inmate, soon to be released, who had been trained as a group leader by a staff member.

The Journal

I had a taste of one of the counselor's transactional analysis groups. The therapist was a black man about twenty-five years old who was short of a release date by approximately two months. He was a very charismatic person, and all the women were very receptive to him. I wonder if some of the acceptance was not due to the fact that this group leader was not a staff person.

Transactional analysis is a very confrontive, direct therapy model. The leader takes an active role and is continually pointing out to the participants what part of the person is speaking at any particular time. It can become very confusing as the conversation continues throughout the constant analysis by the group leader. It can seem like nitpicking also, if the persons involved do not wish to hear what type of person they are at any particular time. The therapy identifies three person types with various subtypes to each: the parent, the child, and the adult. Each type emerges at various times during discussion. Each person relates to other people in all three ways; it is important to realize the type that is projected to understand the dynamics behind the relationship.

This group was dealing with some ambiguous feelings it had toward the correctional counselor. She had neglected to do something for one of the residents in the group, and the resident was extremely upset about it. Other similar instances were brought up by other women. The leader very actively checked out what was going on with each person, confronting at one time and reassuring at another. Transactional analysis can be a very destructive therapy if a person is confronted and made to break down his defenses but is not "put back together" by warmth and support from the rest of the group. The defense destruction must be done in the safe atmosphere of a supportive group. . . .

Editor's Note

In this section, the author describes an exercise in group dynamics and values clarification.

The Journal

The Human Relations Lab group had an exercise in fingerpainting. The group was divided into two and furnished with art supplies to draw a painting of anything at all decided upon by the group, and then try to "sell" the painting to the other group. The exercise had the added element of some values clarification, as the paintings were of things that were very important to each group. One group's theme involved money, while the other's involved a flight away from the institution.

In trying to sell the paintings to each other, the residents saw the dynamics involved when there is a joint investment in the decision to buy something or to decide the value of something. Each group member felt a strong identification with the painting produced by her group, and became deeply involved in trying to sell it.

As to the decision making, the residents saw how quickly the exercise fell into chaos when no real leader emerged and there were no group decisions made as to selling points or method of delivery. Neither group made an impression on the other—indicative of the strong sense of investment the members felt for their own respective paintings—and neither group developed a strong leader. The exchange became a verbal free-for-all. All offered constructive opinions as to what caused the verbal chaos and how the groups might have better handled the exchange. Points that emerged included the fact that leaders failed to emerge, that there was no consensus as to what the strong selling points would be, and that no stock was taken as to what each group was looking for in value.

I held a group session for one of the absent counselors and decided to try a values-clarification exercise. Developed for educational purposes, initially, the exercise neatly applies to any type of group with little modification. The exercise I chose has the residents draw a coat of arms background. The reason for choosing that particular object was not given, however it could relate to the fact that a coat of arms contains things that stand for the family name and are important to the members. The exercise asks the participant to describe something about which he feels strongly, or cherishes as part of himself. The shield is divided into six different parts and the person is asked to write, or draw the answers to these six questions:

> "What was your greatest personal accomplishment?"
> "List three words that describe the person that you are now."
> "What was your greatest personal failure?"

> "What can other people do for you that will make you happy?"
>
> "If you had one year to live and could accomplish anything with guaranteed success, what would you do?"
>
> List three words that you would like to see on your tombstone that describe the person you would have liked to have been."

The participants are asked to draw as well as they can, so that the picture may be described to the others.

The exercise concentrates on the past as it really was, the person as she now is, and what kind of person she would like to be. The questions can be changed to include different areas.

Initially, the exercise was greeted with groans and exclamations that "group" was not supposed to be like this, that you don't write things in "group," and that no one could draw. The people who protested the loudest were the ones who put the most description in their drawings and their narration. Successes were most often family oriented—my children, my husband—or finishing school or a GED program. Failures were most often their presence in prison. If there was one year to live, the main concern was getting enough money to do whatever they wished in that year. This easily led to discussions about what other groups of people hold as valuable, or what is termed successful or a failure according to societal standards and how realistic those values were to the immediate participants. It was really a discussion generator and led to some good and emotional interaction. One woman who had heartily complained at the outset told me, as she was leaving, that she would bring an exercise to the next group meeting. . . .

Editor's Note

In this section, the author reflects on an inmate who feels fairly comfortable as a criminal and is quite convinced that only through crime will she have the opportunities to follow the life style she desires. The author describes the partial success of an aggressive, honest, perceptive counselor in countering the arguments made by this inmate regarding the positive gains of a life of crime.

The Journal

I sat in on one of the counselor's groups, along with the educational specialist. The counselor is very confrontive in her approach. The counselor is continuously asking questions, probing the answers, and disagreeing. But she tempers that with honesty, generous, deserved praise, and consistency. It appears to get results. The women in her groups show up consistently, participate actively, and seek her out individually.

There is one woman in this counselor's group who seems to be a classic example of a sociopathic personality. She was a friendly person, but close to no one, displayed no emotion, and participated only in those activities she wanted to. She did not have a GED, which the staff felt would be desirable, and had no desire to attain one. She frequently admitted, in group, that when she was released back to the community she would continue with the criminal activity that had caused her to be incarcerated. Her interests lay in collecting diamonds, cars, furs, and an endless wardrobe. She was what she owned, that was all that was important.

This woman had been "grouping" with this particular counselor for some time, and while they had reached an impasse, the counselor consistently challenged the woman, who just as consistently parried her questions with emotionless answers. The counselor would get pretty rough with her at times, calling her a loser, superficial, "a woman without insides," and many other things. She did not do so beratingly, or as if to downgrade, but it was as though both of them knew what the counselor thought she was and the expressions became only neutral statements of fact. This woman's only role in life was to look pretty and expensive.

The counselor consistently brought up any negative behavior the woman showed, although she often felt the effort was fruitless. The first time that I sat in the group, however, I noticed a kind of tenseness that seemed to increase as the confrontation continued. When the counselor eventually signaled that the session was over, the woman let out a very distinct, "Yea!" I called this to the counselor's attention and she felt somewhat heartened in her efforts. The signs of anger indicated that the woman was not as emotionless as she purported to be.

This inmate's decision to do just what she wanted to do was costing her some privileges, which she angrily sought. Though she was eligible for a furlough, she was being denied it because she was not "programming." This meant she was not doing what the staff felt was best for her. This could be argued against as a valid reason for denying a furlough; she was also being limited to a certain number of town trips per month, an added attempt to deny her her whims. She was not doing anything to earn an incident report, but she was also not reflecting on her crime and changing her ways. She was flamboyant in her flaunting of the system. Here is another place where the flexibility of this type of institution may be used to stretch the power staff has over residents. Curtailing her activities was a means of control. She totally rejected "rehabilitative efforts." I often wondered why she continued to come to groups as frequently as she did. Perhaps this and her angry emotional reaction were indications of a desire to change after all. I have a feeling, though, that will only be when she decides she needs to change. She is not the type to believe others on something like that.

Editor's Note

Much of correctional work in an institution centers on the day-to-day problems that arise from a large number of men or women who are not related and perhaps have little in common, but nonetheless are forced to interact and cooperate with each other in regard to every facet of their life. In this section, the author describes a "Townhall Meeting," which is essentially a group meeting of the entire unit. The meeting focuses on the problems of life in the institution. The intern expresses her frustration because the meetings tend to become chaotic gripe sessions.

The Journal

I had to hold a Townhall Meeting that afternoon for an absent counselor. Townhall Meetings are for the entire unit; all the women on a unit are required to attend to discuss any concerns that involve the entire unit.

Generally, the group is too large to get anything constructive accomplished, so the session usually becomes a gripe session if the leader is not prepared, ahead of time, with topics that she wants discussed. Today's topic for argumentation was the noise on the floors. There are several circular arguments that surface in this type of discussion—nothing can be said to the person or persons making the noise because you may be attacked later; nothing can be said to a staff person because then you would be "snitching" and would be attacked; it is impossible to catch the people making the noise, or the mess, because no one can possibly be everywhere at the same time. These are the three standard arguments, similar to the "Yes, but . . ." syndrome characteristic of many a therapy session. It becomes a mental obstacle course the worker is supposed to tackle because the inmates will not seriously consider any of the suggested alternative solutions. Getting caught up in trying to think of alternatives for someone else is dangerous and frustrating. Ask each inmate what she thinks is a good thing to do and constructively criticize her suggestions. This saves a lot of frustration.

Editor's Note

In the description of a group session presented in this excerpt, the intern reports what she learned from inmates about staff insensitivity to their problems.

The Journal

In the afternoon, I served as group leader on behalf of a staff member who was involved in other duties. Interestingly, the discussion turned to the prison system, and the women began criticizing the programs. Quickly, the discussion turned into a destructive, name-calling session centered mostly on individual staff members. I pointed out the tone the meeting had taken to the group members and they proceeded to tell me whether they felt the programs at the institution were constructive or not.

With a little direction and a lot of slipping back into the old tone, the group spent an hour thinking about the system and presented some pretty insightful observations. Very apparent to them, and to me, is a tolerance game that many of the staff persons play with the residents. The game consists of denying a legitimate request for what is often no apparent reason. Indeed, several times that I have witnessed such a request and denial, and asked the staff person why the request was denied, the person was at a loss as to why he or she had denied it. It seems to be a kind of contrived test to see how the resident will react to "no." It seems to coincide with a bureaucratic approach that renders some staff members insensitive to their clients' emotions. Just as the doctor, who becomes accustomed to the patients' emergencies and can deal with them quickly and efficiently without personal upset must remember that though the emergency is a routine medical procedure for him, it is not to his client, so must the caseworker, whose sense of urgency over any particular matter has diminished after dealing with the same requests every day, realize that to the client who is currently experiencing the situation it is an especially acute one. The sensitive counselor or caseworker will examine each request in the light of its reasonableness, as well as the realities of the institution's policies and procedures. There must be an empathetic awareness of the feelings that the resident may be experiencing, such as anxiety, frustration, anticipation, or sadness. The feelings cannot be dissociated from those factors that go into making the decisions.

Editor's Note

At the close of her internship, the author summarizes her reactions to the inmates, their response to her efforts, and the insights into the treatment-staff–resident relationship, which she gained during her weeks at the institution.

The Journal

The head of community programs asked me to describe the comfortability, or lack of it, that I had with the residents. I began with the feelings of rejection I had had in the very beginning when stared down by a resident after I had just greeted her. Most residents expect others to "go the extra mile" before they will have anything to do with the other person. It is a sort of trial period the residents feel necessary, but is much more demanding than an ordinary friendship would ask of trust development. Part of the feeling may come from the resentment they have at being arrested, convicted, imprisoned, and told they have a problem and are going to be rehabilitated. They see help being offered that they did not ask for, since they think they do not have any problem. There are only tangible things that they need you for, like getting furloughs approved, and similar other things. As soon as the resident sees that staff can be the deciding factor in many things, she begins to play a game of toleration, being just friendly enough to stay in staff's favor and not jeopardize her position.

That was the way I felt at the very beginning. It was an extremely bleak picture. I still feel the reservation now, but I do not see it in as harsh a light. Consideration and consistency are most appreciated by the residents and do the most for breaking down the reserve they build up.

There is another aspect to the issue, that of developing, as a staff person, a callousness or automatic suspicious nature toward the residents, as if always expecting to be "taken" or used. One cannot be totally unaware that it might happen, but to be expecting it of everyone is also an unhealthy extreme. As a matter of course, policy of the institution protects against such a thing by making certain procedures standard for certain situations. It is a sort of check and balance system for the protection of the staff. . . .

I also had strong feelings about what I perceived as inconsideration and rudeness on the part of the residents. Often, gestures made by staff members that were not required, but were made out of a person's kindness, went unacknowledged. I remember a particular shopping trip I went on where the counselor bought all the residents ice cream at the end of the afternoon, and all silently accepted without any acknowledgement. Another situation involved a picnic that a counselor had arranged for the residents. As soon as the bus arrived at the park, all the residents sat down, griped that there was nothing to do, complained about the food, which none helped to prepare, and had a thoroughly wretched time. I kept wondering all evening why the staff had bothered to organize such an outing in the first place. Several people, including residents and staff, have pointed out to me that I am unrealistic to expect certain gestures of consideration, as, for many, politeness and etiquette were never part of their life style. I can accept that explanation, but I cannot accept the staff's failure, in many cases, to do anything about it. At the times that the situations occurred, I was too angry to say anything constructive, but after a while I specifically mentioned them to several of the people involved. I am not sure what effect this had, but I felt it was something important to discuss.

My supervisor and I also talked about the sympathy pendulum that new staff people and interns often get caught up in. Rather than judging each situation on its own merits, sympathy and understanding seems to cluster exclusively toward staff or toward the residents. Part of this comes from inexperience; going on emotional reaction, initially, the novice tends to sympathize with the one who first tells his or her side of the story. Until all sides are known, judgment should be withheld. I assume that ability comes with practice and experience. I felt it to be so for myself.

My supervisor assured me that I was "growing" professionally, for these were the types of issues many new staff members feel and must deal with. That I was experiencing them as an intern made it even more to my advantage, for some of the growing would already be done when I finally began my career. There is still a long way to go, and a lot of issues yet to be dealt with.

Burnout: Avoiding the Consequences of On-The-Job Stress

Richard M. Morris

Stress and its presence in the workplace are undergoing close examination. Once looked upon as a factor in productivity and creativity, stress is now viewed as a debilitation factor in a worker's performance. The intention of this article is to outline the causal factors in stress and to suggest that the factors be treated as a group.

A certain amount of stress is needed for one to perform at peak ability. Stress is the agent that causes action and reaction, and certain amounts of stress are necessary for life. The same as a banjo string that, if too tightly wound would snap or too loosely wound would produce no sound, the correct amount of tension that give the desired sound can be compared to the factor of stress in daily life.

Most health care professionals know there is an enormous degree of stress engendered in law enforcement and security work. Repeated confrontations in what is perceived as impossible situations requiring a response (damned-if-you-do, damned-if-you-don't situations) create feelings of inadequacy for those who must make ambiguous decisions during constant ambiguous situations. Shift work, constant fear and anticipation of danger and death, confrontation with injury and violence, negative attitudes that prevail during the course of a workday, prejudice, and hostility and suspicion by the general public add to this, invariably causing anxiety, disillusionment, and disappointment with the job.

Correctional officers and others involved in security work are prime targets for this type of stress. Working in a correctional environment can drain one's senses. Because an officer's senses must be operating continuously when on duty in a correctional facility, the drain on his/her senses is also continuous.

Reprinted by permission of the American Correctional Association, Inc. from *Corrections Today* 48 (6) (August 1988): 122-126.

In the private sector, an individual who works 10 or more hours a day and gets the job done quickly is often considered a successful executive. The criterion for success is completing a project in the shortest amount of time. In this atmosphere, the strongest of survivors reaches the top. This type of environment, although successful in the short run, is very costly in its long-term effects. Absenteeism and employee turnover are two of the most immediate symptoms of this work environment. Quite simply, the pressure is too much.

Lately, the analysis of stress has moved into the public sector, with surveys being conducted to determine job burnout. People who work in social programs under government auspices (i.e., programs for the mentally handicapped, physically handicapped, or educationally deficient) often experience what is known as job burnout. Viewed as stress in its most extreme form, job burnout is simply the inability of an employee to continue performing his/her function. Many of the reasons for job stress are reasons for job burnout. Burnout occurs when stress has been so intense for such a long period that is is difficult for an employee to perform even the most basic requirements of his/her job.

Stressors in Correctional Work

There are certain stressors shared by employees in both the private and public sector. Some stressors found in correctional work are also found in other occupations, including administrative policy concerning work assignments, procedures and policy, and lack of administrative backing and support (including the relationship and rapport between correctional officer and supervisor). Stress is also caused by job conflict—a situation in which officers are caught between discrepant situations. Other common stressors in the workplace are inactivity, physical and/or mental work under load and idleness, shift work, working hours other than the normal work schedule, responsibility for the lives and welfare of others, inequities in pay or job status, and being underpaid and under-recognized for one's work.

Correctional officers are also subject to specific stressors including unfavorable attitudes held by the public toward correctional officers, daily crisis situations, daily situations posing a threat or overwhelming officers emotionally, racial situations, confrontations among officers and minority groups, and court rulings that make it seem almost impossible not to violate someone's human or civil rights.

The stressors encountered in security work affect both the organization and individual. Stress can be a prime factor in employee absenteeism, employee turnover, increased costs for overtime, and early retirements. Various studies have indicated excessive stress can lead to alcoholism, drug dependence, heart attacks or other illnesses, divorce, and other family problems.

There are two methods of identifying excessive stress in the workplace. A review of employee sick leave, absentee records, and the job-turnover rate can be used as empirical indicators, but the concerned supervisor will generally recognize that something is wrong. For example, poor or reduced performance, lack of enthusiasm for work, and sudden changes in employee work habits are all common indicators. A review of both the empirical data and the impressions of supervisors is usually the first step in developing a stress management program.

Recommendations for Stress Management

Most stress management programs share three common ingredients. First, the components of stress are defined. Second, warning signals and effects of stress are explained. Third, participants in the program are taught a method of overcoming, reducing and/or dealing with stress. This method can include relaxation techniques, self-hypnosis, and behavior modification. The general principle of stress management is that, although a particular stressful situation cannot be changed, an individual's perception of that situation and his/her subsequent actions can be.

Health maintenance is one further item that is part of most, but not all, stress management programs. Programs focusing on nutritional needs and physical exercise are included in health maintenance. For those individuals who deal in security work, health maintenance is probably an important aspect of a stress management program. An individual in good physical shape may be able to sustain long periods of stressful activity much better than an individual not physically fit.

One factor in stress often overlooked is the physical environment. A stressful environment is generally perceived in terms of an individual's relationship with his/her work and the human contacts in that workplace. The physical environment (i.e., lighting, heating, coolness, dampness, and spacial relationships) can affect individuals in ways that are not readily noticeable. This would seem entirely applicable to those involved in security work. Correctional officers are generally confined to a limited area. A poorly lit area, where the officer is unable to observe the activity of those who are confined, can easily raise the stress level of that officer. Dampness, coldness, or excessive heat can also affect that officer's performance.

Stressful Environments

Ways the organizational structure contributes to employee stress should also be examined. A stress program directed at individuals—and not at the organization—may be effective in the short run, but it will not have any long-term benefits. An employee can be taken out of the stressful environment and recharged, but the stressful environment will once again wear him/her down.

A comprehensive stress management program can also include the family in reducing the level of stress in the individual. Essentially, there are two parts to daily life. The first is the relationship between self and family; the second is the relationship between self and the workplace. For the security officer, this is a severe contrast. He/she moves from a comfortable and friendly environment into one that is the complete opposite. This sudden shift undoubtedly affects the amount of stress in an officer's life, and that amount of stress, in turn, affects that officer's family.

One method of reducing stress in a correctional officer's life may be to include the family in the initial training given to that officer. For example, one or two days in the training program of an officer can be set aside so the type of work the officer will be doing can be explained to spouses and other family members. This way, the family can have a greater understanding of the stress the individual officer is under. At the least, inclusion of family in the officer's training will establish a bond between the two distinct parts of that officer's daily life.

To summarize, an effective and comprehensive stress management program may include, but certainly not be limited to, the following items:

- A definition of the components of stress.
- An explanation of the warning signals and effects of stress.
- A method for overcoming, reducing, and dealing with stress.
- A health maintenance program, including physical fitness.
- An analysis of the physical environment.
- An analysis of the organizational structure.
- The inclusion of the family in a stress management program.

Individuals in the security field involved in stress management programs strongly suggest that the stress program be conducted by fellow officers. They do so for two reasons: 1) officers generally relate better to fellow officers, and 2) the cost of the stress management program can be effectively reduced by using individuals already included in the personnel budget.

As this article indicates, the study of stress in security work has not fully matured. There are people conducting studies, but the scope of the problem almost defies explanation due to over-crowded institutions, changing work forces, changing inmates, court decisions, the question of custody versus treatment, etc. Also, an important first step in a stress program is diagnosis of the seriousness of stress problems in an organization.

It is clear that stress cannot be treated in short training programs. An individual can be told what is happening to him/her, but unless something can be done about it the stress remains.

There is more to stress management than just learning how to stay calm. Personal health management is important. Breaking away from the only-those-inside-can-know attitude is also important. Peer counseling, not just peer instruction, is important. Nobody has a lock on the best method, if there is one.

4 Classification for Correctional Treatment

Introduction

The American Correctional Association defines classification as "the means by which offenders are assigned to different programs in an effort to provide the best available programs to fit the individual offender's needs."[1] Classification of offenders, if properly executed, enables correctional agencies to maximize the use of their personnel and resources to provide treatment that will enable the offender to fulfill his or her specific needs, and to assure, as well, that the concerns of other interested parties are met.

The most basic and familiar classifications of offenders are those made according to sex, age (juvenile or adult), severity of offense (misdemeanor or felony), and types of statutes violated (federal, state, or local). The classification of juvenile offenders has been complicated by rulings that require status offenders (those who have committed offenses that are not illegal for adults) to be housed in nonsecure settings and not be mixed with delinquent offenders.[2]

Classification may be made at a diagnostic or reception center, which receives newly sentenced adults and uses various indicators to assess the level of security at which each offender should be held and the type of treatment that may be given. After an offender is sent to a specific institution an in-house classification may also be made. Juveniles placed in the custody of a State Youth Authority or Youth Commission are customarily remanded to a diagnostic and reception center, where the type of setting in which the youth will be held is decided. However, in some jurisdictions judges have the power to sentence adults or send juveniles to specific institutions.

Classifications made under the guise of treatment are also developed for more effective management of prisoners. Correctional facilities are frequently typified as being maximum, medium, or minimum security; and offenders are placed in terms of their perceived risk to the community and to each other. Maximum security facilities may be surrounded by outside walls or high electrified fences, have internal divisions into cell blocks, and use armed guards. Medium security facilities may be surrounded by walls or fences, but have less intense segregation of prisoners and a lower level of internal surveillance. Minimum security institutions may have no readily visible security measures around the institution and may use cottage living or honors sections for many of the prisoners.

One of the first attempts to develop a prisoner classification system was made by Howard Gill in 1927. His plan included separation of prisoners into distinct groups, either within an institution or by housing them in separate facilities. Gill believed that new prisoners should be isolated from the others for purposes of observing their behavior and determining their potential for rehabilitation. From this point, prisoners would be classified as *tractable*—able to respond to treatment efforts and change their behavior; *intractable*—resistant to change and requiring forcible methods of control; *defective*—mentally ill, retarded, or physically handicapped; and those who could be handled best in some type of work-release or community placement facility.[3]

As classification systems became more refined, it was thought possible, through an elaborate diagnostic process, to match a specific offender with an exact form of treatment that would best suit his needs. Dr. Herbert C. Quay developed a system of classification termed *differential treatment,* which employed such specific matching. First used with delinquents at the National Training School for Boys in Washington, D.C., the program involved testing and then matching of each new student with a counselor who had been trained to "treat" the type of problem behavior this youth was believed to manifest.

When rehabilitation became a paramount goal of corrections, it was necessary to develop treatment modalities to enhance the rehabilitative effort. It was also necessary to ascertain which offenders were likely to benefit from specific treatment programs. The first selection in this chapter, "The Functions of Classification Models in Probation and Parole: Control or Treatment-Rehabilitation?" by Peter C. Kratcoski, notes that highly complex methods of classifying probationers, inmates, and parolees have been developed for administrative and management purposes, as well as for treatment and rehabilitation. The National Advisory Commission on Criminal Justice Standards and Goals, in its *Report on Corrections*, made the point that classification made supposedly for purposes of treatment may in fact be used for control, convenience of the staff, evening out of the number in each treatment program, or cost efficiency.[4]

The range of available correctional treatment is subject to the security level of the institution to which the offender is assigned. For example, total milieu therapy or guided group interaction would not be a likely treatment possibility in a maximum security institution, while behavior modification therapy would be readily available.

On the community level, a probation, parole, or juvenile aftercare officer often divides the caseload into maximum, medium, and minimum supervision levels, after calculating the needs of each offender and the risk each presents to the community. Clients under maximum supervision might be seen rather frequently (once or twice a week), while those in minimum supervision may be required to report monthly, or only if some problem arises.

The second selection in this chapter, "The Case Management System Experience in Ohio," by Clifford W. Crooks, provides information on the step-by-step development, implementation, and revision of a classification system for offenders utilized by the Ohio Adult Parole Authority. Specific instruments illustrate how offenders are assigned to maximum, medium, or minimum supervision, using risk and need assessment scales. Adaptations of the classification system, based on evaluation findings and officer input, are described, and methods for training officers in risk and needs assessment are reported.

The third selection in this chapter, "Intensive Probation: An Examination of Recidivism and Social Adjustment," by Susan Noonan and Edward J. Latessa, describes the manner in which certain clients are chosen for intensive probation as an alternative to incarceration, and focuses on the problems of caseload size, number and frequency of contacts, and methods of measuring program effectiveness.

The final selection in this chapter, "Functional Units: A Different Correctional Approach," describes efforts by the Federal Bureau of Prisons to divide facilities into smaller units of offenders, who are housed together and receive a specific type of treatment under the supervision of a team of staff members permanently assigned to that unit. Such units may be developed to handle offenders with a common problem area (drug, mental health, alcoholism); according to personality types, similar to those used in the Quay system; or to include offenders engaged in specific forms of academic, vocational, or educational training. The authors note the crucial part played by classification in any attempt to operate specialized treatment programs of this type.

Notes

1. Committee on Classification and Casework, American Prison Association, *Handbook on Classification in Correctional Institutions* (Washington, D.C.: American Correctional Association, 1968), 10.

2. Public Law 93-415 (September 7, 1974), Title II, Part B, Sec. 223 (a), (12).

3. Howard Gill, "A New Prison Discipline: Implementing the Declaration of Principles of 1870," *Federal Probation* 34 (June 1970): 31-33.

4. National Advisory Commission on Criminal Justice Standards and Goals, *Report on Corrections* (Washington, D.C.: U.S. Goverment Printing Office, 1973), 202-203.

The Functions of Classification Models in Probation and Parole: Control or Treatment-Rehabilitation?*

Peter C. Kratcoski

The use of classification systems in corrections is not a new development. When corrections moved from a punishment model to a rehabilitation or treatment emphasis in the early 20th century, classifications systems, such as that developed by Howard Gill, were used to separate prisoners according to their potential for treatment or training. Gradually, classification systems became more complex and multipurpose, and today they are used not only to classify offenders within institutions but also to assess the amount of supervision needed by offenders placed on probation in lieu of institutionalization or those paroled from prisons.

Classification systems now in use are complex and multipurpose. A distinction can be made between those that are used for administrative and management purposes and those designed to treat and rehabilitate the offender. Those of a management nature are designed to enhance control and to predict the likelihood that an offender will commit new criminal acts after release. The treatment-rehabilitation systems try to differentiate the offenders on the basis of their needs, attitudes, motivations, and attributes and then provide the treatment necessary to bring about the desired changes in values, attitudes, and skills that will inhibit the offenders from recidivating. The treatment-rehabilitation systems of classification are based on the concept of

*The research presented in this article was funded by a grant to the Ohio Department of Rehabilitation and Correction from the National Institute of Corrections, NIC E-P-6.

Reprinted by permission from *Federal Probation,* 49 (5) (December 1985): 49-56.

differential treatment, which implies that the needs and problems of inmates and those in community supervision must be defined and treated on an individualized basis. The offender is matched with the specific treatment program which best addresses these problems and needs.

According to Edith Flynn, an effective classification system should meet the following criteria:

(1) There must be an explicit statement regarding the function and purpose of the classification system.

(2) The classification system should be dynamic and theoretically based so that it may serve to increase the system's predictive powers and its success in reducing recidivism.

(3) The assumption on which the classification system is based must be explicit.

(4) The critical variables of the classification typology applied must be specific so that the utility of the system can be empirically tested.

(5) The classification system should be useful and feasible and facilitate efficient management and optimum use of available resources.[1]

Classification of offenders within institutions was closely related to programming, while the use of classification for those placed on probation and parole was initially directed toward predicting recidivism, and levels of supervision were set up according to the assessed risk that the offender would become involved in criminal activity after release.

Since 1980, the Federal Probation System has used a Risk Prediction Scale (RPS 80) which classifies offenders for "high activity" or "low activity" supervision. The items used in this scale include completion of a high school education, the age of the offender, arrest-free status for 5 or more consecutive years before the previous offense, few prior arrests, a history of freedom from opiate usage, and a steady employment period of at least 4 months prior to arraignment for the present offense. Each item is weighted, and a cutoff point on the total score determines whether the offender will initially be assigned to low or high activity supervision.[2] Before initiation of this new system, survey data collected by the Probation Division of the Administrative Office of the U.S. Courts in 1974 and by the Research Division of the Federal Judicial Center in 1977 indicated that a variety of caseload classification methods were used by Federal probation officers. These methods ranged from purely subjective assessments to statistical prediction devices.[3]

When the National Institute of Corrections placed the development of statewide classification systems for probation and parole as a high priority funding project, various states developed systems of classification of those under supervision. These statewide systems considered both control and treatment in their classification procedures. One of the earliest states to receive funding for a new classification program was Wisconsin, and a statewide system was put into effect there in 1977. More than 30 other states have now adopted some form of statewide classification model, and the current emphasis in the field is for county level probation departments to incorporate some features of the state models in their supervision programs. Because of its early start in this area and the wide publicity given to its features, the Wisconsin classification system is often considered the prototype for development of new classification systems.

Classification models tend to have common features. One would be an assessment of the risk (danger to the community) presented by the offender. The risk classification device is designed to assess a client's potential for future criminal behavior. Items related to the offender's criminal history and socioeconomic-personal adjustment background are weighted, and a total score is used to place the offender at a specific level of supervision, with the intensity of supervision designed to reduce the threat of recidivism to a minimum. For example, the instrument used to assess risk in the Wisconsin system included the following:

(1) Number of address changes in the last 12 months;
(2) Percentage of time employed in the last 12 months;
(3) Alcohol usage problems;
(4) Other drug usage problems;
(5) Attitude;
(6) Age at first conviction;
(7) Number of prior periods of probation/parole supervision;
(8) Number of prior probation/parole revocations;
(9) Number of prior felony convictions;
(10) Convictions or juvenile adjudications for burglary, theft, auto theft, or robbery, worthless checks or forgery; and
(11) Conviction or juvenile adjudication for assaultive offense within the last 5 years.[4]

When the various states or local probation and parole departments developed their own risk instruments, there was acceptance of the format used in Wisconsin, but each supervising authority tended to vary somewhat in the number of items included, the specific focus of the items, and the weight given to each item in relation to the total score. For example, those responsible for developing a risk instrument for the Tennessee system reasoned that:

> Since laws vary from one state to another, law enforcement varies from one state to another, and people differ from one state to another, those individuals who find themselves in prison and then on parole will differ from one state to another. This . . . requires that the processes of determining levels of risk and need should be reflective of the clientele in the Tennessee Parole System.[5]

This approach of adjusting the instrument to the local conditions seems appropriate. It also apparently does not detract from the predictive power of the instrument. In classifying offenders supervised under the Federal system, several predictive devices used were found to have comparable predictive power, even though the specific items used in the instrument and the method of scoring and assignment to risk levels varied.[6]

Another feature of classification models is use of a needs instrument, which assesses the offender's needs in such areas as family support, employment, emotional problems, or drug or alcohol abuse treatment. As an offender's score on the needs instrument increases, it is assumed that the amount of time and the number of resources directed toward the case will also increase. The needs assessment instrument is most effective when clients are reassessed on a regular basis and determinations are made as to whether progress is occurring in meeting the offender's needs and working on his or her problems.

Both risk and needs instruments allow officers and supervisors the opportunity to categorize all those supervised in a matrix format: offenders with a high risk and high needs levels, those with low risk and high needs, those with high risk and low needs, and those with low risk and low needs. Management and officers get a very clear picture of the distribution of cases which are currently under supervision, and workload distributions can be made according to the intensity of supervision required for the offenders. The models move away from caseloads and incorporate a "work unit" concept, which is set up on the basis of the supervision levels of the offenders, the geographic distribution of the cases, the types of duties required of officers (preparation of presentence investigations or supervision only), and special types of cases handled (transfers or interstate compact cases). Theoretically, this approach should equalize the amount of work expected from each officer. Under past systems, caseloads were defined in terms of the number of cases supervised. Little attention was given to the intensity of supervision required or the amount of time needed for each case.

After assessments have been completed, the classification procedure takes place. Classification in the case management approach involves grounding the specific classification in an evaluation of the interacting forces of the case. The specific classifications of offenders generally include maximum, medium, and minimum supervision levels. They may also provide for cursory levels of supervision, with little or no contact between officer and offender. The specific classification of offenders may vary from jurisdiction to jurisdiction, even though these offenders may have common characteristics. A case perceived as low risk in one jurisdiction may be classified as a medium risk in another because of the small number of serious cases serviced there. The risk score cutoff points may vary significantly, depending on the number of cases supervised and the number of officers available. For example, Ohio and Wisconsin use essentially the same risk and needs instruments, but in Wisconsin the maximum supervision category begins at a score of 15 on the risk instrument, while in Ohio it begins at 26.

In addition to risk factors, other methods are used to classify offenders. Rather than basing classification on criminal activity, other behavioral and personality characteristics of the offender are taken into account. This information is obtained through an interview with the client or from case file information. In Ohio, four Case Supervision Approaches (CSA) are defined, including criminal orientation, multiproblem, socially deficient, and situational offenders. An individual is assigned to one of the CSA's on the basis of a structured interview. After placement at a risk level and a CSA, a case management plan for providing services to the client is developed. The offender is expected to provide input in developing this plan and should agree that the activities required of him or her are appropriate and achievable.

Once the supervision level is defined for a case, the supervision is conducted according to a formula set up for the number and types of contacts required at this level. The specifications of the case plan will direct the officer toward referrals to agencies, the amount of counseling needed, requiring drug presence tests, and setting of special conditions. Case monitoring involves verifying employment, place of residence, participation in required programs, and compliance with probation and parole conditions.

In California, the classification system differentiates both types of offenders and types of parole officers. Offenders are classified as "control," "service," or "minimum-supervision" cases. Those with high risk assessment scores are designated "control" and given intensive supervision by officers who handle only control cases and whose only function is surveillance. "Service" cases, classified by high needs assessment score, are under the supervision of a service officer, who acts as a broker in obtaining referrals to appropriate community agencies. If a service category offender commits a new offense the service officer cannot arrest him—this function is reserved for control officers. Minimum supervision cases (those with low risk and needs scores) are seen only at the time of release from prison and at the end of the year of parole, with monthly mailed-in reports from the offender taking the place of visits to the parole office. Minimum supervision specialists handle these cases, but perform no other functions. In 1981, 84 percent of the parolees were classified as control cases, 8 percent as service cases, and 8 percent as minimum supervision cases. The California parole officers were assigned to control as opposed to service or minimum supervision in a 6 to 1 ratio.[7]

Most classification systems provide for periodic reassessments of the cases. These may take place at specified time intervals (6 months, for example) or if there is a change in jurisdiction from one unit to another or if the person supervised has committed a new offense. The reassessment instruments shift emphasis from past criminal behavior to overall performance or adjustment during the current probation or parole. The reassessment instrument taps the offender's adherence to the rules and special conditions, use of community services recommended, and overall adjustments in the areas of work, family, and personal functioning. At the time of reassessment the level of supervision may be reduced or increased, although there would be a tendency to reduce rather than increase supervision.

At the time of final evaluation before release a summary of the changes and progress which occurred during supervision is developed. Once the case has been terminated, the information available on all of the classification instruments is stored for future access, if needed.

The Effects of Classification Systems on Clients and Staff

Although the majority of states have developed some form of offender classification which attempts to provide a control and treatment formula within the same model, the evaluation of the effectiveness of these models has generally been rather sketchy. Each state has attempted some internal evaluation, and on occasion detailed evaluation by a neutral agent has taken place. The bases for the determination of effectiveness have varied, but recidivism reduction is the primary factor considered. The purpose of this section of the article is to draw attention to areas in which the departments might be affected regardless of the changes in criminal behavior which may occur after the classification system is put into operation. The manner in which the system affects the staff is generally not even considered in evaluations of its effectiveness. In this article we will look at effects of new systems on both clients and officers, including the degree to which administrators and officers accept and commit themselves to the new system, opinions of the new system's efficiency in comparison to prior systems, and the effects of standardization and the reduction of discretion on the officers' perceptions of their role and their job satisfaction. Does the new system remove autonomy and professional discretion, require upgrading of skill levels, vary or consolidate responsibility areas, increase tedious paperwork, improve communications with other officers and superiors, and reduce or enhance overall job satisfaction? For the clients, what is the expectation in regard to recidivism and community adjustment? The new systems are geared to efficiency and productive use of resources. Recidivism is not expected to decline at all supervision levels. Instead, those offenders who are placed in a maximum supervision category and who also have high needs are given the most intense supervision and concentration of services, and for them the model predicts that criminal behavior will significantly decline and that individual and social adjustment will increase. For offenders placed at lower intensity of supervision levels it is predicted that their present level of performance will not deteriorate and that they will not commit criminal offenses at levels greater than their prior performances.

A study conducted by the National Institute of Corrections involved 474 probation and parole officers who were working in nine states in which some new case management system had recently been introduced. In responding to questions about their new system, more than three of every four respondents viewed it as beneficial. The majority of negative comments about the systems dealt with very specific policy issues indigenous to the particular state system. Some of these comments centered on the inability to adequately perform as expected because of an extremely high caseload, the inclusion of juveniles in the system, problems in rural areas related to finding appropriate settings for conducting interviews, and lack of social-community support systems for referrals once the problems of offenders had been assessed. In this study, 32 percent of the respondents rated the system as being "very helpful" in their job, 46 percent considered it "helpful," 14 percent considered it "moderately helpful," and 8 percent regarded it as "not helpful." Seventy-three percent indicated that the system increased their knowledge and understanding of the clients, 53 percent said that it helped improve their case planning, and 54 percent said it helped them improve their ability to anticipate problems on the job.[8]

The degree of satisfaction with new case management systems seems to depend on the commitment to the system by administrators, the preparation for changes, and the ease of the transition from one system to the other. The nature of change is also an important point. In New York City, the Department of Adult Supervision Services had to introduce radical changes in the manner in which it supervised clients because of the influx of more than 13,000 new cases annually and budget reductions. The system introduced, called the Differential Supervision Program (DSP), had three levels of supervision assigned according to risk. However, the minimum supervision level contacts consisted of a monthly telephone call by the offender to a data entry telephone operator. If the call did not occur, a computer-generated letter was sent to remind the probationer to make the call. If the call still was not received, the probation officer was notified and appropriate action taken. Carol Rauh, in evaluating the New York City program, found that two factors were important in determining acceptance or rejection of the model by the rank and file officers. One was whether the automated support services portion of the system performed adequately and actually fulfilled the standardized routine tasks expected of it. The assumption of the program was that the computer would relieve the officers of much of the routine paperwork which was extremely time consuming but contributed to the offenders' welfare. In actual operation, the computer frequently broke down or was in error, and the officers were required to handle a deluge of calls, which led to dissatisfaction and general disillusionment with the system. The second factor mentioned by Ms. Rauh as important in acceptance of the new system was the administration's support and direction. To assess administration and staff commitment, a number of interviews were completed. The higher levels of administrators were very enthusiastic and unanimous in their belief in the importance and effectiveness of the new system. However, satisfaction with the system decreased in the lower levels of administration, and was at its lowest point among the unit supervisors. Only one of six supervisors interviewed spoke enthusiastically about the new system. This lack of belief in the system was reflected in the attitudes of the probation officers. Half of the officers interviewed reported that while it was a good idea in theory they saw little practical value in the new system. Rather than reducing their workloads, they felt that the new system had added to them. About two-thirds of the officers reported that they did not find the forms used to classify clients helpful, and only two of all the officers interviewed felt that the forms helped them focus on client problems.[9]

An extensive evaluation of the Ohio Case Management System was conducted in selected regions of the state one year after the new system had been in operation. I was the person selected to design and carry out this evaluation. As part of the evaluation, officers in one of the first regions to receive training in the new system were asked to complete an Attitude Assessment Questionnaire before they were trained in the new system. They completed the same questionnaire approximately one year after the training was received and the system had been in operation in that region. The questionnaire explored officers' perceptions of administrators' attitudes toward officers, administrators' effectiveness as perceived by the officers, and officers' positive attitudes toward change. Comparison of the results of the two administrations of the questionnaire revealed that in the post-test there was some change toward more positive attitudes, with the most significant change occurring with regard to officers' perceptions of the administrators' effectiveness.

A second phase of the evaluation of attitudes and opinions of personnel involved a qualitative assessment of the system by supervisors and officers in another region of the state in which the new Case Management System had been implemented. A semistructured interview format was used. The supervisors' responses ranged from total acceptance to a somewhat skeptical "wait and see" attitude. Problems identified included the need for an increase in personnel and adjustment in the number of work units allotted for each supervision level case and for emergency situations for cases which involved revocation procedures. The supervisors also saw a need for additional officer training in the development of case management plans. The officers in general accepted the new system as a useful tool, regarded the standardization in the new system as good, and felt it professionalized the officer's position, promoted efficiency, and gave the officers the security of making case management decisions based on objective criteria. Some officers felt that it did involve more paperwork, but the majority felt that the new system was more efficient than the former system because it assisted in developing a case plan earlier and offered direction as to what would be appropriate referrals to social service agencies. Some indicated that it led to an improvement in communications with immediate supervisors. In the past, if there were some confusion or disagreement about how a case should be supervised, the officer would have to accept the supervisors' directions. Now, because of the standardized procedures, it was quite easy to explain to a supervisor how a decision on a case was reached.

In contrast to the New York City probation program, the Ohio case management system was given firm support at all administrative levels. The top administrators supported it through communications and personal appearances to discuss the merits of the system. Regional supervisors and unit supervisors were . involved in the Case Management System Development Committee, which designed the instruments in conjunction with the Research Division of the Adult Parole Authority. This support by the administrators was reflected in the comments by the officers, who indicated that in the beginning they thought the new system was just a gimmick or even a way of increasing caseloads and reducing staff, but after its introduction they believed that the administration was committed to it, that the system was here to stay, and that they might as well work with it.[10]

Perhaps the most drastic change in the role of officers occurred in the California system. We noted earlier that the roles of the officers became quite specialized. The acceptance of the case management model in California by administrators, supervisors, and field officers varied. Administrators and supervisors appeared to accept the model because of its emphasis on the protection of the community. Given the current emphasis on "just desserts" for offenders, and the fact that parole was actually abolished for a period of time in California, a model which emphasizes the control facet of parole work had strong appeal. Some of the field officers also appeared to be quite pleased with the system. They found the concept of the minimum supervision of some cases to be logical and efficient. Some also liked being responsible for only one facet of parole work. Many did not feel competent to handle the dual roles of control and service. On the other hand, some officers lamented the loss of discretion, the ability to use their own judgment in making decisions. This discretionary power was a factor which gave the officer a professional status. Others also felt that the process was more complex and cumbersome than the old system. Their most frequent complaint was that the new system has generated more paperwork, and this detracts from the main job of supervision.[11]

A latent product of extreme specialization by officers only vaguely recognized is a tendency for the department personnel to factionalize on the basis of their assignments. Officers tend to develop a perspective or orientation toward their job which reflects the major goal of their work. The control officers might begin to perceive themselves as law enforcement officers, while the service officers would view themselves as social service workers. The communication gaps and internal dissension between custody and treatment personnel are well recognized in institutional settings on both the juvenile and adult levels. The competition for resources and personnel, in particular when budgets become tight, leads to a general decline in interpersonal relations, morale, and common goal orientation. In most cases, when these conflicts occur the custody factors take priority over treatment.

Recidivism

Although the success or failure of case management systems should not necessarily be dependent on the reduction of recidivism produced, when the basic question, "Does it work?" is asked, reduction in criminal behavior tends to be the criterion which can justify an affirmative response.

The case management models developed by the various states do not suggest that an across the board reduction of criminal behavior will result after the system commences operation. If the model functions according to design, the significant reductions in recidivism should occur in the maximum supervision category. The minimum supervision category should not change, even with the reduction in supervision, and the medium supervision cases might show a reduction in criminal behavior because of the employment of a more individualized case management plan.

Systematic research on the effects on recidivism of new case management plans is trickling in, but the data only give hints regarding the long term effects. Those who have considerable experience in the corrections field are knowledgeable enough to expect dramatic changes in criminal behavior for the maximum supervision cases. An offender whose deviant behavior dates back to childhood and whose life has followed a pattern of repeated offenses, supervision and/or incarceration is not going to change over night because of more intense supervision or a different approach to supervision.

In Wisconsin, a sample of offenders who were placed in the maximum supervision group were compared with a matched sample of cases who had not yet been included in the case management plan. Those in the control group were matched with those in the experimental group in age, sex, race, probation or parole status, employment, and items on the risk and needs instruments. The maximum supervision group under the new case plan had significantly lower recidivism than those in the control group. Thirty-seven percent of those in the control group had a new offense reported, compared to 18 percent of the experimental group. Twenty percent of the control group members had their probation or parole revoked, compared to 11 percent of the experimental group.[12] For the medium supervision cases a smaller percentage of those supervised under the new system recidivated when they were compared with the control group, but the differences were not large enough to be considered statistically significant. The recidivism in the minimum supervision group was quite low for both the experimental and control groups, confirming the hypothesis that this category of offenders can be given only cursory supervision and still not show an increase in their criminal behavior.

The findings that only 18 percent of the maximum supervision group committed a new offense and only 11 percent had their parole or probation revoked appears incredible when compared to the much higher recidivism rates generally considered to be normal for maximum supervision probationers and parolees. However, it should be noted that the Wisconsin Bureau of Community Corrections is responsible for the supervision of all adult probationers and both juvenile and adult parolees[13] and the overall characteristics of this offender population may not be comparable to what one would find in a more urban-industrialized state.

A study by the Wisconsin Bureau of Community Corrections after 2 years of experience with the case management system revealed that there was a strong correlation between the score the offenders obtained on the risk instrument and revocation rates. The higher the risk score, the higher was the revocation rate. For example, of 4,231 probationers and parolees who were terminated within 2 years after commitment to the program, 1,124 (27 percent) had a risk score between 4 and 7 and had a revocation rate of only 2.49 percent. However, at the other extreme 60 offenders (1.4 percent) had a risk score of 30 and above, and they had a revocation rate of 42.55 percent.[14]

In Wisconsin, both risk scores and needs scores were used to assign cases to supervision categories. The risk scores, however, appear to be more predictive of new criminal activity. In Wisconsin, a risk assessment score of 15 and above would lead to a maximum supervision classification, a score of 8 to 14 would result in medium supervision, and a score of 7 and below in minimum supervision.[15] About 50 percent of new clients were placed in maximum supervision.

The evaluation of the Ohio Case Management System I conducted involved a two-faceted research design. In one facet, an experimental region of the state, the first region where the new system was implemented, was used to develop a comparison of recidivism in the region before and after implementation of the system. Cases for the months of September, October, and November 1981, when the new system had been put into effect, were compared with those in the months of September, October, and November 1980. All cases which originated in parole and probation units selected for the experimental region were included. The 1980 sample had 276 cases, while the 1981 sample had 261 cases. The case files of all offenders in the samples were examined, and all criminal offenses which resulted in convictions, all alleged parole and probation violations which were confirmed, and all probation and parole "violator at large" statuses which occurred during a 12-month period from the date that the offender was placed on parole or probation were considered. The offenders were divided according to supervision level (maximum=risk score of 26 or higher; medium=risk score of 18 through 25; minimum=risk score of 0 through 17) and compared with regard to recidivism, as shown in Table 1.

Table 1 *Recidivism of Cases in the Experimental Region by Supervision Level Before and After Implementation of the Case Management System*

Supervision Level	Recidivism 1980		Recidivism 1981	
	N	% of Total[1]	N	% of Total[2]
Maximum	40	70%	50	63%
Medium	26	42%	32	47%
Minimum	27	17%	25	22%
TOTALS	93	34%	107	41%

[1] In 1980, there were 57 maximum supervision offenders, 62 medium, and 157 minimum.
[2] In 1981, there were 79 maximum supervision offenders, 68 medium, and 114 minimum.

As shown in Table 1, recidivism was lower for the 1981 maximum supervision group than for the maximum supervision group in 1980, although the decrease was not statistically significant. Although the recidivism increased from 1980 to 1981 in both the medium and minimum supervision levels, the increases were not statistically significant. This comparison, while not conclusive, gives some support for the assumptions underlying the Case Management System model. In the maximum supervision category, where the intensity of supervision was increased, there was a decline in the percentage who recidivated. At the minimum supervision level, where supervision was decreased, no substantial increase in recidivism occurred. The only group which performed contrary to the model's expectations was the medium supervision level. It was expected that recidivism here would remain constant, but it increased.

Of those parolees who committed new offenses, 58 percent of those in the 1980 sample committed felonies, compared to 49 percent of those in the 1981 sample. The percentage of parolees revoked and sent to prison was slightly higher for the 1980 sample (24 percent) than for the 1981 sample (23 percent). Of the probationers committing new offenses, 50 percent of those in the 1980 sample and 47 percent of those in the 1981 sample committed felonies, and 11 percent of the 1980 probationers in the sample were returned to prison, compared to 9 percent of the probationers in the 1981 sample.

The second facet of the research design involved a comparison of the sample of offenders in the experimental region, where the new Case Management System had been implemented (1981), with a sample in a control region of the state, where the system had not been implemented in that year. Since the offenders in the control region were not classified, the researchers classified them according to maximum, medium, or minimum supervision qualifying status, using the same instruments used by Parole Authority staff to classify the offenders in the experimental region. A comparison of the recidivism of the offenders in the experimental and control regions is given in Table 2.

Table 2   A Comparison of Recidivism by Supervision Level
in the Experimental and Control Regions

Supervision level	Experimental[1] Region		Control[2] Region		Significance
	N	%	N	%	
Maximum	50	63%	28	60%	Not significant at .15 level
Medium	32	47%	34	44%	Chi Square Test
Minimum	25	22%	19	17%	

[1] In the Experimental Region, there were 79 maximum supervision offenders, 68 medium, 114 minimum.
[2] In the Control Region, there were 47 maximum supervision offenders, 77 medium, and 114 minimum.

As shown in Table 2, recidivism was almost three times as great at the maximum supervision level as at the minimum level for both the experimental and control group samples, and the recidivism for the medium level was more than twice that of the minimum. These patterns follow the projections made for the Case Management System model. However, it was projected that the recidivism for the maximum level experimental group would be lower than that for the maximum level control group because of the intense amount of supervision given to the maximum offenders in the experimental group, where the new Case Management System had been applied. This did not occur. The higher proportion of offenders in the maximum supervision category in the experimental group sample, when compared with the control group sample, no doubt had some bearing on the lack of recidivism reduction at this level. For the medium and minimum supervision levels, slight increases in recidivism also occurred in the experimental group sample, although it was projected that recidivism at the medium level would be reduced.

When the severity of new offenses by those who recidivated was compared by supervision level, the maximum level offenders in the control group had a greater proportion of felonies (33 percent) than did the maximum level experimental group (27 percent). In the medium level, the percentage committing felonies was the same for the two groups (25 percent). At the minimum level the experimental group (7 percent) and the control group (8 percent) had similar percentages committing felonies. This offense pattern follows the Case Management System model, with the maximum level offenders in the experimental group having a reduced percentage of serious offenses.

Table 3 compares the offenders revoked and sent to prison in the experimental and control regions.

Table 3 *A Comparison by Supervision Level of Offenders Sent to Prison After a New Offense or Technical Violation in the Experiemental and Control Regions*

Supervision Level	Experimental[1] Region		Control[2] Region	
	N	%	N	%
Maximum	24	30%	17	36%
Medium	14	21%	18	23%
Minimum	6	5%	11	10%

[1] In the Experimental Region, there were 79 maximum supervision offenders, 68 medium, and 114 minimum.

[2] In the Control Region, there were 47 maximum supervision offenders, 77 medium and 114 minimum.

As shown in Table 3, slightly higher percentages of the control region offenders in all supervision levels were revoked and sent to prison. Although these differences are not statistically significant, they support the projection of the Case Management System model that increased supervision of the maximum level cases will have positive results.[16]

One should be cautious about generalizing findings from one state program to another, even if a comparable case management system were used. In Ohio, risk and needs classification instruments were adopted which are quite similar to those used in Wisconsin. However, the cutoff points in the risk instruments used to delineate the Ohio supervision levels were considerably higher (26 and above for maximum supervision, 18 to 25 for medium supervision, and 17 and below for minimum supervision) than those used in Wisconsin (15 and above for maximum, 8 to 14 for medium, and 7 and below for minimum). If one compared Wisconsin and Ohio by supervision level without taking into consideration the actual risk scores used to delineate the various levels, it would appear that recidivism was considerably higher for the Ohio offenders than for those in Wisconsin. However, if the cases from the two states were matched by actual risk scores, the proportion committing new offenses would not vary significantly in the two states.

In conclusion, it is apparent that the case management models should be evaluated in relationship to their utility and not necessarily in relationship to a reduction in criminal activity. The systems work if officers make better decisions on cases, make more appropriate referrals to community service agencies, are more efficient in their work, establish better communications with supervisions, and are more confident and satisfied with their own job performance. If the agency administrators can live with the programs, even though recidivism rates do not drop significantly, case management systems will continue to be refined and this should result in a significant improvement in community corrections.

Notes

1. Edith Elisabeth Flynn, "Classification Systems," in *Handbook of Correctional Classification* (Cincinnati: Anderson Publishing Company, 1978) p. 86.

2. Administrative Office of the U.S. Courts, *Guide to Judiciary Policies and Procedures: Probation Manual,* Vol. x-0 §4004 (February 15, 1979).

3. James B. Eaglin and Patricia A. Lombard, *A Validation and Comparative Evaluation of Four Predictive Devices for Classifying Federal Probation Caseloads* (Washington, D.C.: Federal Judicial Center, 1982), p. 1.

4. S. Christopher Baird, Richard C. Heinz, and Brian J. Bemus, *The Wisconsin Case Classification/Staff Deployment Project* (Madison, Wisconsin: Department of Health and Social Services, 1979), p. 7.

5. James W. Fox, Mitchell Stein, and Gary Ramussen, "Development of the Tennessee Case Management for Delivery of Parole Services." Paper delivered at the 1983 Convention of the Academy of Criminal Justice Sciences, San Antonio, Texas, 1983, p. 7.

6. James B. Eaglin and Patricia A. Lombard, *A Validation. . . Caseloads*, pp. 99-122.

7. Stephen Gettinger, "Separating the Cop for the Counselor," *Corrections Magazine*, Vol. 7, No. 2 (April 1981), p. 35.

8. National Institution of Corrections, *Client Management Classification System Officer Survey* (Washington, D.C.: National Institute of Corrections, 1982).

9. Carol Rauh, "Important considerations in Ensuring the Success of a Case Management/Management Information System Model." Paper presented at the annual meeting of the Academy of Criminal Justice Sciences, San Antonio, Texas, 1983.

10. Peter C. Kratcoski, *An Evaluation of the Case Management System Probation and Parole Sections: Division of Parole and Community Services, Ohio Department of Rehabilitation and Correction*, report submitted September 1983, pp. 171-173.

11. Stephen Gettinger, "Separating the Cop from the Counselor," pp. 36-37.

12. Baird, Heinz, and Bemus, *The Wisconsin Case Classification/Staff Development Project: A Two Year Follow-Up Report* (Madison, Wisconsin: Department of Health and Social Services, 1979), p. 26.

13. *Ibid.*, p. 6.

14. *Ibid.*, p. 10.

15. *Ibid.*, p. 20.

16. Peter C. Kratcoski, *An Evaluation of the Case Management System . . . Ohio Department of Rehabilitation and Correction*, pp. 174-178.

The Case Management System Experience in Ohio

Clifford W. Crooks

Introduction:
The Wisconsin Contribution

The probation and parole case management systems currently in place at the state and county level in Ohio are by no means unique. They are, in fact, based upon the system developed and implemented in Wisconsin in the previous decade. Needless to say, a great deal has been written about the Wisconsin model and its total systems approach to the classification process. In order to fully understand Ohio's case management systems, it is important to summarize the major achievements in Wisconsin.

Responding to a legislative mandate to improve services for offenders and measure the workload of probation and parole agents, the Wisconsin Division of Corrections, Bureau of Community Corrections secured federal funds and formed the Case Classification/Staff Deployment Project (CC/SD Project) in 1975. During development and implementation, every effort was made to maximize staff input and support. Supervisors and line staff worked together, for example, to define standards. Staff were also encouraged to evaluate new procedures and predictive scales and to make suggestions for improvement.

When the Wisconsin Classification System was implemented statewide in 1977, it contained the following integrated components which met the objectives of the CC/SD Project:

1. A risk assessment scale developed by multiple regression analysis to identify and weight offender characteristics and criminal history items that best predict further criminal behavior.

Clifford W. Crooks, M.S., Parole Program Specialist, Adult Parole Authority, Ohio Department of Rehabilitation and Correction.
 This is the first publication of "The Case Management System Experience in Ohio."

2. A risk reassessment scale developed to identify and weight offender items that reflect overall adjustment during the course of supervision.

3. A needs assessment scale and treatment guidelines developed by supervising agents to identify noncrisis, offender problem or need areas, and potential strategies and resources to service them.

4. A Client Management Classification (CMC) system and treatment strategies developed empirically in the form of a semistructured interview and agent impressions to assist in placing offenders in one of five differential treatment groups, and to provide information concerning appropriate treatment strategies for casework planning.

5. A standarized classification and reclassification process was developed for probationers and parolees. At admission to supervision, the risk and need assessment scales are scored and the offender is assigned to one of three supervision levels (specific agent contacts are required at each level). At six month intervals during supervision, the risk reassessment scale and needs scale are scored and an offender is reclassified if appropriate and assigned to the appropriate level.

6. A workload budgeting and deployment system developed as a result of time studies that measured the time required by agents to perform activities and meet supervision standards, and used in the budgetary process and to deploy staff.

7. A management information system generated as a product of the classification and reclassification process and used as a foundation for evaluation, planning, and operations.

In 1979, Wisconsin released a two year followup report and analysis of the CC/SD Project. In part, the report concluded that:

*   Assignment to different levels of supervision based upon risk and needs assessment had a significant impact on probation and parole outcomes. There were fewer new convictions, rules violations, absconding and revocations with high need/high risk offenders as a result of increased contacts. Decreased contacts with low need/low risk offenders resulted in no adverse effects.

*   The risk assessment scale demonstrated effectiveness in predicting success or failure in completing terms of probation or parole supervision.

*   The needs assessment scale demonstrated high inter-rater reliability.

Components of the Wisconsin Model were duplicated in a number of probation and parole agencies throughout the country, including Ohio. The Wisconsin Model became, in fact, a National Institute of Corrections (NIC) Model Probation/Parole Classification System.

The Adult Parole Authority Case Management System (CMS)

The Ohio Department of Rehabilitation and Corrections, Adult Parole Authority staff were first exposed to the Wisconsin Classification System at an NIC funded Case Management Institute in 1979. As a result, federal grant monies were secured and a Case Management Task Force (CMTF), made up of research, management and line staff was formed. It was generally understood that the completed case management product would contain components applicable to both the probation and parole populations serviced by the Adult Parole Authority.

The following is a summary of the integrated CMS components developed by the Task Force:

1. A comprehensive classification process was developed. As in Wisconsin, researchers reviewed a random sample of closed offender cases and used multiple regression analysis to identify strong predictors of future criminal behavior. The resulting risk assessment scale contains ten weighted items. (See Figure 1.)

    A risk reassessment scale, containing eight items, was constructed as well to evaluate an offender's adjustment during supervision. (See Figure 2.)

    Supervisory and line staff developed a needs assessment scale. It contains 13 problem or need areas (two more than the Wisconsin scale), and input for the officer's impressions of the offender's needs. It was designed, like the Wisconsin scale, to be used for classification and case planning. Need treatment guidelines, comparable to Wisconsin's, were devised to assist officers more accurately identifying and treating offender need areas and making appropriate community resource referrals. (See Figure 3.)

    After the risk and need assessment and risk reassessment scales were developed, research staff tested the scales against offender case data to determine ranges of risk and need cut-off scores for three supervision levels:

    Maximum: High failure potential or great number of problem/need areas requiring services.

Figure 1
Assessment of Client Risk

Processor # _____

Client Name _____ Last First Mi	Client Number _____ Date _____
Officer _____ Last Social Security Number	Unit Location Code_____

Select the appropriate answer and enter the associated weight in score column. Total all scores to arrive at the risk assessment score.

Score

Number of Prior Felony Convictions: (or Juvenile Adjudications)	0 2 4	None One Two or more	_____
Arrested Within Five (5) Years Prior to Arrest for Current Offense (exclude traffic)	0 4	No Yes	_____
Age at Arrest Leading to First Felony Conviction (or Juvenile Adjudications)	0 2 4	24 and over 20 to 23 19 and under	_____
Amount of Time Employed in Last 12 Months (Prior to Incarceration for Parolees)	0 1 2 0	More than 7 months 5 to 7 months Less than 5 months Not appplicable	_____
Alcohol Usage Problems (Prior to Incarceration for Parolees)	0 2 4	No interference with functioning Occasional abuse; some disruption of functioning Frequent abuse; serious disruption; needs treatment	_____
Other Drug Usage Problems (Prior to Incarceration for Parolees)	0 2 4	No interference with fuctioning Occasional abuse; some disruption of functioning Frequent abuse; serious disruption needs treatment	_____
Number of Prior Adult Incarcerations in a State or Federal Institution	0 3 6	0 1-2 3 or more	_____
Age at Admission to Institution or Probation for Current Offense	0 3 6	30 or over 18 to 29 17 and under	_____
Number of Prior *Adult* Probation/Parole Supervisions	0 4	None One or more	_____
Number of Prior Probation/Parole Revocations Resulting in Imprisonment (Adult or Juvenile)	0 4	None One or more	_____

Total _____

Figure 2 Reassessment of Client Risk ☐ During Supervision
☐ At Final Discharge

Processor # _____

Client Name	_____	Client Number _____
	Last First Mi	
		Date _____
Officer	_____	Unit Location Code_____
	Last Social Security Number	

Select the appropriate answer and enter the associated weight in score column. Total all scores to arrive at the risk assessment score.

Score

Number of Prior Felony Convictions
(or Juvenile Adjudications)
- 0 None
- 3 One
- 6 Two
- 7 Three or more   _____

Age at Arrest Leading to First Felony Conviction
(or Juvenile Adjudications)
- 0 24 and over
- 2 20-23
- 5 19 and under   _____

Age at Admission to Probation/Parole Supervision
for Current Offense
- 0 30 and older
- 4 18-29
- 7 17 and under   _____

Rate the following based on period since last (re)assessment:

Type of Arrests (indicate most serious
excluding traffic)
- 0 None
- 2 Technical PV only
- 4 Misdemeanor arrest(s)
- 8 Felony arrest   _____

Associations
- 0 Mainly with noncrimnally oriented individuals
- 5 Mainly with negative individuals   _____

Alcohol Usage Problems
- 0 No interference with fuctioning
- 2 Occasional abuse; some disruption of functioning
- 3 Frequent abuse; serious disruption needs treatment   _____

Other Drug Usage Problems
- 0 No interference with functioning
- 1 Occasional abuse: some disruption of functioning
- 2 Frequent abuse: serious disruption; needs treatment   _____

Attitude
- 0 No adverse difficulties/ motivated to change
- 2 Periodic difficulties/ uncooperative/independent
- 5 Frequently hostile/ negative/criminal orientation   _____

Total _____

Figure 3 Assessment of Client Needs

Processor # _____

Client Name _____   Client Number _____
          Last   First   Mi   Date _____

Officer _____   Unit Location Code_____
        Last   Social Security Number

Score

Emotional and Mental Stability

0 No symptoms of emotions and/or mental instability

2 Symptoms limit, but do not prohibit adequate functioning

6 Symptoms prohibit adequate functioning and/or has Court or Board imposed condition

8 Severe symptoms requiring continual attention and/or explosive, threatening and potentially dangerous to others or self _____

Domestic Relationship

0 Stable/supportive relationships

3 Some disorganization or stress but potential for improvement

7 Major disorganization or stress _____

Associations

0 No adverse relationships

2 Association with occasional negative results

4 Associations frequently negative

6 Associations completely negative _____

Drug Abuse

0 No disruption of functioning

2 Occasional substance abuse: some disruption of functioning and/or has Court or Board conditions

7 Frequent abuse; serious disruption; needs treatment _____

Alcohol Usage

0 No disruption of functioning

2 Occasional abuse; some disruption of functioning and/or has court or Board conditions

7 Frequent abuse; serious disruption; needs treatment _____

Employment

0 Satisfactory employment, no difficulties reported; or homemaker, student, retired, or disabled

2 Underemployed

4 Unsatisfactory employment; or unemployed but has adequate job skills/motivation

5 Unemployed and virtually unemployable; needs motivation/training

Academic/Vocational Skills/Training

0 Adequate skills, able to handle everyday requirements

2 Low skill level causing minor adjustment problems

6 No identifiable skills and/or minimal skill level causing serious adjustment problems _____

Financial Management

0 No current difficulties

1 Situational or minor difficulties

5 Chronic/severe difficulties _____

Attitudes

0 No adverse difficulties/motivated for change

2 Periodic difficulties/ uncooperative/dependent

4 Frequently hostile/negative/criminal orientation _____

Residence

0 Suitable living arrangement

1 Adequate living, i.e., temporary shelter

4 Nomadic and/ or unacceptable _____

Mental Ability (Intelligence)

0 Able to function independently

1 Some need for assistence; potential for adequate adjustment

3 Deficiencies severely limit independent functioning _____

Health

0 Sound physical health; seldom ill

1 Handicap or illness; interferes with functioning on a recurring basis

2 Serious handicap or chronic illness; needs frequent medical care _____

Sexual Behavior

0 No apparent dysfunction

2 Real or perceived situational or minor problems

6 Real or perceived chronic or severe problems _____

Officer's Impressions of Needs

A. Low **0**   B. Medium **3**   C. Maximum **5**

Total _____

Medium: Lower failure potential or problem/need areas, but requiring officer involvement.

Minimum: Least failure potential or few significant problem/need areas.

The CMTF added a fourth supervision level, Extended, to be used at reclassification. To be assigned to Extended, an offender must have been under active supervision for at least a year, and at the Minimum level for the previous six months.

Classification is a straightforward process using the risk and need scales. Available information about an offender such as a Presentence or Parole Board Investigation, police reports, interviews or institutional records are reviewed by the officer and the scales are scored. The offender is placed in one of the three supervision levels based upon the higher classification of *either* scale.

The following are current risk and need cut-off scores for the three supervision levels:

Risk Score	Level of Supervision	Need Score
26 and above	Maximum	25 and above
18 to 25	Medium	15 to 24
17 and below	Minimum	14 and below

The following case summary and accompanying scales for Paul S., a 24-year-old male offender on parole supervison for burglary, illustrates the classification process:

Three years ago, Paul and an accomplice went to the apartment of a female known to the accomplice. They forced open a door, entered and ransacked the rooms (the female was not there at the time). They took money, a loaded revolver, a butcher knife, and keys. They stole the female's automobile from a nearby lot.

Both were arrested a short time later in the stolen vehicle. The accomplice had the loaded revolver and Paul had the money and knife. When questioned, Paul admitted his involvement, and told police that he and the accomplice had originally gone to the apartment to "punish" the female for "leaving" the accomplice. Paul was convicted of burglary and sentenced to the Department of Rehabilitation and Corrections. He served three years before he was paroled.

As a juvenile, Paul was adjudicated and convicted at age 14 for the theft of a teacher's purse and placed on indefinite probation. At age 15, Paul threatened a school principal with a hammer, was convicted of menacing and continued on probation. Paul was committed to a Department of Youth Services' institution at age 16 as a result of a burglary conviction and a probation violation finding.

Following release, Paul served a juvenile parole period which terminated at age 18.

As an adult, Paul was convicted of felony theft at age 19 and placed on probation. Within months Paul was arrested while driving a stolen van. He was convicted for receiving stolen property, his probation was revoked and he was sentenced to the institution. Paul was released on Shock Parole and completed his supervision period without major problems. The current offense of burglary occurred when Paul was 21; it is only the second offense committed with an accomplice.

Paul was raised by his older brother. Paul completed high school and a number of basic auto mechanics courses. As a teen, he had a history of acting out when angered. A recent evaluation described Paul as "argumentative, criminally motivated and lacking in positive direction." Paul has an average intelligence.

Paul has worked primarily as a restaurant cook and dishwasher. In the year prior to his arrest for the current offense, Paul worked only three months. He was fired from his last job for chronic absenteeism.

Paul has been unemployed since his release on parole and has resided with his brother. The brother is employed, owns his own home and has no criminal record. The brother is willing to provide Paul with a residence and spending money until Paul is employed and able to rent an apartment. Paul is actively seeking employment according to his brother. (See Figures 4 and 5.)

As the scales indicate, Paul's risk score is 28 and his need score is 24. Thus, Paul would be classified as a Maximum level offender.

There are two classification exceptions. Sex offenders are not classified by the risk or need scale. In addition, officers can override the scales, with supervisory approval, and assign an offender to a higher or lower level of supervision.

Reclassification occurs at six month intervals, when a significant event alters an offender's status, and at the termination of supervision. The risk reassessment and needs scale is scored based upon the offender's adjustment, and the offender is placed in the appropriate supervision level, as determined again, by the higher classification of either scale. Offenders may be placed in the Extended level at reclassification if they meet established criteria. The scales can be overridden at reclassification, as well.

2. A supervision policy was developed. The CMTF discovered that the Adult Parole Authority lacked a cohesive definition of supervision. The CMTF also discovered that the parole and probation sections of the agency had different policies for common tasks such as arrests, violations and the processing of terminations.

Figure 4   Assessment of Client Risk

Processor # _____

Client Name __*Paul S.*_____	Client Number _____
Last First Mi	Date _____
Officer _____	Unit Location Code_____
Last Social Security Number	

Select the appropriate answer and enter the associated weight in the score column. Total all scores to arrive at the risk assessment score.

Score

Number of Prior Felony Convictions:　　　　　0　None
(or Juvenile Adjudications)　　　　　　　　　　2　One
　　　　　　　　　　　　　　　　　　　　　　4　Two or more　　　　__4__

Arrested Within Five (5) Years Prior to Arrest　0　No
for Current Offense (exclude traffic)　　　　　4　Yes　　　　　　__4__

Age at Arrest Leading to First Felony Conviction　0　24 and over
(or Juvenile Adjudications)　　　　　　　　　　2　20 to 23　　　　__4__
　　　　　　　　　　　　　　　　　　　　　　4　19 and under　　__2__

Amount of Time Employed in Last 12 Months　　0　More than 7 months
(Prior to Incarceration for Parolees)　　　　　1　5 to 7 months
　　　　　　　　　　　　　　　　　　　　　　2　Less than 5 months
　　　　　　　　　　　　　　　　　　　　　　0　Not appplicable　__0__

Alcohol Usage Problems (Prior to Incarceration　0　No interference
for Parolees)　　　　　　　　　　　　　　　　　with functioning
　　　　　　　　　　　　　　　　　　　　　　2　Occasional abuse; some
　　　　　　　　　　　　　　　　　　　　　　　disruption of functioning
　　　　　　　　　　　　　　　　　　　　　　4　Frequent abuse; serious
　　　　　　　　　　　　　　　　　　　　　　　disruption; needs treatment　__0__

Other Drug Usage Problems (Prior to Incarceration　0　No interference with
for Parolees)　　　　　　　　　　　　　　　　　fuctioning
　　　　　　　　　　　　　　　　　　　　　　2　Occasional abuse; some
　　　　　　　　　　　　　　　　　　　　　　　disruption of functioning
　　　　　　　　　　　　　　　　　　　　　　4　Frequent abuse; serious
　　　　　　　　　　　　　　　　　　　　　　　disruption needs treatment　__0__

Number of Prior Adult Incarcerations in a State　0　0
or Federal Institution　　　　　　　　　　　　3　1-2
　　　　　　　　　　　　　　　　　　　　　　6　3 or more　　　__3__

Age at Admission to Institution or Probation　　0　30 or over
for Current Offense　　　　　　　　　　　　　3　18 to 29
　　　　　　　　　　　　　　　　　　　　　　6　17 and under　　__3__

Number of Prior *Adult* Probation/Parole Supervisions　0　None
　　　　　　　　　　　　　　　　　　　　　　4　One or more　　__4__

Number of Prior Probation/Parole Revocations　0　None
Resulting in Imprisonment (Adult or Juvenile)　4　One or more　　__4__

Total　__28__

Figure 5 Assessment of Client Needs

Processor # _____

Client Name _Paul S._ _____
          Last   First   Mi

Officer _____
          Last   Social Security Number

Client Number _____

Date _____

Unit Location Code_____

Score

Emotional and Mental Stability

0 No symptoms of emotions and/or mental instability   **2** Symptoms limit, but do not prohibit adequate functioning   **6** Symptoms prohibit adequate functioning and/or has Court or Board imposed condition   **8** Severe symptoms requiring continual attention and/or explosive, threatening and potentially dangerous to others or self

_8_

Domestic Relationship

0 Stable/supportive relationships   **3** Some disorganization or stress but potential for improvement   **7** Major disorganization or stress

_0_

Associations

0 No adverse relationships   **2** Associations with occasional negative results   **4** Associations frequently negative   **6** Associations completely negative

_2_

Drug Abuse

0 No disruption of functioning   **2** Occasional substance abuse: some disruption of functioning and/or has Court or Board conditions   **7** Frequent abuse; serious disruption; needs treatment

_0_

Alcohol Usage

0 No disruption of functioning   **2** Occasional abuse; some disruption of functioning and/or has court or Board conditions   **7** Frequent abuse; serious disruption; needs treatment

_0_

Employment

0 Satisfactory employment, no difficulties reported; or homemaker, student, retired, or disabled   **2** Underemployed   **4** Unsatisfactory employment; or unemployed but has adequate job skills/motivation   **5** Unemployed and virtually unemployable; needs motivation/training

_4_

Academic/Vocational Skills/Training

0 Adequate skills, able to handle everyday requirements   **2** Low skill level causing minor adjustment problems   **6** No identifiable skills and/or minimal skill level causing serious adjustment problems

_2_

Financial Management

0 No current difficulties   **1** Situational or minor difficulties   **5** Chronic/severe difficulties

_1_

Attitudes

0 No adverse difficulties/motivated for change   **2** Periodic difficulties/ uncooperative/dependent   **4** Frequently hostile/negative/criminal orientation

_4_

Residence

0 Suitable living arrangement   **1** Adequate living, i.e., temporary shelter   **4** Nomadic and/ or unacceptable

_0_

Mental Ability (Intelligence)

0 Able to function independently   **1** Some need for assistence; potential for adequate adjustment   **3** Deficiencies severely limit independent functioning

_0_

Health

0 Sound physical health; seldom ill   **1** Handicap or illness; interferes with functioning on a recurring basis   **2** Serious handicap or chronic illness; needs frequent medical care

_0_

Sexual Behavior

0 No apparent dysfunction   **2** Real or perceived situational or minor problems   **6** Real or perceived chronic or severe problems

_0_

Officer's Impressions of Needs

A. Low **0**   B. Medium **3**   C. Maximum **5**

_3_

Total _24_

A supervision mission was defined in terms of a fluid process encompassing information gathering, case assessment, classification, case planning, service delivery, monitoring and evaluation. In addition, nearly every Adult Parole Authority supervision policy was revised to correspond with case management concepts.

3. A process to help officers determine appropriate supervision strategies was selected. A variety of strategies were examined by the CMTF, including negotiated contracts, behavioral objectives, force field analysis and Wisconsin's CMC system. The CMTF chose the CMC system and its accompanying treatment strategies. The CMC is administered to an offender within the first 30 days of supervision.

4. Structured levels of supervision were developed, with criteria for placement and movement between levels. The CMS was designed, like Wisconsin's system, to move offenders to lower supervision levels as problems are resolved or reduced and needs met. A negotiated case planning process was devised that focuses both officer and offender on problem identification, case plan behavioral objectives, the action plan necessary to achieve the objectives and the date when objectives are achieved. The case plan is written and completed by the officer at classification and reclassification. (See Figure 6.)

5. Standards for officer functions were defined. Required minimum standards for the four levels of supervision were developed by the CMTF in terms of face-to-face contacts with the offender and officer's verification of the offender's residence, employment, program participation and compliance with special conditions imposed by the court or Parole Board. Requirements are minimal for an extended case, but increase proportionally as the supervision level increases.

6. A workload system was developed to accommodate the investigative and supervision functions of the agency. Researchers conducted three work/time studies. In one of the studies, a representative number of officers used self-report forms to track time spent with cases in ten standard activities over a four month period. Study results were used to establish specific work units for supervision cases and for court and Parole Board investigations, and to define monthly workload standards.

7. A data system for management information purposes was devised. Supervision forms were designed to collect a variety of data, including demographics, classification, reclassification and

Figure 6 Case Plan

Client Name _____ Client Number _____
(Last)   (First)   (Middle)

Problem/Need (From Instrument)	Objective	Action Plan	Achieved

termination information and workload statistics. Since implementation, the data has been collected and collated manually and used primarily for staff deployment and budgeting.

A computerized, statewide supervision data base with entry and report retrieval capability is scheduled to be on line by 1989. Case management information will be more accessible to staff and can be used for a wider variety of purposes.

In 1980 and 1981, the CMS was implemented throughout the state, one region at a time. As part of the implementation process, staffs were trained in the use of the scales, classification and reclassification, the CMC system and case planning. Ongoing supportive contact was maintained between the CMTF and staff during training and implementation.

An evaluation of the CMS, based upon data generated in the initial implementation region, was conducted in 1984; it yielded mixed findings. The evaluator found, for example, that staff using the system were generally positive about it and that case planning and use of outside community resources by officers had improved. The risk scale was also found to be effective (the needs scale was not evaluated).

However, it was also concluded that officers supervised Minimum and Maximum offenders with the same contact frequency. There were, in fact, too many contacts for Minimum offenders and about half the required contacts for Maximum offenders. Because officer efforts were not concentrated in the appropriate areas, the CMS failed to impact upon the criminal behaviors of Maximum offenders.

Significant steps were taken to strengthen the effectiveness of the system. Followup training was provided to staff to reinforce supervision standards, and emphasis was placed on monitoring officer activities.

A follow-up study of the Case Management System, using methodology from the previous evaluation, was released in 1986. Overall, the findings were positive. The risk scale, for example continued to function as a solid predictive instrument. In addition, a marked increase in the referral of offenders to community service agencies was revealed. This suggested that the need scale and case planning process were effective in identifying with no apparent solution.

As in the 1984 evaluation, it was discovered that officers over-supervised Minimum level offenders and under-supervised Maximum level offenders. Despite these findings, the study documented some decrease in the criminal behavior of Maximum and Medium level offenders.

Transfer of CMS Technology

When fully implemented, the CMS applied to all parolees in Ohio, and probationers (primarily felons) under Adult Parole Authority supervision in 51 of Ohio's 88 counties. The majority of other counties had separate probation departments, each with its own individual organizational structure, policies and practices. In 1981, numerous probation departments expressed an interest in learning more about the CMS to NIC and the Adult Parole Authority. Ultimately, NIC agreed to fund a transfer of CMS technology from the state to the counties but stipulated that the counties and the state work together during the process.

Despite a history of inter-governmental conflict and adverse relations, the Adult Parole Authority and 15 urban and rural counties combined their efforts and expertise within a supportive environment of capacity building. Early in the process CMTF members conducted an orientation session for urban county personnel that focused on the concepts and benefits of CMS. During the technological transfer process, CMTF members collaborated with county staff to solve implementation and resistance problems. NIC acted as both a technical consultant and a catalyst during the transfer process.

County and state staff worked closely together in the training design and system development arena. CMTF members, for example, provided county participants with information about the various classification, reclassification and case planning components of the CMS. Adult Parole Authority staff trained urban county CMC trainers. They, in turn, trained the rural county line staff in CMC interview techniques.

County and state staff also jointly developed a CMS Entrance Training Program. The four day session is designed to provide new county and state officers with an overview of the purpose and function of the risk, risk reassessment and need scales, and the classification process (officers receive specifics concerning policies and procedures when they return to their county department or state unit). The Program also provides practical training in conducting the CMC interview, using the recommended treatment strategies and writing case plans.

In addition to participating in training during the transfer process, the urban and rural counties came together to discuss common issues and problems as they reached the same level of implementation. The county departments also worked with NIC to refine their respective management information and workload systems. County implementation team members first explored creating a professional organization for Chief Probation Officers of Ohio during the transfer process.

By 1984, the 15 urban and rural counties had developed and implemented a CMS for their respective probation departments. Previously tested state classification components such as the risk, risk reassessment and needs scale were duplicated by the county departments (some of the counties later developed their own). A number of counties, however, added an assaultive indicator to their risk and risk reassessment scales. (See Figures 7, 8 and 9.)

The management information and workload technology were transferred from the state to the counties, as well. They too were reshaped to meet the individual needs of the county departments. Wisconsin's CMC system was transferred but not altered.

No formal evaluations of the various county systems have been conducted. However, the transfer of Case Management System technology from the state to county probation departments has undoubtedly resulted in improved inter-governmental relations. More importantly, professional probation practices throughout the State of Ohio have been enhanced significantly.

References and Further Readings

Arling, G., B. Bemus and P. Quigley (1983) *Workload Measures For Probation and Parole.*

Baird, C., B. Bemus and C. Heinz (1979) *The Wisconsin Case Classification/Staff Deployment Project: A Two Year Follow-up Report.*

Farmer, G. (1978) *Final Report: National Institute of Corrections Capacity Building Grant FQ 2.*

Kratcoski, P. (1984) *An Evaluation of the Case Management System.*

Natter, G. (1986) *A Follow-Up Study on the Case Management System.*

Figure 7   Assessment of Client Risk

Name: Risk Level: _____
Case Number:
Date: P.O.'s Name: _____
Select the appropriate answer and enter the associated weight in score column. Total all scores
to arrive at the risk assessment score.

Score

1) Number of Prior Felony Convictions: 0 None
   (or Juvenile Adjudications)   2 One
   4 Two or more   _____

2) Arrested Within Five (5) Years Prior to Arrest   0 No
   for Current Offense (exclude traffic)   4 Yes   _____

3) Age at Arrest Leading to First Felony Conviction   0 24 and over
   (or Juvenile Adjudications)   2 20 to 23
   4 19 and under   _____

4) Number of Prior Adult Incarcerations in a State   0 0
   or Federal Institution   3 1-2
   6 3 or more   _____

5) Age at Admission to Institution or Probation   0 30 or over
   for Current Offense   3 18 to 29
   6 17 and under   _____

6) Number of Prior *Adult* Probation/Parole   0 None
   Supervisions   4 One or more   _____

7) Number of Prior Probation/Parole Revoked   0 None
   or termination Due to Incarceration   4 One or more
   (Adult or Juvenile)   _____

8) Alcohol Usage Problems   0 No indication of alcohol
   abuse
   2 Occasional abuse
   3 Some disruption of
   functioning
   4 Frequent abuse; serious
   disruption; needs treatment   _____

9) Other Drug Usage Problems   0 No indication of drug abuse
   2 Occasional abuse
   3 Some disruption of
   functioning
   4 Frequent abuse; serious
   disruption needs treatment   _____

10) Amount of Full Time Employment in Last   0 More than 7 months
    12 months   1 5 to 7 months
    2 Less than 5 months
    0 Not applicable   _____

Total _____

11) Adult Felony Conviction or Juvenile Felony Adjudi- Yes _____
    cation for Offense Involving Threat of Force, Posses- No   _____
    session of Weapon, Physical Force or Sexual Assault
    within the Last Five Years

If answer to item 11 is yes, then supervision level is
increased to next highest level.

Figure 8 Assessment of Client Risk

Client Name _____ CR_____ Probation
Placement Date _____

Risk: L M H   Reassessment Date _____

Assessing P.O. _____ Date _____

Select the appropriate answer and enter the associated weight in the score column. Total all scores to arrive at the risk assessment score.

Score

Number of Prior Felony Convictions:	0	None
(or Juvenile Adjudications)	2	One
	4	Two or more	_____

Arrested Within Five (5) Years Prior to Arrest	0	No
for Current Offense (exclude traffic)	4	Yes	_____

Age at Arrest Leading to First Felony Conviction	0	24 and over
(or Juvenile Adjudications)	2	20 to 23
	4	19 and under	_____

Amount of Time Employed in Last 12 Months	0	More than 7 months
(Prior to Incarceration for Parolees)	1	5 to 7 months
	2	Less than 5 months
	0	Not appplicable	_____

Alcohol Usage Problems (Prior to Incarceration	0	No interference
for Parolees)		with functioning
	2	Occasional abuse; some
		disruption of functioning
	4	Frequent abuse; serious disruption;
		needs treatment	_____

Other Drug Usage Problems (Prior to Incarceration	0	No interference with fuctioning
for Parolees)	2	Occasional abuse; some disruption
		of functioning
	4	Frequent abuse; serious disruption
		needs treatment	_____

Number of Prior Adult Incarcerations in a State	0	0
or Federal Institution	3	1-2
	6	3 or more	_____

Age at Admission to Institution or Probation	0	30 or over
for Current Offense	3	18 to 29
	6	17 and under	_____

Number of Prior *Adult* Probation/Parole Supervisions	0	None
	4	One or more	_____

Number of Prior Probation/Parole Revocations	0	None
Resulting in Imprisonment (Adult or Juvenile)	4	One or more	_____

Total _____

Officer Override — Alternate level of supervision felt to be appropriate (see reverse side for explanation). ☐

Assault Factor — If client has been convicted of 2 assaultive misdemeanors or 1 assaultive felony (including present offense), the level of supervision is moved up one step. ☐

Figure 9   Reassessment of Client Risk

Client Name _____ CR_____ Probation
Placement Date _____

Risk: L   M   H   Reassessment Date _____

Assessing P.O. _____   Date _____

Select the appropriate answer and enter the associated weight in the score column. Total all scores to arrive at the risk assessment score.

			Score
Number of Prior Felony Convictions	0	None	
(or Juvenile Adjudications)	3	One	
	6	Two	
	7	Three or more	_____
Age at Arrest Leading to First Felony Conviction	0	24 and over	
(or Juvenile Adjudications)	2	20-23	
	5	19 and under	_____
Age at Admission to Probation/Parole Supervision	0	30 and older	
for Current Offense	4	18-29	
	7	17 and under	_____

Rate the following based on period since last (re)assessment:

Type of Arrests (indicate most serious	0	None	
excluding traffic)	2	Technical PV only	
	4	Misdemeanor arrest(s)	
	8	Felony arrest	_____
Associations	0	Mainly with noncriminally oriented individuals	
	5	Mainly with negative individuals	_____
Alcohol Usage Problems	0	No interference with fuctioning	
	2	Occasional abuse; some disruption of functioning	
	3	Frequent abuse; serious disruption needs treatment	_____
Other Drug Usage Problems	0	No interference with functioning	
	1	Occasional abuse: some disruption of functioning	
	2	Frequent abuse: serious disruption; needs treatment	_____
Attitude	0	No adverse difficulties/ motivated to change	
	2	Periodic difficulties/ uncooperative/dependent	
	5	Frequently hostile/ negative/criminal orientation	_____

Total _____

Officer Override—Alternate level of supervision felt to be appropriate (see reverse side for explanation). ☐

Assault Factor—If client has been convicted of 2 assaultive misdemeanors or 1 assaultive felony (including present offense), the level of supervision is moved up one step. ☐

Intensive Probation: An Examination of Recidivism and Social Adjustment

Susan Noonan and Edward J. Latessa

Introduction

According to figures released by the Federal Government, the prison population of this country is at an all time high. (Bureau of Justice Statistics 1985.) Many states have prison construction programs planned over the next ten years costing billions of dollars, but even such programs cannot solve the problems of overcrowding. Some states are also under court orders to reduce or limit their prison population. Consequently, officials are constantly seeking alternatives to incarceration. This article examines the effectiveness of one such alternative; intensive supervision, focusing on a program called the Intensive Supervision Program which operates out of the Montgomery County Adult Probation Department in Dayton, Ohio.

Intensive Supervision Probation

Intensive probation is defined by Clear and Cole as "Probation granted as an alternative to incarceration under conditions of strict reporting to a probation officer with limited caseload" (1986: 518). Bennett describes intensive supervision as an "attempt to place some offenders who had been sentenced to prison in an alternative without danger to the community" (1984: 9). These definitions illustrate the changing nature of intensive supervision. It originally was used to increase

Reprinted with permission from: *American Journal of Criminal Justice*, 12 (1) (Fall, 1987), pp. 45-61.

surveillance of offenders already on regular probation. Today it is being used to reduce prison populations by diverting offenders who would otherwise be in prison (Latessa, 1986). Indeed, intensive probation is not a new concept. There are those that would argue that what is considered intensive supervision today, is really what supervision was meant to be when it was originally conceived (Rothman, 1980).

With this more intense form of probation supervision, both the offender and the probation officer become more accountable for their activities. This is a major factor in making intensive supervision acceptable to judges as an alternative to incarceration (Bennett 1984: 9). The intensive supervision probation officer, because of reduced caseloads, has more weekly contacts with the offender than a regular probation officer. These contacts include visits, telephone calls and help providing services, such as unemployment, welfare, job training, educational assistance, alcohol and drug programs. The combination of closer surveillance and better services places the intensive probationer under tighter control than he/she would be if on regular probation (Hardyman 1984: 2).

Issues in Intensive Supervision

Throughout the years various forms of intensive supervision have been tested. Although there has been a great deal of interest and research on the effects of intensive supervision, (Robinson, et al., 1969; Gottfredson and Neithercutt, 1974; Sasfy, 1975; Banks, et al., 1977; Fallen, et al., 1981; Gettinger, 1983) much of this effort has been of questionable value, (Adams and Vetter, 1974; Latessa, 1979; Fields, 1984).

The three major issues surrounding the use of intensive supervision have been the effectiveness question, the caseload size and classification issue, and the debate over the number and quality of contacts. In terms of effectiveness, the question has gone largely unanswered. Much of the prior research has used recidivism as the primary if not sole measure of effectiveness. There is no conclusive evidence that intensive supervision will result in lower recidivism rates. However, there appears to be some success with "specially" selected offenders (Banks, et al., 1977; Latessa and Vito, 1984), but overall anticipated reductions in recidivism have not materialized. Studies that have included cost, social adjustment and commitment rates as indicators of effectiveness have demonstrated more success and impact (Latessa, 1987, Erwin and Bennett, 1986, and Pearson, 1987).

As far as caseload size is concerned, experiments with intensive supervision have resulted in lower numbers of offenders per officer, with the average caseload around 25. The crucial operational issue has been the dilemma of accurately selecting cases appropriate for higher levels of supervision. The most widely used screening techniques involve either (or both) risk and need assessment instruments (Baird, 1982). This issue has become even more complex as states have attempted to "divert" offenders from prison. If that is a program's goal, then it is important that offenders be diverted from prison, and that intensive supervision not simply be provided to offenders that would normally receive regular supervision.

As expected, the number of contacts with clients has increased under intensive supervision, but the question of whether intensity should simply involve increasing the number of contacts received still remains. The average number of contacts for intensively supervised cases has been about four per month, compared to about one per month under "regular" supervision. This difference in contact levels has not invoked a sense of "intense" supervision. Recently, Georgia and New Jersey have instituted intensive supervision programs that assign two officers caseloads of between ten and twenty-five, with contacts required on at least a daily basis (Bennett, 1984). It appears, however, that the primary purpose of these contacts are for surveillance, not treatment. It should also be noted that both of these states have centralized state probationer services. It is unlikely that local probation departments could provide the same level of service in a cost effective manner without state provided subsidy monies.

The present study adds to this base of knowledge by comparing the performance of probationers placed on intensive supervision to a group of probationers placed on regular supervision. The key issue is whether intensive supervision, through improved service delivery can have an impact on high risk probationers, and thus serve as a basis for a program to divert similar offenders from overcrowded penal facilities.

Montgomery County Intensive Treatment Supervision Program

In November 1984, the Montgomery County Adult Probation Department put into effect the Intensive Treatment Supervision Program (ITSP). This program was part of a probation subsidy agreement entered into with the Ohio Department of Rehabilitation and Correction. The primary goals of the program were to reduce the commitment rate from Montgomery County through the provision of intensive supervision, while maintaining an acceptable level of community safety.

The Montgomery County Adult Probation Department is organized around a team concept, with three geographic service areas; West, East and Central. Offenders are assigned according to the area in which they live. There are four intensive treatment officers, with each assigned approximately twenty-five cases. The intensive officers are responsible to make four face-to-face contacts every thirty days, with at least one in the home. Cases assigned to the program must complete a minimum of six months of intensive treatment supervision. After this period, a case may be transferred to regular supervision provided the ITSP officer believes the defendant is ready to transfer. There are four ways in which cases are assigned to the ITSP:

1. Cases recommended for state commitment and screened by the ITSP officers.

2. Cases assigned by the judge.

3. Cases diverted from the state prison system as a result of an amended sentence (shock probation).

4. Cases supervised under general probation that are potential probation violators.[1]

Screening excluded cases that would normally qualify for regular probation, non-probatable offenders/mandatory sentenced cases, offenders serving a sentence from another jurisdiction, and if the offender refused the MonDay program.[2] In addition to the cases diverted after conviction and recommendation for commitment, the program has accepted shock probationers. Under Ohio law an offender is eligible for shock probation after a short period of incarceration (130 days or less), followed by probation. Findings seem to indicate that even this short period of incarceration has a negative impact on an offender's adjustment.[3] By admitting these offenders into the ITSP, it was hoped that the increased attention and services would make reintegration back into the community more successful.[4]

Research Methods

A quasi-experimental design was utilized, with a comparison group matched and selected from the balance of the department's caseload. The primary matching variables included sex, race, and when possible, risk level. Shock probationers admitted to the ITSP were matched, when possible, to the regular caseloads. Comparison cases were also selected so that cases were being supervised during a similar time frame as the experimental group. This insured that the cases were somewhat similar, at least on some basic parameters.

Data for this study were gathered from the agency files from the beginning of the program through March 1986. Over 200 cases have been supervised in the ITSP since its inception, however, only those cases which were admitted to the program during the first six months were included in this evaluation in order to allow for a sufficient follow-up period. A total of 163 cases were available for this study. One hundred thirty comparison cases were selected from the regularly supervised probation population. In order to simplify presentation, the data were divided into two basic types; in-program and outcome.

In-program information was designed to examine the difference between the two groups at program entry, and to measure the level of service delivery provided. In-program data included information on background characteristics, risk and need assessment, and the number and types of contacts and services provided.

The outcome measures used in this study were designed to determine whether or not the treatment variables had an appreciable effect on offenders in the ITSP. The outcome indicators included recidivism (operationally defined as incarceration in a penal institution), and secondary measures of criminal behavior including arrests, convictions, and technical violations.

In order to measure the severity of criminal offenses and the rate of social adjustment, two separate scales, the Criminal Behavior Severity Scale and the Positive Adjustment Scale were utilized. These scales have been tested and validated in a number of criminal justice settings.[5] The first part of this scale is a continuous measure of criminal behavior based on the severity of offenses as prescribed by the Ohio Revised Code. The second part of the index represents a positive adjustment scale which included factors related to employment, education, residential and financial situation and progress on probation.[6] These two scales were separately analyzed to determine the severity of criminal behavior (for new convictions), and to determine if any advances in social adjustment were made.

Results

In-program Analysis

The primary purpose of the in-program analysis was to measure the differences between the two groups on background variables, and the extent of contacts and service delivery. In order to facilitate presentation of these data the findings pertaining to background and criminal history are summarized.

With regard to the matching variables race and sex, the two groups were almost identical. Males far outnumbered females, and there were more blacks than whites. The two groups were also similar in age, education, marital status and military service. The ITSP reported a lower employment rate at program entry, 34.0 percent compared to 38.7 percent, but the difference was not significant. Only two factors were significant, PSI Recommendation and Risk Classification. Data concerning the PSI Recommendation indicated that the ITSP had fewer cases recommended for probation and more recommended for incarceration than the comparison group. The Risk Classification data likewise revealed that there were significant differences, with over 70 percent of the ITSP classified as high risk versus 44 percent for the regular probationers. These data support the contention that the ITSP cases were more likely to be incarcerated than regular probationers. Surprisingly, however, the data on Need Classification did not result in a significant finding, with an almost equal number of cases in each group classified as high needs. While judges tend to sentence by risk rather than need, the Montgomery Adult Probation Department puts a great deal of emphasis on the Needs Classification, and it appears from these data that the ITSP is not receiving a large number of high needs cases, particularly since 23 percent of their cases were classified as low need. This may be due to the fact that the Department also utilizes the resources of a specialist team that deals exclusively with high need clients such as alcohol and drug abusers, mental health cases and sex offenders.

The data on criminal justice history indicates that there were several significant differences between the groups. The number of times on probation data indicated that 55.2 percent of the ITSP clients had been previously placed on probation prior to diversion into this program compared to 41.5 percent of the regular probationers, however this difference was not significant. The intensive group did report significantly higher juvenile records; 65.8 percent versus 43.4 percent, and more prior arrests for crimes against person; 43.8 percent compared to 23.6 percent. When the current offense was collapsed into the Ohio Revised Code felony and misdemeanor categories, the difference between the groups was significant with the intensive cases reporting convictions for more serious offenses than the comparison group.[7] While these three categories resulted in significant differences, the data related to prior convictions and incarcerations showed no differences between the two groups. The data indicated that the two groups were similar with regard to the number of months incarcerated, total number of incarcerations, convictions and state commitments, and the age at first conviction.

While the ITSP clients had more involvement with the juvenile system, more prior personal offenses and were convicted for more serious offenses than the regular probation group, the criminal history data do not overwhelmingly support the contention that the ITSP cases were significantly "worse." The fact that a substantially higher percentage of ITSP clients were recommended for incarceration and that they were classified higher risk, does imply that many of these cases were in fact diverted. However, given the mixed results of these data, one cannot conclude with certainty that the majority of ITSP cases were diverted from a prison commitment.

In order to examine the level of service provision, data were gathered related to the types of services provided. Table 1 presents data on the services provided to the two samples. These data indicated that the ITSP cases received significantly more service provision in the areas of employment, education, and family counseling. Indeed, the ITSP clients received more services in every area except drug service, however these differences were not statistically significant. Although these data were not conclusive, they do indicate a trend in which the ITSP group received more services in critical social adjustment areas.

Table 1 *Percentage Receiving Services*

Service	Intensive	Control
Vocational Training	16.0%	9.2%
Employment*	53.7%	21.5%
Education*	40.1%	24.6%
Budgeting	16.6%	15.4%
Alcohol	22.7%	19.2%
Drug	17.8%	21.7%
Mental Health	9.2%	6.2%
Welfare	19.8%	15.5%
Family Counseling*	14.7%	6.2%
Group Counseling	5.5%	3.1%
Individual Counseling	83.4%	79.2%

*Significant at the .05 level.

Another critical question pertained to the number of contacts for both the ITSP and comparison samples as shown in Table 2. Contacts were divided into five categories: face-to-face in the office, home visits, jail visits, collateral contacts, and total contacts. Analysis of variance was used to determine if the differences were significant. These data indicated that the ITSP made significantly more face-to-face contacts, home contacts, and total contacts than the comparison group. Overall, the ITSP made 4.09 contacts per month, of which 2.82 were of a face-to-face nature. Besides comparing contacts between the groups, the ITSP contacts were measured against their project goal of four per month, of which one was to be in the home. The ITSP achieved their goal, however, they fell slightly short of providing one home contact per month.

Table 2 *Monthly Probation Contacts Through March 1986*

Group	Type of Contact				
	Face to Face*	Home*	Jail*	Collateral	Total*
Intensive	1.86	.85	.11	1.26	4.09
Regular	1.05	.22	.13	.85	2.15

*Significant at .05 level.

Outcome Analysis

As mentioned previously, a number of different measures were used in order to examine the impact of this unit. Several indicators were considered including recidivism data, and social adjustment.[8] In order to examine the criminal activity of these two groups while under supervision, arrests, convictions, technical violations filed and current status were examined.

The data in Table 3 presents the current status of both the ITSP and regular samples at the end of March 1986. At the end of this period, the ITSP cases had been under intensive supervision an average of 9.17 months while the regular cases had been under supervision 11.4 months. This difference was significant and was statistically controlled for. There were two significant differences with regard to current status data. The ITSP had more cases incarcerated on a new felony: 11.7 percent versus 3.8 percent of the regular cases, but significantly fewer incarcerated on misdemeanors: 1.2 percent compared to 6.2 percent. The regular sample reported a slightly higher percentage of cases absconding, and slightly fewer revoked, but these differences were not statistically significant. Overall, when the first four "failure" categories were combined there were no significant differences between the samples. The ITSP had 22.3 percent incarcerated, revoked or absconding compared to 23.9 percent of the regular probationers.

Table 3 *Current Status of the Intensive and Regular Probationers as of April 1986*

Status	Intensive		Regular	
	N	%	N	%
Released from Probation	12	7.4%	13	10.0%
On Probation	106	65.0	80	61.5
Probation Revoked and Incarcerated	7	4.3	4	3.1
Incarcerated Felony*	19	11.7	5	3.8
Incarcerated Misdemeanor*	2	1.2	8	6.2
Absconded	10	6.1	14	10.8
Other	7	4.3	6	4.7
Total	163	100.0%	130	100.0%

In order to further examine the criminal activity of these two samples, data for arrests, convictions and technical violations were gathered. Table 4 presents the results of the analysis. The ITSP reported a slightly higher percentage of misdemeanor and felony arrests and convictions, but a slightly lower percentage of technical violations filed. None of these differences were significant. The data on arrests and convictions are difficult to interpret. Arrests do not always result in convictions, and multiple convictions may be the result of one arrest. These data also indicated that the majority of cases in each sample have never been arrested or convicted while under supervision.

In addition to the data presented above, the criminal behavior severity scale was designed to measure how well the ITSP has maintained community safety when compared to regular probationers. This scale, along with the positive adjustment scale was founded on the premise that the correctional philosophy of reintegration emphasizes the development of acceptable living patterns to replace the offender's prior reliance on deviant behavior.

Table 4 *Arrests, Convictions and Technical Violations*
Filed for the Intensive and Regular Probationers

Variable	Intensive		Regular	
	N	%	N	%
Misdemeanor Arrests	39	22.0%	36	20.7%
Misdemeanor Convictions	29	15.3	22	13.0
Felony Arrests	26	14.7	20	13.8
Felony Convictions	31	12.2	17	8.4
Technical Violations	43	21.4	32	22.3
Never Been Arrested	107	65.6	87	66.9
Never Been convicted	120	73.6	102	78.4

* the N is based on the total number of offenses while the percentages are based on the actual number of individuals reporting violations.

The results of the Criminal Behavior Severity Scale which weighed the offenses of those offenders from the ITSP and regular probation samples who were convicted of a new crime are presented in Table 5. The overall mean score for the ITSP sample was −2.15 compared to a −2.42 mean score for the regular probation sample. Although the average score was lower for the intensive sample, the difference was not significant. These data indicate that while a higher percentage of ITSP cases were incarcerated for felonies, the level of community safety was at a level comparable to regularly supervised offenders.

Table 5 *Criminal Behavior and Severity Score for the Intensive*
and Regular Probationers

Group	Total Score	Mean	F	N.S.	N
Intensive	346.1	−2.15			161
			.19	N.S.	
Regular	300.0	−2.42			124

The positive adjustment scale was designed to measure several parameters generally considered to demonstrate "acceptable societal behavior." This scale consists of ten items that are considered indicators of successful social adjustment. The total score for each group is presented in Table 6 and is based on measurements taken at the end

Table 6 *Positive Adjustment Scale Score
for the Intensive and Regular Probationers*

Group	Total Score	Mean	F	N.S.	N
Intensive	795.3	4.94			161
			.001	N.S.	
Regular	610.0	4.92			124

of the evaluation period. The mean score for the intensive sample was 4.94 compared to a mean score of 4.92 for the regular sample. This difference was not significant. It appears from these data that while the ITSP sample had a slightly higher score, the increased contacts and services did not result in a significantly better social adjustment.

Conclusions

The results of this initial evaluation highlight the performance of the Intensive Treatment Supervision Program during its first eighteen months of operation. Overall, the results are mixed. The level of treatment is at an acceptable level for a program of this nature, and the data suggests that the program is holding its own with regard to community safety.

There are several possible explanations for these findings. First, despite the attempts at developing an adequate comparison group, important differences remained. Another problem was the relatively short duration of the treatment and follow-up period. As mentioned previously, this is an ongoing program and a more extensive follow-up is planned for the future. While the program did not perform significantly better than the comparison group with regard to recidivism or positive adjustment data, it is reasonable to assume that the effects of the increased contact and treatment will not be fully known for some time. Given the risk levels of the ITSP group, it is also possible that these offenders might have failed at an even higher rate had they not received special attention. In addition, the program did not operate as an ideal example of intensive supervision. The level of contacts did not invoke a sense of intensity, and it was not conclusively demonstrated that the cases supervised were truly diverted from a prison commitment.

Finally, it is important to mention that this evaluation effort was designed to provide information for program improvement. Changes have already occurred that should greatly improve the operation of this program. Hopefully, future research will help answer some of the questions that remain.

Notes

1. Data indicated that 58.8 percent of the ITSP group were recommended for incarceration; 10.6 percent were assigned by a judge; 34.9 percent were granted shock probation or split sentences and; 1.8 percent were probation violators.

2. The MonDay program is a residential treatment facility operating in Montgomery County, and is funded by the state as a subsidy program.

3. For a thorough discussion of shock probation in Ohio, see: Vito G. F. (1978). *Shock probation in Ohio: A comparison of attributes and outcome.* Unpublished doctoral dissertation, Ohio State University, Columbus, OH.

4. There is some data that suggests that increased services and contacts does in fact enhance the social adjustment of the offender, however, there is little evidence that it has a positive impact on recidivism. See: Bennett, L. A. (1987) "A reassessment of intensive service probation. In McCarthy, B. R. (Ed.), *Intermediate Punishments: Intensive Supervision, Home Confinement and Electronic Surveillance.* Monsey, New York: Criminal Justice Press: 113-132.

5. The Criminal Behavior Severity Scale and the Positive Adjustment Scale were developed and validated by researchers at the Program for the Study of Crime and Delinquency at the Ohio State University. These scales have been used in evaluations of numerous programs, including adult halfway houses, institutional drug-alcohol programs, reintegration centers, volunteer programs and juvenile and adult diversion programs.

6. The Positive Adjustment Scale was tested for reliability using Cronbach's alpha. A .87 was obtained, indicating that this scale was extremely reliable.

7. When the current offense data were dichotomized into personal and property offenses there were no significant differences between the two groups. Similarly, when the Criminal Behavior Severity Scale was used on the current offense data no differences were present.

8. A major consideration of this program was to reduce state commitments from Montgomery County. Between January 1985 and March 1986 a total of 163 offenders were diverted into the ITSP, while 470 probatable offenders were committed to the state, resulting in an estimated 25.7 percent reduction in the commitment rate. These figures assume that the 163 cases diverted would have been given a state commitment. If only those 70 cases that were recommended for incarceration on the presentence investigation are used in this computation, the ITSP reduced the commitment rate by 12.9 percent.

References

Adams R. & Vetter, H. J. (1974). Effectiveness of probation caseload sizes: A review of the empirical literature. *Criminology 9,* 333-343.

Baird, C. (1982). Probation and parole classification: The Wisconsin model. In American Correctional Association (Ed.), *Classification as a management tool: Theories and models for decisionmakers.* College Park, Maryland: ACA.

Banks, J., Porter, A. L., Rardin, R., Silen, T. & Unger, V. E. (1977). *Summary, phase I evaluation of intensive probation projects.* Washington, D.C.: U.S. Government Printing Office.

Bennett, L. A. (March, 1984). *Practice in search of theory: The case of intensive supervision.* Paper presented at the meeting of the Academy of Criminal Justice Sciences, Chicago, IL.

Bennet, L. A. (1987). *A reassessment of intensive service probation.* In McCarthy B. R. *Intermediate punishments: Intensive supervision, home confinement and electronic surveillance.* Monsey, New York: Criminal Justice Press.

Bureau of Justice Statistics (1985). *Prisoners in 1985.* Washington, D.C.: U.S. Department of Justice.

Clear T. R. & Cole, G. F. (1986). *American corrections.* Belmont, CA: Brooks/Cole.

Erwin, B. S., & Bennett, L. A. (December, 1986). *New dimensions in probation: Georgia's experience with intensive probation supervison (IPS)* (Research in Brief). Washington, D.C. National Institute of Justice.

Fallen, D. C., Apperson, J. Holt-Milligan, & Roe, J. (1981). *Intensive parole supervision.* Olympia, WA: Dept. of Social and Health Services, Analysis and Information Service Division, Office of Research.

Fields, C. B. (1984). *The intensive supervision probation program in Texas: A two year assessment.* Unpublished doctoral dissertation, Sam Houston State University, Huntsville, TX.

Gettinger, S. (April, 1983). Intensive supervision: Can it rehabilitate probation. *Corrections Magazine*, pp. 7-17.

Gottfredson, D. & Neithercutt M. (1974). *Caseload size variation and difference in probation/parole performance.* Pittsburgh, PA: National Center for Juvenile Justice.

Hardyman, P. L. (March, 1984). *Intensive supervision: What it is and how it can be evaluated.*Paper presented at the meeting of the Academy of Criminal Justice Sciences, Chicago, IL.

Latessa, E. J. (1979). *Intensive Supervision: An Evaluation of the Effectiveness of an Intensive Diversion Unit.* Unpublished doctoral dissertation, Ohio State University, Columbus, OH.

___ (1986). The cost effectiveness of intensive supervision. *Federal probation, 50,* 70-74.

Latessa, E. L. & Vito, G. F. (1984). *The effects of intensive supervision on shock probationers.* Paper presented at the meeting of the Academy of Criminal Justice Sciences, Chicago, IL.

Pearson, F. S. (1987). Taking quality into account: assessing the benefits and costs of New Jersey's Intensive Supervision program. In B. R. McCarthy (Ed.), *Intermediate punishments: Intensive supervision, home confinement and electronic surveillance.* Monsey, New York: Criminal Justice Press.

Robinson, J., Wilkins, L. T., Carter, R. & Wahl, A. (1969). *The San Francisco Project: A Study of Federal Probation and Parole.* Berkeley, CA: University of California at Berkeley, School of Criminology.

Rothman, D. (1980). *Conscience and convenience: The discovery of the asylum and its effects on progressive America.* Boston: Little, Brown.

Sasfy, J. (1975). *An experimentation ot intensive supervision as a treatment strategy for probationers.* Washington, D.C.: Mitre Corp.

Vito, G. F. (1978). *Shock probation in Ohio: A comparison of attributes and outcome.* Unpublished doctoral dissertation, Ohio State University, Columbus, OH.

Functional Units: A Different Correctional Approach

Robert B. Levinson
and Roy E. Gerard

Accepting the proposition that there will always be a need to confine some of society's law violators, advocates for prison reform have persistently stressed the need for humane, rehabilitation-oriented institutions. Cogent arguments have been made regarding the need for facilities with more adequate staff/inmate ratios. This is seen as a major achievement towards reducing the anonymity of offenders; as a critical component in staff coming to view those incarcerated as people and, thereby, fostering a more healthy institutional climate. Limitations on manpower and other resources suggest the need for the most efficient use of those means that are made available. With these considerations in mind, the Federal Bureau of Prisons has initiated a program to restructure the organization of its institutions into Functional Units.

Functional Units

A Functional Unit can be conceptualized as one of a number of small, self-contained "institutions" operating in semiautonomous fashion within the confines of a larger facility. The concept includes the notion

The authors wish to acknowledge the assistance given them in the development of this article by many individuals, both within and outside the Federal Bureau of Prisons. Particularly helpful were: Norman A. Carlson, director, Federal Bureau of Prisons; the staff (and especially John A. Minor, supervisor of case management) at the Kennedy Youth Center, Morgantown, West Virginia; and Dr. Herbert C. Quay, chairman, Division of Educational Psychology, Temple University. Reprinted by permission from Federal Probation, 37(December 1973):8–16.

Reprinted by permission of the *Federal Probation Quarterly,* 37, (December 1973), pp. 8-16.

of: (a) A relatively small number of offenders (50–100); (b) who are housed together (generally throughout the length of their institutional stay or as they near completion—12 to 18 months—of a long term); (c) and who work in a close, intensive treatment relationship with a multidisciplinary, relatively permanently assigned team of staff members whose offices are located on the unit; (d) with this latter group having decision-making authority in all within-institution aspects of programming and institutional living; (e) and the assignment of an offender to a particular unit being contingent upon his need for the specific type of treatment program offered.

While it is preferable to identify a Functional Unit with a single living unit (ideally, one with differentiated quarters within the building), this is *not* a requirement. Given that the above conditions (a–e) prevail, a Functional Unit can encompass two living areas if this more adequately "fits" institutional architecture.

Decentralization

The consequence of organizing a total correctional institution around the Functional Unit concept is to decentralize the facility's organizational structure. This means a "flattening out" of the typical hierarchal pyramid; thereby placing those having the most immediate and direct contact with the residents in close proximity (organizationally) to top-level management. Specialists (such as caseworkers and educators) continue to function at a line and at the supervisory or department head level in both the centralized and decentralized institution. In the centralized facility the generalist, who manages activities which cross departmental lines, is represented on the table of organization at the associate warden (AW) level; in the decentralized institution both the unit manager and the AW are generalists (with the latter functioning in the more "pure" managerial role, while the former individual still gets involved to some degree in the delivery of direct services).

The result of this restructured table of organization is a smaller gap between those who have the most contact with the resident population and the policy, decision-making executive staff. However, decentralization and the establishment of Functional Units can be a mixed blessing.

Perhaps the most difficult aspect of implementing a Functional Unit approach is "getting there." The transition stage—moving from a centralized organization to a decentralized structure—presents a complexity of problems that are not found in either the totally centralized or totally decentralized institution. One problem in the transitional facility centers about the ability of the associate warden to coordinate the programs of the decentralized units with the rest of the institution's centralized operations. Program information has difficulty filtering up to the associate warden. The relationship between the manager of the Functional Unit and the department head who ordinarily would be supervising "his" staff members in each unit becomes one fraught with complications. Unit managers do not relish "interference" with the running of their unit. There tends to be a lack of communication between the various departments and the units. As a consequence, program coordination becomes more difficult. Faced with these problems, the warden must make a definite decision concerning decentralization and Functional Units.

Functional Units: Advantages

The advantages of Functional Units can be clustered under three headings: correction, care, and control.

Correction

The semiautonomous nature of the Functional Unit permits maximum flexibility, both in the initial designing of programs and in later modifications required to meet changing population characteristics. Functional Unit programs may be individually altered, removed, or added with only the most minimal disturbance to the facility's basic organization.

It places services close to the users, thereby allowing decision-making in regard to planning, implementing, managing, and evaluating programs to be in the hands of those most knowledgeable about the resident population.

The Functional Unit concept fosters decentralized case management. This provides continuity of program responsibility by the treatment team, easier recognition of, and greater likelihood for, program assignment to meet the offender's needs. Program fragmentation (which traditionally occurs along department or disciplinary lines) is reduced; which, in turn, results in improved interpersonal relationships among staff members and between staff and residents. Under this organizational structure, those incarcerated receive better treatment, thereby improving their chances of being ready for earlier parole and making a more successful community adjustment.

The staff also benefits by becoming a more integral part of the treatment effort; additionally, they have their immediate supervisors in close proximity. These circumstances lead to greater cohesiveness and better morale.

Care

Functional Units lend themselves to differential allocation of resources. This permits more efficient management of available resources since money, manpower, and material can all be distributed in accord with program needs. That is, special physical facilities (e.g., maximum-security features) and specially trained staff can be optimally utilized with those offenders for whom they are most appropriate. Differing staffing patterns and types of housing can be established for other types of residents for whom the aforementioned features would be inappropriate.

Staff development is also encouraged by adopting the Functional Unit plan. The semiautonomous functioning of the unit (treatment) team which requires lower level staff members to plan, implement, and manage programs, provides an opportunity for these individuals to develop managerial skills. This allows for easier identification of training needs leading to better staff development.

Since all staff members become a more integral part of the Functional Unit's treatment plan, a greater organizational cohesiveness develops. Further, the close working relationship between line and supervisory staff fosters enthusiasm and better morale.

Control

The Functional Unit concept involves maintaining residents in small, independent treatment-relevant groups. This substantially reduces the amount of movement within the facility. Since transfers between units are discouraged, "problem cases" are not passed around. It also permits a more easily achieved physical control of residents since there is a closer working relationship between those incarcerated and the institution staff. The yield is a maximum effort from both groups toward achieving positive goals.

Maintaining control is also aided by the friendly rivalry which tends to develop between Functional Units. Both staff and residents come to feel a sense of pride in "their" unit and its accomplishments. Rather than offenders finding a common cause in organizing against the staff, competition develops along more desirable lines; e.g., which unit has the best record in achieving some positive goal. The resulting learning can be shared among units for the benefit of all.

Functional Units: Disadvantages

The group which most acutely feels the impact of the Functional Unit approach is management—particularly at the department head level. The roles of department heads change as traditional lines of authority are restructured. They need to develop or utilize new and different skills; such changes are often agonizing to undergo.

This change is reflected in a different set of responsibilities for department heads. Their role becomes one of monitoring policy implementation and maintaining performance standards across all of the institution's Functional Units. Other duties and responsibilities are detailed below, but the main point is that some department heads may find their altered role much less satisfying.

The loss of a direct line of authority between the department head and "his people" is reflected in the different table of organization of a decentralized facility. The redesigning process can raise a number of problems for personnel, not only at the department head level, but also at the associate warden level. The redefining of areas of responsibility, the need to clarify vague supervisor-supervisee relationships, the role of the specialist vis a vis the generalist, the writing of new position descriptions and program designs and the implementation of new procedures, all pose difficulties for staff. Feelings of loss of authority or status may result in staff morale problems at the upper echelon level.

Functional Units: Types

It is possible to organize Functional Units around a variety of dimensions; these, then, become the core concept of the unit's program and help identify selection criteria. For example:

1. *Problem area:* drug treatment units, mental health, alcoholism treatment units, etc.
2. *Personality types:* the I-level subtypes described by Warren (1971); Quay's (1972) Behavior Categories, etc.
3. *Work/Training:* grouping together offenders programmed for work or academic training and/or integrating both vocational and educational training with an appropriately designed counseling program.

Implementation of the Functional Unit concept presupposes a "sorting out" process (Admission and Orientation Program) which results in a meaningful assignment of residents to unit programs. Thus, the classification procedure becomes a crucial diagnostic process—involving both staff and offender—attempting to "match" each resident with the most appropriate total program to meet his treatment needs.

Functional Unit: Structure

The concept of a Functional Unit is realized in direct correspondence to the degree that the offender's total correctional treatment plan is designed and implemented by a single, small, integrated group of staff members. This requires a multidisciplinary unit team, i.e., caseworkers, clerical support, correctional counselors, correctional officers, educators, and mental health personnel. Depending upon the number of staff and residents in the Functional Unit, an additional staff member—the unit manager—is needed; he is a "generalist" and may be drawn from any of the fields represented on the unit team.

To a considerable degree, staff activities (next section) are dependent upon the manner in which Functional Units are integrated into the total institution. In a decentralized facility the unit managers function as program directors. As such, they are responsible for the total operation of their unit and report directly to the office of the warden. The role of the department heads changes (see appropriate section below) to that of functioning in a coordinating role between the warden and the Functional Units and between Functional Units. Figures 1 and 2 represent different "model" tables of organization.

The table of organization shown in figure 1 has the department head functioning in a staff role rather than in a direct supervisory relationship. In this model, the associate warden for programs, AW(P), and the associate warden for operations, AW(O), play their traditional roles.

In figure 2 the unit managers as well as the program/training areas, (education, V.T., etc.) all report to a Program Management Committee—composed of five department heads—which functions in the role similar to that of an AW(P). The AW(O) continues to be responsible for coordinating support services throughout the facility in order that the treatment programs can function smoothly.

The within-unit structure and its relationships need to be made explicit. Utilizing the staffing pattern for a 100-man unit—Table 1— the administrative lines of authority are shown in figure 3.

TABLE 1   Functional Unit—Ideal Staffing Pattern

Staff/Unit Size	50 Residents	100 Residents
Unit Manager	a/	1
*Caseworker	1	2
Clerical	1	2
*Correctional Counselors	2	4
Correctional Officers	4+	4+
*Educators	1	2
*Mental Health	1	1

a/One of the asterisked staff serves dual role as specialist and unit manager.

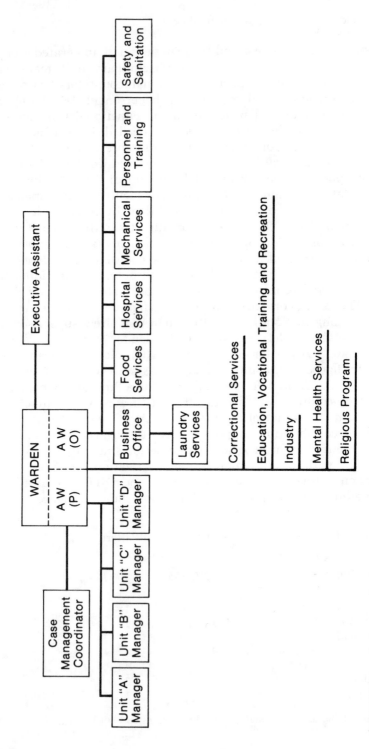

FIGURE 1 Functional Units in a Decentralized Facility

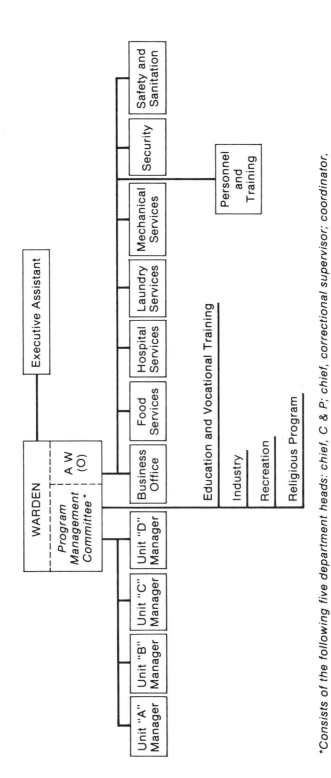

*Consists of the following five department heads: chief, C & P; chief, correctional supervisor; coordinator, mental health services; superintendent, industries; supervisor, education.

FIGURE 2   Functional Units in a Decentralized Facility

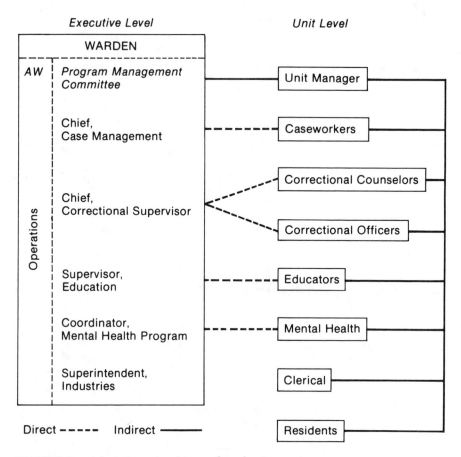

FIGURE 3   Administrative Lines of Authority

Lines of administrative authority flow upward through the unit manager to the office of the warden [i.e., the AW(P) or the Program Management Committee]. That is, members of the unit staff are responsible to the unit manager. He, in turn, is responsible to the office of the warden. The department heads function in a staff role to the warden and have only an indirect relationship with the personnel in the unit staff.

Functional Unit: Staff Activities

The staff members on the unit team are responsible for all aspects of resident program planning and monitoring. This includes initial orientation, admission evaluation, program assignment, implementation of the "in-unit" treatment program (e.g., counseling, therapy, recreation, leisure-time activity, etc.), coordination and liaison with "out-of-unit" activities, both formal and informal program and progress reviews, "promotions" and "demotions" (i.e., handling discipline), Parole Board recommendations, prerelease programming, and so on.

In addition, the unit staff is accountable for the physical condition (i.e., sanitation, orderliness, etc.) of their living unit. They are also responsible for maintaining control in the unit and for observing necessary security measures. In short, each unit is comparable to a small institution which the staff in the unit "run." Within the guidelines formulated by both the executive staff at the facility and those issued by the Central Office, the unit staff are free and expected to formulate a treatment approach appropriate for their "type" of offender. This unit program, in its initial form, is a written proposal subject to review by local executive-level administrators and approval by the Central Office, prior to its implementation.

The Unit Manager

The unit manager's function is to orchestrate the development and implementation of an effective treatment approach in his unit. He is the administrative head of the unit and, as such, the direct-line supervisor of staff assigned to the unit team. In addition to overseeing the within-unit program, the unit manager has important liaison functions throughout the institution. In many ways, he functions in the traditional role of a department head, e.g., attending a variety of administrative meetings (budget, training, warden's staff, etc.), thereby "linking" his unit into the total operation.

The manner in which manpower resources will be expended in the Functional Unit are the responsibility of the unit manager. In establishing work schedules the unit manager should be guided by a number of operating principles: The purpose of the Functional Unit is to find ways to best help offenders, not to set up the most convenient working schedules for the staff. Accordingly, staff should be on duty at those times when residents are most available; e.g., evenings and weekends. Further, since those who are incarcerated are in the institution all year, program activities should not cease during holiday season because all the staff have scheduled themselves for annual leave. It is the responsibility of the unit manager to see to it that staff are available to conduct programs on an extended "treatment day" basis throughout the year.

The unit manager is accountable for the program activities which occur in his unit and should be knowledgeable concerning not only "what's happening" with residents, but with staff as well. It is his responsibility to recognize and remedy program deficiencies. Accordingly, he must be knowledgeable about the treatment philosophy being implemented and capable of either providing himself, or seeing to it that others supply needed needed staff training. In order that he might be aware of his unit's level of performance, the unit manager must place a high priority on the development and implementation of program assessment and monitoring methods. As a "mini-warden," accolades for conducting an effective unit are his due as much as blame for program inefficiencies.

The Caseworker

The caseworker's (and social worker's) responsibilities in a Functional Unit include all the traditional duties required to move an individual through a correctional institution. They include awareness of Central Office policies, possessing the technical expertise to assess correctness of reports, knowledge about Parole Board procedures and the legalities involved, etc. In addition, since caseloads are small, the caseworker takes an active role in direct treatment intervention. That is, he or she will not only function as a full-fledged member of the unit team in all aspects of the programming process as it relates to residents on his caseload, but he will also conduct counseling sessions or whatever other treatment modalities make up the unit's therapeutic approach.

The Correctional Counselor

The correctional counselor serves as a crucial member of the unit's treatment team. He becomes the prime contact between this small group of 25 residents and the rest of the unit and the institution. His role includes being a direct implementer of the agreed-upon treatment modalities, a fully functioning member of the unit team, a liaison between outside-the-unit activities (e.g., work assignment) and their implications for the unit team, an organizer and/or monitor of recreation and leisure-time activities, and so on. In general, he will have the most immediate, prolonged and intensive relationship with many of the unit's residents, of any member on the unit staff. Therefore, he needs training and orientation in the unit's philosophy and methods of treatment implementation. His supervision is the responsibility of the unit manager in consultation with the chief correctional supervisor; his training is the responsibility of the unit staff, other institution personnel, and outside consultants with whom the unit contracts. It is the responsibility of the unit manager to see to it that these staff members receive training in the skills required to conduct the unit's program. He must also be the responsible individual to insure that the correctional counselor's skills are utilized appropriately and that the latter *not* become the "ever-ready" substitute to fill in for absentee staff in other institutional areas.

The Correctional Officer

The correctional officer has the prime role in maintaining security controls in accord with established policies and consistent with the therapeutic nature of the Functional Unit's program. His is the most difficult and least recognized function in any correctional treatment program; yet he is among the most influential in setting the "tone" present in the Functional Unit. Because of his day-to-day interaction with the unit's residents, he becomes a central figure in the establishment and efficient functioning of the "therapeutic community." Therefore, he needs to be oriented to the mission and goals of the unit; he should be an active participant in unit activities; and he should be viewed as a valuable contributor to the unit team of information about an offender's level of progress. In view of the correctional officer's important role in the Functional Unit, care must be exercised to insure that shift rotation is conducted in such a manner that it is not disruptive to program integrity. That is, an orderly, consistent pattern of correctional officer rotation should be established (e.g., relief, morning, day, evening). Every opportunity should be taken to rotate officers within the unit rather than from the day shift in Unit "A" to the Evening shift in Unit "B." Promotion opportunities exist in the direction of either moving up the correctional officer's career ladder or moving into the counselor/unit manager sequence.

The Educator

The role of the educator (academic or vocational training instructor) in a Functional Unit has two major focuses: (1) To function as an education/vocational training guidance counselor—40 percent of his time; (2) to monitor and/or conduct academic or vocational training, ideally within the unit, but more likely in a central school or VT shops building—60 percent of his time. In addition, he is a full member of the unit team and a contributor to this group of information relevant for program assignment. Depending upon the specific needs of the unit's residents, it is the educator's responsibility to recommend training alternatives in order to help each individual reach goals mutually agreed upon in collaboration with the unit team. He may also be required to develop special "classes" which provide the unit residents with information of relevance to the intent of the Functional Unit's program (e.g., "The Social, Psychological, and Physical Effects of Alcoholism" for an alcoholism treatment unit).

The Mental Health Staff Member

The mental health staff member (psychiatrist, psychologist, psychiatric nurse) on the unit team has a multifaceted role. He is expected to be involved in the admission and information gathering process prior to classification; he is a member of the decision-making unit team; he monitors, supervises, and/or conducts therapeutic sessions; he serves as a consultant and trainer for other staff members; and he helps to design and implement program evaluation studies. As with other staff, the mental health worker plays a significant role in the development of the Functional Unit's treatment program. He is expected to become a member of the team in every sense; his activities should be well integrated into the team's functioning in order that the Functional Unit operate as efficiently and effectively as possible.

If there are too few mental health personnel so that the staff pattern in table 1 cannot be adhered to, an alternative structure has the mental health staff serve in a consultative role to the Functional Units. Under these conditions, mental health remains centralized and functions more in a staff role. However, to the extent possible, available mental health staff resources should be "assigned" to a specific unit even though each staff member may cover two or more units.

Clerical Help

Clerical support is critical to the operation of a Functional Unit. Not only is there a high correlation between the smooth flow of paper and an effectively functioning unit, but delays and disruptions in this area have marked negative influence on the therapeutic effort, and staff and resident morale. Further, the need to document program activities and accomplishments, to describe the Functional Unit's program, to prepare brochures to help orient new staff, and to type articles and studies for publication, all argue for capable and adequate clerical support. Message-taking, intra- and interunit communication, and administrative functions such as budgeting, time-keeping, etc., all become clerical functions without which the unit flounders. Further, by including these staff members in training activities, they can become additional treatment resources with the unit.

The Residents

The residents are the *raison d'etre* of Functional Units. Whether they are referred to as prisoners, inmates, residents, or students the purpose of the Functional Unit is to provide better, more intensive, more appropriate, and more effective methods to help them cope more successfully with the problems of living following their release. In achieving this end, programs must be designed which recognize the humanness of those they plan to help. Offenders must be involved in decisions which significantly affect them. Ways must be found to offer opportunities for unit residents to take intramural roles of increasing responsibility both for their own activities, as well as for the smooth functioning of the unit. In the area of decision making, as it relates to a particular individual, he should be viewed as a member of the unit team and have a voice in program decisions affecting him. The "climate" of the Functional Unit should convey a clear respect for the dignity and uniqueness of each of those entrusted to its care.

The Department Heads' Role

In a totally decentralized institution—one comprised entirely of Functional Units—the activities of department heads must, of necessity, change. As indicated in figure 3, they no longer have a line-authority relationship with "their people" in the units. Their function becomes one of a staff role and resource person to both the warden and the unit managers.

As individuals, the department heads consult with and monitor the performance of unit staff members from their area of expertise. Coordination between Functional Units is their prime area of concern; monitoring adherence to policy and standards is of almost equal importance.

Under one model the department heads could function as a Program Management Committee. In this capacity they operate as: an "appeals board" to review unit team decisions; as a policy-recommending, standards-developing group; as an Advisory Council on Treatment; as the Warden's Advisory Research Committee; as a Special Projects Task Force, etc. Either a permanent or rotating chairman of the Program Management Committee could be appointed by the warden.

One of the dangers in a decentralized facility is that the Functional Units may become totally "out of step" with one another, so that the institution appears to be headed in all directions at the same time. The Program Management Committee, therefore, should meet regularly with the unit managers, thereby bringing a broader perspective to program implementation. Despite the change in their role, department heads still have the responsibility to monitor staff activities in their area of expertise, to see to it that standards are maintained and policies adhered to. The warden can expect them to maintain high quality programs, to handle staff problems, and to keep him fully informed.

In those instances where some programmatic areas remain centralized (e.g., vocational training) the department head may function to some degree in the more traditional model; however, even here he will share with the unit manager some of his former authority (e.g., rating VT instructors who also function as part of a unit team).

The Nondecentralized Functions

Up to this point, the article has dealt almost exclusively with those aspects of institutional functioning which are most directly affected by the Functional Unit concept. There remain a number of areas which function much in the same fashion as in a centralized facility. The Business Office, Food Service, Health Services, Laundry, Mechanical Services, Personnel and Training, and Safety and Sanitation, are not significantly affected by this change in organizational structure.

Perhaps the greatest change affects the Correctional Services. In effect, three different areas emerge: the correctional counselors (based in the units and closely tied to the unit manager); the living quarters correctional officers (based in the units but more closely tied to the Correctional Services Department), and security officers (based outside the units and closely tied to the Correctional Services Department). Security operations refer to manning towers, operating the control room, inside patrol, etc. These are characterized by having almost no direct contact with inmates. A second type of security function does have inmate-contact involved—e.g., detail officer; hospital, kitchen, or school officer. Assignments to these latter areas could be distributed among the units with the number of correctional officers attached to the units being increased; rotation through these outside-the-unit situations, then, becomes part of the regular correctional officer rotation sequence.

Thus, the corrections force is required to function in a variety of ways and lines of authority may not always be clear. Care has to be taken to explicate how these separate, but equally important functions will be smoothly integrated, a problem similar to that faced in the dual role played by the education staff.

Evaluation

In any undertaking there needs to be a built-in feedback or evaluation system so that both those conducting the program, as well as those overseeing its operations, have data concerning its level of accomplishment. The development and implementation of assessment methods should be an integral part of a Functional Unit Program Plan.

The unit program plans can become part of a total Master Program Plan for the entire facility. This document details the correctional philosophy, mission, goals and objectives of the total institution in an attempt to describe what a particular institution is trying to accomplish and how all its components contribute towards those ends. Included in the master plan is a measurement and/or evaluation system so that periodic progress reports can be assembled which will provide information regarding the degree to which the facility is meeting its stated objectives. It is the unit manager's responsibility to accord program evaluation high priority in the total activities of his program. While he, himself, may not be knowledgeable in the design of evaluation techniques, such expertise should be accessible either on his own staff or through contracting with appropriate consultants.

Conclusion

The foregoing represents an attempt to describe the concept of a Functional Unit in operational terms. Since the experience of the Bureau of Prisons with this type of unit (and particularly with totally decentralized institutions) is very short, these ideas will no doubt undergo growth and continuing development. This article will have served its purpose to the degree that it provides all concerned with a common frame of reference in discussions about Functional Units, and to the degree that it exposes others to a different approach in the delivery of effective correctional treatment services to incarcerated offenders.

References

Quay, H. C. 1972. Patterns of Aggression, Withdrawal, and Immaturity, in *Psychopathological Disorders of Childhood*, H. C. Quay and J. S. Werry (Eds.). New York: John Wiley & Sons.

Rowitz, L. and Levy L. 1970. The State Hospital in Transition. *Mental Hygiene* 55, No. 1.

Warren, Marguerite Q. 1971. Classification of Offenders as an Aid to Efficient Management and Effective Treatment. *Journal of Criminal Law, Criminology, and Police Science* 62, pp. 239–258.

5 Correctional Counseling and Crisis Intervention

Introduction

Much of the effort of those involved in correctional treatment consists of attempts to discover those factors or occurrences that have some causal relationship to the offender's deviant behavior. Self-introspection helps the law violator uncover his or her motives and motivations and realize the types of reactions, urges, or views of life that have led to problem activity. The offender may also be led to be aware of or develop certain internal strengths, abilities, or qualities that can assist in his or her rehabilitation.

The treatment approach most often used in this form of correctional treatment is termed *casework counseling*. It involves a one-to-one contact between the client and the counselor. The counselor (a therapist, social worker, probation officer, parole officer, or youth worker) seeks to assist the client in becoming better adjusted to his or her current environment and also helps him or her prepare for the future. Hatcher describes correctional counseling as being concerned with the "application of validation techniques designed specifically for bringing about a predictable change in criminal and delinquent behavior."[1]

The specific goals of correctional casework may involve one or more of the following:

1. Increased insight into one's problems and behavior
2. Better delineation of one's self-identity
3. Resolution of handicapping or disabling conflicts
4. Changing of undesirable habits or reaction patterns
5. Improved interpersonal or other competencies

6. The modification of inaccurate assumptions about oneself and one's world
7. The opening of a pathway to a more meaningful and fulfilling existence[2]

Correctional casework does not differ significantly in its goals from casework performed in any of the helping disciplines. The criminal or delinquent has many of the same problems as other individuals who seek counseling. These include facing responsibility, being able to make wise decisions, experiencing self-doubt or anxiety, and developing feelings of self-worth.

There are important differences between casework counseling in corrections and other types of counseling, however. The most profound is that correctional casework counseling *is not voluntarily sought.* The offender is not asked if he desires the counselor's advice and services, nor does he have a choice of caseworkers. This type of counseling, in which a client is required to accept counseling, is sometimes termed coercive counseling. The amenability of offenders assigned to such counseling may range on a spectrum from total rejection and refusal to cooperate to complete acceptance and cooperation. Also, the fact that the counseling is coercive increases the probability that the client will not be completely honest and open with the counselor, but will try to say the kinds of things most likely to speed his release from the institution or from supervision. This makes it much more difficult to establish an open, honest relationship in correctional counseling than in other types of casework.

Nevertheless, the caseworker has certain advantages when counseling is coercive. He can require a client to enroll in an educational or job training program, submit to psychological testing, or become involved in an alcohol or drug rehabilitation program. Although the client may initially resent such direction, the positive outcomes that may result would not have been attained if the offender had been left to his own devices.

Although a correctional caseworker operates under general guidelines set by the courts or the institution (rules of probation or parole, institutional policies), the form of interaction between counselor and client may vary widely, and the counselor's own skills and creativity come into play in the choice of counseling style used with each client. In some instances, the counselor may involve the offender's family in the counseling process as a method of motivating the offender or helping the family change the environment that contributed to the offender's problems. In other cases, the counselor may uncover an area of interest that will open up new employment or educational opportunities for the client and help him to make a new start or turn from criminal associations.

The possible forms of correctional counseling are described in detail in the first selection of this chapter, "Effective Helping—The Human Relations Counseling Model." In this selection, Okun describes a counseling model based on the formation of a helping relationship between counselor and client and the development of strategies for successful resolution of the client's problems and his eventual successful termination from treatment. She notes that the counseling relationship moves through various stages and that certain communications skills are essential for successful implementation of such a counseling model.

A special form of counseling is that termed *crisis intervention*. Any offender who has been remanded to correctional treatment has already experienced a number of personal crises, including arrest, imprisonment, court hearings and trial, sentencing, and imprisonment or assignment to correctional supervision; but it is not likely that the offender received crisis intervention counseling during these events, except for the assistance given by a lawyer. The special, intense counseling called "crisis intervention" is directed primarily at the crises that occur within the setting of correctional treatment. Such a need might arise when a prisoner is subjected to homosexual rape, learns that a loved one has died or is terminally ill, experiences anxiety attacks or other emotional problems as a result of imprisonment, becomes aware that his family is in dire financial straits or that his spouse is divorcing or leaving him, experiences a drug-related episode, or attempts suicide or some other type of self-mutilation. The counseling given in such a crisis is necessarily more intense and of a different nature than counseling designed for long-term, less stressful interaction.

Zusman defined crisis intervention in the following way:

> Crisis intervention is one term that can be used to describe a whole series of recently introduced, brief treatment techniques employing a wide variety of personnel, service organizations, auspices, and formal labels. Crisis intervention includes, for example, suicide prevention services using telephone and in person interviews, teen-age counseling as offered through "hot line" and "drop-in centers," pastoral counseling, brief psychotherapy offered in emergency "walk-in clinics," family dispute intervention provided by specially trained policemen, window-to-window programs, and a host of similar programs.[3]

The premise that at the time of a crisis a client may be more open to positive suggestions and more strongly motivated to change his or her life than at other times is behind much of the current emphasis on crisis intervention. The crisis intervention services available to institutionalized individuals are obviously less wide ranging than the community services listed by Zusman.

The second selection, "The Delivery of Services to Families of Prisoners," deals with the crises suddenly faced by their families when offenders are incarcerated. At the points of arrest, detention, trial, and sentencing the families of offenders are in need of information about what to expect and what could happen; and after imprisonment occurs the families need assistance in redefining their economic dependencies, handling emotional reactions, and planning for the future. Weintraub's article focuses on the possibilities for meaningful crisis intervention activities at these points.

Family therapy is seen as a method of helping an offender adjust within the setting that may have been responsible for creating or intensifying his or her unlawful behavior. Some family therapists, including Virginia Satir, the developer of conjoint family therapy, view the goal of family therapy as the correction of communication problems within the family and teaching of ways to achieve more effective communication.[4] Romig, who reviewed twelve research studies involving 2180 youths, concluded that family treatment focused on improving family communication and that crisis intervention was effective in reducing recurrences of status offenses (truancy, running away, incorrigibility), but was not effective in preventing recurrence of delinquency offenses.[5]

The Northeastern Family Institute, in collaboration with the Massachusetts Department of Youth Services, developed three diagnostic categories of juvenile misbehavior it judged to be related to family dynamics and responsive to family counseling. These included offenses motivated by adolescent rebellion against over-demanding or too-rigid parents, misbehavior triggered by the inability of parents to adequately operate in the parental role because of their own problems, and misbehavior occurring among youths from families broken by death, parental drug or alcohol abuse, mental illness, or desertion.[6]

The National Advisory Commission on Criminal Justice Standards and Goals gave strong approval to the concept of mandatory parental involvement in juvenile court proceedings by recommending that "status offenses" (behavior which is unlawful for juveniles only) be abolished, and that five specific behaviors involving juveniles be categorized as matters coming under the jurisdiction of the courts as "Families with Service Needs" cases. These five behaviors would include:

1. School truancy
2. Repeated disregard for or misuse of lawful parental authority
3. Repeated running away from home
4. Repeated use of intoxicating beverages
5. Delinquent acts committed by a juvenile younger than 10 years of age[7]

Cases involving these matters would be heard with parents, child, and other interested parties present, and the court would have jurisdiction to require the parents, the child, and any public institution or agency to cooperate in dealing with the "Families with Service Needs" problem.

Notes

1. Hayes A. Hatcher, *Correctional Casework and Counseling* (Englewood Cliffs, N.J.: Prentice-Hall, 1978), p. 3.

2. James C. Coleman, *Abnormal Psychology and Modern Life* (Glenview, Ill.: Scott, Foresman, 1964), p. 564.

3. Jack Zusman, "Secondary Prevention," in Alfred M. Freedman, Harold I. Kaplan, and Benjamin J. Sadock, eds., *Comprehensive Textbook of Psychiatry, Volume II* (Baltimore: Williams & Wilkins, 1975), p. 2335.

4. Virginia Satir, *Conjoint Family Therapy* (Palo Alto, Calif.: Science and Behavior Books, 1967), p. 96.

5. Dennis A. Romig, *Justice for Our Children* (Lexington, Mass.: Lexington Books, 1978), pp. 92–93.

6. National Advisory Committee on Criminal Justice Standards and Goals, *Juvenile Justice and Delinquency Prevention* (Washington, D.C.: Government Printing Office, 1977), p. 312.

7. Ibid.

Effective Helping: The Human Relations Counseling Model

Barbara F. Okun

Counseling as referred to in this book encompasses the professional form of helping. The terms "counselor" and "helper" will be used interchangeably, as will the terms "helpee" and "client."

The counseling skills and knowledge covered in this book can apply to different degrees to professional, paraprofessional, or nonprofessional helpers. As the basic communications skills involved in formal or informal helping and in professional, paraprofessional, or nonprofessional helping relationships are the same, much of what constitutes professional training has proven to be effective for paraprofessional and lay helpers. With more training and experience, the helper can deal with a greater variety of people and concerns on a more intensive or theoretical basis.

Many people consider counseling both an art and a science. It is an "art" in the sense that the personality, values, and demeanor of the counselor are important variables (along with the skills and knowledge) that are subjective and difficult to define or to measure. It is a "science" in that much of what we know about human behavior and some of the helping strategies has been developed as structured, measurable, objective systems. Similarly, counseling itself involves a two-part, although overlapping, process. The first part is more an "art" and the second part is more a "science." The process of delivery is perhaps again more an art that runs through the entire helping relationship.

Empathy, defined as understanding another person from that person's frame of reference, is a concept that underlies the entire helping relationship and is necessarily focused upon during the rapport-building initiation of a helping relationship.

The first stage of the counseling process is that of building a trust relationship. The purpose of this relationship building is to create sup-

Reprinted by permission of Duxbury Press from Barbara F. Okun, *Effective Helping: Interviewing and Counseling Techniques*, 1976, pp. 6-14.

port, trust, and open disclosure in order to uncover and explore as much information and as many feelings as possible. This exploration enables the helper and the helpee to determine mutually the goals and objectives for helping and, thus, the direction of the helping relationship. This first relationship stage applies to nonprofessional, paraprofessional, and professional helpers alike.

The skills involved in relationship building on a one-to-one (i.e., one helper with one helpee) basis are fundamental skills that can be used when interacting with others at home, at school, at work, or in your community. These relationship skills are based upon the work of Carkhuff (1967, 1969, 1971, 1972, 1973), Gordon (1970), and others who have developed systematic helper training systems that derive from basic Rogerian client-centered theory.

The second stage of the helping process consists of strategy planning, implementation, and evaluation, leading to termination and follow-up. This stage of the helping process is of some concern to paraprofessional helpers and normally within the province of professional helpers. The nonprofessional helper needs a rudimentary knowledge about the process and application of helping strategies in professional and paraprofessional helping relationships in order to understand and effect appropriate use of human services. The success of this strategies stage depends greatly upon the effectiveness of the communications skills in establishing a positive helping relationship during the first rapport-building stage.

Human Relations Counseling Model

The counseling model upon which this book is based draws upon facets of the major formal theoretical views discussed in chapter 5. It emphasizes a client-centered, problem-solving helping relationship in which behavior changes and action can result from one or both of the following: (1) the client's exploration and understanding of his or her feelings, thoughts, and actions or (2) the client's understanding of and decision to modify pertinent environmental and systemic variables. Cognitive, affective, or behavioral strategies are used alone or in concert when both the helper and the helpee determine the appropriate need and timing.

The theoretical assumptions of the human relations counseling model reflect *existential* as well as behavioristic influences. A list of those influences follows:

1. People are responsible and capable of making their own choices and decisions.

2. People are controlled to a certain extent by their environment, but they are able to direct their lives more than they realize. They always have choices and freedom, along with responsibility, even if they have restricted options due to environmental variables or inherent biological or personality predispositions.
3. Behaviors are purposive and goal directed. People are continuously striving toward meeting their own needs, ranging from basic physiological needs to abstract self-actualization (fulfilling physiological, psychological, sociological, and aesthetic needs).
4. People want to feel good about themselves and continuously need positive confirmation of their own self-worth from *significant others*. They want to feel and behave *congruently*, to reduce *dissonance* between internal and external realities.
5. People are capable of learning new behaviors and unlearning existing behaviors and they are subject to environmental and internal consequences of their behaviors, which in turn serve as *reinforcements*. They strive for reinforcements that are meaningful and congruent with their personal values and belief system.
6. People's personal problems may arise from unfinished business (unresolved conflicts) stemming from the past (concerning events and relationships) and, although some exploration of causation may be beneficial in some cases, most problems can be worked through by focusing on the here and now, on what choices the person has now. Problems are also caused by *incongruencies* between internal (how you see things inside) and external (how you see things outside) perceptions in the present.
7. Many problems experienced by people today are societal or systemic rather than personal or interpersonal. People are capable of learning to effect choices and changes from within the system as well as from without.

The human relations counseling model emphasizes a client-centered helping relationship and the mutual identification of goals, objectives, and intervention strategies that can ultimately be evaluated by observable behavioral change in the helpee's life. It is an eclectic approach in that it utilizes a variety of techniques and strategies, but the major vehicle for change is the development and maintenance of a warm, personally involving, empathic relationship.

The helper is encouraged to learn when and how to use different techniques and strategies and to use different approaches with the same helpee in order to deal with as many areas of concern as possible within the cognitive, affective, and behavioral domains. The goals of helping are to integrate these three domains, to help the helpee become emotionally and cognitively aware of his or her responsibility and choices, and to see this awareness translated into action. When helpees are able to assume responsibility for their feelings, thoughts, and actions and to reduce the contradictions between them, they are able to feel good about themselves and about the world and make choices that reflect the integration of internal and external variables.

The helping relationship is considered the essential foundation of the helping process. It is the *process* of verbal and nonverbal communication, not the content of verbal conversation, upon which this relationship is based. As long as there is an effective helping relationship that communicates the helper's understanding, humanness, strength, and ability to give permission and protection to the helpee, flexibility to select and utilize different strategies remains.

Strategies are secondary to the helping relationship. If a particular strategy does not work but the helping relationship is solid, the helping process is not likely to be negatively affected. For example, if you have developed a trusting relationship with a helpee and you ask her to dialogue (Gestalt technique) with her mother, taking both roles to become more aware of her positive and negative feelings toward her mother, and she is unable to get into it, she will not think you are crazy or incompetent for having tried this strategy. If she trusts and respects you, she will continue to explore with you, seeking strategies that will be more helpful. This helping relationship is reciprocal, in that the helper is considered an equal of the helpee rather than an expert or magician. They work together toward achieving agreed-upon objectives. By equal, I mean that there is reduced social distance and that the responsibility for what occurs is mutual. At the same time, the helper must be able to communicate to clients an understanding of human behavior and the skills to help clients change their behaviors. This relationship aims to increase the helpee's self-understanding and exploration, but it does not provide false reassurance and support. Rather, it is honest and accepts the possibility that discomfort and pain may be involved in the helping process. This honesty enables helpers to tolerate their own and helpees' discomfort without needing to cover it up with false reassurance and distancing.

The major implications for helpers of the human relations counseling model are listed below. This model:

1. defines communications skills as the core of effective human relationships
2. allows that the communications skills can be taught to all helpers in all types of helping relationships
3. provides room for diversity and flexibility for helpers to learn a variety of intervention strategies that can be effective if the basic helping relationship is developed and maintained
4. modifies and integrates a variety of established approaches and strategies
5. provides the versatility and flexibility necessary to meet the needs of a heterogeneous population
6. provides for dealing with feelings, thoughts, and behaviors in a short-term, practical manner relating to the helpee's real life
7. focuses on the positive rather than the negative aspects of the helpee's life (i.e., what one can do to change one's life or environment rather than adjust to given outside pressures)
8. places responsibility for living and decision making upon the helpee while affording as much facilitating as humanly possible

Dimensions of the Human Relations Counseling Model
There are three integrated dimensions of counseling: stages, skills, and issues. Figure 1 shows that helping is encompassed in two overlapping stages of the first dimension. Within this dimension, the two stages of helping are accomplished in the following steps:

1. relationship (development of trust, genuineness, empathy)
   (1) initiation/entry
   (2) clarification of problem being presented
   (3) structure/contract for helping relationship
   (4) intensive exploration of problem(s)
   (5) possible goals and objectives of helping relationship

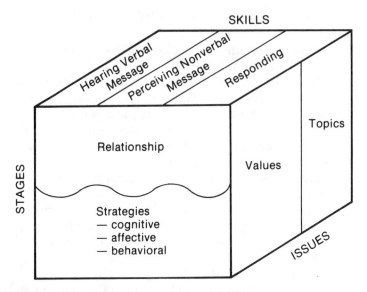

FIGURE 1   The Counseling Model in Dimensional Terms

    2. strategies
        (1) mutual acceptance of defined goals and objectives of helping relationship
        (2) planning of strategies
        (3) use of strategies
        (4) evaluation of strategies
        (5) termination
        (6) follow-up

The top dimension represents communications skills: hearing verbal messages, perceiving nonverbal messages, and responding to verbal and nonverbal messages. These communications skills are required to accomplish the two stages of helping (relationship and strategies) that constitute the first dimension.

    The side or third dimension represents the issues, which are the values and cognitive topics that cut across the other two dimensions. These issues involve not only how an individual relates to others and his or her environment, but also such subjects as sexism, racism, ageism, and poverty. Furthermore, this dimension includes professional matters of ethics, training, and practice, as well as the personal values and attitudes of the helper.

    Outlining a counseling model in diagrammatic form necessitates some formalizing and systematizing that appear rigid and arbitrary. However, this multidimensional view is useful in presenting a simple overview of what happens in and what constitutes effective helping relationships. It thereby provides a useful framework for learning about counseling and developing necessary skills. Naturally, the helper will modify or redesign this conceptual model into whatever form works for him or her.

Stages in Applying the Counseling Model

Relationship. The thesis of this book is that the development of a warm, trusting relationship between the helper and the helpee underlies any strategy or approach to the helping process and, therefore, is a core condition for any effective helping process. Developing a relationship is a time-consuming process; however, a skilled helper can guide this development so that the relationship can aid the helpee within a short period of time.

This development starts with the initial contact between the helper and the helpee. A climate is provided for the helpee to explore concerns and to begin to identify underlying as well as apparent concerns. Later, the client begins to understand these concerns and their implications for living and starts to clarify his or her needs and expectations from the helping relationship in order to facilitate self-exploration, self-understanding, and choices of action. This relationship is crucial to the mutual determination of appropriate goals and objectives and of the limits and nature of the relationship.

Strategies. Once the goals and objectives are mutually decided, the helper reviews all available effective strategies (or courses of action for effective helping) and discusses with the helpee the rationale for a suggested strategy. The possible consequences and ramifications of any strategy are explored.

When agreement on a course of action is reached, the helper applies the strategy, keeping his or her mind open to modifying or refining, depending upon the needs of the helpee. There must be continuous evaluation of the effectiveness of a particular strategy. As stated previously, the effectiveness of any strategy depends more upon the relationship between the helper and the helpee than upon the efficacy of the particular strategy.

When the desired outcomes as agreed upon by both helper and helpee are achieved, the helping relationship is either terminated or attention is focused on another set of objectives and goals. If termination is decided upon, the helper informally or formally checks up on the continued progress of the helpee at a later time.

Skills Needed to Apply the Counseling Model
The communications skills presented in this model are based upon the responsive listening format, which focuses upon hearing verbal messages, perceiving nonverbal messages, and responding to these messages both verbally and nonverbally. The model assumes consistency between the helper's verbal and nonverbal messages. It further relies upon the helper's ability to respond to the helpee by clarifying the latter's underlying feelings and thoughts in such a way as to add to the helpee's self-understanding.

By developing these communications skills, helpers also develop their own self-awareness. As they learn to use their own intuitive feelings as guidelines for hearing other people's messages, they sharpen their helping skills. Helpers are always asking themselves, "What is this person really trying to say to me?", "What is s/he really feeling?" and they are trying to communicate their understanding of this real feeling and message back to the helpee.

Hearing Verbal Messages. Verbal messages are the apparent and underlying cognitive and affective content of the helpee's statements. Understanding the content, implicit and explicit, is usually secondary to understanding the underlying messages and feelings communicated by this content.

Perceiving Nonverbal Messages. Nonverbal messages refer to body language, vocal tone, facial expressions, and other cues that accompany verbal messages. The helper learns to recognize inconsistencies between verbal and nonverbal messages and to develop the helpee's awareness of these incongruencies or inconsistencies.

Responding. Responding requires immediate, genuine, concrete, and empathic reaction to the verbal and nonverbal messages. Both apparent and underlying significances of messages as well as their relationships and inconsistencies affect responses.

Issues Affecting the Counseling Model
Pervasive issues affect both stages of helping. By exposing and clarifying these issues, the helper is able to achieve the type of helping relationship in which these issues do not interfere with helping. Responsive listening skills are effective techniques for discovering and exploring these issues.

Values. Values clarification is a part of helping relationships in that the helper and the helpee both take responsibility for their own attitudes, beliefs, and values. For example, a male counselor in a high school who tells a female student that she cannot enroll or should not consider a carpentry course may be allowing his sexist values to distort or interfere with his counseling. If helpers are not aware of their own biases, the effects will be harmful. However, recognizing your own values will help you avoid imposing them on clients. Research has shown that helpers do communicate their values to helpees, whether or not they do so consciously. Bringing them out into the open and being constantly aware of your values can help you avoid imposing them.

Topics. Some of the pervasive concerns affecting the helping process are issues such as involuntary (or reluctant) clients; helper's dislike of helpees; and ethics, including confidentiality and the helper's responsibility to the sponsoring institution.

Summary

In this chapter we defined the intent and orientation of the book as providing a fundamental introduction to the skills and knowledge necessary for effective helping relationships. These skills and knowledge are needed, to varying degrees, by nonprofessional, paraprofessional, and professional human services workers. Counseling, one important part of human services, is used to represent the helping relationship.

The human relations counseling model consists of three equally important dimensions: stages (relationship and strategies), skills, and issues. These three dimensions are interdependent and cannot be considered mutually exclusive. The helping process depends upon the development of a trusting relationship between the helper(s) and the helpee(s). Effective communications skills enhance this relationship and also provide a way for dealing with controversial issues. Strategies are the various approaches that helpers use to promote self-exploration, understanding, and behavior change with helpees.

References and Further Readings

Carkhuff, R. *The Counselor's Contribution to Facilitative Processes.* Urbana, Ill.: Parkinson, 1967.
———. *Helping and Human Relations,* vols. 1 and 2. New York: Holt, Rinehart, and Winston, 1969.

————. *The Development of Human Resources.* New York: Holt, Rinehart, and Winston, 1971.

————. *The Art of Helping.* Amherst, MA.: Human Resource Development Press, 1972.

————. *The Art of Problem Solving.* Amherst, MA.: Human Resource Development Press, 1973.

Carkhuff, R., and Berenson, B. *Beyond Counseling and Therapy.* New York: Holt, Rinehart, and Winston, 1967.

Gazda, G. *Human Relations Development.* Boston: Allyn and Bacon, 1973.

Gordon, T. *Parent Effectiveness Training.* New York: Wyden, 1970.

Ivey, A. *Microcounseling: Innovations in Interviewing Training.* Springfield, Ill.: Thomas, 1971.

Rogers, C., ed. *The Therapeutic Relationship and Its Impact.* Madison: University of Wisconsin Press, 1967.

The Delivery of Services to Families of Prisoners

Judith F. Weintraub

Traditionally, very few social service agencies, either governmental or voluntary, have identified families of incarcerated individuals as needing specific informational, counseling, and other supportive services. Departments of correction generally formulate their programs only with regard to the offender in their care. When the National Conference of the Association of Social Workers committed themselves in 1973 to working in the corrections field, it totally omitted any mention of families of prisoners. These families, in situations of acute emotional disequilibrium, do require a range of services. They need basic information on which they can proceed to structure their lives. They need counseling to assist them in reformulating their new family unit.

A family member of an incarcerated individual may indeed receive social work services from one of a number of agencies but it is rare that the special problems arising out of the incarceration of the family member will be recognized and dealt with properly. In addition, there is no formal mechanism to deliver basic information about the jails, the courts, the prisons and what is happening to an individual who passes through them. It is therefore necessary to identify the families of the incarcerated individuals as a discrete client group with specific problems and to have the appropriate agencies assume responsibilities for dealing with these problems.

Identification of Crisis Points

Four specific crisis points have been identified for the family of an individual passing through the criminal justice system. They are arrest and arraignment, sentencing, initial incarceration, and immediate/pre/

Reprinted by permission of the *Federal Probation Quarterly* from *Federal Probation*, 40 (4) (Dec. 1976): 28-31.

post release. An examination of the crisis points showed that families experience a twofold need which is common throughout the system.[1] On the one hand is the need for urgent information on what is happening to the family member and how the family can maintain contact with him; and on the other is the need for counseling to help redefine the family unit and deal with all of the problems arising from the incarceration of a primary family member.

Specific Recommendations

Arrest and Arraignment

The obvious first crisis of the family comes when the family member is arrested and arraigned. If the arrested individual is remanded to detention there may be a lapse of time before the family is notified by the inmate. Such notification, when and if it comes, will not necessarily include such important information as the name by which the individual is known to the institution, the exact location of the institution, how to travel there, what restrictive rules govern visiting, writing, and packages, and what requirements apply to bail.

All families of arrested individuals have in common the problems of discovering the name of the defense attorney if he is from the public defender's office or appointed by the court, when the next court appearance will be, what happened at the last court appearance, and what is the approximate period of time it can be expected that the proceedings will take.

To begin to meet these basic informational needs, it is recommended that the institutional authorities provide a preprinted, when appropriate bilingual, form to every individual remanded to a detention facility. The form should include the name and address of the institution, the nearest public transportation, visiting hours, the name by which the individual is known to the institution, and a telephone number to call for further information.

It is further recommended that the governmental agency with the responsibility for maintaining detention institutions should establish a centralized office which can provide information on location of individual inmates, location of institutions, means of transportation to them, visiting hours and regulations, and the names and telephone numbers of voluntary agencies which can provide further services to families. The telephone number of this office should be the one which appears on the forms mailed out by the detainees. This service lends itself to the use of paraprofessionals and/or volunteers.

Sentencing

The second crisis point for the families of individuals going through the criminal justice system is at the time those persons are sentenced to prison. Once again, the families generally cannot obtain information as to which facility their family members will be sent, approximately when they will be transferred there, where the institution is located, how to travel to that institution, what are the regulations for visiting, what must be done to write to the individuals, what are the regulations on sending packages, transfer of money, and most simply, how long is the sentence and when is the earliest possible release. This is in addition to the problems of need for financial assistance, be it welfare or work, problems with housing, and outstanding bills (especially for installment buying). There is also a plethora of internal family problems relating to the need to redefine the family unit in the absence of the incarcerated individual. These problems are especially critical when children are involved. Whether the children remain within the family or with some other family member, or whether they are placed in care, there is still the question of interpreting to them what has happened to the incarcerated parent and why. Questions concerning communication (including institutional visits) must be addressed. The whole continuing relationship between the children and the incarcerated parent must be carefully evaluated on the merits of each individual case.

To meet these problems it is recommended that there be established in the court building itself an office which would assume the responsibility of providing information to families at the time of sentencing. Such an office could be sponsored by a public agency such as probation or the public defender, or by a voluntary agency. The staffing of such offices could well be supplemented by the use of volunteers, especially persons who have been or are at that time members of families of incarcerated individuals. The family would be notified of the availability of this service at the time the defendant is sentenced. At the Family Assistance Office, families would be given a bilingual (where appropriate) printed brochure which would include the location of the facility to which the individual is being sent, how to find out when that transfer has taken place, how to travel to the institution, including reference to free bus services which might be available, regulations on visiting, correspondence, and packages. Staff personnel would give as much of this information as necessary orally, paying particular attention to explaining the minimum release date. If the family so wished, staff would also make an appointment with a private agency for further counseling within as short a period of time as possible.

In order for these to be effective services for families of incarcerated individuals, voluntary agencies doing casework with the general public as well as those programs designed specifically for offenders must be involved.

It is therefore recommended that those voluntary agencies already providing services to the general community identify the members of their clientele who are families of incarcerated individuals. Agencies dealing with children in care should identify which of their clients have incarcerated parents. These agencies should provide orientation and training for staff to enable them to recognize the specific problems of this subgroup and to deal with those problems effectively.

Wherever possible, the voluntary agencies should establish regularly scheduled group sessions for families of incarcerated individuals. These groups, which can effectively utilize volunteer and peer group resources from the community, would focus on problems with children, redefining the family structure, relationships between the family and the incarcerated individual. Any specific problems needing more intensive attention that are identified within the group sessions would be referred to an individual counselor in the same agency or referred to an outside service agency. (It should be noted that provisions for child care and carfare are of essential importance to the success of such a program.)

Further, it is essential that those agencies presently working with offenders recognize that the problems of the family are the problems of the offender also. Whenever possible, a program servicing offenders should work with the individual in the context of his total family.

Institutionalization

The third crisis point occurs at the time that the individual is sent to prison to serve his sentence. The family must redefine itself in the absence of the incarcerated member in such a way as to still include him. In addition, the newly incarcerated individual will rapidly begin to interact with his new milieu. His natural effort to adapt may impose one more strain on the family. The incarcerated person makes demands on the family which they have no way of validating and which they often cannot meet.

In addition to these internal problems, the family must learn to cope with a bewildering new bureaucracy. Traditionally, departments of correction have not established services to meet the needs of families, even on the simplest levels. There is no formal structure to which the family can relate to obtain the information they need about the functioning of the institution and particularly about the status and problems of the incarcerated family member. There is no one to whom the family can give and from whom they can get information. In addition, the varying institutional rules from one facility to another even within one state (or the Federal) system creates confusion.

A far step toward reducing confusion would be accomplished if uniform regulations were established for all institutions within the same system on what can be sent by the family to the incarcerated individual and what constraints are put on visitors with regard to visiting room regulations.

In addition, all reception institutions should provide the inmate with a bilingual (where appropriate) informational mailing containing the location of and traveling instructions for all institutions, rules and regulations on writing, visiting, and packages, and the department in each institution to be contacted if there are any questions. (If all rules are standardized, this can be one mailing from the reception institution.)

Families should be notified *immediately* when an individual has been transferred to another institution and they should be given the reason for the transfer. Family needs should be taken into consideration in any assignment to an institution when possible.

Departments of correction, local, state, and Federal, should accept their responsibility for the families of inmates by:

1. Establishing a coordinating function for all program and services to families. This would include developing and coordinating those programs that exist within a department, such as family visitation services, volunteer and institutional information services, and other department-wide programs for families. It would also include acting as liaison between the department and the community agencies providing services to families of incarcerated individuals.

2. Establishing a family visitation service which would provide at least free transportation from the nearest point of public transportation to a given institution.

3. Initiating programs in the institutions to deal with problems which families may be having with the incarcerated individuals or with the institutions themselves. Such a program can effectively utilize individuals who themselves have been members of families of incarcerated individuals.

4. Developing within the institutional social service units the capability to work with any other program providing service to families or directly with the families themselves. It should serve as a liaison between the inmate with regard to the problems of his

family and those community agencies which can deal with the problems.

Prerelease and Parole

The last crisis point occurs when the individual returns to his family. During the period of incarceration, the family has made an adjustment to continue a stable existence without the presence of that family member. The incarcerated individual has adapted to existence in the prison society. There is presently minimal attention given to preparing the incarcerated individual to return to his family or preparing the family to receive him. There is little or no continuity between planning which may be done for the individual in the institution and agencies which may have been working with the family in the community and the field parole office.

At the time the inmate is to meet the parole board, the department of parole should provide families of prospective parolees with information as to the parole process, how they can possibly influence it, when the inmate will meet the parole board, the amount of time after parole is granted before the individual will actually be released, and the general rules and regulations of parole. The parole officer should also ascertain if the family is receiving any services from a community agency. If not, and the family so wishes, he should refer them to an appropriate agency for prerelease adjustment counseling.

If the family of an incarcerated individual has been known to a community agency, that agency should be invited to submit recommendations to be incorporated in the parole plan for the incarcerated individual.

Community agencies should develop group sessions similar to those described earlier to help families identify those problems which can be expected when the incarcerated individual is released. (Whenever possible, the agency should continue to work with the family and the releasee after his return to the community.)

Prerelease orientation sessions for inmates within the institutions should include discussion of problems to be encountered in reentering the family structure. Whenever possible there should be consultation between those dealing with the families in the community agency and those runnng the prerelease orientations.

Once an individual is approved for parole, a meeting should be arranged between the inmate, his family, and a parole officer who has responsibility for the case at that time. Whenever possible, this meeting should be prior to release, with the inmate attending on furlough. If the individual is being transferred to a Community Residential Facility, a representative from that facility should be present at the meeting.

If an individual's parole is revoked, immediate notice (bilingual where appropriate) should be sent to the family including the name and location of the institution in which the individual is detained, traveling instructions to that institution, regulations for writing and visiting, the date that the hearings will be held and what representation and documentation is permitted at them. Consideration should be given to allowing the family to be present at the revocation hearings.

Conclusion

Many of the suggestions in this article can be implemented at little expense. The primary need is to recognize the families of prisoners as a group with specific problems needing specific responses. It is not necessary for a local bureau of child welfare to hire an expert on the problems of children of incarcerated parents. It would be sufficient to orient the already existing workers that such problems do exist and provide training as to how to deal with them.

Many of the services suggested can be well provided by volunteers, especially ones who themselves have had a family member in prison. More and more departments of correction are establishing volunteer services. It costs no additional money for such an office to establish a volunteer-operated desk in the visiting room of a prison to which families can go for assistance. Many problems can be answered by the dissemination of printed materials. Since most prisons have printshops, it should be an easy matter to have such forms duplicated.

There are no major or insuperable bars to providing many of the services required by prisoners' families. What is needed is the recognition by both private organizations and public agencies that an offender's family will generally have a strong effect on his postrelease behavior. It may be one of positive support, which argues for a maintenance of the family unit during the period of imprisonment. It may be one of negative pressure, which strongly suggests the need for programs to deal with the root problem. Whether for good or ill, the family exists and it behooves the public and private correctional establishment to recognize that fact.

Note

1. Mary C. Schwartz and Judith F. Weintraub, "The Prisoner's Wife: A Study in Crisis," *Federal Probation*, December 1974, pp. 20–26.

6 Reality Therapy and Responsibility Training

Introduction

Reality* therapy is based on the principle that an individual must accept responsibility for his or her behavior, and the goal of the reality therapist is to lead the person being treated to act "responsibly."

According to William Glasser, pioneer of the reality therapy concept, those in need of treatment have been unable to meet their own needs because they deny the reality of the world about them.[1] Reality therapy seeks to help the one being treated to perceive the world as it really is and to behave in a reasonable, responsible manner in the light of this perception. Glasser defines two basic human needs as the key to human behavior— the need to love and be loved and the need to feel that we are worthwhile to ourselves and to others.[2] He regards all irresponsible (socially unacceptable) behavior as caused by the client's inability to fulfill one or both of these needs.

Glasser views a close involvement with other humans as essential to the achievement of responsible behavior, and the reality therapist is called upon to become personally involved with his clients.

Reality therapy differs from other types of therapy in a number of ways. It does not examine the client's past or recognize the existence of mental illness. It views all behavior as conforming to or deviating from the concept of responsible behavior. The concept of morality plays an important role in the therapy, and all acts are defined as being right or wrong. Against this background, the therapist actively instructs the client in ways to become responsible and better fulfill his or her needs.

The use of reality therapy in corrections has a strong appeal for a number of reasons. Since the therapist does not require extensive training and the therapy does not involve complicated terminology, categorizations, or treatment procedures, reality therapy can be implemented by correctional workers who operate on a paraprofessional or volunteer level, as well as by professionals in the field. It follows the basic tenets of common sense and the "golden rule" and does not involve the preparation of detailed case histories, psychological test results, or progress reports.

Critics of reality therapy maintain that it is unrealistic to deny the existence of mental illness and to maintain that any type of individual, no matter how severe his problem behavior has become, can be treated in this manner. As the sole judge of the responsibility or acceptability of the client's behavior, the reality therapist is in a position to guide the behavior of the client without feedback from other professional staff, who might be critical of the manner in which the case is being handled. Finally, the therapist is seen as a strong authority figure, who may alienate those whose criminal behavior is a reaction to or rebellion against authority or the inability to meet the expectations of authority figures.

The two selections in this chapter are designed to introduce the reader to the principles of reality therapy and then provide a discussion of the issues and concerns related to its use. In the first selection, "Reality Therapy: Helping People Help Themselves," Richard L. Rachin describes the step-by-step procedures used by an effective reality therapist to gain the client's trust and lead him or her toward responsible behavior.

In the second selection, "Reality Therapy: Issues and a Review of Research," Carl A. Bersani reviews the success of the application of reality therapy in such settings as schools, corrections, private practice, state mental hospitals, substance abuse centers, and similar programs. Of particular interest is his finding that reality therapy is utilized in 80% of juvenile institutions contacted in a national survey. He also describes the issues and concerns related to the application of reality therapy, including the definition of responsible behavior, and the influence of the moral convictions or preconceived notions and prejudices of the counselor in shaping the client's behavior. Acceptance of the counselor's values and judgments uncritically can lead to a client's overdependence on the counselor and inhibit the client's ability to make independent decisions.

Notes

1. William Glasser, Reality Therapy (New York: Harper & Row, 1965), 7.

2. Ibid., 9.

Reality Therapy: Helping People Help Themselves

Richard L. Rachin

"The realities of mental-health operations," said Anthony Graziano two years ago, "seldom match the idealism with which they are described in the rhetoric."

> *Our professional rhetoric is powerfully reinforcing when it enables us to obscure our own doubts and to disguise our own shortcomings. We seldom actually do what we say we are really doing. Sustained by their own deception, individual clinicians believe they are performing noble functions in essentially bureaucratic, unsympathetic, and doubtfully effective agencies.*[1]

Graziano was not saying anything new. This same message has been delivered, with increasing volume, since the early fifties. Only recently, however, have the efficacy and ethical underpinning of classical treatment procedures been openly attacked.[2] Today it seems almost fashionable to expose, if not castigate, psychoanalysts for defects of character and purpose—faults which they have always shared with the rest of us.[3]

While psychotherapy, particularly of the psychoanalytic type, has never proven to be more effective or dependable than less pretentious kinds of help, orthodox practitioners tend to be as defensive as shamans in examining this incongruity. With certain notable exceptions, there is a remarkable absence of discussion among psychotherapists concerning the efficacy of their treatment techniques in spite of the paucity of evidence mustered to support the belief that psychotherapy is more effective than other treatment procedures.

The influence of mental health practitioners is largely responsible

Reprinted, with permission of the National Council on Crime and Delinquency, from Richard L. Rachin, "Reality Therapy: Helping People to Help Themselves," *Crime and Delinquency,* (January 1974), p. 45-53.

for acceptance of the view that socially disapproved behavior is evidence of emotional illness. Too often the label becomes a self-fulfilling prophecy building impenetrable barriers between *them* (those labeled) and the rest of us.

People in trouble, whether they are patients in mental institutions, drug dependents, or kids who play truant, often are not in a position where they can choose to be treated or not be treated. Public agencies armed with clinical evaluations make the choice for them. The recipient of such public largesse and his family have had little to say about rejecting or terminating treatment, even when the service seems to endanger his health and well-being.[4] Explanations designed to justify these practices are patronizing and lack the evidence that would support continuing them.

Ponder Graziano's theme that American mental health practitioners seem more concerned about improving their status and enhancing their power base than they are about treating. Clinical services have not been freely available to persons needing such care—especially in correction, where both the quality and the quantity of clinical personnel have left something to be desired. Considering juvenile correction alone, the President's Crime Commission reported that, of the 21,000 persons employed during 1965 in 220 state-operated juvenile facilities, only 1,154 were treatment staff. While the accepted national standard required one psychiatrist for every 150 juvenile inmates, the actual ratio in American institutions for children was 1:910. Forty-six psychiatrists (over half of them concentrated in five states) were then listed as the treatment backbone of juvenile correction.[5] As Donald Cressey observed, "The trap is this: We subscribe to a theory of rehabilitation that can be implemented only by highly educated, 'professionally trained' persons, and then scream that there are not enough of these persons to man our correctional agencies and institutions."[6]

Dissatisfaction with the Medical Model

The following are some of the reasons for the accelerating development of alternatives to traditional, medically based approaches to helping troubled people:

1. "The recidivism rate for offenders," writes Seymour Halleck, "remains depressingly high and the number of psychiatrists interested in treating the delinquent remains shamefully low."[7] Publicity given to crime and the problems of our criminal justice system has not led to any significant increase in the number of

clinicians devoting themselves to correction.

2. Even if there were enough conventionally prepared clinicians available, it is doubtful that government would be able or willing to assume the cost of their employment. Psychiatric attention is expensive and psychiatry's patients in the correctional system have never been high on the list of public priorities.

3. Important class, cultural, and racial barriers between those treating and those being treated have hindered the development of rapport and effective treatment programs. This problem has been magnified by our dependence on institutional care and the location of most of the institutions in rural areas, where staff recruitment beyond the surrounding communities (when attempted) is usually unsuccessful. Generally, in a state with a relatively large urban population, few of the staff—but, conversely, a disproportionately large part of the inmate population—are members of city-dwelling minority groups.

4. Research has not demonstrated that people receiving conventional treatment are any better off than those not receiving treatment. While this may be disturbing to advocates of the status quo, it is well to recall Jerome Frank's words: "Comparison of the effects of psychotherapy and placebos on a group of psychiatric outpatients suggests certain symptoms may be relieved equally well by both forms of treatment and raises the possibility that one of the features accounting for some of the success of all forms of psychotherapy is their ability to arouse the patient's expectation of help."[8] We are witnessing an accelerating growth of more humane, socially accountable therapies in which people with problems depend on other people with similar problems for help. The influence that human beings have on one another has long been noted, but has not been applied in practice.[9]

Although middle-class values and standards provide no valid measure for assessing mental health or mental illness, this yardstick has been customarily employed to measure deviation and the need for correctional care, especially in juvenile courts. Fortunately, simple economics has forced a re-examination of the traditional treatment orthodoxy. We have finally come to question the concept of mental illness as behavior that deviates from an established norm and its concept of cure as intervention by professionally trained mental health practitioners.

There should be little argument about the pervasive long-term ineffectiveness of most "treatment" programs. Although poorly trained staff, crumbling and inadequate physical plants, skimpy budgets, and overcrowding contribute to their futility, it is doubtful that unlimited resources alone would make it possible to rehabilitate significantly more offenders. Many private child-care agencies with budgets and per capita costs several times those of their public counterparts have discovered this when they become involved with court-referred children—even though they have been highly selective when deciding which court-committed children they will accept. A major reason for the poor results may be that many of the ways in which most well-adjusted adults once behaved are now viewed as symptomatic of underlying pathology. Two important circumstances are usually overlooked: (1) usually behavior brought to the attention of the courts and other official agencies is disproportionately that of poor and minority group children; (2) as George Vold observed, "in a delinquency area, delinquency is the normal response of the normal individual. . . . The nondelinquent is really the 'problem case,' the nonconformist whose behavior needs to be accounted for."[10]

The imprimatur of the court clinician is usually sufficient to dispose of children whose true feelings and needs are probably better known to their peers than to anyone coming into contact with the child for the first time. As Martin Silver found, "The detection of a 'proclivity to bad behavior' is facilitated by the court's 'treatment' process." Silver goes on to quote Dick Gregory: "Being black is not needing a psychiatrist to tell you what's bugging you."[11]

Offenders who have proved to be poor candidates for traditional treatment approaches in many cases seem responsive to peer group "here and now" therapies. As Carl Rogers expressed it, "It makes me realize what incredible potential for helping resides in the ordinary untrained person, if only he feels the freedom to use it."[12] The medical model for understanding and treating essentially psychosocial, ethical, or legal deviations makes it, as Szasz suggests, "logically absurd to expect that it will help solve problems whose very existence has been defined and established on nonmedical grounds."[13]

Nevertheless, when available in correction and more than just in name, diagnostic and treatment services essentially remain cast from the same orthodox mold. Vested interests and ignorance combine to apply a method of treatment that even Freud himself was to disavow in later life.[14] Ironically, proposals made to improve treatment services are usually accompanied by pleas for more psychiatrists, clinical psychologists, and psychiatric social workers. The influence which mental health practitioners have had on the design and delivery of treatment services seems accounted for not by any greater success in helping people but by seemingly convincing arguments disparaging alternative approaches. Put to the test, conventional treatment practices based upon the mental health/mental illness model have been as unsuccessful with offender groups as they often have been unavailable. Operating in the penumbra of the clinician and frequently in awe of him, legislators and correctional administrators have clung tenaciously to procedures about which they understand little and feel the need to understand less. And this problem has not been restricted to correction.

The development of less costly, more effective, and readily attainable treatment alternatives can be traced to three conditions: first, a quest for involvement, understanding, and clear communication by significant numbers of people—a need which could hardly be met by the small coterie of conventional mental health practitioners; second, voluntary patients' dissatisfaction with the time and expense required for treatment; and third, a crescendo of criticism directed by practitioners and researchers at a treatment methodology that has never been validated.[15]

William Glasser shared this concern. Near the completion of his psychiatric training he began to doubt much of what he had been taught. "Only a very few questioned the basic tenets of conventional psychiatry. One of these few was my last teacher, Dr. G.L. Harrington. When I hesitatingly expressed my own concern, he reached across the desk, shook my hand and said 'join the club.' "[16]

Reality Therapy

Glasser's theories departed radically from classical procedures. He postulated that, regardless of the symptom—be it drug use, fear of heights, suspicion that others may be plotting against one, or whatever—the problem could be traced in all instances to an inability to fulfill two basic needs:

> *Psychiatry must be concerned with two basic psychological needs:* the need to love and be loved and the need to feel that we are worthwhile to ourselves and to others.[17]

Glasser believed that the severity of the symptom reflected the degree to which the person was failing to meet these needs. No matter how bizarre or irrational the behavior seems to be, it always has meaning to the person: a rather ineffective but nevertheless necessary attempt to satisfy these basic needs.

Regardless of behavior, people who are not meeting their needs refuse to acknowledge the reality of the world in which they live. This becomes more apparent with each successive failure to gain relatedness and respect. Reality therapy mobilizes its efforts toward helping a person accept reality and aims to help him meet his needs within its confines.

We fulfill our needs by being involved with other people. Involvement, of course, means a great deal more than simply being with other people. It is a reciprocal relationship of care and concern. Most people usually experience this relationship with parents, spouses, close friends, or others. When there is no involvement with at least one other human being, reality begins to be denied and the ability to meet one's needs suffers accordingly.

Glasser points out that advice given to a person who needs help is of little value. People who deny the reality of the world around them cannot be expected to respond to exhortations to do better or to behave. Involvement means having a relationship with another person who can both model and mirror reality. The reality therapist presumes that people who are experiencing difficulty in living are having difficulty meeting their needs within the confines of the "real world." To help someone adopt a more successful life style, the reality therapist must first become involved with him. Involvement is the reality therapist's expression of genuine care and concern. It is the key to his success in influencing behavior. Involvement does not come easily. The therapist must be patient and determined not to reject the person because of aberrance or misbehavior.

Reality and Traditional Therapy Compared

Reality therapy rejects the classical system whereby problem-ridden people are viewed as mentally ill and their behavior is labeled according to a complex and extensive classification scheme. Instead of the terms "mental health" and "mental illness," reality therapy refers to behavior as "responsible" or "irresponsible." The extensive, ambiguous, and unreliable diagnostic scheme on which conventional practitioners depend is discarded. As diagnostician the reality therapist simply determines whether the person is meeting his needs in a manner that does not interfere with others meeting theirs. If he is, he is acting responsibly; if he isn't, he is acting irresponsibly.

Conventional procedures lead the patient back through a maze of old experiences in search of the origin of his problem, because, the analyst assumes, the patient will be unable to deal with the present until he understands how the problem began in the elusive link in the past. Reality therapy concentrates on the present, on the "here and now" rather than the "there and then." Nothing can change the past, no matter how sad or unfortunate it may have been. The past does not influence present behavior any more than the person permits it to. The focus of the reality therapist, therefore, is on present behavior, about which something can be done.

Conventional therapy emphasizes the process during which the patient relives significant occurrences in his past and projects his past wishes, thoughts, and feelings onto the therapist; through interpretation of these past events the therapist helps the patient understand his present inadequate behavior. In contrast, reality therapy rejects the need for insight into one's past; the reality therapist relates to the person as he is and does not relive the past. The conventional practitioner seeks to uncover unconscious conflicts and motivations and to help the patient gain insight into these mental processes; he de-emphasizes conscious problems while helping the patient understand his unconscious through dreams, free associations, and analysis of the transference. The reality therapist insists that the person examine his conscious self and behavior; conceding that efforts to understand motivation or other complex mental processes may be interesting, he doubts that the results merit the time spent to obtain them: it has yet to be demonstrated, he argues, that these pursuits have anything to do with helping the person.

Conventional practice makes no ethical judgments and frees the patient of moral responsibility for his actions; it views the patient as being under the influence of a psychic illness which makes him incapable of controlling his behavior. In reality therapy the patient is forced to face the consequences of his behavior: Was it right or wrong? What were the results for him?

Finally, the conventionally schooled practitioner insists that his role remain inexplicit, almost ambiguous, to the patient; he does not take an active part in helping him find a more productive way to live. Although the reality therapist does not take over for the person, he helps him—even teaches him when necessary—to learn better ways to meet his needs.

Fourteen Steps

The reality therapist follows certain steps in attaining involvement and influencing responsible, realistic behavior. Responsibility, the basic concept of reality therapy, is defined simply as the ability to meet one's needs without depriving others of the ability to meet theirs.

Realistic behavior occurs when one considers and compares the immediate and remote consequences of his actions.

Step 1: *Personalizes.* The reality therapist becomes emotionally involved. He carefully models responsibility and does not practice something other than he preaches. He is a warm, tough, interested, and sensitive human being who genuinely gives a damn—and demonstrates it.

Step 2: *Reveals Self.* He has frailties as well as strengths and does not need to project an image of omniscience or omnipotence. If he is asked personal questions he sees nothing wrong with responding.

Step 3: *Concentrates on the "Here and Now."* He is concerned only with behavior that can be tested by reality. The only problems or issues that can be confronted are those occurring in the present. Permitting the person to dwell on the past is a waste of time. He does not allow the person to use the unfavorable past as a justification of irresponsible action in the present.

Step 4: *Emphasizes Behavior.* Unlike attitudes or motives, behavior can be observed. The reality therapist is not interested in uncovering underlying motivations or drives; rather, he concentrates on helping the person act in a manner that will help him meet his needs responsibly. Although the person may be convinced that new behavior will not attain responsible ends, the reality therapist insists that he try.

Step 5: *Rarely Asks Why.* He is concerned with helping the person understand what he is doing, what he has accomplished, what he is learning from his behavior, and whether he could do better than he is doing now. Asking the person the reasons for his actions implies that they make a difference. The reality therapist takes a posture that irresponsible behavior is just that, regardless of the reasons. He is not interested in time-consuming and often counterproductive explanations for self-defeating behavior. Rather, he conveys to the person that more responsible behavior will be expected.

Step 6: *Helps the Person Evaluate His Behavior.* He is persistent in guiding the person to explore his actions for signs of irresponsible, unrealistic behavior. He does not permit the person to deny the importance of difficult things he would like to do. He repeatedly asks the person what his current behavior is accomplishing and whether it is meeting his needs.

Step 7: *Helps Him Develop a Better Plan for Future Behavior.* By questioning *what* the person is doing now and *what* he can do differently, he conveys his belief in the person's ability to behave responsibly. If the person cannot develop his own plan for future action, the reality therapist will help him develop one. Once the plan is worked out, a contract is drawn up and signed by the person and the reality therapist. It is a minimum plan for behaving differently in matters in which the person admits he has acted irresponsibly. If the contract is broken, a new one is designed and agreed upon. If a contract is honored, a new one with tasks more closely attuned to the person's ability is designed. Plans are made for the contract to be reviewed periodically.

Step 8: *Rejects Excuses.* He does not encourage searching for reasons to justify irresponsible behavior: to do so would support a belief that the person has acceptable reasons for not doing what he had agreed was within his capabilities. Excuses do not improve a situation; they do not help a person to see the need for an honest, scrutinizing examination of his behavior. Excuses only delay improvement.

Step 9: *Offers No Tears of Sympathy.* Sympathy does little more than convey the therapist's lack of confidence in the person's ability to act more responsibly. The reality therapist does not become inveigled into listening to long sad stories about a person's past. The past cannot justify present irresponsible behavior. The therapist has a relationship with the person which is based upon genuine care and concern; sympathizing with a person's misery or inability to act in a more productive and need-fulfilling manner will do nothing to improve his ability to lead a responsible life. The therapist must convey to the person that he cares enough about him that, if need be, he will try to force him to act more responsibly.

Step 10: *Praises and Approves Responsible Behavior.* People need recognition and esteem for their positive accomplishments. However, the reality therapist should not become unduly excited about a person's success in grappling with problems that he previously avoided or handled poorly. But just as a person's irresponsible behavior is recognized when he is asked what he plans to do about it, so should his responsible behavior be recognized.

Step 11: *Believes People Are Capable of Changing Their Behavior.* Positive expectations do much to enhance the chances of a person's adopting a more productive lifestyle regardless of how many times he may have failed in the past. Negative expectations, on the other hand, serve to undermine progress. It is easier to do things well when others are encouraging and optimistic.

Step 12: *Tries to Work in Groups.* People are most responsive to the influence and pressure of their peers. It is much easier to express oneself with a group of peers than it is to relate to a therapist alone. People are also more likely to be open and honest with a peer group. Problems one often imagines are unique are quickly discovered by group members to be similar to the difficulties others also are encountering. Group involvement itself is immediate and helpful grist for observation and discussion. Learning experiences derived from interaction in treatment groups carry over to personal group encounters.

Step 13: *Does Not Give Up.* The reality therapist rejects the idea that anyone is unable to learn how to live a more productive and responsible life. There are instances when a person may be unwilling to do anything about his life, but this does not mean that, given another opportunity, he will not work to change it. Failure need not be documented in a detailed case record. Case records too often become little more than repetitive and largely subjective harbingers of failure. Sometimes professionals seem more involved with records than with the people the records pretend to describe. The reality therapist does not let historical material interfere with his becoming involved with people or prevent him from beginning afresh.

Step 14: *Does Not Label People.* He does not believe that elaborate diagnostic rituals aid involvement or help the person. Behavior is simply described as responsible or irresponsible. The therapist does not classify people as sick, disturbed, or emotionally disabled.

The principles of reality therapy are common sense interwoven with a firm belief in the dignity of man and his ability to improve his lot. Its value is twofold: it is a means by which people can help one another, and it is a treatment technique, applicable regardless of symptomatology. It is simple to learn albeit somewhat difficult for the novice to practice. Experience, not extensive theoretical grooming, is the key to accomplishment.

Correctional clients who have proven least amendable to conventional treatment methods respond well to reality therapy. That its employment involves only a fraction of the time as well as the cost required by traditional (and not more effective) psychoanalytically oriented treatment modalities only further underscores its value. Until research can demonstrate its relative effectiveness and permanence, these reasons alone make its utilization well worth a try.

Notes

1. Anthony M. Graziano, "Stimulus/Response: In the Mental-Health Industry, Illness Is Our Most Important Product," *Psychology Today*, January 1972, p. 17.

2. *Los Angeles Times*, June 26, 1972, p. 3.

3. Phyllis Chester, "The Sensuous Psychiatrists," *New York*, June 19, 1972, pp. 52–61.

4. Frontal lobotomy, electric shock, and insulin therapy to relieve anxiety were far from being the most humane procedures. See Percival Bailey, "The Great Psychiatric Revolution," *American Journal of Psychiatry*, Vol. 113, 1956, pp. 387–406. Those who have complete confidence in the new wonder drugs should see Richard Elman's "All the Thorazine You Can Drink at Bellevue," *New York*, Nov. 22, 1971, pp. 40–46; also, *New York Times*, July 15, 1972, p. 7.

5. President's Commission on Law Enforcement and Adminstration of Justice, *Task Force Report: Corrections* (Washington, D.C.: Government Printing Office, 1967), p. 145.

6. Donald R. Cressey, remarks on "The Division of Correctional Labor," *Manpower and Training for Corrections*, Proceedings of an Arden House Conference, June 24–26, 1964, p. 56.

7. Seymour L. Halleck, "The Criminal's Problem with Psychiatry," *Morality and Mental Health*, O. Hobart Mowrer et al., eds. (Chicago: Rand McNally, 1967), p. 86.

8. Jerome D. Frank, *Persuasion and Healing* (New York: Schocken Books, 1964), p. 74. See also R. G. Appel et al., "Prognosis in Psychiatry," *A.M.A. Arch. Neurol. Psychiat.*, Vol. 70, 1953, pp. 459–68; O.H. Mowrer, *The Crisis in Psychiatry and Religion* (Princeton, N.J.: Van Nostrand, 1961), p. 121; Hans D. Eysenck, *The Effects of Psychotherapy* (New York: International Science Press, 1966), p. 121.

9. J. Dejerine and E. Gauckler, *The Psychoneuroses and Their Treatment* (Philadelphia: Lippincott, 1913), p. 17.

10. E. Lovell Bixby and Lloyd W. McCorkle, "Discussion of Guided Group Interaction and Correctional Work," *American Sociological Review*, August 1951, p. 460.

11. Martin T. Silver, "The New York City Family Court: A Law Guardian's Overview," *Crime and Delinquency*, January 1972, p. 95.

12. Carl Rogers, *Carl Rogers on Encounter Groups* (New York: Harper & Row, 1970), p. 58.

13. Thomas S. Szasz, "The Myth of Mental Illness," *American Psychologist*, Vol. 15, 1960.

14. J. Wortis, *Fragments of an Analysis with Freud* (New York: Simon and Schuster, 1954), p. 57.

15. Eysenck, *op. cit. supra* note 8, p. 94, quotes D.H. Malan, the Senior Hospital Medical Officer at London's Tavistock Clinic, the locus of orthodox psychoanalysis in England: "There is not the slightest indication from the published figures that psychotherapy has any value at all."

16. William M. Glasser, *Reality Therapy: A New Approach to Psychiatry* (New York: Harper & Row, 1965), p. xxiii.

17. *Id.*, p. 9.

Reality Therapy: Issues and a Review of Research

Carl A. Bersani

Introduction

This introductory section identifies several important characteristics of Reality Therapy. Reality Therapy in action will be discussed in the following section. The primary foci in this section are correctional settings and school settings. A subsequent section identifies a variety of issues and concerns in the application of Reality Therapy. The concluding section briefly reviews Glasser's recent publications.

For those who work with people with a diverse range of problems, Reality Therapy has increasingly become the treatment of choice. Its popularity is evident in school settings, in rehabilitation settings, among the clergy, with offenders, and in private practice. Reality therapy offers us a rather simple but clear approach for growth and behavioral change.

Although trained in psychology and psychiatry, William Glasser's disillusionment led him to devise a practical method in the treatment of clients which he labeled reality therapy. The catalysis leading to the creation of this innovative intervention strategy initially took place during his experiences with confined female delinquents. This led to the first paper dealing with reality therapy (1964), followed by his exceptionally well received book titled Reality Therapy (1965). Reality therapy is distinct from other therapies in a number of ways. We will identify several important distinctions.

Conventional therapy goals do not include client responsibility or personal actions as primary. Rather, the primary thrust of much of our therapeutic strategies is to probe into a client's past thereby gaining insight. Glasser would argue that in the process of continually examining the past in order to understand current behaviors, rationalizations for current behaviors are, unintentionally, given recognition. One of the many distinctions of reality therapy from many other therapies is the treatment focus on the here-and-now. A basic belief of reality therapy, therefore, is that clients refuse to accept responsibility for their current behaviors. Accordingly, reality therapy is designed to enable clients to develop a sense of personal responsibility for their actions and to acquire conscious control over their subsequent behaviors. This process occurs as the reality of their behaviors, their environments, and the consequences of their behavioral choices become known to them. In this therapy, dwelling on unconscious thought processes, feelings, attitudes, and the past are considered self-defeating. Attention is directed instead to the present and into the future. The client-counselor efforts are to explore which current behaviors are self-defeating and what behavioral substitutes better serve the client's needs.

All therapies encounter clients who are depressed, drug addicts, delinquents, spouse abusers and many other categories too numerous to list. However, Glasser is not concerned with the actual symptoms employed by individuals (Ososkie and Turpin, 1985). In describing the central premises of reality therapy, Glasser (1965) identifies another basic belief which underlies and begins to unfold a distinction of his therapy from other therapies. He considers that all the symptomatologies expressed by clients signify they are failures because they have not grasped reality and, therefore, their need satisfactions cannot be achieved. Furthermore, they invite failure for they tend to select ineffective behaviors in their striving to meet their needs. In Glasser's (1965) own words:

> ...all patients have a common characteristic: *they all deny the reality of the world around them.* Some break the law, denying the rules of society; some claim their neighbors are plotting against them, denying the improbability of such behavior. . . . Millions drink to blot out the inadequacy they feel but that need not exist if they could learn to be different: and far too many people choose suicide rather than face the reality that they could solve their problems by more responsible behavior . . . . Therapy will be successful when they are able to give up denying the world and recognize that reality not only exists but that they must fulfill their needs within its framework.

What are these needs? For Glasser, the single, most basic psychological need required by all is the establishment of an identity (Glasser, 1975). The identity is characterized by success and self-esteem. Central in achieving a successful identity are the major psychological routes of loving, being loved and in feeling worthwhile to oneself and to other people. Most important, the shift from a failure identity to a successful identity (and eventual changes in attitudes and beliefs by clients and others) is contingent on changes in the client's behaviors within meaningful interpersonal relationships. In effect, behavioral changes by the client induces behavioral changes in those with whom the client interacts.

Throughout his writings, Glasser continuously reminds us of another major difference between reality therapy and conventional therapies. This difference is the type of client-counselor involvement desired in reality therapy. To varying degrees, conventional therapists remain impersonal and objective. Other therapies view involvement—the therapist becoming a separate and important person in the client's life—as undesirable (Glasser, 1976).

For Glasser, the eventual achievement of involvement (which reduces isolation and facilitates increased need satisfaction) begins with a distinctive type of client-counselor relationship that goes beyond understanding and empathizing with the client. It requires counselors to share openly their own personal struggles with clients, to allow their own values to be challenged by clients, and to confront and challenge clients only when involvement evolves into a special kind of relationship (Glasser, 1965). One earns trust and the privilege of confronting and challenging. It is achieved through a process of involvement where both the counselor and client convey respect, genuineness, and acceptance of each other as unique persons. Without this type of involvement, the underpinnings have not been achieved for a helping process.

Reality Therapy in Action

For over 20 years the helping professions as well as society in general were witness to the intensification of people problems. During this period, the limitations of traditional therapeutic approaches to treatment became apparent. The 1960s to the present can be characterized as a persistent search for demonstrably effective and practical models for intervention (Cohen and Sordo, 1984). Glasser's model of reality therapy and its use in a variety of settings throughout this period is evidence of this search for a practical model of intervention which could be utilized by a wide range of contemporary practitioners.

In the years since the publication of *Reality Therapy* (1965), Glasser's counseling and therapy model has received enthusiastic support and use by highly skilled professionals as well as less skilled workers in service agencies. This popularity is in keeping with Glasser's (1984) statement that the therapy is appropriate to a wide range of behaviors and emotional problems—from mild emotional situations and maladjustments to severe anxieties, perversions and psychoses. Numerous accounts of the successful application of reality therapy with a variety of clientele in diverse settings is evident in the literature (Banmen, 1982a).

Its popularity and application have been reported in settings such as schools, corrections, private practice, state mental hospitals, substance-abuse centers, etc. Two major works convey the successful application of reality therapy by counselors working with a variety of clientele in diverse settings. *The Reality Therapy Reader* (Bassin, Bratter, and Rachin, 1976) brings together accounts of the application of reality therapy in private practice, in education, and in corrections. An edited work by Naomi Glasser (1980) includes two dozen accounts of how reality therapists have worked with a variety of clients. The range of clients helped with reality therapy include: divorced parents, self-destructive adolescents, depressed clients, psychotics who learn to acquire more responsible behavior, clients with severe handicaps, alcoholics, principals helping teachers, and teachers and school counselors helping children (Glasser, N., 1980).

Despite the numerous illustrations mentioned above of the successful application of reality therapy, Banmen (1982b) states that very little formal research evaluating the effectiveness of reality therapy exists. He further states that Glasser and many other reality therapists are increasingly concerned by this lack of formal research. Although reality therapy has not been formally researched in all possible settings and with the full range of potential clients, an examination of the existing limited research could increase our insight regarding the circumstances under which reality therapy appears successful, thereby suggesting promising endeavors and avenues for future research.

In practice, the use of reality therapy is evident in numerous and diverse types of settings. Additionally, general descriptions and testimonies of success by those practitioners utilizing reality therapy are quite apparent in the literature and in conversations with practitioners.

The limited efforts to measure the effects of reality therapy have primarily focused on the correctional and school settings. However, one can offer examples of scattered pieces of research in other settings. Browne and Ritter (1972) selected reality therapy for 16 of the most regressed patients at a V.A. hospital containing 190 psychiatric, medically infirm patients in geriatric wards as a pilot effort. Patients in these wards were diagnosed as long-term, chronic schizophrenics. With the exception of one patient, all achieved personal pride and improved sufficiently in self-care, social abilities, and personal relations making them eligible to be placed in facilities outside the hospital. One study (Zaph, 1974) researched the effects of the use of reality therapy in the community to enhance the personal growth of retarded adult women. Indications of personal growth were measured by improvements in minimum behavioral standards and in goal achievements. Success was achieved on some of these measures.

Another study used reality therapy in efforts to free 65 addicts who were in a methadone dependence program (Raubolt and Bratter, 1976). After one year, significant results in detoxification (remaining drug free, being employed, and no arrests) were achieved.

Correctional Settings

Reality therapy has many supporters among counselors. Its greatest impact appears to be in correctional settings. Vinter (1976) indicates that reality therapy is utilized in 80 percent of the juvenile institutions which were studied in a national survey. It is not known whether the use of this therapy is widespread because it fits the reality as staff understand it or because of the assumption that highly trained professionals are unnecessary in the use of this therapy. Despite its popularity and extensive use in corrections, only a small amount of formal research has been done on reality therapy.

Practitioners have frequently stated that offenders who are alienated by conventional treatment methods respond positively to reality therapy. Using reality therapy in a prison with a group of 43 inmates for 15 weeks, Williams (1976) supports this general impression. All participants found reality therapy to be at least somewhat helpful with 80 percent rating the program as very helpful to them. Many of these inmates felt that reality therapy helped them to take a more realistic and responsible outlook on life in general and prison in particular. Furthermore, none of these inmates received a disciplinary report during the 15 weeks of the program. Williams concludes that reality therapy works because its strengths coincide with many of the weaknesses of incarcerated offenders. One such connection identified by Williams is: "Where many inmates tend to live in a fantasy world of—'if onlys,' reality therapy focuses on the way life is."

One serious problem facing staff is the unrealistic vocational goals of inmates. Prior to release, many inmates avoid facing reality or pursuing a responsible course of action. A main ingredient of the

Maryland Comprehensive Offender Model Program was testing and assessing in order to evaluate training or employment possibilities. Since one goal of this program was to get inmates to face reality and assume responsibility in being available for work possibilities, individual and group counseling were based on the reality therapy model. Within a one-year period 2,795 inmates were in the program; 2,170 of them were released from institutions and available for work. At the time of this report, half of those placed in jobs were self-placements. Bennight (1975) concludes that overall placement of these males exceeded normal placement by applicants who did not have the multiple barriers to employment characteristic of these males.

The research by Falker (1982), German (1975) and Molstad (1981) studied behavioral change. The Magdala Halfway House in St. Louis changed to reality therapy as its primary treatment modality. This facility handles 70 young, adult male offenders per year. Falker (1982) states that previous attempts by staff to control and change the behaviors of residents through positive and negative reinforcements were futile. The reality therapy approach was used to allow both staff and residents an opportunity to examine and evaluate their behaviors.

Among the principles of reality therapy stressed was teaching residents to plan better behaviors when their current behaviors were not fulfilling. Unable to control residents by use of punishment, staff opened new lines of communication leading to cooperative behaviors that fulfilled needs of both workers and residents. For example, "can do—let's try" atmosphere of conciliation along with rules generated by the common group to benefit both staff and clients almost eliminated negativism and various forms of hostile behaviors. Such problems at one time were the norm. Falker found that within a three-year period dramatic reductions by residents in absconding and in terminations occurred, and a significant increase occurred in residents who were successfully released. Successful release meant release to the community with a job, in training, or in school.

Glasser (1965) initially established reality therapy principles within the Ventura School for Girls in California. Considering their prior juvenile history, the Ventura School was the last stop prior to being committed to an adult prison. Of the 370 girls released on parole, only 43 violated parole. German (1975) investigated the effects of group reality therapy on juvenile inmates and staff leaders of the therapy groups. As a consequence of systematic exposure to the principles of reality therapy during group therapy sessions, it was expected that changes in certain behaviors, self-esteem, etc. would occur. German found that the experimental group viewed themselves and were viewed by their teachers as more responsible, more mature, and more acceptable persons. However, self-esteem did not increase. They did exhibit significantly fewer behaviors in the dormitory which required disciplinary action compared to the control group. It was also hypothesized that since staff leaders of the group therapy sessions were exposed to the inmates within a transactional environment, they would change their perceptions of people in general. German's findings indicated that staff leaders changed by viewing people as more positive, complex, and changeable.

Molstad (1981) assumed a position with a residential treatment facility for emotionally disturbed adolescents which had experienced close to total staff turnover. Runaways occurred almost daily; vandalism, theft, fist fights, and other aggressive behaviors were common. Treatment intervention had been based on the Transactional Analysis model. Molstad indicates the new staff felt that TA was too cognitive for these adolescents to understand.

Social workers were given intensive training in reality therapy, and the entire staff (cooks, janitors, etc.) was given a working knowledge of the approach (Molstad, 1981). For the inmates, individual, group, and family therapy were also based on the principles of reality therapy. As long as they remained in keeping with reality therapy principles, policies for each treatment unit were formulated with input from residents. Such involvement (i.e., deciding on rules, tasks, and consequences) increased the likelihood of adhering to the rules. The weekly individual sessions centered on the present, evaluating behavior, developing problem-solving techniques, developing relationships, formalizing resident plans, and developing increased resident responsibility. Daily group reality therapy sessions dealt with school problems, peer problems, family difficulties, problems in the facility, future planning, etc. Each family also experienced group reality therapy sessions. Changes in family relationships, activities, and types of interaction were common areas for discussion. Actual discharge was based on increased level of responsibility in the institution, within the family, within the school setting, and the local community.

Molstad found that behavior in the facility improved greatly when discharge responsibility was turned over to the residents. These adolescents viewed the program more seriously and worked harder toward the goal of discharge. Since accountability was stressed at both the individual and group levels, disruptive behavior and vandalism decreased quickly and drastically.

For the effects of reality therapy on the self-concept of alienated, unmotivated, drug abusing adolescents, see Brown and Kingley (1973). See Thatcher (1983) for a before and after design and a within-group comparison of the effects (for group home delinquents trained in the concepts and practices of reality therapy) on self-concept and locus of control.

There does exist a literature on the use of restitution which we will not review here. Although restitution is clearly grounded on the ideas of reality therapy, the research is not formally structured to examine reality therapy. For a discussion of how reality therapy ideas can be operationalized in traditional restitution programs, see Matthews (1979). Therapists may be especially interested in Lackman's (1986) proposal and operationalization of the behavior equivalent (undoing) to traditional restitution using the steps of reality therapy.

School Settings

The ideas of reality therapy have direct implications in school settings. Glasser first became concerned not only about behavior but also learning, since virtually all the girls at the Ventura School for Girls experienced a history of school failure (Corey, 1977). In his book "Schools Without Failure" (Glasser, 1969), he proposed a program to eliminate failure and other school related problems.

A major problem expressed by teachers in achieving an atmosphere for learning is the issue of serious behavioral problems in the classroom. Several studies have examined the application of reality therapy to classroom discipline problems. Gang (1976) selected two 4th and 5th grade teachers for training in the principles and methods of reality therapy. Each teacher selected three male students whom they considered to be serious behavior problems. Each teacher was trained in reality therapy by the researcher and through participation in a system-wide training program conducted by an associate from Glasser's Educator Training Center. Each teacher met with the researcher at least two times a week and the researcher observed each teacher at least three times a week and provided feedback. Also, trained observers monitored each student in the classroom environment, three times a week, with observations recorded in ten-second intervals.

Gang's study was divided into four phases:

Baseline: In this phase, teachers continued their natural teaching practices in the classroom. This determined where each of the six target students were in relation to the rated behaviors before the beginning of the intervention strategy.

Initial Involvement Intervention: In this phase, teachers were instructed to give each student 15 to 20 seconds of special, personal attention. This was to occur at least three times during each class period. The purpose of this was to develop an ongoing, personal relationship between teacher and student.

Varied Intervention: The teacher continued to give personal attention during this phase, but three modified reality therapy conditions were also used. In the first condition, the teacher responded only to the student's undesirable behavior by following those steps of reality therapy which ask four questions. During the second condition, the teacher responded only to desirable behavior and would follow the steps of reality therapy. In the third condition, the teacher responded to both desirable and undesirable behaviors and followed the steps of reality therapy.

Follow-up: At the conclusion of the intervention phase, trained observers continued recording classroom behavior to determine the durability of any student behavior changes that had occurred as a result of the intervention treatments.

Gang reports that the results clearly supported reality therapy as a solution for those identified as serious behavior problems. For all the target students, a highly significant decrease in the frequency of undesirable behavior occurred; a highly significant increase in the frequency of desirable behavior occurred over baseline conditions during the treatment and follow-up phases of the study. Both teachers felt the establishment of an ongoing, genuine relationship—an outcome of the plan—accounted for the successful outcomes.

The Thompson and Cates (1976) study is similar in goal and method to the Gang (1976) study. Six female elementary teachers each selected the student representing the most difficult discipline problem—a student they would most like to have absent from the school setting. Each teacher received training in a ten-step plan developed by Glasser for teaching discipline to students. The ten-step plan can be divided into three categories. First is the involvement stage. Among other things, it required teachers to stop using unhelpful behaviors and to reinforce helpful behaviors. The counseling stage required teachers to counsel students using the reality therapy process including a written contract with students that outlines a plan for changing behavior. The time-out stage includes logical consequences for misbehavior as well as written plans for correcting misbehaviors. The phases of this study and the method of monitoring/analysis were very similar to the Gang (1976) study. As in the previous study, all six students achieved significant increases in appropriate behavior and decreases in inappropriate behavior during the treatment stage compared to the baseline stage. The two studies taken together appear to support reality therapy as a tool for behavior change. Large gains in appropriate student behavior were achieved through a modest amount of positive behavioral changes on the part of teachers. For the effectiveness of reality therapy on discipline and behavior problems using an experimental and control design, see Matthews (1973).

The primary purpose of the study by Dakoske (1977) was to explore not only the short-term but also the long-term effects of reality therapy on both discipline and self-concept. Thirty selected fifth graders were randomly assigned to either a reality therapy session group or a group which received the Open Language Arts Program. Self-concept and problem behaviors were measured before and after the reality therapy sessions.

Dakoske (1977) indicates reality therapy sessions were led by a classroom teacher with assistance by the elementary school counselor. On a weekly basis, fifteen sessions were held for one hour each week. Classroom topics as recommended by Glasser (1965, 1969) were discussed by the students. The teacher provided encouragement to students to explore their ideas, feelings, and values. The principles of Glasser's approach were followed in the classroom discussions and included efforts to build interpersonal relationships and provide mutual support.

Dakoske found significant differences in favor of the group exposed to reality therapy sessions on post-test versus pre-test measures of problem behaviors and self-concept. However, post-test one year later which included no treatment for either group revealed no significant difference between the groups on self-concept. For additional studies using experimental/control groups with a pre- and post-testing design reporting favorable effects of the reality therapy process on self-concept, see Omigo and Cubberly's (1983) study of learning disabled children and Slowick, Omizo and Hammet's (1984) study of Mexican-American adolescents. Other studies which have measured the effects of the reality therapy process on school achievement, locus of control, and self-concept are: Hawes (1971), Thatcher (1983), Matthews (1973), and Shearn and Randolph (1978).

Banmen (1982b) has commented on the issue of the practitioners' skills in using reality therapy. He offers this as a possible explanation for some of the inconsistencies in some of the findings on reality therapy. In reviewing reality therapy studies, Banmen (1982b) found that positive results were more likely for behavioral changes. This review also finds increasing positive results for changes in self-concept but mixed results on locus of control. Thus, we can identify areas where reality therapy appears promising. We should also recall that in many settings and populations reality therapy is the primary treatment mode despite the lack of research validation. Thus, more research is needed in those settings and populations virtually ignored by formal research.

Issues and Concerns in the Application of Reality Therapy

When one views edited works (Bassin, et al., 1976; Glasser, N., 1980), volumes by William Glasser, and diverse monographs, the numerous virtues of reality therapy appear to be common knowledge. Yet, like other therapies, reality therapy in practice is only as good as the individual counselor using it (Trojanowicz and Morash, 1983). Considering the particular mode of intervention used in reality therapy, it is one of the methods especially subject to misuse and misunderstanding, despite the fact other therapies may encounter similar problems (Ivery, 1980).

In the application of reality therapy, therefore, issues and concerns have been expressed. A number of writers raise a variety of concerns. For example, what constitutes responsible behavior? If behavior does not harm others, who decides? What is moral and correct? In practice, who really decides? Is the counselor expected to function as a value catalyst and as a model for responsible behavior? Do the principles of reality therapy contain ingredients both for involvement and for rejection? In his more recent works (see references), Glasser increases the emphasis on a nonjudgmental, noncritical, and supportive therapeutic relationship (Corey, 1986). Nevertheless in the applying of principles of reality therapy, a number of writers continue to express the concerns just mentioned. (For example, see Corey, 1986; Peterson, 1976; May, 1967; Ivery, 1980; and Arbuckle, 1975.) Ivery (1980) also cautions that reality therapy must achieve a balance in working with clients which includes environmental circumstances. What follows are some of the major problem areas with reality therapy and its application.

All counselors adhere to moral standards particular to them. Clients are confronted with the disparity between a variety of behaviors which the counselor deems conventional and acceptable versus the specific behavior of the client. Distinct from some therapies, Glasser's (1965, 1972) position is that people are failures not because their standards are too high, but because their performances (irresponsibilities) are too low. Accordingly, there is the need to enhance greater maturity to reduce irresponsible behavior. (As an aside, reality therapy is appropriate for over-socialized clients, but the statement above does not appear appropriate to this category of client.)

We should be concerned with moral standards because therapy counselors are free to incorporate their own values into the interaction process. At times counselors unconsciously incorporate their values because they assume these are the preferred ones. Clients can be especially victimized when they do not have firm convictions with regard to the allocation of responsibilities within their family, aspirations for their children, or attitudes toward homosexuality. The client may be victimized for being involved in a lifestyle not consistent with the counselor's preferred values. Reality therapy counselors continually evaluate the current behaviors of clients and may unduly assist in suggesting options for future behavior—based more on personal value sets than on those which could emerge from clients. To the extent this occurs, it is the preconceived notions and prejudices of these counselors which shape future planning. Thus far, Glasser's writings do not provide a systematic methodology for clearly separating the moral standards of the counselor from that of the client. Those who should be best able to cope with this dilemma are reality therapists who are experienced and certified.

This apparent lack of reasonable amount of uniformity by diverse counselors in the application of reality therapy creates other concerns troublesome to many adherents of reality therapy. Attention will be given to a selected number of those concerns which are central when one attempts to implement reality therapy. Beyond moral standards, another concern deals with the issue of involvement. Essentially, the problem involves the importance of the uncritical acceptance of the client as the central feature in establishing involvement. Sometimes, a subsequent shift occurs toward critically evaluating a client's future behavior. Because of this shift, the possibility does exist that the underpinnings for the relationship and for changing behavior may have changed. The mandate to accept or at least to give recognition to much of what the client has to say initially offers a solid foundation for establishing a firm emotional and cognitive relationship. After the counselor determines that the special type of involvement desirable in reality therapy has been achieved, the counselor revises the relationship in the eyes of the client by also becoming a person whose acceptance of the client appears, now, to be highly conditional on successfully achieving agreed upon behavioral changes. The counselor becomes a judge, and, perhaps, unconsciously conveys that love comes as a result of good behavior.

Thus, the concern here is the potential for the client to perceive the counselor's behavior and statements as rejection. For a client with a history of failures in relationships, this relationship is then like all others. Worse, because it may not be as apparent, in order to sustain acceptance from the counselor, the client makes behavioral changes to please the counselor. But this occurs at the expense of enhancing the client's self-determination which is the reason for the therapy and the relationship. These scenarios also bring into question whether the client is developing involvements with others beyond the therapist. The whole purpose of planning responsible behavioral changes is to become involved with others, not to expend one's energies on rescuing the involvement with the therapist.

The question of dependency as well as the termination of therapy are issues for many therapies. For reality therapy, these are serious concerns when we consider its ideas and that it is short-term therapy. Central to reality therapy is that self-worth can only be achieved by becoming involved with others in the client's real world. Despite the successes of the therapy in helping clients become more behaviorally responsible, (as the earlier research review suggests) not all clients achieve independence. Some practicing reality therapists were aware early on that some clients concluded that the counselor's evaluation and guides for behavioral changes had greater validity than their own judgments. Yochelson and Samenow (1977) state that a shortcoming of reality therapy is the lack of specifics in teaching processes of decision making that would apply beyond the immediate situation. We need to acknowledge the problem of dependency and include as part of reality therapy a strategy for learning that enables what is learned to transfer beyond the immediate behavioral change. If the counselor is perceived as the expert and concrete behavior changes are not generalized to other aspects of life, then clients are likely to sustain a dependency relationship. They are also likely to experience a crumbling of the degree of self-confidence they have attained when therapy does end.

Szasz, like Glasser, feels strongly that mental illness is not an illness. Immediately upon publication of *Reality Therapy* (1965), Szasz (1966) expressed concern that Glasser had merely relabeled everything called mental illness as irresponsibility. It is clear even in Glasser's recent writings that he continues to view all behaviors as the sole creation of the inner workings of the individual. Further, if the behavior is disruptive to elements of conventional society, one is behaving irresponsibly.

It is not difficult to concur with Glasser's major thrust. However, behavioral expressions stem from greater complexities than choosing to be irresponsible. We will identify only a few issues here. At times what others are doing is vastly more important than the irresponsible behavior of the client. The labeling processes directed toward one individual may be so pervasive that the irresponsible behavior of the client is but a symptom of a larger problem. This issue is not adequately dealt with by the principles of reality therapy.

Also, given insufficient recognition are subcultures. Indeed, some people do behave irresponsibly toward others. Yet, they may believe they possess successful identities, not failure identities. Some persons are simply happy not conforming. Some pimps may illustrate this point. Drug trafficking provides another example. Can we really assume that they consider themselves to be failures or concur with our standards of responsible behavior? Glasser does not adequately deal with this issue except to say that if the client does not critically assess existing behavior, therapy can be of no help.

Another principle of reality therapy is: "Accept no excuses." Many practitioners have difficulty following this in practice. The principle is critical since many clients have histories of using excuses as rationalizations so as not to conform. In effect, excuses are used to sanction irresponsible behavior. Yet, who does not need self-esteem defenses to preserve credibility—to smooth over interactional encounters? Those who don't are few in number. Eliminate the use of excuses for a month from the thousands of interactions experienced during that period. Now what is the status of your informal and formal relations? How are you perceived? It is apparent that valid and even invalid excuses are vehicles for orderly social interaction and relationships. In fact—at least in our society—a major feature among members is to use excuses when expectations are not fulfilled. Therefore, literally permitting no excuses can affect relationships. No excuses permitted in the "problem" area is absolutely crucial. On the other hand, permitting *normal* usage of excuses in marginal areas around the core problem is realistic and is in keeping with how people normally behave.

There is the question of whether reality therapy should explicitly include a principle dealing with the client's social relations. It would be helpful if a principle existed which emphasized and provided guidelines for the counselor to monitor what others, in addition to the client, are doing in the relationship. Explication here is critical if the counselor is to be effective in helping the client plan strategy. One walks a precarious path when the plan for action is based mainly on what ability the client possesses in grasping and in conveying what others are like in the relationship. For this reason, some counselors have contacts with others in the relationship.

The negative influences of environmental circumstances is not directly dealt with in the steps of reality therapy. This is a major concern to therapists who incorporate this therapy in their actual practice. Reality therapy does attempt to help the client to accept and to meet the circumstances which actually surround the client. For emotional stability and to establish a successful identity, one must learn to cope with certain environmental circumstances which cannot easily be changed. Nevertheless, for many ex-cons the actual adjustments to the neighborhood can be overwhelming. Despite the plan for behavioral change, there are basic questions about the availability of appropriate associates, available employment, and the holistic exposure to an environment kindly described as negative.

The above suggests that reality therapy lacks a guide for addressing the all-embracing roles and positions within which clients are physically and mentally entrapped. What should be done after one grasps the client's relationships? At the very least we should attempt revisions, after client consensus evolves, in the fabric of the client's social web. However, once the counselor does grasp the reality of our multiple worlds, realistically achieving a successful identity should not be equated to living a conventional lifestyle.

What constitutes some of the elements of a comprehensive approach? There are some elements which are immediately apparent. But these hardly exhaust all possible elements. First, reality therapy at the individual level is primary. All other elements are supportive players for achieving the goals of the therapy. Environmental "manipulation" is a necessary tool for therapists. After client consensus evolves, the client is assisted in gradually securing appropriate relationships through groups/associates, work, and residential placement. There comes a time when group counseling serves well clients with similar problems, and those to whom the client must relate. In our society many may be striving for identity first, then goals as Glasser (1975) states. Eventually, the core of who we can be is supported and reinforced by job satisfaction. Therefore, it is the responsibility of the therapist that the maximum vocational and educational potential of the client is understood and acted upon. Lastly, any good therapist would grasp the disabilities (including social skills) and potentials of clients and routinely take advantage of the extensive network of social services actually available. Far too many therapists are not really aware of all the types of services which are available to their clients. On this point, Bratter (1976) similarly argues that the counselor's role should be one of advocate to help the client obtain needed services. Glasser (1972) has proposed a Community Involvement Center to serve failing people. Although the CIC is restricted in vision, many of the elements proposed in this comprehensive approach can easily be included in an expanded version of Glasser's center.

Recent Works

Recent works by Glasser are consistent with his discussions in his earliest writings about the principles of reality therapy. Thus, the basic beliefs conveyed in earlier writings such as *Reality Therapy* (1965);

Schools Without Failure (1969); and *Identity Society* (1975) have not been subject to profound revisions. It does appear that Glasser's recent writings give more emphasis on particular points. For example, Corey (1986) concludes that these writings encourage the counselor to be less critical, less judgmental, and to be more accepting, less confrontational in the therapeutic milieu. This shift addresses a few concerns mentioned previously. But these concerns are not fully resolved by Glasser's recent statements. Certainly, they are unresolved in the actual practice of reality therapy.

Some of Glasser's recent writings are consistent with his earliest writings, others complement or expand reality therapy. In *Positive Addiction* (1976), Glasser appears to enrich reality therapy by recognizing the difficulties of developing one's potential including the entrapment of self-involvement which leads to *negative* addiction (drugs, overeating, etc.). Glasser's solution is addiction. The addiction to which he refers is *positive* addiction. Glasser recognizes the needs of clients to cultivate strength if reality therapy plans for behavioral change are to be successful. Positive addictions to Glasser are unlimited and very regular: running, studying, meditating, volunteering, and so on. Glasser states this lets the client's "brain spin free" (the brain becomes free from the undesirable consequences of negative addiction). Heavy involvement with positive addiction is fruitful because this mental achievement generalizes to the individual's overall pleasure and competence in other areas of life. Accordingly, Glasser would encourage the counselor to use this approach as a means for the client to acquire the needed strength to accomplish the goals of reality therapy.

Other recent works by Glasser which extend beyond reality therapy but are useful as a resource for reality therapists are *Stations of the Mind* (1981), and *Control Theory* (1984). Control theory and elements of brain functioning are combined to involve theory of perception. Stated very briefly, the heart of the theory is the relation between our inner world perceptions which are internally motivated and external happenings which have no meaning until we internally interpret external happenings. It is not external forces which cause us to behave in a certain way. Instead, it's what our inner behavior makes of external behavior. In effect, we choose our emotions. For example, others are reacting to us. Others may view us as short or ugly. We may have been deceived. Reactions of being depressed or being hostile are not the only outcome. Why? Because we ought to satisfy our inner needs and therefore it is we who should control how we desire to perceive the external. It is we who choose how we perceive and that determines our view of external reality. In short, Glasser feels we cannot let the external world shape the personal world within us. We take control, interpret and interact with the external; we thereby, in turn, influence external elements in the course of satisfying our inner needs.

For reality therapists these two recent works appear to be far more practical and useful than is traditional behavioral psychology. These writings complement Glasser's reality therapy and are worth the attention of those counselors committed to this therapy.

References

Arbuckle, D.S. 1975. *Counseling and psychotherapy—an existential-humanistic view*, 3rd ed. Boston: Allyn and Bacon.

Banmen, J. 1982a. *Reality therapy bibliography.* Los Angeles: Institute for Reality Therapy.

_____. 1982b. "Reality therapy research view." *Journal of Reality Therapy,* 2(1): 28-33.

Bassin, A., Bratter, T.E., and Rachin, R.L., eds. 1976. *The Reality Therapy Reader.* New York: Harper and Row.

Bennight, K. C. 1975. "A model program for counseling and placement of offenders." *Journal of Employment Counseling,* 12(4): 168-173.

Bratter, T. E. and Raubolt, R. R., 1976. "Treating the methadone addict." In *The Reality Therapy Reader,* Bassin, A., Bratter, T. E., and Rachin, R. L. (eds.). New York: Harper and Row.

Brown, L. J. and Ritter, J. I. 1972. "Reality therapy for the geriatric psychiatric patient." *Perspective in Psychiatric Care,* 10(3): 135-139.

Brown, W. and Kingley. 1973. "Treating alienated, unmotivated, drug abusing adolescents." *American Journal of Psychotherapy,* 27(4): 585-598.

Cohen, B. Z. and Sordo, I. 1984. "Using reality therapy with adult offenders." *Journal of Counseling Services and Rehabilitation,* 8(3): 25-39.

Corey, G. 1986. *Theory and practice of counseling and psychotherapy,* 3rd ed. Monterey, Calif.; Brooks/Cole Publishing Company.

Dakoske, T. J. 1977. "Short- and long-term effects of reality therapy on self-concept and discipline of selected fifth grade students." Ph.D. diss., University of Cincinnati. *Dissertation Abstracts International,* 1977, 2338.

Falker, F. (1982). "Reality therapy: a systems level approach to treatment in a halfway house." *Journal of Reality Therapy,* 1(2): 3-7.

Gang, M. J. 1976. "Enhancing student-teacher relationships." *Elementary School Guidance and Counseling,* 11(2): 131-137.

German, M. L. 1975. "The effects of group reality therapy on institutionalized adolescents and group leaders." Ph.D. diss., George Peabody College for Teachers, 1975. *Dissertation Abstracts International,* 1975, 1916b.

Glasser N., ed. 1980. *What are you doing? How people are helped through reality therapy.* New York: Harper & Row.

Glasser, W., 1964. "Reality therapy: A realistic approach to the young offender." *Crime and Delinquency,* 10, 135-144.

_____. 1965. *Reality therapy: A new approach to psychiatry.* New York: Harper & Row.

_____. 1969. Schools without failure. New York: Harper & Row.

_____. 1975. *The identity society.* Rev. ed. New York: Harper & Row.

_____. 1976a. "Notes on reality therapy." In *The reality therapy reader.* Bassin, A., Bratter, T. E., Rachin, R. L., (eds.) New York: Harper & Row.

_____. 1976b. *Positive addiction.* New York: Harper & Row.

_____. 1981. *Stations of the mind.* New York: Harper & Row.

_____. 1984a. *Control theory.* New York: Harper & Row.

_____. 1984b. "Reality therapy." In *Current psychotherapies.* Corsini, R. (ed.). Itasca, Ill.: Peacock.

Hawes, R. M. 1971. "Reality therapy in the classroom." Ph.D. diss., University of the Pacific, 1971. *Dissertation Abstracts International,* 1971, 2483.

Ivery, A. E. 1980. *Counseling and psychotherapy: Skills, theories and practice.* Englewood Cliffs, N.J.: Prentice-Hall.

Lachman, S. J. 1986. "Restitution: A behavioral analog for undoing." *Journal of Reality Therapy,* 5(2): 3-10.

Matthews, D. B. 1972. "The Effects of reality therapy on reported self-concept, social adjustment, reading achievement, and discipline of fourth and fifth graders in two elementary schools." Ph.D. diss., University of South Carolina, 1972, *Dissertation Abstracts International,* 1973, 4342-4843.

Matthews, W. G. 1979. "Restitution programming: Reality therapy operationalized." *Offender Rehabilitation,* 3: 319-324.

May, R. 1967. *Psychology and the human dilemma.* Princeton, N.J.: D. Van Nostrand Company.

Molstad, L. P. 1981. "Reality therapy in residential treatment." In *Journal of Reality Therapy,* 1(1): 8-13.

Omizo, M. M. and Cubberly, W. F. 1983. "The effects of reality therapy meetings on self-concept and locus of control among learning disabled children." *Exceptional Child,* 30(3): 201-209.

Ososkie, J. N. and Turpin, J. O. 1985. "Reality therapy in rehabilitation counseling." *Journal of Applied Rehabilitation Counseling,* 16(3): 34-37.

Peterson, J. A. 1976. *Counseling and Values—A Philosophical Examination.* Cranston, R. I.: Carroll Press Publishers.

Raubolt, R. R. and Bratter, T. E. 1976. "Treating the methadone addict." In *The Reality Therapy Reader,* Bassin, A., Bratter, T. E. and Rachin, R. L. (eds.), New York: Harper & Row.

Shearn, D. F. and Randolph, D. L. 1978. "Effects of reality therapy methods applied in the classroom." *Psychology in the Schools,* 15(1): 79-83.

Slowick, C. A., Omizo, M. M., and Hammett, V. L. 1984. "The effects of reality therapy process on locus of control and self-concepts among Mexican-American adolescents." *Journal of Reality Therapy,* 3(2): 1-9.

Szasz, T. S. 1966. "Equation of opposites." *The New York Book Review.* Feb. 6:6.

Thatcher, J. A. 1983. "The effects of reality therapy upon self-concept and locus of control for juvenile delinquents." *Journal of Reality Therapy,* 3(1): 31.

Thompson, C. L. and Cates, J. T. 1976. "Teaching discipline to students." *Elementary School Guidance and Counseling,* 11(2): 131-137.

Trojanowicz, R. C. and Morash, M. 1983. *Juvenile delinquency,* 3rd ed. Englewood Cliffs, New Jersey: Prentice-Hall.

Vinter, R. D., ed. 1976. *Time out: A national study of juvenile correction programs.* Ann Arbor: National Assessment of Juvenile Corrections.

Williams, E. W. 1976. "Reality therapy in a correctional institution." *Corrective and Social Psychiatry and Journal of Behavior, Methods and Therapy,* 22(1): 6-11.

Yochelson, S. and Samenow, S. E. 1977. *The criminal personality—The change process,* Volume II. New York: Janson Aronson.

Zapf, R. F. 1974. Group therapy with retarded adults: A reality therapy approach Ph.D. diss., Fordham University, 1973. *Dissertation Abstracts International,* 1974, 4889-4890.

7 Behavior Modification

Introduction

Of all the treatment techniques described in this book, behavior modification holds the distinction of being the most debated. Proponents of this technique applaud its ease of implementation; clearly observable results; and applicability to a wide range of populations, ranging from autistic or hyperactive preschoolers through nursing-home residents troubled by problems of senility. Those who oppose or would severely restrict its use argue that it borders on "thought or mind control," reduces the production of acceptable human behavior to the level of training an animal, or has such a strong potential for abuse that it must be carefully monitored.

The truth about behavior modification's benefits and hazards certainly lies somewhere between these two extremes. Much of the criticism of behavior modification has arisen from public confusion about what it is and references to use of electric shocks and drug therapy in some types of behavior modification. The first selection in this chapter, "Behavior Modification: Perspective on a Current Issue," clearly defines just what behavior modification is and is not, gives examples of the types of positive reinforcement and aversion stimuli common to behavior modification programs, and discusses the special considerations attendant upon use of behavior modification programs in a correctional institution.

The use of behavior modification in an institution poses special problems. A therapist must walk the line between working to modify the inmates' behavior in a manner that will make them more law-abiding citizens after they leave the institution and simply changing the inmates' behavior within the walls—that is, making them more docile, easier to handle, or respectful of authority. The correctional setting provides opportunities for abuse of behavior modification techniques that would not be likely to occur elsewhere. For example, the "time out" method of aversion stimulus, which amounts to removing the offender to a room, alone, for a short period of time, could easily be expanded to punitive periods of solitary confinement. Denial of privileges could be misused in the same manner.

On the positive side, the institution offers the most controlled environment for behavior modification, since inmates are less open to outside influences or able to obtain substitutes for the positive reinforcements offered as part of a behavior modification program.

Students and evaluators of behavior modification therapy generally conclude that the individual doing the reinforcing or applying aversion stimuli is the key factor in the program's success. A number of studies of behavior modification involving delinquents discovered that positive reinforcement is most important at the beginning of a program;[1] that the personalities of the therapists providing the reinforcement or aversion were important factors in behavioral changes;[2] and that the more clearly defined the expected behaviors were, the greater the chance of achieving them.[3] After reviewing and summarizing fourteen studies of behavior modification programs involving almost 2000 delinquents in the United States, Romig reached the following conclusion:

> *Behavior modification is certainly no panacea for juvenile delinquency. Behavior modification did work to change certain behaviors, such as school attendance, test scores, promptness, and classroom behavior. However, it did not affect something as global as delinquency or arrest rate.*[4]

This chapter's second selection, "Establishing Behavioral Contracts with Delinquent Adolescents," explores the strategies that have proven most successful in this type of contracting. Input from the adolescent into the design and setting of rewards and regulations was found to be very important. Examples of behavioral contracts that utilize positive influences already available in the adolescent's life and are designed to fit various types of delinquent activity are given in this article.

In the third selection, "Behavioral Family Contracting: Helping Families Change," by James S. Stumphauzer, the concept of contracting is applied in the family setting. The process of family contracting, with the counselor taking the role of negotiator, is presented in a step-by-step process, with case studies and specific contract illustrations.

Notes

1. R.L. Bednar; P.F. Zelhart; L. Greathouse; and W. Weinberg, "Operant Conditioning Principles in the Treatment of Learning and Behavior Problems with Delinquent Boys," *Journal of Counseling Psychology* 17 (1970):492–497.

2. V. Tyler and G. Brown, "Token Reinforcement of Academic Performance with Institutionalized Delinquent Boys," *Journal of Educational Psychology* 59 (1968):164–168.

3. S.B. McPherson and R.S. Cyrille, "Teaching Behavioral Methods to Parents," *Social Casework* 52 (1971):148–153.

4. Dennis A. Romig, *Justice for Our Children* (Lexington, Mass.: Lexington Books, 1978), p. 20.

Behavior Modification: Perspective on a Current Issue

Bertram S. Brown

Louis A. Wienckowski

Stephanie B. Stolz

Introduction

In the history of civilization, people have continuously tried to control their environment and to find ways of teaching themselves and their children better means of acquiring new skills and capabilities. Commonsense notions of the ways that reward and punishment can change behavior have existed since time immemorial. Thus, elements of what is now referred to as behavior modification were used long before psychologists and other behavioral scientists developed systematic principles of learning.

As behavior modification procedures are used ever more widely, many different concerns have been expressed. On the one hand, the public and mental health professionals are concerned about whether behavior modification procedures are sufficiently well demonstrated through research for these procedures to be generally recommended and widely disseminated. On the other hand, behavior modification has acted as a conceptual "lightning rod" in the midst of stormy controversies over ethical problems associated with attempts at social influence, drawing to it such highly charged issues as fear of "mind control" or concerns about the treatment of persons institutionalized against their will. Apparent or actual infringements of rights, as well as some abuses of behavioral procedures, have led to litigation and calls for curbs on the use of behavior modification.

Published by the U.S. Department of Health, Education and Welfare, National Institute of Mental Health (Washington, D.C.: U.S. Government Printing Office, 1976).

Everyone tries continually to influence his own and others' behavior, so that the individual using behavior modification procedures is distinctive only in that he is attempting to influence behavior more systematically. Commenting on this issue, one attorney has said that to be opposed to behavior modification is to be opposed to the law of gravity. Rather, the key issue is what sort of care, caution, and control should be exercised when behavioral principles are applied precisely and systematically.

This report is intended to provide an objective overview of the history and current methods of behavior modification and to review some critical issues, in an effort to aid the reader in differentiating between warranted and unwarranted concerns. We will also make some suggestions regarding ethical standards and practices.

What Is Behavior Modification?

To understand behavior modification, it is helpful first to clarify its relationship to a broader concept, behavior influence.

Behavior influence occurs whenever one person exerts some degree of control over another. This occurs constantly in such diverse situations as formal school education, advertising, child rearing, political campaigning, and other normal interpersonal interactions.

Behavior modification is a special form of behavior influence that involves primarily the application of principles derived from research in experimental psychology to alleviate human suffering and enhance human functioning. Behavior modification emphasizes systematic monitoring and evaluation of the effectiveness of these applications. The techniques of behavior modification are generally intended to facilitate improved self-control by expanding individuals' skills, abilities, and independence.

Most behavior modification procedures are based on the general principle that people are influenced by the consequences of their behavior. The current environment is believed to be more relevant in affecting the individual's behavior than most early life experiences or than enduring intrapsychic conflicts or personality structure. Insofar as possible, the behaviorally oriented mental health worker limits the conceptualization of the problem to observable behavior and its environmental context, rather than including references to hypothesized internal processes such as traits or feelings.

In professional use of behavior modification, a contractual agreement may be negotiated, specifying mutually agreeable goals and procedures. When the client is an adult who has sought therapy, the contract would be between him and the mental health worker. When

the behavior modification program is to benefit a mentally disadvantaged group, such as the retarded, senile, or psychotic, the contract is
often between the individuals' guardians or other responsible persons
and the mental health worker. Parents, who usually make decisions
affecting their young children, generally are consulted by the mental
health worker regarding treatment for their children. Who the appropriate person is to make the contractual agreement for a prisoner is a
complex and unsettled issue, taken up later in this report in connection with the discussion of the use of behavior modification procedures
with prisoners.

Behavior therapy is a term that is sometimes used synonymously
with behavior modification. In general, behavior modification is considered to be the broader term, while behavior therapy refers mainly
to clinical interventions, usually applied in a one-to-one therapist-
patient relationship. That is, behavior therapy is a special form of
behavior modification.

Behavior modification typically tries to influence behavior by
changing the environment and the way people interact, rather than by
intervening directly through medical procedures (such as drugs) or
surgical procedures (such as psychosurgery). Thus, behavior modification methods can be used in a broad range of situations, including the
child-rearing efforts of parents and the instructional activities of
teachers, as well as the therapeutic efforts of mental health workers in
treating more serious psychological and behavioral problems. The effects of behavior modification, unlike the results of most surgical
procedures, are relatively changeable and impermanent.

Behavior modification procedures require that the problem behavior be clearly specified. That is, the mental health worker must be able
to define objectively the response that the service recipient wants to
learn or to have reduced. Thus, certain kinds of problems treated by
dynamic psychotherapy are simply not appropriate candidates for behavior modification. In particular, the patient who seeks therapy because of an existential crisis—"Who am I? Where am I going"—is not
an appropriate candidate for behavior modification. This quasi-philo-
sophical problem does not lend itself to an approach that deals with
specific identifiable behavior in particular environmental contexts. It
is possible that a patient who describes his problem in this way actually has some specific behavioral deficits that may underlie his existential difficulties or occur alongside them. Whether a careful behavioral analysis of the patient's difficulties would reveal such deficits is
not now known, however.

While it has been alleged that secret, powerful psychotechnological
tools are being or would be used to control the masses, researchers in

behavior modification point out that they have encouraged the dissemination of information about behavior processes. In fact, workers in this area believe that increased knowledge will help people to understand social influence processes in general and actually would enable them to counteract many attempts at control, if such attempts occurred. Many persons using behavior modification methods not only evaluate the effectiveness of their procedures, but also measure the consumers' satisfaction with the behavior modification program used.

Is Behavior Modification Merely Common Sense? Many persons who learn about the general procedures of behavior modification say that they seem to be nothing more than common sense. To some considerable extent, this is true. For example, parents are using these techniques whenever they praise their children for good report cards in the hope of encouraging continued interest and application. On the job, promotions and incentive awards are universally accepted as ways of encouraging job performance. The very structure of our laws, with specified fines, penalties, and the like, is intended to modify behavior through aversive control.

Behavior modification, however, like other scientific approaches, imposes an organization on its subject matter. While common sense often includes contradictory advice (both "out of sight, out of mind," and "absence makes the heart grow fonder"), the principles of behavior modification codify and organize common sense, showing under what conditions, and in what circumstances, which aspect of "common sense" should be applied. The mothers and grandmothers who use what could be described as behavior modification procedures may often do so inconsistently, and then not understand why they have failed.

What Behavior Modification Is Not. As more publicity has been given to this approach, the term "behavior modification" has come to be used loosely and imprecisely in the public media, often with a negative connotation. Thus, behavior modification has sometimes been said to include psychosurgery, electroconvulsive therapy (ECT), and the noncontingent administration of drugs, that is, the administration of drugs independent of any specific behavior of the person receiving the medication. However, even though procedures such as these do modify behavior, that does not make them "behavior modification techniques," in the sense in which most professionals in the field use the term. In this report, the use of the term "behavior modification" will be consistent with its professional use; that is, behavior modification will be used to refer to procedures that are based on the

explicit and systematic application of principles and technology derived from research in experimental psychology, procedures that involve some change in the social or environmental context of a person's
behavior. This use of the term specifically excludes psychosurgery,
electroconvulsive therapy, and the administration of drugs independent of any specific behavior of the person receiving the medication.

History of Behavior Modification

Even though behavior modification is new within the behavioral sciences, the basic experimental work designed to obtain a precise understanding of the principles of learning dates back at least 75 years.
Pavlov's first book, *Work on the Digestive Glands*, was published in
Russian in 1897. Since then, those initial studies have been followed
up with extensive laboratory experiments on learning in both animals
and humans. It is on this broad foundation of experimental research
that behavior modification principles are based.

The clinical use of behavior modification has a somewhat shorter
history, since reports in the scientific literature of such applications
have occurred mainly within the past 15 years, although some work was
done as early as the 1920s and 1930s (e.g., Jones 1924; Mowrer and
Mowrer 1938). Building on animal research by Skinner and his students, the pioneering work of Lindsley (Lindsley and Skinner 1954) and
Ferster and DeMyer (1961) demonstrated that the behavior of even such
severely disturbed individuals as adult psychotics and autistic children
actually followed the same psychological laws as that of normal persons. Wolpe (see, e.g., 1958), working from a more neurophysiologically
based theory, developed the method of systematic desensitization, a
technique for treating neurotic behavior patterns. Psychologists and
psychiatrists in England (Shapiro 1961; Eysenck 1952) also contributed
to the early growth of behavior modification.

Once these and other researchers had shown that the principles of
learning applied to severely disturbed persons, the development of the
field of behavior modification began to accelerate. On the whole, applied researchers have found that the principles developed in laboratory research can be applied effectively to many behavior problems in
the real world.

Behavioral treatment interventions were first used with regressed
psychotics and neurotic adults (Ayllon and Michael 1959; Ayllon and
Azrin 1965; Wolpe and Lazarus 1966). Extensive clinical work has
shown that behavior therapy techniques can be effective in eliminating many incapacitating neurotic fears, such as fear of flying in

planes. Behavior therapists working with regressed psychotics have been able to develop a variety of adaptive behaviors in these patients so that the patients' lives were enriched by the availability of many new choices (e.g., Ayllon and Azrin 1968).

From these beginnings, the field of behavior modification has expanded to new clinical populations and new settings, including delinquents in halfway houses, the retarded, preschool and deaf children, and drug abusers. Some autistic children, who might otherwise be continuously restrained in straightjackets because of their attempts at severe self-mutilation, have been helped by properly designed programs to control their own behavior effectively (e.g., Lovaas et al. 1973). Severely retarded children previously considered incapable of any learning other than the most basic, have, in some instances, been shown capable of acquiring some intellectual skills (e.g., Baer and Guess 1971). Delinquents who would otherwise have been incarcerated at great cost to themselves and to society have often been successfully helped in behaviorally oriented community settings, their own homes, and schools (e.g., Phillips et al. 1971). Some of the drug abusers who have chosen abstinence as a goal have been helped to attain this objective and carry on a normal life without opiates (e.g., Thomson and Rathod 1968).

A large amount of behavior modification research has been done with normal children, including research on improving classroom management, teaching methods, and parent-child relations. Children whose behavior is only mildly maladaptive can be treated by their parents or teachers, because behavior modification lends itself to use by persons not professionally trained in therapy. Most recently, behavior modification has been extended to social problems such as the facilitation of cooperative living in a public housing project, decreasing littering, encouraging the use of public transportation, and enabling unemployed persons to find jobs.

Behavior modification procedures are now used by psychologists, psychiatrists, educators, social workers, speech therapists, and members of other helping professions.

Current Practice of Behavior Modification

Behavior modification is a family of techniques. The diverse methods included under the general label have in common the goal of enhancing persons' lives by altering specific aspects of their behavior. Ideally, the mental health worker and the service recipient decide together on a mutually agreeable set of treatment goals and on the

means for attaining these goals. The service recipient or his representative should be kept fully informed of the results of the treatment as
it progresses, and also participate in any modification of goals or
techniques.

The initial analysis of the problem typically should begin with a
detailed description of the behavior that is causing distress or interfer-
ing with optimal functioning of the individual in familial, social, vocational, or other important spheres of activity. The behavioral goals are
to be viewed in the context of everything the person is able to do, and
also in terms of what kinds of support his usual environment is capable of providing over the long term.

This description, whenever possible, should be based on observations of the individual in the setting in which he reports that he is
distressed. These observations may be careful quantitative records, or
they may be statements about the relative frequency of various behaviors. The person making the observations may be the therapist or his
agent, a peer of the individual receiving the service, or the individual
himself. For example, a parent might be trained to tally the frequency
with which a child stutters, a teacher or hospital aide might keep a
record of a child's aggressive outbursts, and a well-motivated individual can count the frequency of occurrence of an unacceptable habit
such as nail-biting.

In addition to obtaining this description of what the individual
does and does not do, the behavioral mental health worker should try
to find how the individual's behavior relates to various events and
places in his current and past experiences. Relevant for behavior
modification are the events that immediately precede and that immediately follow the behavior. The goal should be to determine the circumstances under which the behavior seems to occur and the environmental consequences that might be maintaining it.

Behavior modification, then, involves the systematic variation of
behavioral and environmental factors thought to be associated with an
individual's difficulties, with the primary goal of modifying his behavior in the direction that, ideally, he himself (or his agent) has chosen.

Transition to the Nontreatment Setting

The goal of all treatment is the maintenance of improvement after
the termination of therapy. The ideal behavior modification program
would include a specification of the environment in which the individual normally would be living, and a provision for establishing and
strengthening behavior desired or useful in that environment. Generalization to the natural environment is helped if the behavior modifica-

tion program includes a planned transition between the therapeutic program and the natural environment. The following example illustrates this principle:

> O. Ivar Lovaas (UCLA) has been studying autistic children for a number of years.[1] He has found that when parents have been trained to carry on with a behavior modification program, children continue to improve after they have left his special treatment ward. On the other hand, the children regress if they are returned to institutions after leaving the ward, and no longer participate in a special training program.

Examples of Behavior Modification Methods

This section briefly describes some of the most common behavior modification methods. This is a young field, and other techniques are continually being developed and evaluated by clinical researchers. Thus, the methods included here should not be considered an exhaustive list.

Methods Using Positive Reinforcement. Positive reinforcement is a technical term that is roughly synonymous with reward. A positive reinforcer is defined as any event following a given response that increases the chances of that response recurring. Typical positive reinforcers include tangible items, such as money or food; social events, such as praise or attention; and activities, such as the opportunity to engage in recreation or to watch television. However, what is reinforcing or motivating for some people—what they will work for—is not necessarily reinforcing for others. As a result, when using behavior modification procedures with any individual, the mental health worker needs to determine what particular items and activities will reinforce that person's behavior at that time.

Methods that use positive reinforcement form the major class of methods among behavior modification techniques. In general, positive reinforcement is used to develop and maintain new behavior, and the removal of positive reinforcement is used to decrease the frequency of undesired behavior. Positive reinforcement has been used in teaching social behavior, in improving classroom management, in motivating better and faster learning of academic materials, in maintaining necessary weight loss, and in teaching new skills of all sorts.

> Positive reinforcement is being used to help disruptive under-achieving children, in one research project.[1] Among a variety of procedures being used, teachers praise the children for appropri-

ate behavior, and send home daily reports. The children's parents reward them for good daily reports. The researcher, K. Daniel O'Leary (State University of New York, Stony Brook), reports that the children's disruptive behavior has been reduced as a result of this program.

Although some positive reinforcers are much more effective if a person has been deprived of them for a while, others continue to be reinforcing virtually regardless of how often an individual is exposed to them. Thus, by carefully selecting reinforcers, it should not be necessary to deprive an individual beyond the natural deprivations that occur in daily life in order to be able to reinforce him positively.

One increasingly common use of positive reinforcement is in the group management procedure called a *token economy* (Ayllon and Azrin 1968). In a successful token economy program, the participants receive tokens when they engage in appropriate behavior, and, at some later time, exchange the tokens for any of a variety of positively reinforcing items and activities, just as money is used in society at large. Thus, the token economy is basically a work-payment incentive system. As such, it can be used with institutionalized persons to strengthen behavior that is compatible with that needed in the society at large, such as regular performance on a job, self-care, maintenance of one's living quarters, and exchange of currency for desired items.

One advantage of the token economy, given the limitation in professional manpower, is that nonprofessional personnel are typically the actual agents of therapeutic change. If therapeutic procedures are going to be extended to the many persons who require help, professional personnel must make increased use of those who are in direct contact with the persons requiring service. Those persons who can administer a token economy without special advanced training include nurses, aides, correctional officers, and friends and family members of the individual receiving the service. Such persons should, of course, receive appropriate professional supervision.

The early development of the token economy system took place almost exclusively in closed psychiatric wards. Token economies were found quite useful in preventing or overcoming the deterioration of normal social behavior, or what Gruenberg (1967) has called the "social breakdown syndrome," that accompanies prolonged custodial hospitalization, whatever the initial diagnosis. The token economy method is now being extended to acute psychiatric programs, to public school classrooms, and to classrooms for disadvantaged, hyperactive, retarded, and emotionally disturbed children (Anderson 1967; O'Leary and Drabman 1971). Such programs have also been used with delinquents and persons with character disorders to enhance educational achievement and to improve adjustment to military or civilian environments (Cohen and Filipczak 1971; Colman 1971). Tokens have been used to increase children's attention span and to improve self-help skills in retardates (e.g., Minge and Ball 1967).

In the behavior modification technique of *shaping,* a desired behavior is broken down into successive steps that are taught one by one. Each of the steps is reinforced until it is mastered, and then the individual is moved to the next one. In this way, the new behavior is gradually learned as what the individual does becomes a closer and closer approximation of the behavioral goal.

New behavior can also be taught by means of *modeling.* In this method, a person who already knows how to engage in some desired behavior demonstrates it for the individual who is learning. For example, if a client were learning socially appropriate ways to greet members of the opposite sex, another person might demonstrate them for the client.

> *The model demonstrating the appropriate behavior can be an actual one or an imaginary one. Alan E. Kazdin (Pennsylvania State University) is conducting a study of some facets of imaginary or covert modeling.[1] Subjects in his study are college students who have problems in assertiveness. They are taught to imagine one or several other persons engaging in the sort of assertive behavior that the subjects hope to learn, and then are tested to see how much their own assertiveness has increased.*

In *contingency contracting,* the mental health worker and the client decide together on the behavioral goals and on the reinforcement that the client will receive when the goals are achieved. For example, a parent and child might agree that it would be desirable if the home were neater, specifically, if the child's playthings were appropriately stored after a certain time in the evening. The child might request that the parent agree to take him to a favorite activity after the child had put away his playthings for a specified number of days. A contract often involves an exchange, that is, each person entering into the contract agrees both to change his own behavior and to provide reinforcement for the changes that the other person makes. Such a mutual contract is frequently used in marriage counseling.

> *The methods of contingency contracting are being studied by Henry M. Boudin (University of Florida) to see how they can be made effective for dealing with the special behavior problems characteristic of drug abusers.[2] The goal of this project is to reduce*

drug dependence in addicts who are being treated in an outpatient setting. The contracts made between the drug abusers and the therapists cover a large number of aspects of the addicts' lives. For example, an addict might agree to set up a joint bank account with his therapist, to which the addict deposits his own money. If a urine test indicates that he has broken his promise not to use illegal drugs, funds are taken from that account by the therapist and sent to some organization that the addict strongly dislikes. Contracts work both ways: If the therapist is late for an appointment with the addict or misses a therapy session, he can be required to deposit money to the addict's account. A contract involving positive reinforcement might specify that if the addict completes some amount of time on a job, he would receive a few movie passes or discounts on some number of phonograph records.

Aversive Control.   Some types of inappropriate behavior, such as addictions and certain sexual behaviors, appear to be maintained because their immediate consequences are naturally reinforcing for the individual. In such cases, aversive control techniques are sometimes used to combat long-term consequences that may be much more detrimental to the individual than the aversive methods themselves. Aversive methods are also used for behaviors that are life-threatening, such as severe self-mutilation.

In general, an aversive stimulus, that is, something that is unpleasant to the person, is used to help the person reduce his desire to carry out the inappropriate behavior (Rachman and Teasdale 1969). After aversive therapy, for example, a man who formerly became excited sexually only when thinking of women's shoes, might report that he had lost interest in the shoes. With aversive techniques, the aversive stimulus will not occur, that is, the individual is able to avoid it, as long as he does not perform the behavior that he and the mental health worker have agreed is undesirable. When aversive therapy is appropriately conducted, it is accompanied by positive reinforcement of normal behavior.

Perhaps the most commonly used aversive stimulus in behavior modification is a brief, low-level electric shock. This type of aversive stimulus has been highly effective in ameliorating severe behavioral problems such as self-injurious behavior (see, e.g., Bucher 1969). When properly used, the shocks are very brief. Shock used this way causes no lingering pain or tissue damage and can be administered with precise control (Baer 1970). The use of shock as an aversive control procedure is entirely different from its use in electroconvulsive therapy, a procedure completely outside the scope of behavior modification.

A different type of aversive control method is the removal of positive reinforcement, such as a loss of privileges following a given behavior. This is a technique commonly used by American parents (Sears, Maccoby, and Levin 1957). One example of a technique involving the removal of positive reinforcement is the *time-out* procedure, in which an inappropriate behavior is followed by a period of brief social isolation.

> *The time-out procedure is one of a number of behavior modification techniques being used in a study of preschool children with poor social, language, and cognitive skills.*[1] *The goal of the investigator, Donald M. Baer (University of Kansas), is to reduce these children's hyperactive and rebellious behavior. When a child engages in disruptive behavior, he is placed for a brief period in a small room adjoining the classroom. This aversive control for disruptive behavior is combined with a wide variety of positive reinforcing procedures for appropriate behavior. Positive reinforcers used in this study include attention, praise, access to preferred activities, and snacks.*

Fines are another example of aversive control; fines require the individual to give up some positive reinforcement following an instance of inappropriate behavior.

One common use of aversive stimuli is in attempts to reduce excessive drinking by associating the drinking experience with an aversive stimulus. For example, recent research on alcoholism has employed electric shock as an aversive stimulus to teach the alcoholic patient to avoid continued drinking beyond a criterion blood alcohol level. This has reportedly been successful in helping problem drinkers learn to limit their intake to moderate levels typical of social drinking (Lovibond 1970).

> *In research by Roger E. Vogler (Patton State Hospital and Pacific State Hospital, California), alcoholic persons being treated either in the hospital or as outpatients receive electric shock if they drink too much alcohol in a bar-like setting in the hospital.*[3] *Shock is also used to train the patients to discriminate when their blood alcohol concentration exceeds a specific level, and to teach them to drink slowly.*

Drugs such as Anectine and Antabuse have also been used as aversive treatment for alcoholic persons (see section on Methods Using Drugs, below).

The other relatively common use of aversive stimuli is to control self-injurious and self-destructive behavior such as head-banging or tongue-biting. Such behavior can apparently be eliminated with a brief application of a strong aversive stimulus immediately after the response (Risley 1968; Bucher and Lovaas 1968).

> *Occasionally, infants, young children, and some mentally retarded persons "ruminate," that is, they apparently voluntarily eject food from their stomachs into their mouths where it may be reswallowed or further ejected from their mouths. When this problem is severe, it can be life-threatening and may have serious detrimental effects on the physical, emotional, and social development of the child. Thomas Sajwaj (University of Mississippi) has developed a procedure using lemon juice as a mild aversive stimulus to control the ruminative behavior: when the infant or child regurgitates, a small amount of lemon juice is immediately squirted into his mouth by an attendant.[1] Preliminary results with a few children suggest that this aversive therapy eliminates the rumination, and that no other maladaptive behavior appears.*

A consistent finding from research on aversive control is that the effects of the therapeutic use of aversive stimuli seem to be restricted to the particular behavior that is associated with the aversive stimulus, in that particular situation, with that particular therapist. That is, the effects of aversive stimuli do not seem to generalize very much (Risley 1968; Bucher and Lovaas 1968).

In contrast to the somewhat limited effects of aversive stimuli in controlling undesirable behavior, the positive side effects of this treatment seem to be rather widespread. For example, it is commonly reported that once the use of aversive stimuli has eliminated a patient's self-injurious behavior, he avoids people less and is more responsive to other therapy aimed at teaching him adaptive responses.

While the effects of aversive stimuli may, in many cases, be only temporary, the individual will not make the undesirable response for at least some period of time. During that time, he is more amenable to learning new, appropriate responses. On the whole, research suggests that the most effective way of eliminating inappropriate behavior is to follow it with aversive stimuli, while at the same time positively reinforcing desired behavior. If the environment then continues to support the new, desired responses, the inappropriate behavior will soon cease to occur. Since the aversive stimuli are used only following inappropriate behavior, they will no longer be administered. The effects of the initial aversive control will, however, be lasting, because the individual will now have learned to make appropriate responses.

It is important to note, however, that in the absence of rewarded alternatives, the response that had been suppressed by an aversive technique is likely to recur. To ensure that it does not, the individual being treated should learn behavior that will be maintained by rewards that occur naturally in his environment. In some instances, simply stopping the undesirable behavior enables the individual to get natural rewards. For the "ruminating" child, for example, stopping the ejection of food in itself allows proper digestion of food, greater comfort, and normal eating, growing, and developing. In addition, the infant is now more receptive to normal learning experiences.

Overcorrection. Overcorrection is a behavior modification method combining positive reinforcement and aversive control that is used to discourage inappropriate or disruptive behavior. In this procedure, the person who has engaged in the inappropriate behavior not only remedies the situation he has caused, but also "overcorrects" it. That is, the person is required to restore the disruptive situation to a better state than existed before the disruption. For example, a violent patient in a mental institution who overturns a bed in a dormitory might be required not only to right that bed and make it up again, but also to straighten the bedclothes on all the other beds in that dormitory. Making up the bed that was overturned corrects the situation that the violent behavior disrupted; making up all the other beds is, then, an "overcorrection."

Often an inappropriate or disruptive behavior has been receiving some sort of reinforcement. For example, stealing results in the thief acquiring goods he desires; turning over a bed might get a patient attention and concern from an otherwise busy ward staff. Thus, one function of the overcorrection procedure is to terminate any such reinforcement associated with the inappropriate behavior: the thief must return the stolen goods, for example.

Moreover, overcorrection is an aversive stimulus, because it requires effort to complete the overcorrection, and because the person cannot be engaging in other behavior while he is completing the overcorrection task. In addition, the overcorrection procedure itself may often be educative, in that the process of restoring the original situation generally requires the individual to engage in appropriate behavior.

Overcorrection has been a particularly effective technique in eliminating aggressive and disruptive behavior in institutionalized patients (Foxx and Azrin 1972; Webster and Azrin 1973). One of the advantages of overcorrection over other methods for dealing with these problems is that severe aversive stimuli may not be involved in overcorrection.

Systematic Desensitization. Gradual, progressive exposure to feared situations has long been advocated as a means of eliminating or reducing maladaptive anxiety or avoidance behavior. In systematic desensitization, the exposure is preplanned in graduated steps. In general, this procedure involves teaching the patient to relax, and then having him imagine or actually encounter increasingly disturbing situations. The patient usually does not move on to a more disturbing item until he can remain deeply relaxed with a less disturbing one. Recent research, however, has suggested that some degree of forced exposure can also be effective in reducing fears.

If a patient is afraid of heights, for example, the therapist works together with the patient to develop a list of increasingly fearful situations. For example, the patient might say he is very afraid of looking out from the top of the Empire State Building, but hardly afraid at all of climbing a small ladder. He then is trained to relax, and the therapist asks him to imagine each of the series of situations, starting with the one he is least afraid of, the one arousing little or no tension or fear. Over a series of therapy sessions, the patient will be exposed systematically to the whole list of fearful situations, and, at the end of treatment, will be able to maintain his relaxed state even while imagining scenes that were initially extremely fearful. Patients are usually encouraged to try out their newly learned ability to relax in the face of the formerly fearful situation outside of the therapy setting. Generalization of the effects of systematic desensitization from the treatment setting to real life is typically found, especially when the patient has done the "homework" of gradually facing what used to be fearful.

Systematic desensitization has been used clinically by behavior therapists to treat unreasonable fears, frigidity, insomnia, interpersonal anxiety, and other clinical problems in which anxiety is a core problem.

> *Systematic desensitization is being used with a variety of problems. For example, Thomas L. Creer (Children's Asthma Research Institute and Hospital, Denver) has demonstrated the effectiveness of systematic desensitization in the treatment of children's asthma.[1] As a result of the treatment, the children learned to be less afraid of having asthma attacks and used significantly less medication. Desensitization is also being used as a treatment for insomnia (Richard R. Bootzin, Northwestern University)[1] and as a component of treatment for marital sexual dysfunction (Joseph LoPiccolo, State University of New York, Stony Brook).[1]*

Assertive Training. When a person fails to stand up for his rights in an appropriately firm manner, he may not have acquired appropriate assertive behavior, or he may not be engaging in behavior that he actually knows how to do. Similarly, persons who do not express positive feelings in appropriate situations also may lack appropriate assertive skills or an appreciation of the situations in which those skills should normally be used.

Assertive training is taught by a combination of methods, including modeling of appropriate behavior by the therapist or some other person, and reinforced practice by the patient. The overall goal of this type of behavior therapy is the alteration of the patient's interpersonal interactions.

Methods Using Drugs. On the whole, behavior modification procedures emphasize environmental manipulation. However, drugs have occasionally been used as an integral part of a behavioral treatment, either following a particular behavior, or as an adjunct to a behavioral program.

A few case studies in the literature report the use of drugs as aversive stimuli, when the therapist was attempting to reduce some inappropriate behavior. For example, succinylcholine chloride (Anectine) was given to one individual who had a severe dependency on sniffing various substances such as airplane glue. In the treatment, the patient sniffed one of these substances and was immediately injected with Anectine, which produces an extremely unpleasant sensation of drowning and suffocating. The treatment was conducted under the supervision of an anesthesiologist. After this treatment, the patient refrained from sniffing the substance that had been associated with the Anectine (Blanchard, Libet, and Young 1973).

Anectine, and emetic drugs such as Antabuse, have also been used as aversive treatment for alcoholic persons, although the evidence suggests that they are not strongly effective treatments.

When drugs are used as part of an aversive control program in behavior modification, they must take effect immediately after the occurrence of a specific inappropriate behavior. This temporal relationship between the behavior and the aversive action of the drug is considered to be an essential aspect of the therapy. As noted later in this paper, giving aversive drugs independently of a person's behavior is not behavior modification, in the sense in which we are using that term.

Drugs are also sometimes used to facilitate the progress of a behavioral program. Brevital is a drug that enhances relaxation. Some practitioners who do systematic desensitization give their patients small doses of Brevital, if the patients are otherwise having trouble learning to relax in the therapy session (Brady 1966). Usually the dosage level of the drug is gradually adjusted so that the patient soon relaxes without the assistance of the drug.

Evaluation of Behavior Modification

Collecting evidence that would show whether behavior modification is effective is not as easy as it would seem. Several conceptual issues first need to be resolved. In order to evaluate behavior modification, the types of problems for which it is appropriate must be delimited, suitable outcome measures must be selected, and appropriate comparison conditions must be chosen.

While therapists who use behavior modification feel that it is appropriate for a wide range of problems, other persons have questioned the appropriateness of a behavioral approach to many mental health problems because of their belief that the therapy for a particular problem must direct itself to the root cause of the problem. In that view, disorders of biological origin should be treated with biologically based principles, while those of psychological origin should be treated psychotherapeutically.

A substantial body of opinion insists that there need not be a relationship between the etiology of a problem and the nature of the treatment that is effective in ameliorating it (Birk et al. 1973; London 1972). A disorder with an organic or neurophysiological etiology may be responsive to a biological therapy, but it may also be markedly improved by one of the procedures based on behavior modification. Similarly, difficulties that have an environmental origin may be responsive to biological intervention, such as psychopharmacologic treatment, as well as to a behavioral treatment. Behavior modification is based on learning principles, and so is particularly suitable for those problems, whatever their etiology, where the appropriate treatment involves retraining or learning new skills.

Therapists who use behavior modification methods would choose an objective, preferably quantifiable, measure of behavior as the outcome measure for evaluating the efficacy of treatment procedures. This selection contrasts with the outcome measures preferred by classical psychodynamically oriented therapists, who feel that personality tests reflect the changes that they seek to achieve in therapy. These psychotherapists may, in fact, regard as "mere symptoms" what the behaviorally oriented therapists regard as the focus of treatment. One of the consequences of this difference in viewpoints is that it is extremely difficult to obtain general agreement on a set of outcome measures for a comparison of the effects of behavior modification and psychotherapy.

The ideal evaluation of the effectiveness of behavior modification would tell us whether behavioral procedures bring about improvement more often, more quickly, to a greater degree, longer, or at less cost than do alternative procedures, such as psychotherapy. Unfortunately, at least in part because of the difficulty in obtaining agreement among professionals on what constitutes "improvement," this sort of direct comparison has been made systematically in only a few studies.

Despite the conceptual problems in making comparisons of different kinds of treatments, however, researchers have recently begun to conduct comparative evaluations in which one group of individuals receives a standard, well-accepted treatment, conscientiously applied, while another receives some kind of behavior modification, again conscientiously applied. This kind of research is aimed at answering the important questions of relative therapeutic efficacy and cost-effectiveness. By comparing results obtained on a variety of outcome measures with existing, standard procedures and with behavior modification, researchers will begin to provide the evidence necessary for deciding whether the costs of introducing new procedures, training staff in those procedures, and making changes in supervision and record-keeping, will be adequately repaid with a significant improvement in the functioning of the persons treated.

Although few comparisons have been made of behavior modification with other forms of treatment, large numbers of case studies and systematic evaluations of behavior modification have been reported in which the researchers have shown experimentally that the behavior modification methods were responsible for the improvements obtained. To summarize these many reports briefly, behavior therapy has been shown to be effective with some persons suffering from unjustified fears, anxiety reactions, and stuttering. Problems that have shown some improvement when individuals have been treated by behavior therapy procedures include compulsive behavior, hysteria, psychological impotence, frigidity, exhibitionism, and insomnia.

Behavior modification procedures have been used to analyze and produce significant changes in the language of institutionalized retardates who were initially deficient in language skills. Control of self-destructive and self-mutilating behavior has been achieved in a number of cases through behavior modification, as has the elimination or great reduction of milder forms of disruptive behavior, such as tantrums, whining, screaming, fighting, and destruction of property. Positive behaviors developed in institutionalized persons with behavior modification procedures include proper eating techniques and the complete range of self-care skills frequently absent in such persons. In otherwise normal preschool children, behavior modification has been used to facilitate the development of those motor, social and cognitive skills thought especially appropriate to the preschool environment, yet not appearing in the normal course of events in that setting. For example, social isolates have acquired social skills, and silent children, a readiness to speak. Hyperactive children have been taught to attend to tasks, and predelinquents have been taught friendly speech and have learned to perform skills necessary for school achievement, to take appropriate care of their living quarters, to interact cooperatively with their families, and to stop stealing and aggressive behavior (Baer 1973).

Token reinforcement systems have been shown to be effective in many classrooms for modifying behavior problems such as classroom disruption, failure to study, and low academic achievement. Chronic mental patients on wards throughout the country have learned a wide variety of appropriate social behaviors after the introduction of a token economy. The token economy has recently been introduced in a few nursing homes and wards for senile patients, and the early results appear promising. When the behavioral program is in effect, the patients come to interact more with each other and engage in more activities. Studies have shown that careful implementation of behavioral techniques can often produce improvements in the verbal and nonverbal behavior of psychotic and schizophrenic children.

Behavioral treatments have been quite successful with toilet training and most nervous habits, but somewhat less successful with alcoholism, smoking, and tics other than in a few special cases. To the extent that the symptoms of asthma are maintained by environmental consequences, the number and severity of asthmatic attacks can be reduced by behavioral programs designed to rearrange those consequences. Systematic desensitization has also been effective with some asthmatics (Price 1974).

Overall, then, much more evaluative research needs to be done with the behavioral treatments, although they do show considerable promise. With many clinical problems, behavioral procedures have been used only on a few individual cases, so that experimental evidence is lacking for the efficacy of the specific methods used. Thus, while a great range of problems appears to be responsive to behavioral treatment, for many types of problems, validating data are yet to be obtained. The existing evidence is strong enough, however, that an expert task force of the American Psychiatric Association recently concluded that behavior therapy and behavior principles employed in the analysis and treatment of clinical phenomena "have reached a stage of development where they now unquestionably have much to offer informed clinicians in the service of modern clinical and social psychiatry" (Birk et al. 1973).

Current Behavior Modification Programs: ADAMHA

The Alcohol, Drug Abuse, and Mental Health Administration (ADAMHA) is supporting behavior modification research in a wide variety of areas; the amount of that support exceeds $3 million a year, out of a total of over $121 million spent on research. Behavior modification research being conducted with ADAMHA support covers a wide range of problems and populations. Research is being done on the behavioral problems of children and adults, on persons with mild behavior problems and quite severe ones. Researchers are attempting to develop better behavioral techniques for dealing with asthma, insomnia, and hypertension, as well as evaluating new child-rearing techniques and classroom management methods. Behavioral treatments for problems of alcoholism, drug addiction, and juvenile delinquency are also being studied.

Many current projects have been described above as examples of specific behavior modification procedures. A few other projects will be described here, as further indication of the range and scope of support currently being provided.

Montrose M. Wolf, Elery L. Phillips, Dean Fixsen, and others (University of Kansas)[1] have developed a halfway house for predelinquent adolescents that uses procedures of behavior modification. This halfway house, called Achievement Place, is a community-controlled, community-based, family-style residential home for six to eight adolescents who have typically been adjudicated there by the juvenile courts. The program is designed to provide a maximum amount of motivation and instruction to the youths when they first enter, and then, as they develop skills and self-control, to reduce the amount of structure, replacing it with more natural reinforcement conditions. Behavior modification procedures include a token economy; positive reinforcement to shape appropriate social, academic, prevocational, and self-care behavior; and fines for inappropriate behavior. In addition, the adolescents' parents are trained in child management procedures so that the parents can be more successful in guiding their children toward productive lives.

Preliminary findings indicate that Achievement Place youths progress far better than do comparable youths placed on probation or sent to a State training school. This model has been copied widely, and there are now more than 30 such homes in operation in eight States, supported by State and local funds.

Nathan H. Azrin (Anna State Hospital, Illinois) has developed an extensive life-intervention scheme for alcoholic persons, based on behavior modification principles.³ In this treatment program, vocational, family, and other social reinforcers are rearranged so that the alcoholic person learns new behavior patterns incompatible with drinking. The clients are given marital and job counseling and are introduced to alcohol-free social situations especially established for them. The effectiveness of this treatment package is being compared with that of existing hospital procedures.

A.J. Turner is receiving support for a project in which behavior modification procedures are being used in all possible service areas of the Huntsville-Madison County (Alabama) Mental Health Center.¹ The results obtained on a wide variety of measures administered to the patients in this center are being compared with results on the same measures obtained from patients in a comparable community mental health center that uses standard procedures. Thus far, the experimental community mental health center has reported a much greater decline in State hospitalizations from their catchment area than that shown by comparable counties, as well as decreases in other measures, such as average number of days in the hospital.

Critical Issues in Behavior Modification

Recently, concerns have been widely expressed over the ethical and legal aspects of behavior modification techniques.

The Fear of Control

Some people fear behavior modification and control because of prevalent contemporary attitudes of distrust and skepticism of authority in general, and "mind control" in particular; others have more specific concerns that are related to the practice of behavior modification or, often, to myths and misconceptions about the practice of behavior modification.

General Concerns About Control. Behavior modification is most often criticized when it is used to alter the behavior of persons who are involuntary participants in therapy. Involuntary patients or subjects include those who are disadvantaged, vulnerable, or powerless because of institutionalization, age, social position, or discrimination.

Perhaps the most frequent complaints are in connection with the treatment of hospitalized mental patients and institutionalized delinquents and criminals. There has been a growing sensitivity to the ambiguity that can underlie diagnosis and choice of treatment goals for these populations. According to this view, a thin line separates social deviance from a mental illness that requires hospitalization. Society can often find it more convenient to institutionalize the deviant individual than to deal with the problem he represents. The hospitalization or incarceration thus may be more in the interest of social control than in the interest of the person's welfare.

The growing distrust of the exercise of control over the helpless and the disadvantaged even challenges the legitimacy of the authority of those who attempt to treat these persons. The authority to treat the institutionalized mentally disordered, for example, has been eroded by the growing dissemination of the notion that mental "illness" is a myth. According to this view, people should accept responsibility for their own behavior, including behavior that might otherwise be termed "mentally ill." Further, an emerging sociological model views the mentally disordered patient as a victim of stresses and strains that reside primarily within the social structure, rather than within the individual.

Credence has been increasingly given to the picture of the mental patient as a victim who is hospitalized for the convenience of society. In that view, treatment is seen as either a form of punishment or a procedure designed to make the patient conform to the requirements of an oppressive society. The mental health worker who proposes to modify the patient's behavior thus can be seen as serving the interests of the oppressor, rather than favoring the right of the person to express his individuality.

The news media, popular books, and movies have given voice to these general concerns. Also, several organizations have, in the last few years, called conferences to explore these issues. For example, the Institute of Society, Ethics, and the Life Sciences, of the Hastings Center (Hastings-on-Hudson, New York), held a series of meetings between 1971 and 1973 in which leaders in mental health research, practice, and public policy explored the problems of behavior control by drugs, the media, and physical manipulation of the brain, and discussed issues relating to the use of behavior control in education and in total institutions such as prisons and mental hospitals. The Institute has released reports summarizing these discussions.

Specific Fears of Behavior Modification. The general concerns mentioned above are relevant to all types of psychotherapy, as well as to behavior modification. In addition, people have expressed other concerns that are more specific to behavior modification procedures.

Behavior modification has been criticized with respect to its theoretical foundation, its goals, and its methods. Some mental health professionals have attacked behavior modification on the grounds that its underlying assumptions are at variance with their basic values and tend to dehumanize man (see, e.g., Carrera and Adams 1970). Contingency contracting, for example, has been said to foster a manipulative, exchange orientation to social interaction, and token economies, an emphasis on materialistic evaluation of human efforts. Mental health professionals, including persons with a behavioral orientation, have also questioned the appropriateness of accepting a patient's definition of his own problem, on the grounds that the patient's self-attribution of deviance can, like his behavior, be seen as learned behavior that is a function of consequences provided by society (Davison 1974; Begelman, 1977).

Another type of concern about the goals of behavior modification was expressed in a detailed law review critique which argued that behavior modification could be used to impose "an orthodoxy of 'appropriate conduct' " on the community (Heldman 1973), and thus to silence social and political dissent. Extremist activist organizations have described the procedures of behavior modification as "crimes against humanity."

The media and literature have incorrectly linked behavior modification with techniques such as psychosurgery, chemotherapy, electroschock, and brainwashing. The fantasied potency of imaginary or untested mind-controlling techniques, popularized in such works as *Brave New World, 1984, The Manchurian Candidate,* and *A Clockwork Orange,* has been extended to encompass standard, carefully evaluated behavior modification techniques.

Further, procedures that are encompassed within behavior modification can be misused. When this happens, critics decry behavior modification, even though the misuse is such that the procedure can no longer accurately be called "behavior modification." For example, Anectine, a drug that produces the sensation of drowning or dying, and Antabuse and other emetic drugs, have occasionally been used as components of behavior modification procedures. In aversive therapy for problems such as glue-sniffing and alcoholism, such drugs may be used as the aversive stimulus. However, these drugs have also been seriously misused, especially in prison settings, where they are given to persons in retribution for real or imagined lack of "cooperation" on their part, or as a way of keeping recalcitrant persons "in line." The noncontingent use of drugs lies outside the purview of behavior modification.

A Perspective On the Issue of Control.   Like any technology, behavior modification can be used ineptly, or for ends that could be considered immoral. The technology of behavior modification, says Skinner (1971), "is ethically neutral. It can be used by villain or saint. There is nothing in a methodology which determines the values governing its use" (p. 150). When psychoanalytic therapy was first introduced, it too raised the spectre of unethical authoritarian control. It is likely that any approach to the alteration of human behavior raises these same questions.

In the view of persons working in the field of behavior modification, it is the nature of social interaction for people to influence each other. In other words, behavior is continually being influenced, and it is inevitably controlled. Therapy without manipulation is a mirage that disappears on close scrutiny (Shapiro and Birk 1967). That is, in all kinds of therapy, the therapist hopes to change the patient in some way. Bandura (1969) formulates the issue in this way: "The basic moral question is not whether man's behavior will be controlled, but rather by whom, by what means, and for what ends." Behavior modification, then, involves altering the nature of the controlling conditions, rather than imposing control where none existed before.

Behavior modification is not a one-way method that can be successfully imposed on an unwilling individual. By its very nature, behavior modification will succeed only when the individual who is receiving the consequences is responsive to them and cooperates with the program. If the environmental events following an individual's behavior are not reinforcing to him or are less reinforcing than some alternative, his behavior will not change. Similarly, if the aversive consequence that follows his behavior is less unpleasant to him than some alternative, his behavior will not change. For many persons, it is highly reinforcing to be resistant to attempts to alter their behavior and highly aversive to succumb to external control. Even though such an individual may be participating in a behavior modification program, the person conducting the program may not be able to find any consequence strong enough to compete with the individual's desire to remain unchanged. Thus, in the long run, each of us retains control over his own behavior.

This characterization is equally true, whether the persons in the behavior modification programs are voluntary, adult, clinic patients, or institutionalized individuals with senile psychotic syndrome. Even for the latter group of persons, environmental consequences will succeed in altering their behavior only if the new consequences are more reinforcing than some alternative. Because mentally disadvantaged groups, such as the senile, often are in settings lacking an array of alternative reinforcers, special care needs to be exercised in developing programs for them. Later in this paper, some procedures are suggested that might help protect disadvantaged groups from inappropriately designed programs.

Although aversive therapy procedures seem more coercive than those using positive reinforcement, the individual still must cooperate fully with the procedures in order for them to be effective. While aversive procedures may reduce the individual's motivation to engage in the undesirable behavior, the motivation probably will not be reduced to zero. Rather, the goal of the therapy generally is to reduce the motivation to the point where the individual is able to exercise self-control and avoid engaging in the undesirable behavior.

Recent fiction has dramatically portrayed individuals supposedly unable to overcome the effects of aversive therapy. This, however, is not realistic. If coercion is used in therapy—whether positive or aversive—that may indeed force the individual's cooperation for a time. But, in real life, once this coercion is removed, the individual will be able to return to his former ways if he is motivated to do so.

It is important to remember that in addition to its emphasis on environmental control, the behavioral approach also assumes that persons are able to learn behavioral principles and understand how environmental events can control their own behavior (Ulrich 1967). As behavioral principles are more widely disseminated, an increasing number of persons will have access to them. Hopefully, through the knowledge that people gain from discussions of behavioral principles in courses, workshops, articles in the public press, television "talk shows," and other such sources, they will have a better understanding of their own behavior.

As public awareness increases, the likelihood of behavior being manipulated by more knowledgeable individuals lessens. Just as a professional in behavior modification may use his understanding of behavioral principles in an attempt to alter other persons' behavior, so those other persons can make use of their own understanding and control of themselves and their environment to resist, or indeed to counterinfluence the behavior of the professional. The behavior influence process is always a reciprocal one: The behavior manager attempts to shape the behavior of some other person through changing the consequences of that person's behavior, but, at the same time, the manager's behavior is in turn shaped by the other's response. Control always results in countercontrol.

In the ideal situation, the mental health worker using behavioral procedures would plan the goals and methods of the therapy together with the client. Persons using behavioral approaches would follow the same generally accepted ethical principles guiding other therapists, and so would strive to maintain a suitable balance between the rights of individuals and of society.

Thus, when there is controversy over the application of behavior modification, it often seems to be in instances in which these ideal conditions have not, for some reason, been met. One important benefit of the public attention to and criticism of behavior modification has been increasing sensitivity on the part of all mental health workers to issues that were formerly often neglected. For example, many therapists are only recently becoming aware of the need to involve the client or his representative more realistically in the planning of the treatment program, including the selection of both goals and methods. In the past, the mental health worker often used simply his own clinical judgment and experience as the basis for determining treatment goals and methods.

Also, the significance of the imbalance in power that is usually found between the therapist and the client is only now coming to be understood by mental health workers. Typically, the therapist comes from the more powerful classes or has a higher status within an institution, while the client is from a less powerful class or is of a lower status. In all mental health fields, including behavior modification, therapists have tended to view problems from their own perspective, so that treatment goals chosen were those that they would want for themselves or that would benefit those to whom the therapist had allegiance. In many instances, the inclusion of the client or his representative in the decisionmaking process is beginning to redress this imbalance. The power imbalance is a particularly serious problem, however, when the clients are involuntarily confined in an institution. Later in this report, the issues surrounding the use of behavior modification in prisons are discussed in detail.

On the whole, the goal of behavior modification, as generally practiced, is not to force people to conform or to behave in some mindless, automation-like way. Rather, the goals generally include providing new skills and individualized options and developing creativity and spontaneity.

Persons working in behavior modification have tried to be sensitive to the issue of control and to face the issue directly. Task forces on ethical issues in behavior modification have been established by each of the major professional societies whose members work in this field— the American Psychiatric Association, the American Psychological Association, and the Association for Advancement of Behavior Therapy. The first of these has published an extensive report (Birk et al. 1973).

In summary, people do fear control of their behavior, and they fear any method that seems to be effective in changing behavior. However, people need an understanding of what controls behavior and how behavior can be changed. Skinner (1971) has a thoughtful statement on this issue: "Good government is as much a matter of the control of human behavior as bad, good incentive conditions as much as exploitation, good teaching as much as punitive drill. . . . To refuse to exercise available control because in some sense all control is wrong is to withhold possibly important forms of countercontrol" (pp. 180–181). Dissemination of information about behavior modification methods will make techniques of resisting oppressive control generally available, so that new methods of control can be met by new methods of countercontrol (Platt 1972).

The Use of Aversive Control

Aversive procedures can be and have been seriously misused so that they become means by which a person in power can exercise control or retribution over those in his charge. The abusive treatment may then be justified by calling it therapeutic and labeling it "behavior modification."

A Perspective on Aversive Control. While many behavior modification aversive techniques, such as shock and time-out, are effective, it is unfortunately true that they are also cheap and easy to apply, requiring little if any specialized knowledge on the part of the person using—or misusing—them. Further, aversive techniques are widely known to be included in the family of behavior modification methods. Thus legitimized, these simple aversive methods are subject to indiscriminate use and other abuses, without regard for individual rights. For example, time-out, which appropriately used should be for only short periods of time, has, in some settings, involved extraordinarily long periods of isolation in small quarters.

Aversive techniques have been used successfully to eliminate life-threatening self-destructive behavior in clinical populations. Although the techniques themselves are unpleasant to consider, the gain from their use can be potentially great, especially when compared to the alternative, which may be long-term confinement in an institution or prolonged periods in total restraint. Thus, aversive techniques are appropriately used when the risk to the patient of continuing the self-injurious behavior is serious, alternative treatments appear to be ineffective, and potential benefits to the patient from the treatment are great. On the other hand, aversive methods should not be used to enforce compliance with institutional rules.

Suggested Procedures. When aversive methods are used, appropriate safeguards should be included for the protection of the rights and dignity of those involved. Severe aversive methods, involving pain or discomfort, should be used only as a last resort, when the person's behavior presents immediate danger to himself or others, and when nonpainful interventions have been found to be ineffective. Aversive therapies should be conducted only under the surveillance of an appropriate review panel, preferably one including representatives of the group to which the person receiving the treatment belongs; and they should be used only with the continuing consent of the person receiving them, or of his representative. The person supervising the use of aversive methods should continually monitor the results, which should also be available to the review panel. Any method not providing significant help should be abandoned. The technique used should not violate generally accepted cultural standards and values, as determined by the review panel.

Behavior Modification in Prisons
Behavior modification has become an increasingly controversial yet important law enforcement tool. Many persons feel that the use of behavior modification in prisons conflicts with the values of individual privacy and dignity.

Persons using behavior modification procedures have been particularly criticized for their attempts to deal with rebellious and nonconformist behavior of inmates in penal institutions. Because the behavioral professional is often in the position of assisting in the management of prisoners whose antagonism to authority and rebelliousness have been the catalyst for conflict within the institution, the distinctions among his multiple functions of therapy, management, and rehabilitation can become blurred, and his allegiance confused. While the professional may quite accurately perceive his role as benefiting the individual, he may at the same time appear to have the institution, rather than the prisoner, as his primary client.

Frequently, the goal of effective modification in penal institutions has been the preservation of the institution's authoritarian control. While some prison behavior modification programs have been designed to educate the prisoners and benefit them in other ways, other programs have been directed toward making the prisoners less troublesome and easier to handle, adjusting the inmates to the needs of the institution.

A related problem is that in prisons as elsewhere, the term "behavior modification" has been misused as a label for any procedure that aims to alter behavior, including excessive isolation, sensory deprivation, and severe physical punishment. Behavior modification then becomes simply a new name for old and offensive techniques.

The question of voluntary consent is an especially difficult problem when the persons participating in a program are prison inmates (Shapiro 1974). It is not clear whether there can ever be a "real volunteer" in a prison, because inmates generally believe that they will improve their chances for early parole if they cooperate with prison officials' requests to participate in a special program. There are other pressures as well; for example, participation in a novel program may be a welcome relief from the monotony of prison life.

The use of behavior modification in the prisons came to national attention recently when the Law Enforcement Assistance Administration (LEAA) withdrew its support from some behavior modification programs. According to a spokesman for LEAA, this was done because the agency staff did not have the technical and professional skills to screen, evaluate, or monitor such programs. The termination of the programs was criticized by the American Psychological Association (APA) as an injustice to the public and to prison inmates. The APA's news release (Feb. 15, 1974) said that the LEAA decision would tend "to stifle the development of humane forms of treatment that provide the offender the opportunity to fully realize his or her potential as a contributing member of society."

A similar point of view has been expressed by Norman A. Carlson, Director of the Federal Bureau of Prisons, in discussing the difficulty of determining which programs should be described as behavior modification: "In its broadest sense, virtually every program in the Bureau of Prisons is designed to change or modify behavior. Presumably, the Federal courts commit offenders to custody because their serious criminal behavior is unacceptable to society. The assumption is that during the period of incarceration, individuals will change their patterns of behavior so that after release, they will not become involved in further criminal activity." In general, when behavior modification programs are introduced in Federal prisons, it is important that they be consistent with this philosophy.

A Perspective on the Use of Behavior Modification in Prisons. A major problem in using behavior modification in prisons is that positive programs begun with the best of intentions may become subverted to punitive ones by the oppressive prison atmosphere. Generally, behavior modification programs are intended to give prisoners the opportunity to learn behavior that will give them a chance to lead more successful lives in the world to which they will return, to enjoy some sense of achievement, and to understand and control their own behavior better. Unfortunately, in actual practice, the programs sometimes teach submission to authority instead.

Thus, critical questions in the use of behavior modification in prisons are how goals are chosen for the program and how continued adherence to those goals is monitored. Behavior modification should not be used in an attempt to facilitate institutionalization of the inmate or to make him adjust to inhumane living conditions. Further, no therapist should accept requests for treatment that take the form "make him 'behave,'" when the intent of the request is to make the person conform to oppressive conditions.

Currently, a common position is to recommend the elimination of behavior modification programs in prisons, on the grounds that such therapy must be coercive, since consent cannot be truly voluntary. However, before this drastic step is taken, careful consideration should be given to the consequences. If constructive programs were eliminated, it would deny the opportunity of improvement for those inmates who genuinely want to participate and who might benefit from the programs. It would seem far better to build in safeguards than to discard all attempts at rehabilitation of prison inmates, whether behavior modification or any other rehabilitative method is involved.

Suggested Procedures. The appropriate way to conduct treatment programs in prisons, and, in fact, whether such programs should even be offered, are matters by no means settled. Because of the custodial and potentially coercive nature of the prison setting and the pervasive problem of power imbalance, special procedures are needed to protect the rights and dignity of inmates when they engage in any program, not only behavior modification. Some procedures are suggested here, in an attempt to add to the dialogue about ways to give prisoners the option of participating in programs and yet not coerce them into doing so.

A review committee should be constituted to pass on both the methods and goals of proposed treatment programs, and to monitor the programs when they are put into effect. The committee should be kept continually informed of the results of the programs, including short- and long-term evaluations, and of any changes in goals or procedures. A meaningful proportion of the members of this committee should be prisoner representatives, and the committee should also include persons with appropriate legal backgrounds. The person conducting the behavior modification program should be accountable to this committee, and ultimately, to all the individuals participating in the program.

As is always the case with such review panels, conflicting philosophies and differing loyalties may make it difficult for the panel members to agree unanimously on decisions. Such a panel does, however, provide a regularized opportunity for conflicting points of view to be expressed, an opportunity generally not otherwise available. Thus, the group's discussions can, at a minimum, sensitize program administrators and prison officials to the critical issues.

When this committee, including both prisoners and staff members, has chosen the goals and methods of the program, each potential participant should have a realistic right to decline participation. If a prisoner does refuse to cooperate, he should neither lose privileges he already has, nor receive additional punishment, for so declining. The presentation of the program given to him should include a description of the benefits of participation, both in the institution and after the prisoner has left there. Ideally, the prisoner should be offered a choice among several different kinds of programs, rather than the single alternative of a behavior modification program or nothing.

Implications for Behavior Modification of Emerging Legal Rulings

In the last few years, the courts have begun to make rulings on the rights of institutionalized persons, including the mentally ill. The emerging law may have a major impact on behavior modification programs, in particular, because the recent rulings extend rights that are considered basic and that must presumably be available to all persons. While even the major decisions apply legally only in the jurisdiction where they are announced (unless they are ratified by the U.S. Supreme Court), often other areas will adopt rules or pass legislation that is consistent with the decisions, so that they often have impact far beyond a circumscribed geographic area.

The recent decisions are an important step forward in defining the rights of patients more clearly. In particular, the identification of specific items and activities to which the patients are entitled under all circumstances seems to be a major advance. Even though these legal rulings have the effect of requiring the behavioral worker to be far more ingenious in selecting reinforcers for use in institutions (as explained below), this professional inconvenience is far outweighed by the gain in human rights for the patients. No therapeutic program should have to depend for its existence on the continuation of a dehumanizing environment.

Judicial rulings are not necessary to emphasize that aversive techniques are neither legally nor ethically acceptable when they are used solely for oppressive purposes or without the consent of the person on whom they are used, or his guardian. The recent legal reinterpretations relating to human welfare have been concerned mainly with limiting possible abuses of positive reinforcement.

For example, one of the most common ways for mental hospital patients to earn money or tokens for token programs is by working in on- and off-ward jobs. Such employment is justified by mental health professionals on the grounds that it has an educational purpose: It teaches the patients skills needed in the outside world. The decision in *Wyatt* v. *Stickney*[4] seems to have restricted the use of hospital work as a means of earning money or tokens. In that decision, the court barred all involuntary work by mentally handicapped patients on hospital operations and maintenance, and specifically said that privileges should not be contingent on the patients' work on such jobs. A similar ruling was made in *Jobson v. Henne.*[5]

Usually when patients work on hospital jobs, they are compensated at a level far below the prevailing wage, or even below the minimum legal wage. This practice of employing institutionalized persons without normal compensation to perform productive labor associated with the maintenance of the institution has been called "institutional peonage" (Bartlett 1964). The *Wyatt* decision specified jobs that may be done by mentally handicapped patients and held that the patients must be compensated for that work at the prevailing minimum wage. Another recent case, *Souder* v. *Brennan,*[6] extended the principle of minimum wage compensation to all institutionalized persons in non-Federal facilities for the mentally ill and mentally retarded. While the minimum wage requirement may seem reasonable on the face of it, it may be a problem for many mental institutions and institutions for the retarded that cannot afford even the minimum wage. Under *Wyatt,* apparently the only types of work exempt from minimum wage coverage are therapeutic work unrelated to hospital functioning, and tasks of a personal housekeeping nature (Wexler 1973).

Among the reinforcers used in some token economies are such basic aspects of life as food, mattresses, grounds privileges, and privacy. That is, in these programs, the patients have been able to have these items or engage in these activities only if they were able to purchase the item or activity with their tokens. According to recent legal developments, such as the *Wyatt* v. *Stickney* case, patients have a constitutional right to a residence unit with screens or curtains to insure privacy, a comfortable bed, a closet or locker for personal belongings, a chair, a bedside table, nutritionally adequate meals, visitors, attendance at religious services, their own clothes or a selection of suitable clothing, regular physical exercise including access to the outdoors, interaction with members of the opposite sex, and a television set in the day room. In other cases (*Inmates of Boys' Training School* v. *Affleck*[7] and *Morales* v. *Turman*[8]), similar kinds of activities and amenities were ordered to be available to juveniles in residential facilities. Thus, these legal rulings appear to have defined as basic rights many of the items and activities that have till now been employed as reinforcers in token economies.

The *Wyatt* decision was upheld on appeal by the U.S. Court of Appeals for the Fifth Circuit.[9] Even before that action, the ruling was already influential. However, because of inconsistencies among rulings, it is not clear at the moment just how much these rulings entitle the members of various institutionalized populations to have, and what sorts of items and activities can be restricted to those persons with sufficient tokens to purchase them (Wexler 1973).

Further, the new rulings do not totally prevent the inclusion in a token economy of the various items and activities named in the rulings. Rather, the result of the rulings is to permit the restriction in availability of these items and activities only with the consent of the patients or representatives of the patients. That is, these constitutional rights, like other constitutional rights, can be waived in suitable circumstances by the individuals involved. For example, a patient may consent to having his access to television restricted so that television programs might be available to him only following changes in his behavior that he desires to make.

Mental health workers who want to use the token economy procedure are now beginning to search for new types of reinforcers or new methods of reinforcement delivery that will not require special waivers of the constitutional rights of the patients. Suitable reinforcers would be those beyond which any patient would ordinarily be entitled, or to which he would normally have access. Many professionals believe that such new types of reinforcers will be developed, that behavior change can be produced without depriving patients of the basic necessities or asking them to waive their constitutional rights, and that this entire legal development is a significant step forward. The rulings, however, are recent ones, and extensive changes in practice have yet to occur.

Recent legal rulings have implications for behavior modification procedures other than the token economy. For example, *Wyatt* specified in detail the conditions under which electric shock devices could be used with mentally retarded residents. That ruling, and *New York State Association for Retarded Children* v. *Rockefeller*[10] also, set limits on the use of seclusion with mentally retarded and mentally ill patients.

Other legal rulings (e.g., *Rouse* v. *Cameron*[11] and *Donaldson* v. *O'Connor*[12]) have held that patients have a right to treatment. Possible implications of this might be an extension of patients' rights with concomitant restrictions on the use of some behavior modification techniques. At the same time, a right to effective treatment might result in a requirement that all therapies include the sort of continual monitoring of effectiveness that is generally standard practice in behavior modification. Judicial rulings in this area have been inconsistent, however, some supporting a right to treatment (e.g., *Rouse* v. *Cameron* and *Wyatt* v. *Stickney*), and some holding that there is no legal obligation to provide treatment (e.g., *Burnham* v. *Department of Public Health of the State of Georgia*[13] and *New York State Association for Retarded Children* v. *Rockefeller*). In the 1974 appellate court decision upholding *Wyatt*, the court also overruled the lower court decision in the *Burnham* case. Thus, the Fifth Circuit Court has ruled that, for that jurisdiction, mental patients as a class have a Federal constitutional right to adequate treatment when they are committed against their will to State institutions. Inconsistencies remain, however, especially in decisions regarding voluntary hospitalization (Budd and Baer, in press). It is still too early, also, to draw clear implications for behavior modification from the appellate court decisions on right to adequate treatment.

Ethics in Behavior Modification

Recently, many persons have expressed increasing concern that those who conduct behavior modification programs should take special care that their methods are ethical and that the individuals undergoing behavior change are protected. While, on the whole, researchers and therapists using behavior modification methods have exercised normal caution, some aspects of the problem have not always received the attention that they deserve.

One difficulty in establishing ethical standards for behavior modification is that the issues and problems are different for different populations in different settings. Informed consent, for example, is clearly meaningful when a normal adult voluntarily goes to an outpatient clinic to obtain guidance in altering a specific behavior that he wants to change. However, when prisoners are offered the opportunity of participating in behavior modification, it is by no means clear that they can give truly voluntary consent.

A further difficulty in this area is that the appropriate person to determine the means and goals of treatment is different for different populations in different settings. The mental health professional must decide in each instance who his client is, that is, who the person or group is with whom he should negotiate regarding the choice of means and goals for a behavior modification program. It is often both obvious and correct that the ostensible client is the actual one. For example, a neurotic patient comes to a clinic to be relieved of his fear of flying in planes: The patient, determining for himself the goal of therapy, is the true client. Or, when a husband and wife are referred to a mental health worker to learn contingency contracting as a method of improving their marriage, it is generally clear that both partners have chosen the goal of improvement of their interpersonal relations. The mental health worker's responsibility is to assist them in achieving this goal.

On the other hand, when a behavioral consultant is asked to help a teacher keep her pupils in their seats, working quietly at all times, the ethical situation is less clear. Are these the optimum classroom conditions for learning, and are the children's best interests served by teaching them to be still, quiet, and docile (Winett and Winkler 1972; O'Leary 1972)? The mental health professional may want to suggest alternative goals, or work together with the class and the teacher in developing appropriate goals.

Similarly, when an administrator of an institution for the retarded asks a behavioral professional to establish a token economy so that the inmates will be motivated to work on jobs for the hospital, the professional may want to work together with an advisory committee to determine the relative value of that work activity for the hospital and for the retardates. While he is being asked to have the hospital as his client, he needs also to consider the rights of the patients, the potential benefits to them of the activity, and any risks that may be involved. The professional may decide, for example, that such hospital jobs have minimal benefit for the patients, and thus may feel that the institution's goal is an inappropriate one. Identifying the true client is also a critical problem when behavior modification programs are used in prisons.

Suggested Procedures. Ethical safeguards for behavior modification programs need to take a number of factors into account: client involvement, a balance of risk and benefit, appropriate review by outside persons, the efficacy of the proposed procedures, and the plans for accountability of the program.

In discussing these complex issues, we are aware that the procedures we suggest have relevance for all types of mental health programs, not just for behavior modification. In this paper, we do not attempt to address these complex issues in that broader context. However, we recognize that the full range of concerns mentioned here applies in all mental health settings.

Ethical responsibility demands that members of the client population or their representatives be seriously consulted about both the means and the goals of programs, before the programs are introduced to change behavior. The persons planning the program need to evaluate the extent to which the members of the target population can give truly informed consent to the program. This involves (1) preparation of a description of the program and its goals so that the persons will know what is to be involved, (2) an assessment of the extent to which they are competent to understand the proposal and make an appropriate judgment about it, and (3) an evaluation of the degree to which their consent can be truly voluntary.

The client himself, or the advisory committee, together with the mental health worker, should weigh the potential benefits to the client of the change that is expected to result from the proposed behavior modification program, against an evaluation of possible risks from using the procedure. This balance can be a difficult one to reach, because the various persons involved may well each see the situation from his own point of view. Thus, the mental health worker might find a proposed technique acceptable because it produces rapid improvement in seriously maladaptive behavior, while client representatives might object to the same technique because it violates the client's rights or restricts his freedom, however briefly, and regardless of ensuing benefits. The client may disagree entirely with the goal of the program that has been chosen by the institution in which he is confined, on the grounds that he is not interested in the supposed benefits offered.

The definitions of risk and benefit will be different in different settings and will also change over time, as customs, knowledge, and values change. Thus, while all the members of an advisory committee may share the goal of helping the client, reaching consensus on how to achieve that goal may involve considerable compromise by persons representing differing points of view.

In many cases, the individual whose behavior is to be changed will be able to negotiate the proposed means and goals directly with the professional personnel. In that way, mental health worker and client can arrive at a mutual agreement or contract that would specify the rights and responsibilities of each of them. However, when the program concerns individuals who have been shown to be incapable of making their own decisions, it will be necessary for the mental health worker to deal with a representative or surrogate for the specific persons who would participate in the proposed program.

The less directly the persons are involved in the initial determination of means and goals, the more protections of those persons should be built into the system. Thus, when the mental health worker is not directly accountable to his client, an advisory committee should be established that would cooperate with the mental health professional in choosing the methods and goals of the behavior modification program. This committee should include either representatives of the persons whose behavior is to be modified, their guardians, or advocates.

The establishment of a suitably constituted review committee does not automatically guarantee that approved programs will include appropriate protections. The official guardians of the persons in the program may, for example, have a vested interest in controlling those persons in a way more convenient for the guardians than beneficial for the persons in the program. The mental health professional, too, cannot be viewed as an entirely disinterested party, especially when he is employed by the institution charged with the care of the persons in the program. In general, members of review committees need to be aware of the conflicting interests involved, and sensitive to the factors influencing their own and each other's behavior, so that subtle coercions are not used to manipulate the decision.

Effectiveness and accountability are other key elements of ethical responsibility in behavior modification. The results of the behavior modification program must be carefully monitored to ensure that the goals agreed on by the advisory committee, or by client and therapist, are being achieved. If they are not, sound practice requires a reevaluation and revision of the methods being used. In addition, the persons conducting behavior modification programs must be accountable to those whose behavior is being changed, or to their representatives. Information on the effectiveness of the program should be made available to the consumers on a regular basis.

Behavior modification programs have an additional special ethical problem because the procedures are generally simple enough to be used by persons lacking the training to evaluate them appropriately. Thus, a further safeguard that should be built into behavior modification programs is a limitation on the decisionmaking responsibilities of program staff to those matters in which they have expertise. Persons with appropriate professional qualifications, such as a suitable level of training and supervised clinical practice, are able to design and organize treatment programs, develop measurement systems, and evaluate the outcome of behavior modification programs. Such persons should be familiar with the ethical guidelines of their particular profession. Technicians, paraprofessionals, and other workers with only minimal training in behavior modification generally can function in the setting in which behavior is being modified, but should not initiate decisions affecting the welfare of other individuals, unless those decisions are reviewed by the professional staff (Sulzer-Azaroff, Thaw, and Thomas 1975). Given such a delegation of responsibility, review of behavior modification programs should be concerned both with the individuals who make the critical treatment decisions and with the adequacy of supervision of nonprofessional staff.

Ethical Safeguards: The Professions. The need to adhere to sound ethical practices is accepted by all trained mental health practitioners. Practitioners using behavior modification methods are expected to adhere to existing codes of ethics formulated by their professions. In addition, the Association for Advancement of Behavior Therapy (AABT) is currently formulating a set of standards for practice. The Behavior Therapy and Research Society publishes a list of behavior therapists whose qualifications have undergone peer evaluation.

The AABT also has a system of consultative committees that are coordinated by the president of the Association. Persons who are associated with institutions or programs and who are concerned about present or proposed behavior therapy procedures can ask the AABT president to appoint a committee of persons to go to the site, investigate, and make an advisory report. These reports are compiled into a casebook of standards of practice.

Ethical Safeguards: DHEW Policy and Protections. Much of the biological, medical, and behavioral research conducted in this country is supported by funds from the Department of Health, Education, and Welfare (DHEW). According to the current DHEW policy, which was established by the May 30, 1974, regulations (Chapter 45, Code of Federal Regulations, Subtitle A, Part 46), in activities involving human subjects, the rights and welfare of the subjects should be adequately protected; the risks to an individual from participation should be outweighed by the potential benefits to him and by the importance of the knowledge to be gained; and informed consent should be obtained by methods that are adequate and appropriate.

According to DHEW policy, risks are defined to include not only potential physical harm, but also adverse psychological reactions or social injury. The policy gives as the basic elements of informed consent: a fair explanation of the procedures to be followed and their purposes, including an identification of those that are experimental; a description of any expected discomforts and risks; a description of the benefits to be expected; a disclosure of appropriate alternative procedures that would be advantageous for the subject; an offer to answer any inquiries concerning the procedures; and an instruction that the subject is free to withdraw his consent and to discontinue participation in the project or activity at any time without prejudice to himself.

As applied to research on behavior modification, this policy means that the person receiving the service or his representative should be told that the person will be receiving behavior modification treatment, and what the treatment program will involve. He should be told what problems might arise, if any, and what the goal of the treatment is. It should be made clear to him that he should feel free to drop out of the study at any time. Not mentioned in the official regulations, but part of recommended practice in this area, is that the client or his representative should cooperate with the mental health worker in specifying the goals of the behavior modification treatment.

The DHEW regulations place primary responsibility for safeguarding the rights and welfare of subjects on the organization conducting the activities. The responsibility, however, is shared by the organization's review committee and the DHEW staff and advisory committees, each of whom determines independently the adequacy of proposed procedures for the protection of human subjects. According to the regulations, any institution conducting DHEW-funded research, development, or related activities involving human subjects must establish a committee with responsibility for reviewing any application for support of such activities, to insure that the protocol adequately fulfills the policy for the protection of the subjects.

The National Institutes of Health established a study group that is charged with reviewing various aspects of the DHEW policy on human subjects. The group drafted proposed rules dealing with protection of subjects in prisons and mental institutions, and with protection of subjects in research involving pregnant women, abortion, fetuses, and products of *in vitro* fertilization. Public comment on these proposals has been received.

Many hospitals and research institutions have used the DHEW regulations as a model for structuring their own policy for the protection of human subjects. Others have gone beyond the regulations to require, for example, the presence of the subject's personal physician, personal lawyer, and immediate kin, with specific periods of time being allocated for discussion before consent is given. This is an area that is receiving increasing attention.

The National Research Act (PL 93–348) provided for a National Commission for the Protection of Human Subjects of Biomedical and Behavioral Research, which will be in existence for 2 years, beginning in 1974. This Commission is charged with investigating a number of issues, including the problems of obtaining informed consent from children, prisoners, and the institutionalized mentally infirm when they are asked to participate in experiments. The Commission has also been asked to determine the need for a mechanism that will extend the DHEW regulations beyond DHEW-funded research activities to all activities with human subjects, including research and health services.

Summary and Conclusions

Behavior modification currently is the center of stormy controversy and debate. We have attempted to put these problems in perspective, through a discussion of what behavior modification is and what it is not, and a review of the major issues.

Many years of laboratory research provide the basis and rationale for the development of behavior modification techniques and behavioral treatments. The behavior modification methods currently being used include procedures suitable for use in the clinic, such as desensitization, and in the mental institution, such as the token economy. The procedures can be used with normal adults and children and with the mentally disadvantaged, including the retarded, the senile, and the psychotic. Behavior modification methods have been used to ameliorate a wide range of problems, including mutism, self-destructive behavior, inappropriate fears, and nervous habits. Also, behavior modification methods have been used to teach a great variety of appropriate, normal behaviors, including normal speech, appropriate social behavior, and suitable classroom skills.

The Federal Government continues to support and encourage research and demonstrations that test new behavior modification techniques, that seek to refine existing ones and apply them to new clinical populations and new settings, and that promote the dissemination of techniques that have been positively evaluated. A particularly strong need is for additional research comparing the efficacy of behavior modification methods with that of alternative treatment approaches. Research is also needed on ways to deliver behavior modification techniques to larger numbers of persons in less restrictive settings than the institutions where much of the research, until now, has been done.

Concern has been expressed that behavior modification methods may be used by those in power to control and manipulate others. Some critics have charged that the use of behavior modification methods is inconsistent with humanistic values. However, all kinds of therapies involve attempts to change the patient in some way. Behavior modification, like other therapeutic methods, requires a cooperative individual in order for it to be effective. Countercontrol, especially countercontrol based on knowledge of behavioral principles, is a major way that individuals can respond to any attempted manipulation.

The concerns that have been expressed about behavior modification have stimulated a reexamination of the assumptions and ethics of all psychosocial therapies. Ethical problems are particularly serious when therapies are used within institutions such as mental hospitals and prisons, or with the institutionalized mentally retarded and senile. In these settings, mental health workers have to be sensitive to the implications of the imbalance in power between them and their clients.

Aversive procedures, easy to abuse, have also raised serious concerns. These methods can, however, be used to benefit patients greatly, as when aversive techniques are used to eliminate life-threatening self-destructive behavior. Appropriate safeguards need to be provided, whenever aversive control techniques are proposed. Greater involvement of clients or their representatives in decisions about the means and goals of treatment programs will help protect persons participating in the programs.

Perhaps the most controversy has arisen in connection with the use of behavior modification in prisons. Behavior modification programs have, in some places, been designed to preserve authoritarian control and discipline, rather than to teach skills that would benefit the prisoners, once they are released. It is not clear whether prisoners are ever able to be true volunteers in any experimental program held in a prison. Here, too, safeguards must be built into the structure of any behavioral program.

Recent legal rulings have provided significant gains in human rights, especially for involuntarily committed patients. The rulings have called attention to possible abuses of the use of positive reinforcement and have extended the limits of institutionalized persons' basic rights.

In addition to discussing these issues, we have suggested some ways that safeguards might be designed for behavior modification programs. The issues are relevant to all types of mental health programs, and many of our proposed solutions would be applicable more generally as well. They are discussed here, however, only as they apply specifically in behavior modification.

Ethical responsibility demands that members of the client population or their representatives be consulted about both the means and goals of programs, and that these persons have an opportunity to weigh the balance of risk and benefit in any proposed program. Programs should be monitored to ensure that they are effective, and those persons conducting the programs should be accountable to those whose behavior is being changed, as long as the program is continued.

The Department of Health, Education, and Welfare is currently developing new regulations for the protection of human subjects, and the National Commission for the Protection of Human Subjects of Biochemical and Behavioral Research is also investigating related topics.

Public debate will surely continue concerning the issues that surround the use of behavior modification techniques. Professional evaluation of these techniques and public discussion of them can help prevent abuses in the use of behavior modification procedures, as well as foster public understanding and acceptance of beneficial procedures. London (1974) contends that " . . . a decent society regulates all technology that is powerful enough to affect the general welfare, at once restricting the technicians as little as possible and as much as necessary." In that context, both continued monitoring of behavior modification by the public and further research on this important technology are needed to serve society and the individuals who make it up.

Notes

1. This project is being supported by the National Institute of Mental Health.

2. This project is being supported by the National Institute on Drug Abuse.

3. This project is being supported by the National Institute on Alcohol Abuse and Alcoholism.

4. 325 F. Supp. 781 (M.D. Ala. 1971), 334 F. Supp. 1341 (M.D. Ala. 1971), 344 F. Supp. 373 (M.D. Ala. 1972), and 344 F. Supp. 387 (M.D. Ala. 1972). This case was known as *Wyatt* v. *Aderholt* on appeal.

5. 335 F. 2d 129 (2d Cir., 1966).

6. 367 F. Supp. 808 (D.D.C. 1973).

7. 346 F. Supp. 1354 (D.R.I. 1972).

8. 364 F. Supp. 166 (E.D. Tex. 1973).

9. *Wyatt* v. *Aderholt*, No. 72–2634 (5 Cir., Nov. 8, 1974).

10. 357 F. Supp. 752 (E.D. N.Y. 1973).

11. 373 F. 2d 451 (D.C. Cir., 1966).

12. 493 F. 2d 507 (5 Cir., 1974).

13. 349 F. Supp. 1335 (N.D. Ga. 1972), appeal docketed, No. 72–3110, 5 Cir., Oct. 4, 1972. This case was consolidated for argument on appeal with *Wyatt*.

References

Anderson, R.C. Education psychology. *Annual Review of Psychology*, 18, 129–164, 1967.

Ayllon, T., and Azrin, N.H. The measurement and reinforcement of behavior of psychotics. *Journal of the Experimental Analysis of Behavior*, 8, 357–383, 1965.

Ayllon, T., and Azrin, N.H. *The Token Economy*. New York: Appleton-Century-Crofts, 1968.

Ayllon, T., and Michael, J. The psychiatric nurse as a behavioral engineer. *Journal of the Experimental Analysis of Behavior*, 2, 323–334, 1959.

Baer, D.M. A case for the selective reinforcement of punishment. In Neuringer, C., and Michael, J.L., eds. *Behavior Modification in Clinical Psychology*. New York: Appleton-Century-Crofts, 1970.

Baer, D.M. The control of developmental process: Why wait? In Nesselroade, J.R., and Reese, H.W., eds. *Life-span Developmental Psychology: Methodological Issues*. New York: Academic Press, 1973.

Baer, D.M., and Guess, D. Receptive training of adjectival inflections in mental retardates. *Journal of Applied Behavior Analysis*, 4, 129–139, 1971.

Bandura, A. *Principles of Behavior Modification*. New York: Holt, Rinehart and Winston, 1969.

Bartlett, F.L. Institutional peonage: Our exploitation of mental patients. *Atlantic*, 214(1), 116–119, 1964.

Begelman, D.A. Ethical and legal issues of behavior modification. In: Hersen, M.; Eisler, R.; and Miller, P., eds. *Progress in Behavior Modification*. Vol. 1. New York: Academic Press, 1977.

Birk, L. et al. *Behavior Therapy in Psychiatry*. Washington, D.C.: American Psychiatric Association, 1973.

Blanchard, E.B.; Libet, J.M.; and Young, L.D. Apneic aversion and covert sensitization in the treatment of a hydrocarbon inhalation addiction: A case study. *Journal of Behavior Therapy and Experimental Psychiatry*, 4, 383–87, 1973.

Brady, J.P. Brevital-relaxation treatment of frigidity. *Behaviour Research and Therapy*, 4, 71–77, 1966.

Bucher, B. Some ethical issues in the therapeutic use of punishment. In Rubin, R.D., and Franks, C.M., eds. *Advances in Behavior Therapy*, 1968. New York: Academic Press, 1969.

Bucher, B., and Lovaas, O.I. Use of aversive stimulation in behavior modification. In Jones, M.R., ed. *Miami Symposium on the Prediction of Behavior*, 1967. Coral Gables: University of Miami Press, 1968.

Budd, K., and Baer, D.M. Behavior modification and the law: Implications of recent judicial decisions. *Journal of Applied Behavior Analysis*, in press.

Carrera, F., III, and Adams, P.L. An ethical perspective on operant conditioning. *Journal of the American Academy of Child Psychiatry*, 9, 607–623, 1970.

Cohen, H.L., and Filipczak, J. *A New Learning Environment*. San Francisco: Jossey-Bass, 1971.

Colman, A.D. *Planned Environment in Psychiatric Treatment.* Springfield, Ill.: Thomas, 1971.

Davison, G.C. Homosexuality: The ethical challenge. Paper presented at the meeting of the Association for Advancement of Behavior Therapy, Chicago, November 1974.

Eysenck, H.J. Discussion on the role of the psychologist in psychoanalytic practice: The psychologist as technician. *Proceedings of the Royal Society of Medicine,* 45, 447–449, 1952.

Ferster, C.B., and DeMyer, M.K. The development of performances in autistic children in an automatically controlled environment. *Journal of Chronic Diseases,* 13, 312–345, 1961.

Foxx, R.M., and Azrin, N.H. Restitution: A method of eliminating aggressive-disruptive behavior of retarded and brain damaged patients. *Behaviour Research and Therapy,* 10, 15–27, 1972.

Gruenberg, E.M. The social breakdown syndrome—some origins. *American Journal of Psychiatry,* 123, 12–20, 1967.

Heldman, A.W. Social psychology versus the first amendment freedoms, due process liberty, and limited government. *Cumberland-Samford Law Review,* 4, 1–40, 1973.

Jones, M.C. The elimination of children's fears. *Journal of Experimental Psychology,* 7, 382–390, 1924.

Lindsley, O.R., and Skinner, B.F. A method for the experimental analysis of behavior of psychotic patients. *American Psychologist,* 9, 419–420, 1954.

London, P. The end of ideology in behavior modification. *American Psychologist,* 27, 913–920, 1972.

London, P. Behavior technology and social control—turning the tables. *APA Monitor,* April 1974, p. 2.

Lovaas, et al. Some generalization and follow-up measures on autistic children in behavior therapy. *Journal of Applied Behavior Analysis,* 6, 131–165, 1973.

Lovibond, S.H. Aversive control of behavior. *Behavior Therapy,* 1, 80–91, 1970.

Minge, M.R., and Ball, T.S. Teaching of self-help skills to profoundly retarded patients. *American Journal of Mental Deficiency,* 71, 864–868, 1967.

Mowrer, O.H., and Mowrer, W.M. Enuresis—a method for its study and treatment. *American Journal of Orthopsychiatry,* 8, 436–459, 1938.

O'Leary, K.D. Behavior modification in the classroom: A rejoinder to Winett and Winkler. *Journal of Applied Behavior Analysis,* 5, 505–511, 1972.

O'Leary, K.D., and Drabman, R. Token reinforcement programs in the classroom: A review. *Psychological Bulletin,* 75, 379–398, 1971.

Phillips, E.L., et al. Achievement Place: Modification of the behaviors of pre-delinquent boys within a token economy. *Journal of Applied Behavior Analysis,* 4, 45–59, 1971.

Platt, J. Beyond Freedom and Dignity: "A revolutionary manifesto." *The Center Magazine,* 5(2), 34–52, 1972.

Price, K.P. The application of behavior therapy to the treatment of psychosomatic disorders: Retrospect and prospect. *Psychotherapy: Theory, Research and Practice,* 11, 138–155, 1974.

Rachman, S., and Teasdale, J. *Aversion Therapy and Behaviour Disorders.* Coral Gables: University of Miami Press, 1969.

Risley, T.R. The effects and side effects of punishing the autistic behaviors of a deviant child. *Journal of Applied Behavior Analysis*, 1, 21–34, 1968.

Sears, R.R.; Maccoby, E.; and Levin, H. *Patterns of Child-Rearing.* Evanston, Ill.: Row, Peterson, 1957.

Shapiro, D., and Birk, L. Group therapy in experimental perspective. *International Journal of Group Psychotherapy*, 17, 211–224, 1967.

Shapiro, M.B. The single case in fundamental clinical psychological research. *British Journal of Medical Psychology*, 34, 255–262, 1961.

Shapiro, M.H. Legislating the control of behavior control: Autonomy and the coercive use of organic therapies. *Southern California Law Review*, 47, 237–356, 1974.

Skinner, B.F. *Beyond Freedom and Dignity.* New York: Knopf, 1971.

Sulzer-Azaroff, B.; Thaw, J.; and Thomas, C. Behavioral competencies for the evaluation of behavior modifiers. In Wood, W.S., ed. *Issues in Evaluating Behavior Modification.* Champaign, Ill.: Research Press, 1975.

Thomson, I.G., and Rathod, N.H. Aversion therapy for heroin dependence. *Lancet*, ii, 382–384, 1968.

Ulrich, R. Behavior control and public concern. *Psychological Record*, 17, 229–234, 1967.

Webster, D.R., and Azrin, N.H. Required relaxation: A method of inhibiting agitative-disruptive behavior of retardates. *Behaviour Research and Therapy*, 11, 67–78, 1973.

Wexler, D.B. Token and taboo: Behavior modification, token economies, and the law. *California Law Review*, 61, 81–109, 1973.

Winett, R.A., and Winkler, R.C. Current behavior modification in the classroom: Be still, be quiet, be docile. Journal of Applied Behavior Analysis, 5, 499–504, 1972.

Wolpe, J. *Psychotherapy by Reciprocal Inhibition.* Stanford, Calif.: Stanford University Press, 1958.

Wolpe, J., and Lazarus, A.A. *Behavior Therapy Techniques.* Oxford: Pergamon Press, 1966.

Establishing Behavior Contracts with Delinquent Adolescents

Robert Bruce Rutherford, Jr.

The effectiveness of behavior modification (applied behavioral analysis) principles and techniques has been demonstrated repeatedly with children and adults in a variety of learning environments. Some behavioral techniques are more effective than others depending upon the environment where intervention is to take place. The custodial or institutional setting has the potential for controlling the widest range of variables competing with the intervention strategy. Intervention strategies which originate in the home, school, or community, on the other hand, may be limited in their behavioral influence because the individual will have access to many other sources of reinforcement. Older subjects such as delinquents may be more adept at developing alternate strategies for obtaining reinforcers and avoiding manager- or mediator-imposed interventions. It appears, especially with the more sophisticated adolescent, that in order to maximize the effectiveness of the behavioral intervention, and to bridge the gap between the institutional setting and real life, the adolescent must be given the power to negotiate various aspects of the tasks and reinforcers included in the intervention strategy. The strategy which lends itself most appropriately to the adolescent's involvement is behavioral contracting.

Behavioral Contracting

Behavioral contracting involves the systematic negotiation between mediator (parent, teacher, probation officer, social worker, unit counselor, or supervisor) and a target (delinquent adolescent) of the behav-

Reprinted by permission of the *Federal Probation Quarterly,* 39 (1) (March 1975): 28-32.

iors to be performed within a given environment, and the specific reinforcing consequences or "payoffs" to be provided when performance requirements are met.

Behavioral contracting is based upon an applied behavior analysis model whereby the environmental dynamics which maintain behavior are assessed. In behavioral contracting, a behavioral analysis involves specifying: (A) the antecedents which will cue the contract behavior, (B) the contract behavior to be developed, (C) the consequences which will maintain the contract behavior (see figure below).

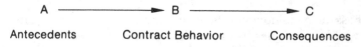

Figure 1   Behavioral Analysis of Contract Behavior

The "antecedents" are events which are present in the environment to cue behaviors. They include those stimuli, cues, directions, or prompts that set the occasion for a given behavior and a specific, predictable consequence. The antecedent cues for doing 20 arithmetic word problems at home may be a math book, a sharp pencil, 3 sheets of paper, directions at the top of the page, and a quiet, well lighted room. These cues may signal that the "consequences" of completing the "contract behavior," e.g., math problems done correctly by 9:00 a.m. the following morning, will be positive. The positive consequences may be a higher letter grade, praise from teacher and parents, and/or a specifically contracted item or event such as a coke or 20 minutes of free time at midday. Behavioral analysis makes the assumption that consequences which are positive will result in an increase in the frequency of the desired behavior.

In summary, behavioral analysis involves planning before the fact and behavioral programming after the fact of a given behavior. Sound behavioral contracts specify systematically each of the three steps of the behavioral analysis model.

Rules for Establishing Behavioral Contracts

The following are steps which appear to be most crucial for the development of sound behavioral contracts:

1. A behavioral analysis must be made of the behavior to be

contracted. As mentioned earlier, analysis must be made of the antecedents and consequences of the contracted behavior, as well as of the behavior itself.

2. The behavioral contract must be precise and systematic. Each condition of the contract must be specified. Dates, times, criterion behaviors, amounts and/or range of consequences, names of contractor and contractee, and names of others involved in the contract should all be included. The terms of the contract must be adhered to strictly and systematically at all times.

3. The behavioral contract must be fair to both the contractor and the contractee. A contract implies the power of both parties to negotiate terms. If the terms are unfair, the contract will fail. The contracted behaviors and the consequences must be balanced to the satisfaction of both parties.

4. The terms of the behavioral contract must stress the positive. A behavioral contract which implies positive reinforcement for appropriate behavior rather than punishment for inappropriate behavior will be more readily adhered to by the contractee. Positive reinforcement strengthens the behavior which it follows; punishment only temporarily suppresses behavior.

5. The concept of "shaping" may be used when establishing behavioral contracts. If a behavior initially does not exist or exists at only a minimal level, the contract must reinforce approximations of a final specified behavior. Opportunities for easy initial success must be enhanced. It should be emphasized that behaviors that are already in the contractee's behavioral repertoire *must* be built into the contract.

6. A consultant or arbitrator may be helpful at first in the negotiation of behavioral contracts between the contractor and the contractee. In many contracts, both the contractor and the contractee must change their behaviors; under these circumstances a consultant or arbitrator permits the terms of the contract to be fair to both parties.

7. The behavioral contract should be a formal written document which specifies all privileges and responsibilities of the parties involved. It should be signed by both parties. The behavioral contract is a negotiated agreement between two people which allows the contractor and the contractee to predict the consequences of the contracted behaviors. Signatures enhance the formality and commitment of the contract.

8. Both the consequences which follow the completion of the contracted behavior (*the A clause*), and the consequences which follow the noncompletion of the contracted behavior (*the B clause*),

must be specified. By specifying the consequences for completing and not completing the contract, the possibilities for misinterpretation of the contract are reduced. Inclusion of both the A and B clauses reduces the chances of error.

9. Reinforcing consequences must always follow the completion of the contracted behavior and must be delivered immediately. In establishing a behavioral contract, the opportunity should be available to receive some portion of the reinforcing consequence immediately upon completion of the contracted behavior. Contracts are often negotiated which allow for small but continuous payoffs for daily behaviors, while at the same time making a large payoff contingent upon completion of a whole series of daily behaviors.

10. Behavioral contracts should progress from contractor-initiated to contractee-initiated as rapidly as possible. While behavioral contracts are negotiated documents, it is generally true that the terms of the initial contracts are designated and controlled by the contractor (parent, teacher, probation officer, unit supervisor, etc.). Behavioral contracting will have more generalized results when the contractee (adolescent) proposes the privileges and responsibilities to be included in the contract.

Case Studies and Sample Behavioral Contracts in Four Settings

In order to demonstrate the diversity of the environmental settings where behavioral contracts may be negotiated with delinquent adolescents, four cases are presented along with sample behavioral contracts. The contracts described include a family contract (between mother and son); a school contract (between teacher, counselor, and student); a community contract (between probation officer and probationer); and an institutional contract (between unit supervisor and inmate).

Family Contract

John is a 15-year-old boy. His parents have been separated for several years and he lives with his mother and younger brother and sister. John's mother is concerned that John has been suspended from school because of his poor attendance record. His mother has been trying to reason with him because the school counselor has told her that unless he attends for the rest of the semester and turns in all work assignments, John will not be readmitted to that school. His work assignments consist of two take-home assignments per week. Only 4 weeks remain until the end of the semester. As a last resort, John's mother has threatened to withhold enrollment in a driver's education course unless he can stay in school. John has expressed a strong interest in the driver's education course and in getting his driver's permit in August.

Several other problems exist in the home. John has been going out on weekends without permission and staying out past curfew, a situation which worries his mother because he has been picked up twice by the police and brought home. In order to try to gain John's confidence, his mother has started buying him cigarettes by the carton. She has discovered John is selling unused cigarettes to his friends.

When John is not at home, he frequently visits his mother's friend, Rick Blackley, who lives a few houses away. Rick has a garage full of tools and an old car on which John has worked since his suspension from school. However, the work that John was doing on the car was completed several weeks ago.

CONTRACT

Date _____

1A For each day that John attends all classes, he will earn the privilege of ten (10) cigarettes per day or one (1) package of cigarettes every other day.

1B For each day that John does not attend all classes, ten (10) cigarettes per day will not be earned.

2A If John attends 90 percent of the *full* school days between Monday, May 21, 1973, and Friday, June 14, 1973 (20 days), he will earn one (1) driver's education course. The driver's education course will begin on June 18, 1973.

2B If John does not attend school for 90 percent of all classes between May 21, 1973, and June 15, 1973 (20 days), the privilege of the driver's education course will be withdrawn.

3A For each take-home assignment that John turns in to his teachers between Monday, May 21, 1973, and Friday, June 15, 1973, John will earn one evening out on the weekend, provided his mother knows his whereabouts and the time that he will return home.

3B For each take-home assignment that John does not turn in to his teachers between Monday, May 21, 1973, and Friday, June 15, 1973, John will stay in one evening during the weekend.

As negotiator and overseer of this contract, Mr. Rick Blackley will see that all sections of this contract are followed and that said consequences will be paid.

As representative of the Central High School, Mr. Tom Anderson, counselor, will act as the monitor of the behaviors in the school (i.e., attending classes and turning in assignments).

Mr. John Wright, Student	Mrs. Judy Wright, Mother
Mr. Rick Blackley, Negotiator	Mr. Tom Anderson, Counselor

School Contract

Ron is a 16-year-old boy of above average intelligence who is quite disruptive in all of his 10th grade classes except math. His grades, in all but the math class, have been D's and F's for the last two 6-week periods. He is currently maintaining an A in math. He enjoys being with his math teacher, Mr. Leigh, as demonstrated by his appearances in Mr. Leigh's classroom before and after school to discuss math problems and backpacking (a hobby both he and Mr. Leigh have in common). When Ron is not actively disrupting his other classes, he is usually doing math problems rather than the assigned task.

Ron was arrested twice in the last 4 months for selling pills after school near the high school. In addition, he was accused of beating a 14-year-old boy for allegedly failing to make good a debt related to his drug sales. The charges were eventually dropped. However, Ron is still on probation for the drug arrests and his probation officer has stated that if he does not pass all of his courses at the end of the school year, Ron will remain on probation.

Ron's disruptive classroom behavior includes being verbally abusive to his teachers and his peers, making loud noises when others are speaking, walking around the classroom and poking constantly at his classmates. Presently he is excluded from English and machine shop classes due to his behavior. His counselor, Mr. Quinlin, and his math teacher, Mr. Leigh, have discussed establishing a contract with Ron to facilitate his getting back into English and machine shop classes and raising all of his grades to passing level.

CONTRACT

1A If Ron returns to both his English and machine shop classes and attends at least 4 days out of 5 days each week, he will be allowed to spend his last period (formerly a study hall) in Mr. Leigh's intermediate math class as a math assistant and tutor.

1B If Ron either fails to return to his English and machine shop classes or fails to attend at least 4 out of 5 days, he will not be allowed to be Mr. Leigh's math assistant and tutor.

2A If Ron's behavior in both his English class and his machine shop class is judged appropriate by the teachers (criteria of appropriateness to be determined before this contract is to be initiated), he will earn one chit per class per day to be turned in to Mr. Quinlin, the school counselor. Thus a maximum of 10 chits per week can be earned for attendance.

Ron will earn one chit per letter grade on the math, the social studies, the English and the machine shop tests each Friday. An F = 0 chits, a D = 1 chit, a C = 2 chits, a B = 3 chits, and an A = 4 chits. These chits will also be turned in to Mr. Quinlin. Thus a maximum of 16 chits per week can be earned for grades.

For each week that Ron earns at least 18 chits, Mr. Quinlin will issue Ron a pass to spend one half hour a day for three days of the following week with Mr. Leigh, after school. These three ½-hour periods will be spend discussing any topic Ron wishes.

2B If Ron does not earn a total of 18 chits per week, he cannot spend the ½-hour periods after school with Mr. Leigh.

All terms of this contract have been negotiated freely between me, *Ron Chan*, and Mr. Leigh, my math teacher, and Mr. Quinlin, my counselor. I also understand that Mr. Mock, my machine shop teacher, and Mrs. McGlothlin, my English teacher, will assist in this contract.

_____ Ron Chan   _____ Mrs. McGlothlin

_____ Mr. Leigh   _____ Mr. Mock

_____ Mr. Quinlin   _____ Date

Community Contact

Pamela is 14 years old. She has a record of being a runaway for periods of up to 1 year. When she leaves it is usually to be with older men. When she was 9 years old she had her first sexual experience with a 19 year old. She now has a 4-month-old baby, fathered by her

21-year-old ex-boyfriend. She has also been treated a number of times for venereal disease.

Pamela's mother is mainly concerned with two of Pamela's problems. The first of these problems is her constant running away from home. Pamela says that the argument that usually precedes her running away deals with the mother's placing too much responsibility for household chores on Pamela. She has three sisters in the home, but she is expected to do the major portion of the work. The second problem area that the mother identifies deals with the $96.00 which Pamela receives every 2 weeks from the County for her baby. Pamela thinks that she should have control of it. Currently the County is making the check payable to the mother.

Pamela enjoys parties with her friends, watching television, and listening to music. She has shown a great deal of interest in going to Disneyland and going out to a nice dinner. She also greatly enjoys the peer group activities that are periodically provided by the County Probation Department, i.e., trips to the mountains, beaches, sports events, museums, and movies.

CONTRACT

Date: _____

1A Pamela receives $96.00 every 2 weeks. Of that $96.00 she will pay her mother, every 2 weeks:

Food	$30.00
Board	20.83
Utilities	3.00
Total	$53.83 Every 2 weeks

2A For following the chore chart each week (which divides the household chores evenly between Pamela and her sisters), Pamela will be able to attend any and all group activities provided by the Probation Department that week.

2B For not following the chore chart each week, Pamela will not be able to attend group activities provided by the Probation Department that week.

3A For each Friday or Saturday night that Pamela goes out and is home by 1:00 A.M. her mother will provide free baby sitting for the baby that evening.

3B For each Friday or Saturday night that Pamela goes out and is not home by 1:00 a.m., she will pay her mother fifty cents (50¢) per hour for the time that she is gone past 1:00 a.m.

4A Pamela will receive free baby sitting from 9:00 a.m. to 1:00 p.m. from her mother on weekdays when Pamela is attending summer school.

4B Pamela will pay fifty cents (50¢) per hour to her mother for baby sitting if she does not attend summer school.

As negotiator and overseer of this contract, Mr. Glen Hamilton, County Probation Officer, will see that all sections of this contract are followed and that said consequences will be paid. Mr. Hamilton will see that both Pamela and her mother are treated fairly by the contract.

_____

Ms. Pamela Brooke, Student

_____   Mr. Glen Hamilton,
Ms. Sue Brooke, Mother   Probation Officer

Institution Contract

Unit III of the County Detention Facility contains 20 girls whose ages range from 13 to 17 years. The average length of confinement is 13 months. The major reasons for confinement include drug use, incorrigibility, theft, assault, and prostitution.

Problem behaviors on the Unit include fighting, refusal to obey staff orders, attempts to run away, refusal to go to school, refusal to work on Unit projects such as group behavioral counseling sessions and Unit cleaning and decorating activities, destroying property in the dayroom and in the dormitory, and stealing from the staff and the other girls.

Possible positive reinforcers available include shortened sentences, having one's own room, weekend passes home, staying up late, special materials to decorate rooms, radios and televisions in one's room, and items from the token economy store.

A token economy system has been established in order to reinforce the girls systematically for performance of appropriate behavior. All of the girls earn tokens for specific behaviors: 5 points for being at breakfast at 7:30 a.m., 3 points for each 20 minutes on-task in the school classroom, 5 points for brushing teeth and hair in the evening, etc. Each girl can also negotiate individual contracts to deal with behaviors unique to herself.

Barbara is a 13-year-old who was placed in the County Detention Facility for being an accomplice to an armed robbery committed by her 19-year-old boyfriend. Barbara, who has lived in nine foster homes since she was 18 months old, was at the County Detention Facility 5 weeks when the first contract was negotiated with her. She participated in the basic token economy of Unit III, but she refused to take part in either the school program or the daily group counseling sessions on the Unit. When she was forced by the staff to attend these activities, she did not speak or in any way acknowledge the other participants.

Barbara has expressed a great deal of interest in visiting her current foster parents. She has been with them over a year and they seem to be as attached to Barbara as she is to them. Also, Barbara has beautiful long black hair which she spends a great deal of time brushing and combing. Barbara's hair is very important to her as she has received many compliments on it both before she entered the Detention Facility and in the Facility itself.

BEHAVIORAL CONTRACT

Date: _____

1A I, _____, agree to attend the school from 9:00 a.m. to 12:00 noon for at least 4 out of the 5 days of the week contingent upon receiving 25 *bonus* points per day and being allowed to stay up until 9:30 to watch TV or play cards with staff.

1B I, _____, agree that if I do not attend school from 9:00 a.m. to 12:00 noon for at least 4 out of 5 days of the week, I will not receive 25 *bonus* points per day and I will have to go to bed at 8:30.

2A When I, _____, am in school, I will complete, 80 percent correctly, 5 of 6 lessons per day contingent upon 5 *bonus* points per lesson and the use of the hairdryer for 30 minutes each evening.

2B When I, _____, am not in school or do not complete, 80 percent correctly, 5 of 6 lessons per day, I will not receive 5 *bonus* points per lesson nor will I be allowed to use the hairdryer that evening.

3A When I, _____, attend each behavioral counseling session, I will receive 5 *bonus* points and the use of all of the hair conditioner, shampoo, curlers, hairnets, bobby pins, and scotchtape I need to do my hair that evening.

3B When I, _____, do not attend a behavioral counseling session, I will not receive 5 *bonus* points and I will not get to use the hairsetting materials.

4A If I, _____, contribute to the behavioral counseling session (as judged by Mr. Denison, the behavioral counselor, and the other girls on a scale of 1 to 15) with an average score of 10 or above, I will receive 10 *bonus* points.

4B If I, _____,receive a score below 10 on my contribution to the behavioral counseling session, I will not receive 10 *bonus* points.

5. When I, _____, receive 3150 *bonus* points, I can visit my foster parents at home from 4:00 p.m. Friday until 4:00 p.m. Sunday of the weekend following my earning the 3150 *bonus* points.

Ms. Barbara Russell   Teacher

Unit Supervisor   ·   Behavioral Counselor

Conclusion

Applied behavioral analysis, in the form of written behavioral contracts, can be an effective intervention strategy with delinquent adolescents. The contract provides the adolescent with: (1) maximum negotiation power, (2) directly observable contractor responsibilities, and (3) a system for predicting the behavior of the contractor. The contract provides the contractor or mediator with: (1) the power to negotiate change in the adolescent's behavior, (2) observable contractee behaviors and contingencies, and (3) a system for predicting contractee behavior.

Behavioral Family Contracting: Helping Families Change

Jerome S. Stumphauzer

The family plays a key role in the child's development. Certain methods of parenting or childrearing can change or even prevent delinquent behavior. Generally, the younger the child, the greater the influence of the family. In adolescence the family often plays less of a role and the peer group may have the greater influence. In part, this is necessary for healthy human development as young people prepare themselves to become independent adults. Often with delinquent youth, however, something has gone wrong in this process. They may not have had consistent parenting from which to learn stability when they were young children, the family may be losing even its limited influence on the child in adolescence, and peers may be shaping or "teaching" delinquent behavior through modeling and reinforcement. By the time we see families of delinquent children in the clinic, counseling session, or probation office they often have taken years to "fall apart" and become ineffective systems. These families are frequently chaotic; the adolescent is labeled "bad" or "out of control." The parents often report "we have tried everything but nothing works." In fact, as Stuart (1970) and other researchers have found, the parents have not tried everything but rather have used punishment as a parenting approach and inconsistently at that. Punishment alone doesn't work. In these families there are no rules or agreements spelled out; no consistent demands or expectations (antecedents); and no follow-through, especially no positive reinforcement (consequents). Coming home very late may result in nothing one night and a family fight followed by "nagging" the next night. Many times this chaotic family process can be reversed through a social learning process called behavioral family contracting.

Reprinted from *Helping Delinquents Change* by Jerome S. Stumphauzer, pp. 91-102. Reprinted by permission of the publisher, The Haworth Press, New York.

A behavioral family contract is a formal agreement (often spelled out on paper) *which gives the family the very thing it is lacking: a specific plan and method for changing behavior in this family today.* The goal is usually a *series* of agreements between the youth, his or her family, and often others (such as teacher or probation officer) that will change behavior. The program is based on reciprocal rewards ("If you will do this . . . we will do that . . ."). Behavioral family contracting gives families four things they didn't have before:

1. structure: family members will know what behavior is expected from each other and, perhaps for the first time, what results to expect;

2. learning: a system of natural rewards and punishments arranged to maximize change or the learning of more productive behavior for the youth and more effective family interactions;

3. commitment: families who reach agreements and sign their names to them are more committed to change: "there *is* something we can do about our problems and this contract is it;"

4. responsibility: in contracting it becomes clear where the responsibilities for change lay: in the family; it is no longer "it is his fault" or "please doctor, fix my kid," but "*we* need to do this and this *today.*"

A major aspect of this approach should be underscored—the adolescent does have a say in the contracting as an "equal partner" and his or her wishes and wants are respected (perhaps an unusual event!). Remember, we are not forcing change but rather are helping the delinquent change. The therapist or counselor takes the role of *negotiator* and this is where the "art" of contracting comes in. Skill and experience (together what I meant by "art") are required to achieve a balance in each family meeting so that the parents *and* youth get what they want, the youth does not feel "ganged up on," so that compromises can in fact be reached, and the family keeps coming to sessions. This sounds like a formidable task—it is, but it can be done.

In the beginning the counselor/negotiator may have to side somewhat with the adolescent, to underscore their rights to "a point of view," and otherwise to reinforce his or her assertiveness (speaking up without taking away the rights of others). This helps considerably in avoiding "resistance" and noncompliance. The following is an example of such a negotiation session between a therapist, a seventeen-year-old boy and his parents.

Sample Negotiation of a Family Contract

Therapist: So one of the problems is what time Bill comes in at
night...

Mother: Yes, we tell him to be home early and we never know
when he'll come in.

Bill: Not always.

Father: No, not always, but you come in when *you* feel like it.

T: Is there any set rule of when Bill is to be in on weekday
nights and weekend nights that you all have agreed is fair?

F: There isn't much we agree on.

M: No, there's no rule but he knows I worry and want him home
at a decent hour so he won't get in trouble again.

T: Let's work on this together today. Let's see if we can come up
with hours for Bill to come in that are acceptable to all of
you.

B: Acceptable to me?

T: Acceptable to you *and* your parents.

B: It won't do any good, they won't listen.

T: They're listening now. Do you all think there should be a
different time to be home on weeknight and weekend nights?

B: Definitely *late* on weekends.

F: I guess there should be a difference.

M: Well, yes, school nights should be earlier.

T: Well, we have agreed on that already! You all think Bill should
be home earlier on week nights than on weekends. Now, let's
get more specific. What time should the hours be?

B: One o'clock on weekends.

F: Out of the question! A seventeen-year-old should not be out
that late.

T: Your father doesn't think *that* is quite fair or acceptable.

M: I don't either. Eleven-thirty is late enough.

B: No way! You can't do anything and be home on a Saturday by
eleven-thirty. Some parties don't start until ten.

T: Well, let's see if we can work out a compromise here. Bill,
what would be a compromise that you could live with.
Perhaps, one late night a weekend? What do *you* think is fair?

B: Midnight one weekend night.

F: Too late. Eleven-thirty is late enough.

T: It seems to me that many seventeen-year-olds are permitted to
stay out *one* weekend night, but let's come back to that. Bill,
would you be willing to come in by 10:00 *every* weekday night
in order to earn the privilege of staying out until 12:00 on
Friday or Saturday.

B: I think so, yeah.

T: *Don't agree to it unless you will really do it.*

B: Yeah, *I'd* do it, but *they* won't go for it.

T: Maybe they will. You won't be staying out too late, and they will know when to expect you home.

T: Now, what do you two think of this. Would you agree to this compromise?

M: Well, I don't know.

F: What if he didn't stick to it?

T: If he is later than 10:00 on weekday nights, then he couldn't stay out late on either weekend night. But he has already agreed he would to it.

M: I think we would be willing to try it. It would be the first time we agreed on anything in a long time.

F: Yes, ok, *if* he will do it.

T: Bill, you agree to this plan?

B: Yeah.

T: Bill will be doing what you want and Bill, you will get what you want. It sounds like a pretty fair exchange to me. Now let's put it on paper and sign it before we finish today and you and your parents will get copies to take with you. Then next week we will talk about how it worked, but I think this family is off to a good start already!

Effective family contracts should contain some basic ingredients—each of which adds an important aspect. The six important basic ingredients are:

1. The *date* the agreement is made.

2. A *general agreement*—a simple statement that the people involved agree to work together on such a program. Without it, the contract won't work because it is one-sided or coercion or perhaps no one really wants to do it. With it you have alliance, partners who are problem solving, and motivation. Achieving this general agreement is most important and may even take a whole first family meeting to negotiate. Only *after* a general agreement is achieved should you move on to the specific "who will exchange what" below.

3. The *specific privileges* or rewards are placed on one side of the contract. These are the activities or things the adolescent wants (like "staying out until midnight on weekends," "use of the car one night a week," "$5.00 a week," etc.). It is best to write these in this way: "In order to stay out until 12:00 on Fridays and Saturdays . . ."

4. The *specific responsibilities* that go with or are linked to each privilege are spelled out in detail. Note that these are often the

things the parents want, their rewards as determined in the counseling session. The counselor/negotiator must help the family arrive at specific responsibilities that are acceptable to all parties: asking for "enough" to satisfy parents without asking for so much from the teenager that he or she won't do it. Each completes the "In order to . . ." sentence started in privileges with ". . . I agree to . . ." For example, "In order to stay out until midnight on Friday and Saturday nights . . . I agree to go to school every day the week before."

5. Who is to *keep a record* of the behaviors? A form may be posted on the ever-popular refrigerator door and the adolescent may "sign in," bring notes from school, or a parent may keep a chart on each behavior. Measurement, as seen in Chapter Three, *is* critical. The record should then be brought in to the next contracting session to see what worked, what didn't, and what may need to be adjusted in a new contract for continuing success and improvement.

6. Finally, *signatures* of all involved should be added at the bottom. This adds to the commitment and responsibility of each party and shows that each really does agree to the contract, to do these things now. You may want to add your signature for further emphasis, a "legal seal," or whatever might add to the contract's importance. Others involved, such as teachers or probation officers, might add their signatures as well. Carbon or photocopies should be made for each party (one for your records) and suggestion made that it is to be posted at home—the refrigerator door is a good "public" place, but the teenager's bulletin board is another good location.

Some Examples of Behavioral Family Contracting

Behavioral contracting with families of delinquents appears to have begun about 1970. Since that time there have been many published reports. Applications have differed somewhat and results have varied with programs, measures, and settings.

An early report by Stuart (1971) presented extensive rationale and a case example. Two important assumptions he underscored were (a) that in interpersonal exchanges, receipt of a reward is a privilege rather than a right, and (b) effective contracts are governed by *reciprocity* (that something is exchanged for something). The case involved a 16-year-old girl (with extensive history of delinquent behavior) and her family. The detailed contracting, carried out in the home, focused on exchanging privileges of going out (places and hours) for letting parents know where she was and returning home on time. Noteworthy is the use of natural *bonuses* (extra privileges for completing the contract or for several successful compliances) and sanctions (punishments "fitting the crime" like "If she is 10 minutes late one night . . . she must come in 10 minutes early the next"). The family contracting worked very well in this difficult case. However, after treating 79 families, Stuart and Lott (1972) questioned whether successful contracting depended upon the characteristics of contracts, clients, or therapists. They suggested that the counselor's skill in encouraging compromises may be as important, or even more important, than the actual paper document.

Alexander and Parsons (1973) appear to have further emphasized this point in a form of behavioral family contracting which focused on "reciprocity of communication." Specifically, they described the contracting as: "therapists actively modeled, prompted, and reinforced in all family members: (a) clear communication of substance as well as feelings, and (b) clear presentation of 'demands' and alternative solutions; all leading to (c) negotiation, with each family member receiving some privilege for each responsibility assumed, to the point of compromise" (p. 220). Their program was successful with a large number of families of delinquents—more successful than a "client centered" approach or a "no treatment" control group. Success of contracting was demonstrated both by improvements in family interactions as well as in lower rates of recidivism by the adolescents.

Robin and Foster (in press) have combined problem-solving with communication training in their approach to therapy with the families of adolescents. They regard families as social systems which are held together by bonds of affection and exercising mutual control over each other's contingency arrangements and behavior. Problem-solving, also utilized in the social skills training program described in Chapter Seven, here involved the following steps:

1. defining the problem (e.g., adolescent or parent behavior which causes disagreements);
2. listing the solutions (generating alternatives);
3. evaluation of alternatives (looking at and weighing possible consequences); and
4. planning and carrying out the best solution.

Communicative training stressed the clear expression of opinions in assertive but nonoffensive ways, listening to and "decoding" messages from other family members, and reflection of thoughts and feelings (through verbal acknowledgements and body posture). In this approach as well, the therapist was teacher, negotiator, and source of social reinforcement.

A case simulation practice manual called *Writing Behavioral Contracts* has been developed by DeRisi and Butz (1975) who have extensive experience with such programs in the California Youth Authority (CYA) institutions. The manual is recommended reading for "where to begin," gathering data, negotiating, "trouble shooting," and practicing the skill of behavioral family contracting. In one sample contract a youth's agreement to take part in two thirty-minute role playing sessions that week was exchanged for discussion of any subject of the youth's choice for thirty minutes following each session. In another sample contract if the boy attended at least three of his assigned classes each day that week, then he would be allowed to work in a store for three hours a day at two dollars an hour. To this second contract a "bonus pass" good for a hamburger and soft drink was added for every two classes over the fifteen specified in the contract for a week. Also, a penalty was added: if the boy missed more than two days of school he would lose his weekend late-night privileges for one week.

Another such program has been developed as an adjunct to the Dallas Police Department—the Youth Services Program reported by Douds, Engelsgjerd, and Collingwood (1977). Behavioral family contracting has been utilized routinely for 1200 youths and their families. Notable results based on follow-ups that are 74% of youths improved in following rules at home, 72% improved in communicating with parents, 63% did better in school attendance, and 45% increased participation in organized activities. Of the 1200 completing the program only 10.7% have been arrested (compared to 42.7% in a control group).

Behavioral contracting has been used successfully not only with families, but also in probation, schools, employment programs, and in group homes.

Application of Behavioral Family Contracting: Contracting Form and Two Case Examples

A sample contract form, similar to that used by Stuart (1971), is provided in Table 1. It can be used with families or contracts can be written out by hand. At times it is best to have the adolescent write the contract in their own handwriting. They may have more commitment to it. Two case examples from the author's work with families of problem youth follow.

1. Steve

Steve, a 15 year old, was referred to our mental health clinic by probation following a "breaking and entering" and "vandalism" of his own school. Initially, he attended ten sessions of the social skill training program. While he successfully completed that program, it became clear that there were conflicts between him ("She bugs me. She's crazy. She won't even let me use the telephone.") and his mother ("I worry about him. I worry he will get in trouble again. He's on the telephone too long — until I yell at him."). The following contract (Table 2) developed during the first family meeting, focused on a mutual concern (telephone use) and a compromise was negotiated. Steve said, "It will never work; she will never change." Both agreed and the simple agreement seems to have made a big difference in this family. A week later they were both pleased (and surprised) at the success: "Doctor, it's amazing...the phone rings, he picks up the clock, talks, and when ten minutes are up he says 'I have to go now'!" At this point I turned to Steve, said "great, and saying 'I have to go now' and ending the telephone conversation is what I call being assertive" (something he learned in the social skills group), and he smiled in approval. In fact, at six month follow-up this agreement was still working.

Table 1

date _____

Behavioral Contract

Privileges	Responsibilities
General Contract: In order to	we agree to
Specific Contracts:	
1. In order to	1. _____ agrees to
2. In order to	2. _____ agrees to
3. In order to	3. _____ agrees to
4. In order to	4. _____ agrees to

Bonuses and Sanctions:

Who will measure what:

Signatures: _____

_____

_____

2. Tammy

Tammy, a twelve year old, was referred to the clinic by her parochial school for "repeated and uncontrolled stealing" over the last five years. This case is reported in detail elsewhere (Stumphauzer, 1976). The following family contract (Table 3) was negotiated after a behavioral analysis determined that stealing was heavily reinforced by teacher and parent attention, little or no reinforcement was given for either "good behavior" or periods of not stealing, and all agreed to work together in improving the family (a general contract).

The behavioral family contract (with this key shift in reinforcement), combined with self-control training, resulted in an almost immediate cessation of stealing. Stealing did not occur again over eighteen months of follow-up while productive, nondelinquent behavior increased.

Table 2

Family Contract on Telephone Use Contract

date: 4-29-85

General Agreement: In order to improve things, the family, we agree to work on a program together.

Specific Contract

Specific Privileges

Specific Responsibilities

1. In order to use the telephone and not have his mother "bug him" while he is on the telephone. . .

1. Steve agrees to use the telephone (calls in or out) for only *10 min.* each time.

Record

Mrs. W. will keep a record of telephone use (approx. min. per call each day) and bring it in next week.

Signatures

Steve _____

Mrs. W. _____

Dr. J. _____

Table 3

date ___May 6___

Behavioral Contract

Privileges	Responsibilities
General Contract: In order to help Tammy stop stealing	we agree to work together on this program

Privileges	Responsibilities

Specific Contracts:
 	
1. In order to
   get 20¢ for ice cream. . .
2. In order to
 	
3. In order to
 	
4. In order to
	1. ___Tammy___ agrees ^not^ to steal or
	   borrow in school the day before.
	2. _____ agrees to
	
	3. _____ agrees to
	
	4. _____ agrees to

Bonuses and Sanctions:
As a bonus, Tammy will get special Sunday pancakes. . .if she does not steal or borrow in school *all week*.

Who will measure what: Tammy will carry *Daily Behavior Card* back and forth to school; she will count number of times she steals and Sister Louise will countersign the card if she agrees with the count.

Signatures:	___Tammy___
___Therapist___	___Mr. and Mrs. P.___
	___Sister Louise___

Summary

Families play a key role in child development (including delinquency) and families, as presented in this chapter, can help delinquents change. Behavioral family contracting refers to the application of the social learning approach in a series of family agreements or contracts.

The counselor or therapist takes the role of negotiator and teacher, helps the family understand delinquent behavior, and helps provide and negotiate a specific plan for changing behavior in that family starting that day. Behavioral family contracting provides structure, a natural system for learning and changing, commitment (signed agreements), and responsibility (in effect, the family agrees to change itself).

Ideally, each family contract contains key ingredients: that day's date, a general agreement to work together, specific privileges (reinforcers or rewards), specific responsibilities linked to each privilege, a system of record keeping (assessment), and signatures of all involved. For example, a privilege such as "use of the family car one night a week" could be exchanged for a responsibility such as "agree to attend school every day the week before." At times one contract can help a family change delinquent behavior, but more often a series of contracts are necessary as behavior changes and as other problems are worked on. Others have combined behavioral contracting with family communication training. A negotiation transcript, a contracting form, and two case examples from the author's work were presented.

Social learning principles have been applied to delinquents in groups to teach behavior incompatible with youth crime.

Readings

1. Alexander, J. F., & Parsons, B. V. (1973). Short-term behavioral intervention with delinquent families: Impact on family process and recidivism. *Journal of Abnormal Psychology, 81,* 219-225.

2. De Risi, W. J., & Butz, G. (1975). *Writing behavioral contracts: A case simulation practice manual.* Champaign, IL: Research Press.

3. Robin, A. L., & Foster, S. L. (in press). *Parent-adolescent problem solving and communication.* New York: Guilford.

References

Alexander, J. F., & Parsons, B. V. (1973). Short-term behavioral intervention with delinquent families: Impact on family process and recidivism. *Journal of Abnormal Psychology, 81,* 219-225.

DeRisi, W. J., & Butz, G. (1975). *Writing behavioral contracts: A case simulation practice manual.* Champaign, IL: Research Press.

Douds, A. F., Engelsgjerd, M., & Collingwood, T. R. (1977). Behavior contracting with youthful offenders and their parents. *Child Welfare, 56,* 409-417.

Stuart, R. B. (1970). Assessment and change of the communicational patterns of juvenile delinquents and their parents. In R. D. Rubin (Ed.), *Advances in Behavior Therapy*. New York: Academic Press.

Stuart, R. B. (1971). Behavioral contracting within the families of delinquents. *Journal of Behavior Therapy and Experiemtal Psychiatry, 2,* 1-11.

Stuart, R. B., & Lott, L. A. (1972). Behavioral contracting with delinquents: A cautionary note. *Journal of Behavioral Therapy and Experimental Psychiatry, 3,* 161-169.

Stumphauzer, J. S. (1976). Elimination of stealing by self-reinforcement of alternative behavior and family contracting. *Journal of Behavior Therapy and Experimental Psychiatry, 7,* 265-268.

8 Group Counseling in Corrections

Introduction

In chapter 5 we discussed family therapy and crisis intervention counseling for the entire family. In this chapter we will explore other types of group counseling, and discuss their advantages and disadvantages.

Group counseling, which involves group activity under the direction of a therapist or group leader, differs from individual, one-to-one interaction between counselor and client in a number of ways. Hatcher defines it in the following manner.

> Group counseling is a planned activity in which three or more people are present for the purpose of solving personal and social problems by applying the theories and methods of counseling in a group. It can be either structured or relatively unstructured in regard to purpose or leadership. It can be an intensive emotional experience or a superficial "bull session." Its primary focus, ideally, is upon the presentation of personal and interpersonal reality in such a way that one has an opportunity to learn about self and others.[1]

Group counseling and group treatment techniques evolved during World War II and in the postwar years. A type of group therapy termed "guided group interaction" was developed by McCorkle and Wolf as a method of treating offenders who were members of the armed forces. Following World War II, the technique was modified and adopted by civilian institutions. The most notable experiment using the guided group interaction technique was undertaken by McCorkle and Bixby in the early 1950s, as part of a delinquency treatment program known as the Highfields Experiment. In this project, as in earlier group work of this type, the group members were called upon to help each other set and work toward specific goals; to lend strong peer support to efforts at positive change; and to exert sanctioning power over negative behavior. The key element of guided group interaction is the problem-solving activity that takes place in the group meetings.[2]

Group counseling was introduced into the correctional system in the 1940s and 1950s for reasons of increased efficiency in handling prisoners rather than because treatment personnel had strong convictions that it would be more effective than individual counseling. California led the way in adopting group counseling, and by 1961 the California prison system had 10,000 inmates and 700 counselors involved in group counseling each week.[3]

Initially, group counseling had a strong educational or training emphasis and only dealt incidentally with efforts to assist offenders in solving their emotional problems. Two new types of group therapy emerged in the 1950s. Although not specifically developed for correctional treatment, they proved to be readily adaptable to correctional settings. Moreno originated "psychodrama," a type of group counseling in which the subject acts out his problems while other group members serve as the various "characters" for the "drama."[4] Psychodrama episodes might include simulations of dialogues with spouses, parents, or acquaintances, with other group members acting the parts of these significant others in the subject's life. Role playing, a similar technique used by Slavson, calls upon various group members to assume certain roles and simulate situations, under the guidance of a therapist or counselor.[5]

The 1960s provided two additional forms of treatment that can be applied in a group setting, reality therapy and transactional analysis. In chapter 6 we noted that reality therapy involves having the correctional client gain an idea of what his immediate needs and behavior requirements are and accept responsibility for them. A group may be the ideal setting for a client to learn just how his behavior is perceived by others, realize that others care what happens to him, and develop a plan for better behavior in the future. Transactional analysis was originated by Berne and modified by Harris. Berne believes that behavior is directed by one of three "ego states": the "Adult" ego state, characterized by rational, mature, responsible behavior; the "Parent" ego state, which is judgmental of the behavior of others; or the "Child" ego state, which involves emotional, self-centered responses.[6] In transactional analysis, the dialogues taking place in the group situation are constantly analyzed and categorized by the group and group leader as representative of one of these ego states. The goal of TA is to help group members learn to interact at the "Adult" ego level.

The 1970s witnessed another development in group counseling. Harry H. Vorrath, who was involved in the earlier Highfields Experiment in guided group interaction, modified and redeveloped this technique into what he called "positive peer culture." This approach, used with juveniles, involves interaction of small groups (approximately nine) of youths under the guidance of a group leader. The influence of peers is brought to bear in identifying problems, deciding how to solve them, developing interest in and concern for all members of the group, and feeling a stake in the success of others. Those involved in positive peer culture groups define their difficulties and seek to solve them with the aid of a list of general and specific problems, which are defined when they exist and when they are solved. The list is given below.

Positive Peer Culture Problem-Solving List

1. *Low self-image:* Has a poor opinion of self; often feels put down or of little worth.
   When solved: Is self-confident and cannot easily be made to feel small or inferior. Is able to solve his problems and make positive contributions to others. Doesn't feel sorry for self even though he may have shortcomings. Believes he is good enough to be accepted by anybody.
2. *Inconsiderate of others:* Does things that are damaging to others.

When solved: Shows concern for others even if he does not like them or know them well. Tries to help people with problems rather than hurt them or put them down.

3. *Inconsiderate of self:* Does things that are damaging to self.
   When solved: Shows concern for self, tries to correct mistakes and improve self. Understands limitations and is willing to discuss problems. Doesn't hurt or put down self.

4. *Authority problem:* Does not want to be managed by anyone.
   When solved: Shows ability to get along with those in authority. Is able to accept advice and direction from others. Does not try to take advantage of authority figures even if they can be manipulated.

5. *Misleads others:* Draws others into negative behavior.
   When solved: Shows responsibility for the effect of his behavior on others who follow him. Does not lead others into negative behavior. Shows concern and helps rather than taking advantage of others.

6. *Easily misled:* Is drawn into negative behavior by others.
   When solved: Seeks out friends who care enough about him not to hurt him. Doesn't blindly follow others to buy friendship. Is strong enough to stand up for himself and makes his own decisions. Doesn't let anyone misuse him.

7. *Aggravates others:* Treats people in negative, hostile ways.
   When solved: Gets along well with others. Does not need to get attention by irritating or annoying others. Gets no enjoyment from hurting or harassing people. Respects others enough not to embarrass, provoke, or bully them.

8. *Easily angered:* Is often irritated or provoked or has tantrums.
   When solved: Is not easily frustrated. Knows how to control and channel anger, not letting it control him. Understands the put-down process and has no need to respond to challenges. Can tolerate criticism or even negative behavior from others.

9. *Stealing:* Takes things that belong to others.
   When solved: Sees stealing as hurting another person. Has no need to be sneaky or to prove himself by stealing. Knows appropriate ways of getting things he wants. Would not stoop to stealing even if he could get away with it.
10. *Alcohol or drug problem:* Misuses substances that could hurt self.
    When solved: Feels good about self and wouldn't hurt self. Does not need to be high to have friends or enjoy life. Can face his problems without a crutch. Shows concern for others who are hurting themselves by abusing alcohol or drugs.
11. *Lying:* Cannot be trusted to tell the truth.
    When solved: Is concerned that others trust him. Has strength to face mistakes and failures without trying to cover up. Does not need to lie or twist the truth to impress others. Tells it like it is.
12. *Fronting:* Puts on an act rather than being real.
    When solved: Is comfortable with people and does not have to keep trying to prove himself. Has no need to act superior, con people, or play the show-off role. Is not afraid of showing his true feelings to others.[7]

In addition to the obvious cost-efficiency factor of treating more than one offender at the same time, group counseling has been rated as having a number of other advantages in the correctional setting. Chief among these is the fact that it can be used to counter the influence of the inmate subculture, which makes strong demands for the prisoner's loyalty and attention. The types of openness and amenability to change that can be developed in group treatment can work to counter the strong pull of the inmate code. In addition, the brain-storming or problem-solving experience of the group as a whole may provide solutions that offenders may not have thought of or may be reluctant to accept from staff members, but will try because peers who have "been there" suggest them. Another advantage of group counseling is that many members of the staff may become involved and have a stake in the treatment outcome. Although trained therapists are needed for certain types of group work, other groups can be ably directed by regular staff, student interns, or even offenders who have received training in the treatment techniques.

There are certain disadvantages to group counseling as well. These include the fact that, unless guided skillfully, sessions may become little more than occasions to air grievances. Offenders, who have the one constant goal of "getting out," may see the group setting as an appropriate spot for "conning" staff members, and may display little sincerity. Deep-seated fears of revealing information that may delay release or result in physical reprisals or ostracism by other inmates can prevent candor in a group setting. Finally, personality characteristics of some offenders make it very difficult for them to feel comfortable or to participate in group sessions.

The choice of the specific treatment technique to be used in a group setting is dependent upon the leader's training, preference, assessment of the group's needs, and the goals set for the group activity. Treatment possibilities for groups designed to be primarily instructive or to attack a specific problem (alcohol or drug addiction, for example) are necessarily more limited than for groups structured for the more general purpose of improving offenders' adjustment within the correctional setting. Problem-solving group work, such as reality therapy, guided group interaction, or positive peer culture, may involve role playing or psychodrama; while group counseling geared to improving the offender's general adjustment to life would be more likely to use such techniques as transactional analysis.

The effectiveness of group counseling in a correctional setting has not been definitively demonstrated. We noted in chapter 2 that Martinson found no indication that group counseling was highly effective in preventing recidivism. Romig, who reviewed the findings of twenty-eight studies involving over 1800 juveniles who took part in group treatment, concluded that:

> The results of the majority of studies were that group counseling did not result in significant behavior changes. At best, group

counseling allowed for the verbal ventilation of negative feelings of institutionalized delinquents. Such emotional catharses did at times positively affect the youths' immediate institutional adjustments. However, institutional behavior changes did not transfer outside the institution.[8]

In analyzing the reasons why the wide variety of group counseling programs he examined failed to change the behavior of youths outside the group itself, Romig decided that the group leaders failed to help the youths transfer what they found out about themselves in the group sessions to their own lives and plans for the future.[9] In the first selection of this chapter, "The Process of Group Counseling," Trotzer notes that an effective group process must involve five stages, if the knowledge gained in the group is to be transferred to activity outside it. These stages are: (1) the security stage, in which the group member is made to feel comfortable and not threatened in the group setting; (2) the acceptance stage, in which the group member comes to know that he is an important part of the group, that others care about him, and that he has certain problems; (3) the responsibility stage, in which the group member takes responsibility for his or her own actions and for finding solutions to his problems; (4) the work stage, during which things found to be unsatisfactory in one's life must be changed; and (5) the closing stage, when the group member accepts the support and encouragement of the group as he or she gradually detaches himself from it.[10] Romig's findings about the ineffectiveness of the majority of group counseling programs seems to indicate that many of the groups failed to get beyond the "acceptance stage" and did not plan specific procedures for the "work stage," when the problems that had been defined by the group should be attacked.

In the second selection of this chapter, "Transactional Analysis: A New Method for Helping Offenders," Nicholson gives a detailed account of the application of the transactional analysis technique in a correctional setting. Various "games" played by those who must make adjustments to prison life are described, and the unique nature of the transactional analysis dialogues that take place in correctional treatment is apparent.

Although group treatment commonly involves from three to twelve participants, the concept of group work can embrace a much larger number of participants. Those who speak of the "therapeutic community" envision the entire institutional setting as a place where professional staff, correctional officers, and inmates are involved in the treatment process. The Highfields Experiment in guided group interaction sought to establish such a therapeutic community. In this chapter's last selection, "Ideology and Correctional Intervention: The Creation of a Just Prison Community," a truly therapeutic atmosphere is proposed. The reasons for the failure of certain other forms of treatment in an institutional setting are examined, and a model for an ideal therapeutic community, based on development of a moral ideology and social awareness on the part of both prisoners and staff, is presented.

Notes

1. Hayes A. Hatcher, *Correctional Casework and Counseling* (Englewood Cliffs, N.J.: Prentice-Hall, 1978), p. 152.

2. Lloyd McCorkle, *The Highfields Story* (New York: Holt, Rinehart and Winston, 1958).

3. Norman Fenton, *An Introduction to Group Counseling in State Correctional Systems* (New York: American Correctional Association, 1961), p. 54.

4. J.L. Moreno, *The First Book on Group Psychotherapy* (New York: Beacon House, 1957).

5. S. R. Slavson, *An Introduction to Group Therapy* (New York: Commonwealth Fund, 1950).

6. Eric Berne, *Transactional Analysis in Psychotherapy* (New York: Grove Press, 1961), p. 19.

7. Harry H. Vorrath and Larry K. Brendtro, *Positive Peer Culture* (Chicago: Aldine, 1974), pp. 37–38.

8. Dennis A. Romig, *Justice for Our Children* (Lexington, Mass.: Lexington Books, 1978), p. 68.

9. Ibid., p. 74.

10. James P. Trotzer, *The Counselor and the Group* (Monterey, Calif.: Brooks/Cole Publishing, 1977), pp. 53–63.

The Process of
Group Counseling

James P. Trotzer

Background

The process of group counseling presented in this chapter has emerged from experience in a variety of settings and with a wide range of clients and age groups. Contributing to this model have been my involvement and leadership experience in schools with upper elementary, junior high, and senior high students, at the Minnesota State Prison working with inmates and staff, at the university level working with undergraduate and graduate students, in numerous human-relations workshops with a variety of educators, in church-related youth retreat groups, in interracial groups, and in other diverse settings as a consultant. Contrary to what might be expected from reading the previous chapter, this process model was developed first (Trotzer, 1972), and the rationale supplied later. In this sense the model is experience-based rather than theory-based and is rooted in observation of actual group interaction rather than in empirical assessment of hypothetical constructs.

Nature of the Process

The model described presents a developmental perspective of group counseling, which is intended for use as an aid in understanding and directing the group process and as a framework for many different theoretical approaches and techniques. The group process itself is divided into five stages. However, the stages are not autonomous or independent of each other. Each stage has certain characteristics that

From The Counselor and the Group: Integrating Theory, Training, and Practice, by J.P. Trotzer, Copyright © 1977 by Wadsworth, Inc. Reprinted by permission of the publisher, Brooks/Cole Publishing Company, Monterey, California.

distinguish it, but their meaning and impact are obtained only within the context of the total group process. The duration of each stage is dependent on the nature of the leader and group members. In some cases, the stages turn over very rapidly; in some, the stages are almost concurrent; and in others, a particular stage may continue for a long period of time and can lead to stagnation in the group process, especially if this occurs early.

Rogers' (1967) description of the group process correlates well with this idea of stages emerging and submerging in group interaction.

> *The interaction is best thought of, I believe, as a varied tapestry, differing from group to group, yet with certain kinds of trends evident in most of these intensive encounters and certain patterns tending to precede and others to follow [p. 263].*

Each stage of the group is like a wave that has momentary identity as it crests but whose beginning and demise are swallowed up in the constant movement of the sea.

The Group Process and Problem-Solving

The stage cycle of the group process reflects characteristics of our basic human needs and depicts the essential qualities of good interpersonal relationships. The model also mirrors a basic pattern for successful problem-solving. The integration of the stages into a conceptualization of a method for resolving problems is readily evident. The stages of security, acceptance, responsibility, work, and closing are easily translated into a step-by-step procedure for resolving personal concerns. First of all, as we experience problems we can't solve, there is a natural tendency to hide or deny them because we don't want negative repercussions in our self-image or in reactions of others around us. Problems threaten our security as persons and our relationships with others. Therefore problems are only shared with others if an atmosphere of safety is part of our relationship with them. Feelings of trust and confidence reduce risk and facilitate our sharing of personal concerns with others. The amount of trust necessary for disclosing our problems is a product of the combined emotional seriousness of the problem and the quality of our relationships. Some problems we experience force us to use disclosure as a means of developing a trusting climate. For example, a client who has recently undergone a traumatic experience—say a close friend was injured while riding in a car the client was driving—may be motivated by intense emotional feelings to share the problem without first determining if the atmosphere is safe. Such risks are sometimes taken without a foreknowledge of trust in the relationship. However, other problems may have emotional or social overtones that demand an atmosphere of confidentiality before any self-revelations occur. In these cases the relationship must develop first and self-disclosure follows. Examples of these kinds of problems include sex problems, drug problems, and difficulties in relationships with significant others such as parents, teachers, or marriage partner. In any event, step one in resolving our problems is to find a safe place in which we can talk about them.

The second step is associated with acceptance. Although the term *acceptance* encompasses a broad range of concepts, such as acceptance of self, acceptance of others, and acceptance by others, a key point in solving a problem is to accept that problem as a part of ourselves. Until we recognize that the problems we experience are part of us, we cannot act constructively to resolve them. Denial and unwillingness to face our problems are the biggest deterrents to their resolution. In order to accept our problems, we need to know that recognition of them as our own will not be devastating to ourselves or to our relationships with others. In other words, our own acceptance of our problems is contingent to a large degree on the reactions or the perceived reactions of others. If we are accepted by others in total, if we feel we can show them all of ourselves including our problems and be received with an empathic ear, we are more willing to identify, share, and acknowledge our problems.

Taking responsibility is the third step in the problem-solving process. After we acknowledge our problems, we must also admit to our part in their cause and shoulder the responsibility to act positively to resolve them. Responsibility brings into focus the action phase of problem-solving. The realization that problem-solving is an active process and that the individual with the problem is primarily responsible for that action is a difficult but necessary step toward resolution. Clients often hope that once they have admitted to, identified, or accepted their problems something almost magical will occur and the problem will be resolved. They sometimes feel that because they have made the courageous effort to reveal themselves, their reward should be instant resolution, or at least that the counselor should take over. Therefore the process of getting clients to take responsibility for themselves is another key step in successful resolution.

The fourth step is to work out the means whereby the problem can be solved. This involves understanding the problem, identifying alternative solutions, evaluating them, planning and practicing new attitudes or behaviors, and trying them out in the real world. The helping relationship at this point is a working relationship in which all parties exert energy and intelligence toward helping the individual find and implement a successful solution.

The final step is to terminate the relationship when clients begin to experience success more than failure in their attempts to integrate changes into their lives. Terminating counseling clients should not only realize their problems are resolved but should have learned the problem-solving process and increased their confidence to use it. The following discussion will describe the life cycle of a group in which the problem-solving characteristics just detailed will be related to the group-counseling process. Each stage will be discussed separately, considering factors such as major identifying characteristics, focus, leader role, and resulting impact.

The Security Stage

The initial stage of the counseling group is characterized by tentativeness, ambiguity, anxiety, suspicion, resistance, discomfort, and other such emotional reactions on the part of both the members and the leader. The members experience these reactions because they are entering a new situation in which they cannot predict what will occur, and they are not confident of their ability to control themselves or relate well to the group. Even though orientation procedures are used, once the group comes together and interaction begins, the cognitive preparation gives way to the normal emotional reactions experienced in new social situations. Uncomfortable feelings also arise because each member is aware that he or she is in counseling and has personal concerns that are not easily shared under any circumstances.

An example of the inner turmoil a group member experiences was demonstrated by a young woman who requested admittance to a therapy group at a university counseling center. During the first session she paced and stood outside the room, struggling with the decision of whether to enter or not. The group leader, aware of her fears and misgivings about the group, left the door open and indicated to her that she could come in when she was ready. Toward the end of the session she entered the room and stood against the wall but did not join the group until the second session. So extensive was her discomfort that she did not participate until the fourth session and did not risk disclosing anything about herself until much later. Although most group members do not experience reactions to that extent, feelings of discomfort in the early sessions are always prevalent.

The security stage is a period of testing for the group members, and much of this testing takes the form of resistance, withdrawal, or hostility. Bonney (1969) points out that "resistance and hostility toward the leader and conflict among group members are ... expected outgrowths of the basic insecurity of procedural direction and uncertainty concerning the capacity of the group to achieve its proposed aims" (p. 165). The testing takes many forms and is aimed in many directions but the most common challenges are leveled at leader competency, ground rules, and other members' actions. Rogers (1967) feels that negative expressions are a way of testing the trustworthiness and freedom of the group. All persons in the group experience some form of nervousness that generates defending types of behaviors rather than the authentic sharing of feelings.

The focus during this initial period must take into account these insecure feelings of the members. Underlying concerns that brought the members to the group should be set aside for the moment, and the here-and-now discomfort facing the group should be worked with. Some leaders like to use group warm-ups to help members express and work through these initial feelings and to establish a comfortable rapport within the group. The individual problems of the members, though they may be categorically similar, are most likely quite dissimilar in the perception of each member at this point. Thus it is important to establish a common ground so that members can make contact with each other and open lines of communication.

Since each member is preoccupied with dissatisfactions in his or her own life, an immediate focus on any one problem would lead to a rather disjointed process, which would run a high risk of losing the involvement and cooperation of all the members. This type of emphasis might also allow some members to go too deeply too quickly and scare off others. Cohn (1973) warned leaders to avoid this possibility and stressed that one essential feature of the group process is that members must be moved to deeper levels of interaction together. By initially focusing on the discomfort that all are experiencing, a common ground is established, which moves the group toward more cohesiveness. This identification with one another helps members overcome feelings of isolation and lays the foundation for the development of trust (Trotzer, 1972).

A significant aspect of the security stage is the leader's part in sharing the discomfort. Seldom will a leader enter a group without some feelings of uneasiness and hesitancy. These feelings do not reflect the skill and experience of the counselor but rather are indicative of the effort involved in working toward closeness between people and helping people with problems. If leaders do not enter groups with some of these feelings, they are probably not prepared to become involved in the very personal worlds of the members.

The leader's role in the security stage is to perform what Lifton (1966) calls "security-giving operations." Leaders must be able to gain the confidence of the members, display warmth and understanding, provide for the various needs of the members, and create and maintain a friendly and safe atmosphere in the group. Sensitivity, awareness, and an ability to communicate feelings and observations to the group without dominating it are important qualities of group leadership at this stage of the group's development.

As the group resolves the discomfort of the artificial situation, members can begin delving into the problems in their lives, and as members share their common feelings and perceptions, trust develops. Cohn (1964) emphasizes this concept of trust, suggesting that once group members trust and are trusted the groundwork is laid for making the effort needed to improve their real-life situations. Rogers (1967) states that the "individual will gradually feel safe enough to drop some of his defenses and facades" (p. 8). The members will become more willing to show their inner selves rather than just their outer selves. They will begin to direct energy toward expression— communication that allows oneself to be known to others authentically and transparently—rather than impression—communication that involves putting on a face in order to attract others (Schmuck & Schmuck, 1971).

Ohlsen (1970) also described the impact of the security stage:

> When clients come to feel reasonably secure within their counseling group, they can be themselves, discuss the problems that bother them, accept others' frank reactions to them and express their own genuine feelings toward others [p. 91].

In other words, the development of trust provides the basis for getting down to the business of working on one's problems. Vorrath (n.d.) adds that the most dynamic experience members "gain from the group is that they learn to trust people" (p. 9). So trust has a process dimension and an outcome dimension, which give it a two-fold impact in the group process. During the security stage the development of a trusting, nonthreatening atmosphere is the primary objective. This objective is in accord with each member's basic human need for security. As trust increases, the willingness for personal involvement and commitment increases. Members are more likely to risk letting themselves and their problems, frustrations, joys, and successes be known. Because of the atmosphere created by the movement toward trust, the individual members feel freer to be themselves. When this occurs the transition into the second stage of the group-counseling process takes place.

The Acceptance Stage

The acceptance stage is directly related to our need for love and belonging and therefore has many derivatives that influence the direction of the group process. Generally this stage is characterized by a movement away from resistance and toward cooperation on the part of group members. As members begin to overcome the discomfort and threat of the group, the grounds for their fears dissipate and they become more accepting of the group situation. As they become more familiar with the group's atmosphere, procedures, leader, and members, they become more comfortable and secure in the group setting. They accept the group structure and the leader's role. This acceptance does not mean the purpose of the group is clear to members, but it does mean they are accepting the method. The meaning and purpose of the counseling group must be derived from the group members not from the group structure.

Inherent in the group members' acceptance of the group as a vehicle for their interaction is their need to belong and the need for relatedness. The members' desire to be a part of the group emerges as an important motivating factor. This desire is inwardly evident to the individual from the outset of the group. But at first it's stifled for fear of acting in a manner that might ultimately jeopardize that belonging. However, with the foundation of trust established, the members are more willing to be their real selves and risk being known for the sake of being accepted. A journal entry of a 24-year-old Vietnam veteran who chose an alcohol treatment center rather than jail effectively depicts the acceptance stage of the group process:

> At first there was no way I was going to admit to being an alcoholic or even that I had a drinking problem. But as I listened to the other guys talk about booze in their lives I began to realize they were all talking about many of the same experiences I had. The first thought that came to me was "Hey, you can't fool these cats because they've been there." I felt lots of pressure to 'fess up' but still held back because I wasn't sure how they (the group) would take me nor was I sure I could stomach myself if I did. I finally decided to share my drinking problems when I saw the group treat another Nam vet in the group in a sensitive way,

> *giving him support and help with a problem I thought was even*
> *worse than mine. When I did admit I had a drinking problem*
> *the group seemed to open up to me and let me in, and I also liked*
> *myself better.*

As acceptance is experienced, relationships grow, and cohesiveness develops. Cohesiveness is important to the group process because it makes group members more susceptible to the influence of each other and the group. It also provides the impetus for group productivity. It is a key factor in the helping process in groups because "those who are to be changed and those who influence change must sense a strong feeling of belonging in the same group" (Ohlsen, 1970, p. 88). Thus group cohesiveness meets the members' needs to belong, provides them with a temporary protective shield from the outside world, and is a potent therapeutic factor in the change process.

The therapeutic influence of cohesiveness makes use of peer-group dynamics as its key resource in the group. As members experience genuine acceptance by fellow members, self-esteem is enhanced, ego is strengthened, self-confidence is bolstered, and they develop more courage in facing up to their problems. The impact of feeling accepted by a group of one's peers is stated succinctly by Gawrys and Brown (1963):

> *To be accepted and understood by the counselor is a satisfying*
> *experience: to be accepted and understood by a number of indi-*
> *viduals is profound (p. 106).*

Within this context, then, the potential of peer-group influence can be used in a positive manner by the counselor. The group leader's role in this stage is no small factor in generating an accepting atmosphere in the group and contributing directly to the individual members' experience of feeling accepted. Leaders must be models of acceptance from the onset of the total group process. They must demonstrate a genuine caring for each of the group members. Their leadership must be characterized by acceptance of each person regardless of the behaviors he or she has exhibited outside the group. The process of acceptance is initiated by leaders who practice Rogers' (1962) concept of unconditional positive regard. As the members experience acceptance from the leader, they feel more accepting of themselves and follow the leader's model in their actions toward one another. As members feel more accepting of themselves and other members, a total atmosphere of acceptance is created.

This brings us to the primary objective of the acceptance stage from a problem-solving perspective—developing acceptance of self.

For members' problems to surface in the group they must feel free to be truly themselves without fear of rejection or reprisal. As already stated, members cannot deal effectively with their problems without recognition that the problems are a part of them. Further, they must know that even though they have problems they are still persons of worth and importance. All people have the desire to like and accept themselves and to be liked and accepted by others. It is this desire that the group utilizes in helping members deal with their problems. When each member can accept feelings, thoughts, and behaviors, whether good or bad, as part of themselves and still feel accepted and respected as a person of worth, a big step has been taken in the helping process of the group.

The focus during the acceptance stage should be on the whole person and not just on isolated problem areas. In order to attain self-acceptance and acceptance of others, members must work with the total picture of themselves and others. Getting to know oneself and each other, engaging in "who am I?" and "who are you?" activities, serve to promote self-disclosure. As individuals share themselves and describe their problems, accepting problems as part of themselves occurs more naturally and is less threatening. Many leaders like to incorporate the first two stages of security and acceptance, using structured personal-sharing activities and techniques to do so. In this way sharing promotes trust, and trust encourages sharing. And members find that many of their concerns are similar to those of other members. This similarity among members leads to identification with each other and the group and facilitates openness. As members can speak more freely about their problems, they find they can embrace them without losing self-esteem or position in the group; and this experience paves the way for the more individualistic stage of responsibility.

The results of the second stage of the group-counseling process include acceptance of the group structure and the leader's role, meeting individual needs for love and belonging, acceptance of self, acceptance of others, and acceptance of problems as part of oneself. This may sound like a big order to fill, and it is. But acceptance is also a powerful force in facilitating the problem-solving process. When established, it removes many of the roadblocks in the counseling process. It enables the group to begin constructive individual help. The development of acceptance accomplishes three main objectives (Trotzer, 1972).

> *1. It aids the group in becoming cohesive and close thus meeting Gendlin and Beebe's (1968) guideline that "closeness must precede unmasking."*

2. *It helps each individual feel accepted as a person of worth even though life is not satisfactory at the moment. This meets Gendlin and Beebe's (1968) guideline of putting "people before purpose."*
3. *It releases the potential of peer-group influence to be used in a positive rather than negative manner.*

The Responsibility Stage

The third stage of the group-counseling process is characterized by a movement on the part of group members from acceptance of self and others to responsibility for self. There is a subtle but distinct difference between acceptance of and responsibility for self. Acceptance helps members realize and admit that problems are a part of their selves. However, acceptance alone leaves members with an avenue of retreat away from working on their problems. Members can say "yes, that's the way I am" or "that's my problem" but can disclaim any part in its cause or rectification. Acceptance allows members to claim no fault and negates any responsibility for doing anything about changing. The inclusion of responsibility, however, moves members toward resolution. The combination of acceptance and responsibility encourages members to state "yes, that's my problem, and I have to do something about it." The ground is thus made fertile for constructive change to take place.

A single mother with two children who shared her problems and frustrations in a women's counseling group at a mental-health center exemplifies the difference between acceptance and responsibility. During the fourth group meeting she talked extensively about the pain of her divorce and the subsequent difficulties of trying to raise her children alone. She became very emotional at times, and the group facilitated catharsis in a very sensitive manner. At the end of the session the group leader helped the woman put herself back together emotionally and solicited feedback from the group couched in terms of support. During the following session she was again the focus of attention, but this time members began to suggest alternatives that could possibly help her improve her life. To each alternative she responded by saying, "I already tried that" or "I don't think that would work." After several attempts to get her to consider alternatives failed, one member observed that maybe she really didn't want to do anything different in her life to overcome the problems. The woman denied that but soon afterward asked that the focus of group attention be directed elsewhere. During the following sessions this woman's problem was brought up several times by herself, other group members, or the leader, but the discussion always stalemated at the point of her taking any responsibility for the problems or for initiating changes. Eventually she told the group that she felt her problems were the result of others being unfair and insensitive to her and that she was a victim and not a cause in her situation. Soon afterward she left the group. She was willing to share her problems in the group but was not able to see herself as a contributor or take the initiative to work toward resolving them.

The issue of responsibility in the group emanates from both our needs as human beings and the nature of the problem-solving process. Members can only meet their need for esteem and respect through actions and achievements that require the person to take responsibility. If members feel causes are external they will also feel the cures must come from sources external to themselves and not from within.

Our needs are reflected in the pressure of the counseling group to move on. The social aspect of cohesiveness developed in the acceptance stage wears thin after a while, and there is a natural tendency toward getting down to the business of problems. This tendency, according to Bonney (1969), is a mark of group maturity in that group members begin to accept responsibility for the management of the group and exert their energies to the task of problem-solving. As members take increased responsibility for themselves and the therapeutic process, their chances for growth within the counseling group improve. In fact, Lindt (1958) found that only those who accepted responsibility in the helping process of the group benefited from their experience.

During the early stages of the group process the task is to develop trust and acceptance by focusing on similarities among members. This process universalizes. It helps members recognize that their problems are experienced by others (universalization), even though individual differences are apparent (Dinkmeyer and Muro, 1971). During the responsibility stage the focus changes to individualization and differentiation based on each person's uniqueness and responsibility. The atmosphere of the group provides for considerable personal freedom with the implication that members have permission to explore their weaknesses, strengths, and potentialities, to determine a way of working on problems, and to express feelings. The here-and-now emphasis is a key component in the responsibility stage, but it takes on a broader, problem-oriented perspective. During the early stages of the group the here-and-now is restricted to present feelings about the group and one's part in it and to help members focus on their here-and-now problems outside the group as well. This can be done in a step-by-step process in which expression of feelings is the starting point. The expression of personal feelings and perceptions about self and others is one basis for learning responsibility in the group. To emphasize taking responsibility for what one feels, leaders can ask members to state their own perceptions and to tack on the statement "and I take responsibility for that feeling." In this manner members learn to take responsibility for expressing hostility and caring without the threat and risk usually associated with the expression of such feelings.

As the members learn to accept responsibility for their personal feelings it becomes easier to accept responsibility for their actions and eventually their problems. These steps must be taken if the counselor and the group are to have any significant impact on the individual member's life. Mahler (1969) emphasizes the importance of responsibility for oneself:

> Counselees must realize the importance of being responsible for their own lives, behavior, and actions, making their own decisions and learning to stand on their own perceptions [p. 140].

He adds that:

> People need opportunities to learn that only by taking actions, making decisions, and accepting responsibility for their own lives can they become adults in the full sense of the word [p. 141].

Group counseling gives them that opportunity.

The leader's role during this stage centers around helping members realize self-responsibility. Lakin (1969) and Glasser (1965) stress the modeling nature of the leader role in which the counselor's actions must depict the proper attitude toward responsibility. Glasser feels that responsibility can only be learned through involvement with responsible people. Therefore the member's primary example to follow in the group is the leader. The leader must help members maintain a focus on themselves and their problems at this point, rather than on events, people, or situations external to the group and beyond its influence. The counseling group can only affect people and situations through its effect on the person in the immediate presence of the group. The counselor must stress an internal frame of reference rather than an external one. The question that ultimately must be faced is not "what can others do?" but "what can I do?"

The leader faces a crucial issue during the responsibility stage, and a word of caution is apropos. In our concern for our clients to "make it on their own," we often see opportunities in the group process that could be used to "teach" members responsibility. This situation must be avoided. For group members to become responsible they must experience responsibility, not be told about it. It is appropriate at times to bring up the issue of responsibility or even to confront members with it, but the choice to be responsible should be left to the members. Mahler (1969) feels that "counselors who teach in group counseling violate the concept that basic responsibility for management of one's own life is up to the individual" (p. 103). Therefore leadership should be directed toward helping members feel accepted and responsible without domination. When successful, members will feel more personal, individual responsibility and will exhibit less dependency.

The responsibility stage sets the tone for the remainder of the group-counseling process. Once members realize their responsibility for themselves and understand that neither the leader nor the group will infringe upon it, the members can direct their entire attention to problem-solving. The responsibility stage affirms the inherent worth of the members, assures them of respect as human beings, and points out the qualities necessary to enhance self-worth and resolve problems. Those qualities are self-assessment, congruence, honesty, responsibility, and commitment. When the members willingly engage in the introspective process, self-disclose, demonstrate their acceptance of others and willingness to help others, and—with very little or no help from the leader—take responsibility, the work stage of the counseling process is imminent.

The Work Stage

The character of the work stage organizes itself around the individual problems and concerns of the group members. As trust, acceptance, and responsibility are experienced and learned, it becomes increasingly evident that there are some areas in each members' life that are not satisfactory and could benefit from change. When these areas are pinpointed and discussed specifically, the work stage goes into full operation. Vorrath (n.d.) feels that the core of the group process is reached at this point, because the goal of this type of group is to work on problems and get them solved.

The work stage of group counseling is exemplified by the interaction of a human-relations group designed to improve communication and relationships between racial groups in a large urban high school. The members decided that the basic problem was not knowing how to approach students who were racially different from themselves. They tended to be hesitant, fearing overtones of prejudice might be communicated. To work on this problem, the leader first had racially similar members discuss their perceptions of racially different groups and then make suggestions that they felt would facilitate better relationships. After each subgroup had discussed their perceptions and made their suggestions, a comprehensive list of suggestions was developed in terms of skills. The leader than formed racially mixed dyads to try out the suggestions. During their work stage, partners were rotated periodically to give members the experience of trying out alternatives and building their skills and confidence with all racial groups represented.

The basic purposes of the work stage are to give group members the opportunity to (1) examine personal problems closely in an environment free of threat, (2) explore alternatives and suggestions for resolving the problems, and (3) try out new behaviors or attitudes in a safe setting prior to risking changes outside the group (Trotzer, 1972). The energy of the group is concentrated on accomplishing these three purposes through the use of feedback, clarification, and information-giving. Once in motion the productivity of the group is quite amazing and at times needs to be held in check because of the tendency to begin to solve problems before they are fully understood.

The leader role in the work stage is extremely vital from two perspectives. Leaders must be both facilitator and expert. They must be able to facilitate the discussion of problems, bringing out as many facets as possible, and create an atmosphere where alternatives can be suggested. These two processes entail mustering the total perceptual and experiential resources of the group. After a particular problem has been discussed and alternative solutions suggested, leaders must use their expertise to provide vehicles for examining the consequences of the suggestions as a means of aiding the decision-making process. These activities can take the form of role-playing, sociodramas, communication exercises, or discussion. In this way alternatives can be assessed and evaluated, thus avoiding shot-in-the-dark failures. This type of reality testing in the group provides the group member with an idea of both the feasibility of a specific alternative and the effort involved in using it to resolve the problem. It also provides the member with an opportunity to develop self-confidence before attempting to make any specific changes in the more threatening world outside the group.

Another important facet of the group process that surfaces during the work stage is the dual role of the group member as both the helper and the helped. When any one member of the group is working on a particular problem, the other members provide help through their feedback, sharing, suggestions, discussion, and participation in group activities. The experience of being in the helper role increases the members' feelings of self-worth because now they are in the position of giving rather than receiving. The giving of assistance to others also produces a more congenial attitude toward receiving assistance from others. The two-way process of helping and being helped is thus established. This process makes good use of members' altruistic tendencies, as well as allowing them to engage in "spectator therapy" where they benefit from watching others work out their problems.

During this stage the group also represents "society in microcosm" (Gazda, 1968c); that is, group members represent, as best they can, the forces, attitudes, reactions, and ideas of the world outside the group. Through the process of feedback the group helps each member develop realistic alternatives to problems that can reasonably be applied in their lives outside the group. This minisociety function is important because of its transitional value in preparing members for the task of implementing changes.

In the work stage the "healing capacity" (Rogers, 1967) of the group emerges, and the specific goals and objectives of the counseling group are dealt with. Each group has different objectives based on the diversity of the group membership and the setting in which the group is formed. However, since most counseling groups are usually organized to deal with specific problems, it is at this point in the group process where efforts are focused on resolving them. The work stage prepares members for reentry into the world where they are experiencing their problems. They are armed with a well-conceived and evaluated plan, and self-confidence has been shored up through practice and personal encouragement. However, individuals do not have to make the changes and implement their plans without some support, which brings us to the final stage of the group process, closing.

The Closing Stage

The final stage of the group-counseling process is mainly supportive in nature and is characterized by feedback, encouragement, and perseverance. Although group members may successfully work through their problems within the group, they still face the difficult task of modifying their behavior and attitudes outside the group. The expectations of significant others outside the group are still based on past experience with the group member, thus making it difficult to give encouragement or reinforcement to the member for acting in new or different ways. The group is a place where members can share their frustrations, successes, and failures and also reassess their actions for possible changes that will increase their effectiveness. Without a source of support, the chance of regression to old ways is greater.

The group also serves as a motivator. Part of this function entails rejecting excuses and confronting members with their own lack of commitment and effort if need be. Sometimes members need to be pushed out into the real world when they cannot venture forth on their own. The group has uncanny competence in assessing whether members are authentic in their efforts and whether they have performed up to their capability. During this stage the group can be both a sounding board and a control board.

Group support facilitates the integration of change into the client's life. Efforts to change and the change process itself are supported until reinforcement occurs in members' lives outside the group. As the changes become more natural parts of their life-styles, the difficulty of adapting new behaviors, feelings, and attitudes decreases. The support of the group is only necessary until the balance between ease and difficulty in implementing change swings to the ease side of the scale.

The focus of the group thus turns to members' behavior and experience outside the group and deals with progress they are making. The leader helps members discuss their experiences and feelings, offering support, understanding, and encouragement. The leader also helps members begin to take credit for their own changes instead of giving credit to the group or the counselor. In this way the individual members can integrate their new behaviors and attitudes into their everyday lives and can feel reinforcement from within themselves rather than from the group.

The closing stage for individuals may take many different forms. For example, a student who had been a member of a therapy group at a college counseling center for three years began to miss group meetings, showing up periodically but with longer time lapses between attendance. As she entered the final semester of her senior year, she relied less and less on the group for feedback and support taking more and more responsibility for herself. Her need for the group and her involvement in the group lessened, with termination coinciding with graduation.

Another example of the closing stage is the standard procedure used at an alcohol treatment center when individual patients are preparing to leave treatment. The patient's group holds a graduation ceremony for the departing member during which that person makes a commencement address reviewing and summarizing the treatment and describing goals and objectives for the future. The group then engages in a serenity prayer during which group members give support, feedback, and encouragement to the graduating member. The person is then presented with a coin that has a missing piece symbolizing the unending process involved in rehabilitation and growth. The ceremony thus serves to summarize and reinforce changes that have occurred but also prepares the person for the rigors of adjusting to life outside of the treatment center.

The point at which a group or individual member should terminate is sometimes difficult to determine. For this reason groups are often terminated on the basis of a preset time schedule, for example, after ten sessions or at the end of a quarter or semester. However, ending a group is also appropriate when group members experience more success than failure in solving their problems and feel intrinsic rather than extrinsic reinforcement for their actions in doing so. As members become more dependent on themselves, they lose their dependence on the group. As they resolve their problems and learn how to solve problems, they no longer need the group. When any of these situations occur the group has run its course and should be disbanded.

A Precautionary Note

Viewing group counseling as a developmental sequence of a set number of stages raises the possibility of unnecessary and undesirable rigidity in conceptualizing the group process. To circumvent this and maintain flexibility in this group model, it is necessary to remember that within each stage there can be many levels. Different degrees of trust, acceptance, and responsibility are reached by the group and its members at different times. Some problems discussed in the group require less trust than others. At other times it may be necessary for the process to recycle, developing deeper levels of trust, acceptance, or responsibility in order to deal with a particular problem. Bonney (1969) refers to this occurrence as the retransition stage in which the group goes back through the early phases of group development before proceeding to a deeper level. At any one time and with any one problem or person the group may have to retreat to a previous stage before it can move on to the next one. In fact, all stages may recur several times before the group has run its course.

Another consideration is that components of two or more stages may be prominent in the group at the same time. The group may be learning trust, acceptance, and responsibility while working on a particular problem. The group does not develop in a lock-step manner even though general trends can be noted and specific characteristics consistently appear at certain points in the group's development. Neither can the group process be forced to conform to an external standard or model. Rather it is a responsive and flexible process that is influenced by the leader's personality, by differences between people and their problems, and by variations in the rate at which different people develop relationships and work out individual change.

Concluding Comments

Group counseling brings into perspective the relationship between psychological needs and the socialization process, whereby human learning and problem-solving occurs through interaction. It accentuates the social learning process by focusing on the dynamics of the group itself rather than on some environmental context. Group members are given the opportunity to learn how they function individually and interpersonally. They can do this because the leader and other members have created a climate or atmosphere characterized by psychological safety and acceptance where they can take responsibility for their own lives. In such a situation members can experience the healthy attributes of individuality or uniqueness and relatedness or conformity. They learn both independence and interdependence.

Members can express themselves freely and engage in open and honest interaction with other members without the fear of rejection or reprisal that so often tempers interaction in one's environment. Within the group members can experience and learn responsibility. They can confront problems openly, knowing they will obtain support and assistance as needed. Members experience the interchanging role of being the helper and the helped as they work on their own problems and assist others with theirs. The member can discover and evaluate alternative solutions to personal concerns while at the same time building self-confidence and personal security, which serve as enabling factors in implementing change outside the group. Thus group counseling provides both a setting and a process whereby the basic objectives of a counseling program can be attained.

Learning Activities

The exercises presented here are organized in sequence to relate to the stages of group development discussed in this chapter. Although the primary characteristic and use of each activity is stage-related, there are also many other purposes for which they can be used. These activities are versatile and adaptable, depending on the leader's approach and the nature of the group.

Trust Ring[1]

Option I. This exercise is useful in demonstrating the characteristics of trust and confidentiality that are necessary for a group to work effectively. Have all group members stand in a circle in an area that is free of material objects such as chairs or tables. Members should have a strong grip on each of their partners' hands or wrists. Then have the group extend out as far as possible forming a taut circle. Instruct all members to lean back exerting pressure on the circle and slowly move their feet toward the center of the circle creating a centrifugal pressure on the group. Have the group move in a clockwise direction maintaining this centrifugal pressure. After a few moments reverse the direction. Follow the exercise with a discussion of each person's reaction in terms of the amount of pressure they were personally willing to place on the group and their feelings regarding their partners and the total group. Stress the importance of the whole group going to the aid of individuals who were slipping in order to protect them and maintain solidarity in the group. Discussion can also focus on the amount of pressure the group as a whole exerted relating it to risk-taking in self-disclosure and feedback.

Option II. A variation of this exercise is to have members stand in a circle shoulder to shoulder. Instruct the members to interlock their arms around the back or waist of the persons beside them. Then have the group members lean inward and slowly move their feet away from the center of the group creating a centripetal force on the group. Have the group move alternately in a clockwise and counterclockwise manner. At the conclusion of the exercise have the group members retain their interlocking positions in the circle and discuss the reactions in the same manner as described above. An added feature of this discussion can be the impact of closeness created by the "arms around each other" dimension, relating it to the effect of warmth and closeness in developing cohesiveness and trust in the group.

Option III. This exercise is useful in working with individual members who are having difficulty developing, feeling, or understanding trust in the group. It is particularly effective in working with individuals who wish to trust the group but are having difficulty doing so. Stand one member in the center of the group and have the other members form a standing circle around him. The initial distance between the person in the center and the circle members should be relatively small but large enough to allow freedom of movement. Instruct the member in the center to close his eyes and place his feet together.

Then instruct him to fall toward the circle without moving his feet and allow the group to move him back and forth and around. The outside circle should vary the distance they allow the person to fall and the roughness they use in handling him but always be responsible for the member's safety. Follow-up discussion should center on the individual's feelings and reactions. The main thrust is to help the individual come to grips with feelings about trust and to point out the important group dynamics associated with individuals sharing problems or disclosing themselves in a group situation.

Closed Fist[2]

This activity lends itself to a consideration of the strategies used by people in negotiating trust in human relationships. It is particularly applicable to group counseling because of the risk intrinsic to the process of sharing. Break the group down into dyads. Ask the partners to exchange some material object that they value (such as a ring, a picture, or a wallet). Have each partner put the object away out of sight for the time being. Then instruct the members to think of something that is extremely valuable to them, something they would not wish to give up under any circumstances. Give the group a few minutes to choose something. Then ask one of the partners to figuratively place the thing of value in a closed fist without telling the partner what it is. Instruct the other partner to try to get it. Allow this process to proceed for a time without any intervention. Then ask for an account of what happened, noting the different strategies that were used to obtain the object and pointing out their relevance to the group process. After this discussion ask the members to try to get back the actual objects they exchanged initially.

Important factors to consider in this exercise are the type of exchange strategies that produce competitiveness, cooperation, ill will, and positive interpersonal feelings. Strategies that are conducive to positive relationships should be used in the group. Also, the value of the objects exchanged reflects the amount of commitment and trust in the relationship. Members will share more willingly and at a deeper level if there is reciprocal sharing by other members.

Life Story

Vorrath (n.d.) uses this technique to introduce new members into the group. It is especially appropriate for ongoing counseling groups that experience member turnover. New members after a brief period of time in the group are asked to tell their life stories as completely and as accurately as they possibly can. The life stories should include a description of the problems that brought the new people into the group. The other group members have the responsibility of facilitating the new member's efforts. Under no circumstances should the views of the person be challenged at this point. After the story is completed the group can begin to work with discrepancies or other factors that might relate to solving the member's problems. The main impact of this technique is that members realize their side of the story is going to be heard first. They receive guarantees that their frame of reference is important and will be considered by the group. They experience acceptance and find the group is a safe place to air their problems.

Poem of Self

This exercise helps establish a minimum level of self-acceptance for each group member and helps the group become involved in introspection and self-disclosure essential to the group process. Use the following directions in carrying out the exercise.

1. List four words (adjectives) that describe what you look like.
2. List four words (adjectives) that describe what you act like (personality).
3. List five words ending in "ing" that describe things you like to do (if you like to read, put reading).
4. List six things (nouns) that would remind people of you (for example, possessions, such as a guitar, or roles you play, such as a student).
5. List four places you would like to be.
6. On a sheet of paper draw the following diagram (you may want to hand out a mimeo form).

$$
\begin{array}{ccc}
& \underline{\quad} & \\
\underline{\quad} & & \underline{\quad} \\
\underline{\quad} & \underline{\quad} & \underline{\quad} \\
\underline{\quad} \quad \underline{\quad} & \underline{\quad} & \underline{\quad} \\
& \underline{\quad} \quad \underline{\quad} & \\
& \underline{\quad} &
\end{array}
$$

7. On the first line of the diagram write your full name.

8. Choose one word from list 1 (what you look like) and one word from list 2 (what you act like) and place them in the blanks in line 2.
9. Choose three words from list 3 (things you like to do) and insert them in the blanks in line 3.
10. Choose four words from list 4 (things that remind people of you) and write them in the blanks in line 4.
11. Choose two words from list 5 (places) and write them in the blanks in line 5.
12. On the bottom line write a nickname or any name by which you are called other than your given name. (This may be a derivative of your given name, such as "Toni" for Antoinette.)

On completion of the poem have each member read his or her poem to the group twice, the first time quickly with rhythm and the second time slowly so that they can catch all the words. After everyone has read and explained the meaning of the words in their poems discuss how the exercise contributed to getting to know one another.

Coat of Arms

The coat of arms has more depth to it than the poem of self and can be used in conjunction with it. This activity gets at more varied aspects of each person's life and provides a good beginning for the actual counseling process. It also combines the medium of illustration with verbal description, which makes sharing an easier process. Give each person a sheet of paper with the illustrated diagram on it or have the people draw it. Then have them fill in the numbered sections of the shield according to the following instructions.

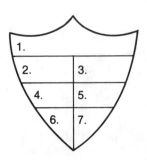

1. In the section numbered 1, write a motto or phrase that describes how you feel about life or that is a guide to your life-style. (Some people create their own; others use quotations, poems, or Bible verses.)
2. In section 2, draw a picture that represents your greatest achievement or accomplishment (no words).
3. Draw a picture that represents something other people could do to make you happy (no words).
4. Draw a picture that represents a failure or disappointment (no words).
5. Draw a picture that represents the biggest goal in your life right now (no words).
6. Draw a picture that represents a problem you would like to work on in this group (no words).
7. Write down three things you would like people to say about you if you died today.

After all the members have completed the shield, have each member describe his or hers to the group, explaining the meaning of each section. This exercise has the positive impact of acceptance since it deals with each person's strengths, weaknesses, goals, relationships with others, and problems. The instructions for the various parts can be changed to meet the demands of the situation and the needs of the members, thus making this exercise a flexible and effective tool in the hands of the group leader.

Strength Bombardment
One means of helping group members accept responsibility for themselves is to approach it from a perspective of strengths, assets, and accomplishments the member is already aware of. This exercise uses the process of self-disclosure and feedback to help members take responsibility for their behavior. First, have each group member develop a list of all positive accomplishments or achievements. Encourage the members to feel completely free about the list and not to think about the reactions of others or about the ego-related emotional connotations such a request usually conjures up. On completion of the list, have the members write a paragraph, starting with "I am," that describes their positive qualities. Assure them that no one else will see the paragraph, but indicate that they should include only positive qualities and not put in any negative ones. When the paragraph is completed have members put it away, stating that they can do what

they want with it. Now have the members share their initial list of accomplishments with the group. Then place two chairs facing each other in the center of the circle. Ask one member to volunteer to take one of the chairs in order to receive positive feedback from the other members. When one person has taken a chair, each other person in turn gets up, sits in the opposite chair and gives the first person only positive feedback. There should be no "I would like you if" or "I like you but" comments, and the person receiving the feedback can only respond with expressions of appreciation, not with denials or counter remarks. This process continues until each person has received positive feedback from every other person in the group. On completion of the activity, relate the experience to the issue of responsibility and discuss how one's positive qualities can be used to help overcome one's negative qualities and problems.

Awareness and Responsibility

This technique has developed out of the Gestalt approach to group therapy and combines the concepts of personal awareness and individual responsibility. It has relevance to group counseling because it clarifies where members are personally and helps them take responsibility for their own thoughts, feelings and behavior in the group. Each group member is asked to share with the group present thoughts, feelings, and perceptions or observations using the format: "Right now I am aware . . . [members complete the statement describing what they are aware of], and I take responsibility for that." The last part of the statement is added to get individuals to affirm their own part in feeling, acting, or thinking the way they do and to prevent them from putting responsibility on others. A leader can effectively use the last part of the statement by simply asking members to add it to any statement involving a personal emotion, accusation, interpretation, or perception. In this way, the impact of the statement becomes just one person's frame of reference and allows other members the freedom to respond as they see fit without feeling threatened by the imposition of another person's point of view on them.

Gestalt Interventions

One of the ways we avoid being responsible for ourselves and in control of our own lives is through the words we use in communication (Stevens, 1971). The following intervention techniques drawn from the Gestalt approach to group therapy can be used to help group members take responsibility for their own thoughts, feelings, and behaviors and ultimately for their problems.

1. *Questions or Statements.* Many questions that group members ask are really camouflaged statements. Before responding with an answer ask the questioner to change the question into a statement that expresses personal perceptions, observations, or feelings.

2. *I Can't/I Won't Statements.* Members often use the words "I can't" in discussing problem situations, which give the impression that control is really outside of themselves. When you hear an "I can't" statement ask the member to repeat the statement using "I won't," which conveys the message that the person has a choice in the matter. "I just can't talk to my father" changes to "I just won't talk to my father."

3. *I Have to/I Choose to Statements.* Have group members make a list of "I have to" statements describing all the things in their lives that they feel they have to do. Have them share their lists in the group. Then have them change "I have to" to "I choose to" and discuss the differences between the two lists. Discussion usually pinpoints quite clearly the issue of personal responsibility and choice. As a group leader you can also ask members to substitute "I choose to" for "I have to" during group discussions. In doing this the members realize that they are responsible and that they do have a choice.

4. *I Need/I Want Statements.* Group members often express desires as needs, creating the impression that severe personal consequences will result if needs are not met. They say "I need," which depicts whatever it is as essential to their well-being. To define more accurately what really is needed and what can be done without, have members change "I need" statements to "I want" statements and discuss which is more appropriate, incorporating feedback from other members as to the accuracy of the statement.

Problem Identification and Rating

The work stage is the point in the group process at which problems should be dealt with directly. This exercise pinpoints problems that are pertinent to individual members and are relevant to other members' lives as well. Have the members anonymously write down a description of a problem they would be willing to discuss with the group. Stress the "willing to discuss" aspect. When the descriptions are finished, read them one by one to the group. After each problem is read ask members to individually rate it on a scale (5 is high and 1 is low), showing their interest in discussing the problem and their identification with it. Record each individual rating and after reading and rating all the problems, add up the totals. A hierarchy of problems develops based on the scores. Reread the highest rated problem and ask the person who wrote it to describe it in detail. The group can then work with that specific person and problem.

This procedure results in a hierarchical agenda, but if the group is particularly effective in helping the first person, other members may decide to reveal deeper problems they want help with. The problem agenda and hierarchy should be adhered to only if it is in the best interests of the group. Rigid structuring of the group focus could deter progress.

Go-Round

One of the simplest and yet most versatile and effective exercises that can be used in group counseling is the "go-round." As the name implies this technique involves going around the group person by person, giving each a specific opportunity to respond. This technique has many variations and purposes and fits at any stage of group development. For instance, a "go-round" is a good way to begin with a group to find out what everyone is thinking or feeling and to get some cues about how to proceed. A "go-round" when a group ends gives members the opportunity to say what they have not had a chance to say and is a good way to tie up loose ends. During the group sessions, go-rounds immediately following critical incidents are useful to air feelings and release tension, as well as to move the group on to the next phase of the process.

Notes

1. The Trust Ring exercises of Options I and II were developed by Jim Ross and demonstrated in my group-counseling class at the University of Wisconsin-River Falls.

2. This exercise was demonstrated by Dr. Dan Ficek in a Human Relations Workshop he and I led at Red Wing, Minnesota in the spring of 1974.

References

Bonney, W.C. Group counseling and developmental processes. In G.M. Gazda (Ed.), *Theories and methods of group counseling in the schools.* Springfield, Ill.: Charles C. Thomas, 1969.

Cohn, B. Group counseling with adolescents. In B. Cohn (Ed.), *Collected articles: The adolescent and group counseling* (unpublished). Board of Cooperative Educational Services, Yorktown Heights, N.Y. 10598, 1964.

Cohn, B. *Group counseling presentation*. Spring Group Guidance Conference, University of Wisconsin-Oshkosh, 1973.

Dinkmeyer, D.D. and Muro, J.J. *Group counseling: Theory and practice*. Itasca, Ill.: F.E. Peacock, 1971.

Gawrys, J., Jr., and Brown, B.O. Group counseling: More than a catalyst. *The School Counselor*, 1963, *12*, 206–213.

Gazda, G.M., and Larson, M.J. A comprehensive appraisal of group and multiple counseling research. *Journal of Research and Development in Education*, 1968, *1*(2), 57–132.

Glasser, W. *Reality therapy*. New York: Harper & Row, 1965.

Lakin, M. Some ethical issues in sensitivity training. *American Psychologist*, 1969, *24*, 923–928.

Lifton, W. *Working with groups* (2nd ed.). New York: Wiley, 1966.

Lindt, H. The nature of therapeutic interaction of patients in groups. *International Journal of Group Psychotherapy*, 1958, *8*, 55–69.

Mahler, C.A. Group counseling in the schools. Boston: Houghton Mifflin, 1969.

Ohlsen, M.M. *Group counseling*. New York: Holt, Rinehart & Winston, 1970.

Rogers, C.R. The interpersonal relationship: The core of guidance. *Harvard Educational Review*, 1962, *32*, 416–429.

Rogers, C.R. The process of the basic encounter group. In J.F.T. Bugental (Ed.), *Challenges of humanistic psychology*. New York: McGraw-Hill, 1967.

Schmuck, R.A., and Schmuck, P.A. *Group processes in the classroom*. Dubuque, Iowa: Brown, 1971.

Stevens, J.O. *Awareness: Exploring, experimenting, experiencing*. Moab, Utah: Real People Press, 1971.

Trotzer, J.P. Group counseling: Process and perspective. *Guidelines for Pupil Services*. Madison: Wisconsin Department of Public Instruction, 1972, *10*, 105–110.

Vorrath, H.H. *Positive peer culture: Content, structure and process*. Red Wing, Minn.: Red Wing State Training School.

Transactional Analysis:
A New Method for
Helping Offenders

Richard C. Nicholson

"I'm okay; you're okay!" If a group counselor feels this way about himself and his clients, the social transactions within the group can become straightforward and free of games. This is the position recommended by Eric Berne, M.D., author of *Transactional Analysis in Psychotherapy*.* He likens the successful group therapist or counselor to a "cowboy." By that he means that the therapist should be relaxed, alert, adaptable as well as a straight shooter. Unlike the tense therapist, the "cowboy" does not believe that the members of his group will get better faster if everyone remains serious. He considers that laughter is as much an expression of feeling as is hostility: "We like laughter; our patients like laughter."[1] Another feature of Transactional Analysis is that it employs colloquial terms that are easily understood by all. Doctor Berne has introduced a new way of talking about human behavior. His terminology is simple and direct:

> *Transactional Analysis because of its clearcut statements rooted in easily accessible material, because of its operational nature, and because of its specialized vocabulary (consisting of only five words: Parent, Adult, Child, Game and Script), offers an easily-learned framework for clarification.*[2]

Since its development, Transactional Analysis[3] has attracted international interest. Over 1,000 professionals have received formal training in Berne's methods. He is perhaps more popularly known for his best seller, *Games People Play*, but in professional circles he is also acclaimed for such works as *Principles of Group Treatment* which serves as an excellent textbook for persons interested in the application of his method; and *The Structure and Dynamics of Organizations*

Reprinted by permission of the Federal Probation Quarterly, from *Federal Probation Quarterly*, 34 (1) (Sept. 1979).

and Groups, which offers a systematic framework for group treatment.

After receiving his degree in medicine at McGill University and serving his residency at Yale's Psychiatric Clinic, Eric Berne received specialized training in psychoanalysis in the respective institutes at New York and San Francisco. Sometime later, during a session of one of his therapy groups, one of his patients commented that he felt like a little boy. Traditionally, a psychoanalyst would have given a different interpretation to such a comment, but Berne, who had previously observed the same person being quite adult, later queried, "Who's talking now, the adult man, or the little boy?"[4] Subsequent observations led him to believe that there are three "ego states" operative in all of us. Berne has colloquially called them the Parent, Adult, and Child. His conclusions were also based upon the hypotheses suggested by Wilder Penfield's study and treatment of epileptic patients.[5]

Penfield discovered that when he applied mild electric stimulation to the exposed cortex of his patients, that they would re-experience past events, usually from childhood, in as fresh and animated form as when they first happened. Apparently, our brain functions very much like a three-track, high-fidelity tape recording, that can reproduce the past events in our lives, including the interpretations that we gave them and the emotions felt at the time. Our "memory tapes" are available for replay today, and they can greatly influence our present behavior.

From Penfield's experiments Berne perceived the existence of two "ego states," one based upon the present, external, and psychological situation; the other based upon the "re-living" of occurrences going back as far as the first year of our life.[6]

Parent, Adult, and Child

While watching and listening to his patients, Berne noticed that they would change right before his eyes. He observed changes in facial expressions, postures, gestures, voice intonations, vocabulary, and body functions (blushing, etc.). A father's face will harden when his son defies him; a person turns pale and trembles when stopped by the red light and siren of a pursuing traffic officer; an adult person shouts with child-like excitement when his slot machine hits the jackpot and the winning bell clangs. Such changes can be observed in the same person. "He changes from *what* to *what?*"[7]

According to Berne, these changes are shifts from one "ego state" to another, like the previously described patient who would feel like a small child at one time, and like an adult at another time. The shifts occur between our Parent, Adult, and Child (PAC).

The Parent

We have said that the external events that occur in a person's life are recorded in the human brain pretty much like a high-fidelity tape recording. Such events are recorded during our early years (about 0–5 years) and are, for the most part, provided by the significant persons in our lives—our own parents, or those who substitute as our parents.

In selecting the name "Parent" for these recordings, Doctor Berne was mindful of the examples that our own parents give: their advice and admonishments; their nurturence, assistance, and affection; and all of the traits that one's parents exhibit, including their prejudices. During our early years we know very little about word formations. Our ability to make realistic evaluations and judgments is therefore quite limited. We take in these "Parent" recordings or tapes just as we perceive them—without any processing based upon what is real and correct. Our future behavior is highly influenced by our "Parent" tapes. We might hear others say, "He's like his father, you know." When a drunken father lashes out at his own feelings of depression and guilt by striking the small child, or by verbally abusing him, all that the child can record is that "Daddy doesn't love me; I can't be any good," and he later may come around to feeling that persons possessing authority are also abusive and unloving. Such as "Parent" tape may sound very familiar to people in corrections.

The Child

At the same time our "Parent" tapes are being recorded, the internal events occurring in early childhood are being recorded also. These recordings are described as:

> The responses of the little person to what he hears and feels. Thus, an evoked childhood recollection is not an accurate reproduction of what occurred but of what the person saw and heard and felt and understood.[8]

Such recordings or "Child" tapes are therefore full of misconceptions, fusions, and emotional conflicts. The reactions of the small child are mostly *feelings*. His ability to make reality judgments is limited by his incomplete knowledge of word formations. He is small, clumsy, and unable to control his body functions. Since he is constantly being corrected by the significant adults in his life, he comes to feel that he is the object of their disapproval. Our "Child" tapes play back many "not okay" feelings. Where parents have been rejecting, too demanding, or harsh, the "not okay" feelings will predominate. These negative feelings are easily evoked when we perceive signs of disapproval from others—when our friends or co-workers do not respond to our "good morning"; or when the boss is grumpy; or when we hear the police siren and fear that we have been singled out for a traffic arrest. In TA we say that such incidents "hook the Child." By that we mean there is a replay of the "not okay Child tapes."[9]

On the positive side, the Child is creative, curious, explorative, affectionate, and playful. Our "happy" Child can also be hooked, as when our "good morning" begets a favorable response. A man who is skilled at hooking the "happy Child" of others can become a good husband, father, or boss.

The Adult

When the little person begins to feel the power of movement, starts moving out, starts handling objects, and when he starts exploring his environment, he is freeing himself from his original inertia. It is at this stage of development that our Adult comes into being. As we mature, our Adult functions more and more effectively, despite the commands and blockings of our parents and despite the anxieties they have aroused in the small child. The Adult can be described as a sort of computer that processes reality data. "Mommie is wrong, school isn't all fun," or "Mommie is right, the cars in the street can hurt me."

The primary goal in Berne's treatment is to emancipate the Adult, enabling it thus to examine the Parent in order to determine whether the recordings are realistic or correct (see figure 2). The Adult can accept or reject the "Parent" tapes depending upon their validity. The Adult may not be able to erase the "not okay" feelings uncovered in the Child, but it can shut them off. In TA the patient or client is encouraged to place his Adult in command of his personality, or to make it the executive, so to speak. With the Adult in command, we are able to activate the Parent or let out the Child when appropriate to the occasion. If we do not bring out our restraining Parent when junior threatens a tantrum, we may beget a "problem child." Our Adult rejects dictums from the Parent that tell us "The only good Indian is a dead Indian," but it accepts and employs wise sayings such as, "A stitch in time saves nine." Our Adult does not allow the Child to express sexuality in public, but it does allow its levity to come out when our duties at work become too burdensome.

Conception	Biological Birth	Psychological Birth	Social Birth (school)
(9 months)	(estrangement)		(age 5)

FIGURE 1

The Four Life Positions

Referring to figure 1, we see a continuum depicting a life span from the moment of conception to the age of about 5 years.

The first 9 months of our existence is the most perfect situation that a human being can experience. At biological birth the infant is pushed out and into a situation of terrifying contrast and presumably exposed to extremes of temperature, noise, light, separateness, and abandonment.[10]

This "birth trauma" is recorded and stored in the brain cells. Soon after birth, a rescuer wraps the infant in a blanket, comforts him, and strokes him. Without this he will die—as foundling infants sometimes do from progressive emaciation. By the rescue and by receiving "strokes," the infant finds out that life on the outside is at least endurable. Depending upon the gap between biological birth and the rescue (psychological birth), the quality and frequency of stroking, the child will develop a "central emotional position to which he will automatically return for the rest of his days as a major safeguard of the major vulnerability of his life."[11]

There are four life positions:

1. *I'm not OK; you're OK:* The environment of the growing infant can be likened to that of a Lilliputian living in a land of giants. He finds himself dependent upon his giant-like parents for strokings and for feelings of being OK. The child-rearing policies of his parents, although necessary, leave him with many "not OK" feelings. He is always being corrected, and eventually finds himself in the life position of "I'm not OK; you're OK." This is the neurotic or depressed position, and is the most common one in our society. Although we can rise above it, we will find that it continues to have a profound effect upon the way we handle our everyday social transactions. All correctional workers have encountered cases in which the offender is trying to prove that, in fact, he is "not OK."

2. *I'm not OK; you're not OK:* This is the position occupied by the autistic child—the child whose early experiences denied him a timely rescue or sufficient stroking. Such a child has little will to live. Schizophrenia may be the outcome of this position.

3. *I'm OK; you're not OK:* This is a denial of position number 1, frequently adopted by a child who wants to retaliate. It is the sociopathic or psychopathic position so often observed in the incorrigibles.

4. *I'm OK; you're OK:* This position requires a statement of faith, and it is the basis for getting well. The first three positions are assumed at the preverbal stage and are based upon feelings. The fourth position results from thought, confidence in ourselves and others, and willingness to venture out of our defenses. It is a decision that we have to make. In some respects it is like a religious conversion.[12]

The most common position is "I'm not OK; you're OK," and may be expressed by the playing of "games." Later, we will go into Berne's definition and description of games. For the moment it is important to emphasize that our "not OK" Child stays with us. Through TA a person can be enabled to collect new recordings or "tapes" through the experiencing of successful outcomes in his Adult transactions and through successes gained by arriving at proper judgments. Patience and perseverence are required to secure the position of "I'm OK; you're OK" because our previous "bad tapes" and social inadequacies cannot be overcome immediately. Our Child wants immediate results; our Adult can exercise patience. Berne's method of treatment takes time, but less time than do the traditional therapies.

Structural Analysis

Before a client can profitably participate in TA, he must first understand something about Structural Analysis. Although social transactions are complex, TA enables us to diagram such transactions, thus making them more easily understood.

1. *Ideal:* We all have a Parent, Adult, and Child, but the working relationships among these ego states may differ. Ideally, as in figure 2, the lines or boundaries between Parent, Adult, and Child are clean-cut and relatively impermeable.

The Adult, although holding the executive position, is nevertheless able to admit the "examined Parent" and the "adapted Child," when appropriate. Berne's treatment aims at clearly separating the three "ego states," and at determining just what is each client's Parent, Adult, and Child. His treatment goals are easily understood by everyone. Thomas A. Harris, M.D., cites the example of a deprived and unsuccessful school dropout (a teenage girl) who indi-

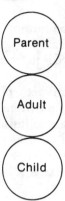

FIGURE 2

cated her understanding of PAC after the initial interview, thus: "It (PAC) means that we are all made up of three parts and we'd better keep them separated or we're in trouble."[13]

2. *Contaminations:* Instead of the ideal situation, as presented in figure 2, we most often find that the boundaries or circles overlap each other. Such an overlap is called a contamination (see figure 3).

The (a) overlap depicts a contamination of the Adult by a "dated and unexamined" Parent with the recorded parental data deemed to be true and accurate. A person thus contaminated suffers from prejudice. "Negroes are inferior; all Germans are mass murderers; law-enforcement officials are sadistic; court judges are stupid, prejudicial and corrupt," etc. We all have encountered persons whose prejudices are unshakeable. The only way to elimi-

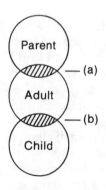

FIGURE 3

nate our prejudices is by realizing that it is no longer dangerous to disagree with one's parents, or to modify the data that one has in his "Parent."

The (b) overlap represents an Adult contaminated by the Child. When this contamination is at its worst, the Adult is seldom in control and the person is liable to suffer from delusions or halluci-nations. A person who views the world as a grim, ugly place is probably seeing it as it appeared to him during childhood. A little child who lives in fear of angry, unpredictable parents can, when grown up, experience the same fear in stressful situations.[14] By decontaminating his Adult, a person becomes able to process real-ity data. Hallucinations develop when the boundary between the Child and Adult breaks down and the original haranguing dialogue between a child and his parents is projected outward as real. "While the voice emanates from the Parent the audience consists of the Child and sometimes the contaminated Adult as well."[15]

3. *Exclusions:* According to Berne, "an exclusion is manifested by a stereotyped, predictable attitude which is steadfastly main-tained as long as possible in the face of a threatening situation. The constant Parent, the constant Adult, and the constant Child all result primarily from defensive exclusion of the two complemen-tary aspects in each case."[16]

Figure 4 depicts the person who cannot play. He works late at the office; duty dominates his activities; he is all business. He has been so overpowered by stern, unrelenting parents that he feels secure only when his Child is completely turned off. His theme is, "Children should be seen and not heard. . . . Didn't I tell you . . .

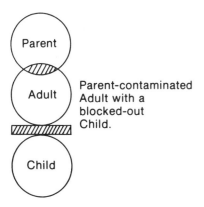

Parent-contaminated
Adult with a
blocked-out
Child.

FIGURE 4   Parent-Contaminated Adult with a Blocked-Out
Child

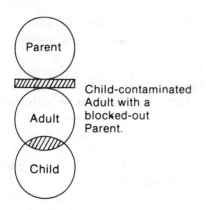

Child-contaminated
Adult with a
blocked-out
Parent.

FIGURE 5 Child-Contaminated Adult with a Blocked-Out
Parent

grow up!" He has very little happiness recorded in his Child tapes. By freeing his Adult and firming up the boundaries between Parent and Adult, the Parent can be then examined and some of its unrealistic and harsh dictums rejected. The result: Our duty-dominated client is enabled to cut down on his office hours, listen lovingly to his children's fantasies, and start sharing his life with his family.

Figure 5 is of particular interest to correctional workers. It represents the person without a conscience, the dyssocial or sociopathic (antisocial) personality. If his parents have been frightening, brutal, indifferent to his feelings or unpredictable, he preserves himself by turning them off. From the "I'm not OK; you're OK" position, he retaliates with "I'm OK; you're not OK." By excluding the painful parent he also excludes, unfortunately, what little good was in them. Feelings of guilt, embarrassment, or remorse are noticeably absent. Treatment of such a person is admittedly difficult. According to Dr. Harris, "He may never have an operational Parent to back up his Adult, but his Adult can be strong enough to carry him through a successful life wherein he gains the approval and even the esteem of others. It is on this possibility that all our rehabilitative efforts in the field of corrections must be based."[17]

Analyzing Transactions

"A unit of social intercourse is called a transaction. If two or more people encounter each other . . . sooner or later one of them will speak, or give some indication of acknowledging the presence of the others.

This is called a *transactional stimulus*. Another person will do or say something which is in some way related to the stimulus. This is called the *transactional response.*[18] The response may in turn become another stimulus inviting a new response, chain fashion. The important purpose of transactional analysis is for the participating clients to determine which part of our PAC—Parent, Adult, or Child—is providing the stimulus and which is giving the response. Clues that the Parent is providing either the transactional stimulus or response include finger and head wagging; clucking and sighing; tightening of the lips, tilting the head, etc. For the Child: words signifying refusal, or wants; "mine's better," etc. For the Adult: a vocabulary indicating why, who, where, when, how. The clues for each ego state consist of differences in gestures, facial expressions, postures, voice intonations, vocabulary, and body functions (blushing, etc.).

Complementary Transactions

Figure 6 shows examples of complementary transactions.

In example (a), we find a couple of elderly persons complaining about times and morals. Their discussion is without any consideration of new data so that the Adult never enters into their conversation. They might, for example, consider the "why's" of changing times. At any rate the vectors, both stimulus and response, are Parent to Parent. This brings us to Berne's first rule of communications: *When stimulus and response on the PAC transactional diagram make parallel lines, the transaction is complementary and can go on indefinitely.*

In situation (b), Adult to Adult, we might find a person asking another for street directions. Situation (c) might be two members of a fraternity plotting initiation rights (Child to Child). We might get a situation as diagrammed in (d) if hubby were to ask wifey to help him control his cigarette habit.

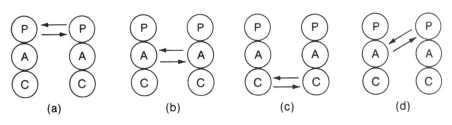

(a)   (b)   (c)   (d)

FIGURE 6

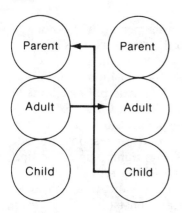

FIGURE 7

Crossed Transactions
These transactions bring about trouble in our interpersonal relations.

Referring to figure 7, Berne gives the example of a transaction between a husband and wife in which he asks: "Dear, where are may cuff links (Adult stimulus)?" A complementary response (parallel vectors) from his spouse might be, "In your top dresser drawer." But if wifey has had a rough day, storing up her resentments, she might respond with, "Why are you always picking on me?" The result is a crossed transaction as seen in figure 7. His stimulus is Adult to Adult; her response is Child to Parent, and the vectors cross. This brings us to Berne's second rule of communication: *When the stimulus and response on the PAC transaction diagram cross, communication stops.*

The husband and wife won't talk about cuff links anymore, but rather something like the game of "uproar." Or, wifey could have replied: "Why don't you put things where they belong?" As shown in figure 8, we would then get another crossed transaction of Parent to Child, and again, the communications cease, and the games begin.

The origin of non-Adult responses is in the life position of the "not OK" Child. This can be seen when a person "reads" into another's statements, thus: "Where did you get these steaks?" says the husband. "Why, is there something wrong with them?" wifey retorts. The individual with the "not OK" Child cannot handle Adult transactions, if the Child is in control. The primary requirement in Adult transactions is that we deal with reality.

The "not OK" position can also be expressed in the stimulus. Figure 9 offers an example wherein hubby asks, "Where did you hide the

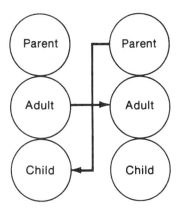

FIGURE 8

can opener?" An attempt to get this information via Adult stimulus would be a straight, verbal question (Adult to Adult). But in our example, the husband not only wants to get information, but his Parent is also covertly saying (Parent to Child), "You're a lousy housekeeper." Whether or not we get a crossed transaction would hinge upon how the wife would respond. If she feels OK enough not to be threatened, her response would be parallel or complementary, thus: "I hid it next to the forks, darling." But if her response were to be, "Don't get smart with me," the search for the can opener terminates and the wrangling begins.

Central to the possibility of change is whether or not the Adult can

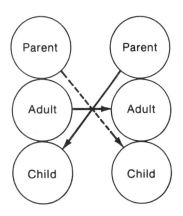

FIGURE 9

be strong enough to keep the Child in control. According to Dr. Harris, "First of all a conscious effort is required, built on a conscious plan which rests on a set of values adopted by the Adult. It is said that you cannot teach navigation in the middle of a storm. Likewise, you cannot expect to carry through a successful transaction with your Adult in charge if you never thought about, or never built, any set of values which gives it purpose."[19]

The Structuring of Time

We hear that our average life span is three score and 10 years, but today's trend is to increase this expectancy. We are frequently concerned with what to do with the smaller periods of time, next week, today, the next hour, or right now. People who do not structure their own time look to others to tell them what to do.

Berne has concluded that there are six ways of structuring time which includes all of the transactions: withdrawal; rituals; activities; pastimes; games; intimacy.

Withdrawal

This is not a transaction in a strict sense, but it always occurs in a social setting. A schoolboy's withdrawal into fantasies in order to escape classroom tedium is one example.

Rituals

"A ritual is a socially-programmed use of time where everybody agrees to do the same thing."[20] In rituals we risk no involvement with others, the outcome is predictable, and the activity makes us feel we are doing something that is expected. Our salutatory activities are examples, e.g., "good morning!" This is worth about one stroke. Rituals are found everywhere, at cocktail parties, at church, in courtrooms, etc.

Pastimes

Usually are in the form of "semiritualistic" discussions on common topics. Pastimes may be engaged in for their own sake, but with "not OK" individuals they are used exactly for what the term implies, i.e., a way of passing time: To sweat out an hour, a day, until it is time to retire for the night, until work or school commences, until some cure is obtained, or until death rescues them from feelings of guilt, despair, or boredom. At best, pastimes are enjoyed for their own sake, serving as a means to develop acquaintanceships and intimacy.

Berne's high sense of humor shows in his descriptions of certain pastimes, conversations that often occur at luncheons, cocktail parties, or club meetings: "General Motors" (comparing cars) and "who won" (man talk); or "morning after" (hangover); "What became of" (good old Joe).

Activity
An ordinary, comfortable way of structuring time by dealing with reality, e.g., building a house, washing a car, etc.

Games
Berne has published a book devoted solely to games. Like pastimes, his games have some amusing titles such as "NIGYSOB" (now I've got you; you S.O.B.); "If it weren't for you;" "Ain't it awful;" "Schlemiel;" and "ITHY" (I'm only trying to help you—played by social caseworkers and correctional workers). He defines games as:

> An ongoing series of complementary ulterior transactions progressing to a well-defined, predictable outcome. Descriptively, it is a recurrent set of transactions, often repetitious, superficially plausible, with a concealed motivation, or more colloquially, a series of moves with a snare, or "gimmick." Games are clearly differentiated from procedures, rituals and pastimes by two characteristics: (a) their ulterior quality, and (b) the payoff. Procedures may be successful, rituals effective and pastimes profitable, but all of them are by definition candid; they may involve contest, but not conflict, and the ending may be sensational, but it is not dramatic. Every game, on the other hand, is basically dishonest, and the outcome has a dramatic, as distinct from exciting quality.[21]

Games are played for primary and secondary gains and these are what Berne terms "payoffs" for the players. Some of these gains are the relief of tension; the avoidance of noxious situations; internal and external psychological advantages, etc.

Berne points out that most studies of criminality are unproductive and ambiguous. The reason for this, he says, is that most criminologists fail to detect that there are two basic types of criminals, a) the big-money maker whose Child does not want to be caught and who rarely is caught. This is the "professional" criminal who is careful to obliterate any evidence resulting from his crime. He calls this type the "compulsive winner." He is the untouchable for whom a fix is often made; b) the "compulsive loser" who plays the game "cops and robbers." He is usually caught; and if he does realize some profit through his criminality, it is the result of chance rather than skill.

There are many games: "Uproar" (a sexual game); "Schlemiel" (a party game); "Courtroom" (a marital game), and "I'm only trying to help you" (consulting room game), to name a few. Of interest to correctional workers are those described by Berne as "Underworld Games." One of these is "Cops and Robbers."

The latter game reflects the offender's hatred of authority, particularly the police whom he tries to outwit. In fact, the primary motive for playing "cops and robbers" is not to obtain stolen property, but rather to get caught, making it either difficult or easy for the police to catch up with him, according to the game player's individual preference. True, at the Adult level the offense is committed for material gains, but at the Child level it is the thrill of the chase, or the getaway and the cool-off that motivates the player. Berne sees the prototype for "cops and robbers" in the childhood game of hide-and-seek. When father is "it," the little boy or girl shows chagrin if caught too easily. If father plays the game well and holds off on finding the hidden boy or girl, they will give him a clue as to their whereabouts. If father gives up, the children are disappointed, for "being caught" is the actual payoff.

"Cops and robbers" is a battle of wits and yields a more satisfying payoff when each player does his best. Yet at the psychological level the offender's Adult must lose in order for his Child to win. Not being caught is actually the antithesis, for the offender is thus eliminating the Child element and turns the whole game into an Adult procedure, as professional criminals will do.

Intimacy

Consists of an accepting affection and understanding between persons that are "OK" enough to give, take, and share. From the "I'm OK; you're OK" position we come to realize that each person is unique or "something special." In intimacy our emotional expressions are spontaneous as well as appropriate, and not merely role-like responses to what is socially programmed. The "OK" person is not afraid to give strokes or to risk involvement.

Methods of Transactional Analysis

The goal of TA is social control which is achieved by the freeing of the client's Adult, thus making it the executive of the personality. By consciously examining his Parent and Child, the client's Adult can then make the decision as to when his Parent or Child can be released, and when the Adult should resume its primacy. The Adult may call upon the Parent, for example, to determine whether any planned behavior is socially appropriate, ethical, and legal. Transactional Analysis lends itself easily to group treatment, primarily because, "... the natural function of therapy groups is transactional analysis."[22] It also has an application in one-to-one counseling. It appears particularly helpful in the treatment of offenders, because the liberated Adult in command of the personality is able to circumscribe tendencies to "act out," can learn to stand firm in the face of evil and hostile impulses, or to repress them, if necessary. With the Adult in command we become responsible for what happens to us in the future, regardless of what has happened in the past.

We are cautioned that the analysis of games and scripts (similar to life themes) is a useful therapeutic device when employed by a professional who has received clinical training in Transactional Analysis, but these techniques do not occupy as important a position in treatment as do structural and transactional analysis. For a person to "know his game" or "script" does not necessarily make positive change possible. Not only does structural and transactional analysis hold more promise for change in short-term treatment, but it also avoids the danger of depriving a client of a defense before he has come to understand his position, as well as the situation in childhood when it was first established. Unless the group leader has experienced complete training in Berne's treatment methods, he should confine his treatment techniques to structural and transactional analysis. True, the leader must be aware of what games are being played by the group members, but only for the purposes of breaking up the games, and for leading the group into the more productive activity of analyzing the group's transactions, determining whether the stimuli and responses are from the Parent, Adult, or Child. The group's training and exercises strengthen the primacy of the Adult.

Treatment of Offenders

Berne's methods are used in group treatment afforded to probationers and parolees in the federal probation office for the Eastern District of California. Participants are selected on the basis of their own requests, or in cases where the supervising officer believes that a need exists for such treatment. Otherwise the selections are made without regard to sex, age, type of offense, or whether the participant is on probation or parole. A series of 12 weekly meetings is held on Tuesday evenings for an hour and a half, with the agreement that the participants can enroll for the next 12-week series. However, once the participant attends the first meeting, he is obliged to complete the series by attending 11 more meetings. There are three rather firm rules that all members must observe: (a) no fraternization with other group members; (b) during treatment sessions a member may say anything he wishes, but he cannot make any physical contact with other members, except for the handshake that is permitted at the beginning and end of each meeting; (c) a member is not obliged to answer any questions put to him by the rest of the group.

The first meeting is handled almost exclusively by the group leader who discusses the organizational aspects of the group: the goals of group treatment, the selection of the membership, and, more important, Berne's theory of Structural Analysis. A blackboard is a necessary item for the application of Berne's treatment methods. Transactions occurring within the group are thus diagrammed for explanation and study purposes. The organizational aspects of the group as each member is related to the authoritarian structure of federal corrections is also outlined on the blackboard. In line with the recommended limitations placed on the use of Berne's methods, the group is advised that TA is not group therapy but "group treatment"; that we do not explore psychological cellars, so to speak, and they are told that the aims of TA treatment are to help each member in his relationships with others, and to help him become the master over his own behavior. Stated more colloquially, "We are here to make winners out of losers." Often a specific contract is made between the group leader and a client, such as, "My contract with you is to help you get along on the job," or "to quit drinking," or "to control your frightened child," etc.

The group soon becomes familiar with the three ego states, Parent, Adult, and Child (PAC), and begins to perceive which state is active in group interactions, in themselves, as well as in other members. It is important that the group leader diagram on the blackboard some of the more important transactions.

Offenders are Unique in Group Treatment

Berne regards therapy as a kind of contest involving four persons, the patient's Parent and Child acting as warring factions against the Adult, with the therapist holding the role of "auxiliary Adult." This situation presents even odds that the patient will do better, but if the therapist finds a triumvirate of the patient's Parent, Adult, and Child working against him, as in the treatment of sociopathic individuals, the odds are three against one that the outcome will be successful. The group leader who attempts to treat offenders, should be prepared for alliances formed against successful outcomes, since each offender group will have in it at least one sociopathic type. By seeing to it that the group becomes more and more efficient in analyzing its transactions, these "anti-get-well" alliances will eventually dissolve.

Franklin Ernst, M.D., has employed Berne's methods for over 9 years in treating groups of prisoners at the California Medical Facility. Besides discovering the "Underworld Game," "How do you get out of here," he has also observed other games or maneuvers played by inmate groups. Some members will "rat pack" another member ("the hot seat technique"), or a single member will pull a "stick-up job" using the group's time ("You better get me what I'm asking for or—").[23]

Likewise, special maneuverings and games can be observed in the group treatment of probationers and parolees, i.e., persons living in free society: "Why do we have to attend these meetings," and "What do *you* get out of this Mr. Group Leader?" (both variations of NIGY-SOB); "Now let me tell *you* why I hate probation officers" (Courtroom); and, "I'm a good boy, aren't I papa?' (Santa Clause fantasy—"If I do what is expected, I'll be presented with the magic orb").

The following transactions occurred at one of our earlier meetings and are offered as a good example of how quickly the members learn how to analyze them.

Jerry, an alcoholic, comes into the meeting room, already partially occupied, before the meeting commenced. He is obviously under the influence of alcohol. Upon being introduced to Larry who wears his hair long, and adorns himself with beads, Jerry slurs out something about a "hair do" and "hippie." The group leader is smoking a cigar. Jerry asks him, "Aren't you afraid that cigar will make you sick or something?" The group leader offers Jerry a cigar. After the meeting has commenced Jerry first tells how he wrestles with his sons, how they are going to become real "he-men." He then turns to Larry:

> *Jerry:* If my kids wore their hair long, I'd kick the s——— out of them.
> *Larry:* Well, OK. You'd kick the s———out of 'em. What I'm concerned about is getting a job. . . .
> *Jerry (interrupting):* Wanta job—cut your goddam hair! Let me ask you, do you think you're cute with your long hair and beads?
> *Larry:* No, I just wear it this way (clears throat). . . .
> *Jerry (winking at other group members, apparently to let*

them in on the "sport"): Tell me, bud, why do you wear your hair long?

Larry: Why do you drink?

Jerry: Why do *I* drink . . . hmm.

Larry: I'm not listening to you, anyway.

Jerry (eyes narrowing, pitch of voice raising): Why aren't you listening to me?

Larry (tilting his head, strengthening his voice): Because you've been drinking. My mother was a lush. I don't like lushes.

Jerry (voice higher yet): You calling me a lush?

Larry: If you want it that way. . . .

Doug (probably our sincerest and best motivated client): Boy, Jerry! He sure hooked your Child! You started out being the big, bullying Parent, trying to hook Larry's Child, but instead you hooked his Parent.

Barbara (Jerry's spouse, pointing her index finger to the ceiling): That's right, Doug he *is* a bully when he's drunk—an *Irish* bully!

Doug: OK, Barbara, but now you're being a punishing Parent.

Barbara (voice raising, eyes moistening): OK, so I'm a Parent, but if *you* had to—Well, I am working at being an Adult. Anyhow, Larry, if you want to wear your hair long, do it. You're still OK.

The meeting ended on a friendly note, with the group giving Larry some "strokes." Jerry remained subdued and depressed.

The following transactions, occurring at a later meeting involving the same group, illustrate how the group leader may receive the "hot seat" technique. The meeting commences with a brief discussion by the group leader on the four life positions. The desirability of striving for the position, "I'm OK; you're OK" was stressed. Billy, a check-writer, recently reparoled, attempted to maneuver the group into playing a game:

Billy: I can't buy this I'm OK; you're OK, because it's just brainwashing stuff, because *nobody's* OK. I just read where a probation officer was convicted of taking a bribe. . . .

Leader (interrupting): Of embezzlement.

Billy: So what! He's a crook! They're *all* crooks! A guy

comes up on a check rap in front of a crooked judge and gets 5 years. . . .

Judy (interrupting): Are you saying you're OK and the rest of us are not? You're perfect?

Billy: You're damn right.

Don: Well, these federal probation officers haven't done *me* a bit of good. And those stupid bastards in the employment agencies! They're drawing their pay checks, and when you ask for help . . . what a runaround. . . .

Jerry (referring to group leader): Mr. Nick's a probation officer and I think he's OK. He always played it straight with me . . . (I'm a good boy, aren't I, papa?)

Billy: Oh Yeh? What *goodies* are you *getting* out of this, Mr. Nick?

Group
Leader: My Adult gets a salary. My Parent is trying to do something about helping people free up the Adult and making it the boss—and protecting society; and my Child is curious about what comes out of TA.

Jerry: Don't you *resent* what Billy's saying? I would!

Group
Leader: What's important for us to do is to analyze what part of us—Parent, Adult, Child—is doing the talking.

Judy: I think it was Billy's Parent talking just now—and, well I guess it was my Parent telling him *he* thinks *he's* perfect (laughter).

Doug: Well, Billy, you're *acting* like a Parent, but I picked up a lot of Child in what you *and* Don said.

Don: Child!

Doug: Yeh, a not OK Child and a scared Child.

The discussion went on with Billy protesting that he isn't afraid of anything. The noteworthy thing coming out of this session is Billy's confirmation of his life position of "I'm OK; you're not OK" which actually represents his reversal of the position, "I'm not OK; you're OK." His unloved and frightened Child sought group support for his need to rehearse his defenses. An attempt was made to entice the group leader into playing games, but Billy's maneuver was diverted into the more productive activity of analyzing group transactions. Billy never returned.

Summary

Transactional Analysis does not have all the answers and many of our group members do not profit by their participation, but those who do use it profitably have demonstrated remarkable improvement in their life positions and in their vocations, recreations, and interpersonal relationships. A former nomadic and depressive parole violator is now studying to become an IBM computer analyst; an alcoholic probationer has voluntarily committed himself for treatment in a state hospital; another probationer without trade skills is studying to become an automobile mechanic. And there are others making similar attempts at improving themselves. Transactional Analysis helps a person to become responsible for his future; to feel "OK."

Notes

*Dr. Berne died unexpectedly July 15, 1970, from a cardiac disorder.—*The Editors.*

1. Eric Berne, 'Analyzing 'Games' and "Scripts' in Transactional Psychotherapy," *Frontiers of Clinical Psychiatry*, October 1945, p. 1.

2. Eric Berne, *Principles of Group Treatment* (New York: Oxford University Press, 1966) p. 214.

3. Hereinafter to be designated as TA.

4. Berne, *Group Treatment*, p. 2.

5. W. Penfield, "Memory Mechanisms," *Archives of Neurology and Psychiatry* 67 (1952):178–179.

6. Eric Berne, *Transactional Analysis in Psychotherapy* (New York: Grove Press, 1961), p. 19.

7. Thomas A. Harris, *I'm OK–You're OK* (New York: Harper & Row, 1969), p. 16.

8. Ibid., p. 25.

9. Ibid., p. 27.

10. Ibid., pp. 37–53.

11. Ibid., p. 42.

12. Ibid., pp. 50–51.

13. Ibid., pp. 97–98.

14. Ibid., pp. 98–99.

15. Eric Berne, *Transactional Analysis in Psychotherapy*, p. 62.

16. Ibid., p. 44.

17. Harris, *I'm OK*, p. 104.

18. Eric Berne, M.D., *Games People Play* (New York: Grove Press, 1964), p. 29.

19. Harris, *I'm OK*, pp. 94–95.

20. Ibid., p. 116.

21. Eric Berne, *Games People Play*, p. 48.

22. Eric Berne, *Transactional Analysis in Psychotherapy*, pp. 90–91.

23. Franklin H. Ernst, M.D., and William C. Keating, M.D., "Psychiatric Treatment of the California Felon," *The American Journal of Psychiatry*, April 1964.

9 Special Areas of Correctional Counseling

Introduction

In Chapter 4, we noted that classification models have been introduced, tested, and refined to assist probation and parole officers and treatment personnel in supervising the client population more effectively. These models are based on the risk presented to the community by the offender, but they also contain components which examine the needs of the offender with regard to job opportunities, medical treatment, substance abuse counseling, mental health assessment, and other factors. The risk element is always the overriding consideration in determining classification as to the need for maximum, medium, or minimum intervention of the officer and counselor in the offender's life. The needs of the offenders, although apparent and identified, become a secondary consideration.

In this chapter, we will consider counseling for various types of offenders whose needs are so paramount that they must be included in any treatment plan. These include the retarded, handicapped, and mentally ill, sex offenders, and those involved in severe substance abuse.

Public Law 94-142, the Education of All Handicapped Act of 1975, has important implications for both juvenile and adult correctional treatment, because it mandates free and appropriate education for all handicapped persons 21 years of age or younger. Handicapped individuals are defined in the law as mentally retarded, hard of hearing, deaf, orthopedically impaired, other health impaired, speech impaired, visually handicapped, seriously emotionally disturbed, or learning disabled requiring special education and related services.[1] Because of the age range covered in the law's mandate, many offenders incarcerated in adult institutions, as well as those held in juvenile facilities, are required to receive services.

A survey of 85 state departments of youth and/or adult corrections and all fifty state departments of education was conducted by the Correctional/Special Education Training Project to determine the number of handicapped institutionalized offenders. It was found that 28% of the institutionalized juveniles and 10% of the adult inmates had been identified as handicapped, and that 92% of these handicapped juveniles and one percent of these handicapped adults were receiving special education services.[2] The Project noted that such offenders, in addition to the correctional and special education programs they receive in institutions, will need transitional programs to assist them in community job placements and tie them in to community programs which can continue to assist them once they leave the institutions.[3]

In the first selection in this chapter, "Group Counseling with Retarded Offenders," Joseph Steiner describes a group counseling program for retarded offenders in a jail setting. In this facility, inmates identified as having borderline to moderate retardation were kept in a separate section on the jail's psychiatric floor and provided with entry to group counseling on a voluntary basis. The author described the group process here as "cognitive casework," defined as a helping process for dealing with clients whose low-level cognitive deficits deprive them of the basic tools or skills necessary for thinking.[4] The correctional officer who supervised these inmates was also involved in the group sessions, which generally included 5 to 10 inmates, the counselor, and the officer. Steiner discusses the difficulties in establishing an atmosphere of trust, and in overcoming the group members' difficulties in making their needs known. The group process and content are described, and the outcomes of the group activities over a four-year period are assessed.

Handling mentally ill and mentally retarded offenders in institutional settings is difficult for many reasons. They must be protected from victimization by the general inmate population, and they require additional attention to help them understand the significance of what is happening to them and reduce the traumatic effects of the incarceration experience. Community treatment, whenever possible, would seem to be the most appropriate setting for retarded or mentally ill offenders who do not pose a threat to the community. The second selection, "Halfway Houses Meeting Special Needs," by Robert A. Lippold, describes a program which has been used effectively for residential treatment of such a population. The program utilizes a closely monitored program of behavior control, recreational activities, vocational training, and individual counseling, monitored by correctional supervisors, a developmental disabilities specialist, a consulting psychiatrist, and a nurse.

Sex offenders also present unique difficulties for correctional counseling and treatment. Many of the disorders and dysfunctions experienced by such offenders are too complex to be treated adequately by counselors who are not specifically trained to work with them. When the offender's family is closely involved, as is frequently the case, the need for family therapy may be readily apparent, but not easily accomplished. Although treatment for severe disorders, such as sexual psychopathy, is now mandated in many states, sex offenders involved in less dramatic behavior may not be offered the treatment quality or intensity needed to prevent recurrence of their offenses. The third and fourth selections in this chapter describe the varieties and types of treatment currently available and the roles offenders' family members can play in the treatment process.

In the third selection, "Treatment of the Sex Offender," DeZolt and Kratcoski note that many activities formerly defined as improper sexual behavior subject to criminal penalties are no longer liable for criminal prosecution. State codes have been revised to specifically define sexual offenses, and most of these can be categorized as sexual assaults and displays. In this article, particular attention is given to the characteristics of sexual psychopaths, rapist typologies, and typologies of sex abusers of children. The legality of treatment such as psychosurgery-castration or drug therapy is reviewed, and counseling therapies of various types are described. Institutional and community group treatment of sex offenders is discussed and evaluated, and characteristics of therapies which have been effective with sex offenders are described. Group therapy which follows the technique known as rational-emotive therapy is discussed.

In the fourth selection, "Northwest Treatment Associates, Seattle, Washington, A Comprehensive, Community-Based Evaluation and Treatment Program for Adult Sex Offenders," Knopp describes specific techniques used to retrain adult sex offenders to deal with and overcome their tendencies toward unacceptable sexual behavior and to develop appropriate sexuality. Guided group work is utilized, and behavioral treatment, geared to the specific needs of individual offenders, is included. Impulse control techniques which can be applied by the offenders themselves and stronger intrusive types of controls which may need to be applied are described. The roles offenders' spouses and victim counselors can play in changing the behavior of adult sex offenders are given detailed consideration.

Another special area of offender behavior, substance abuse, has always been recognized as closely involved with or contributing to unlawful behavior. The U.S. Department of Justice reported that drug use is far greater among offenders than among non-offenders. It noted that 75% of jail inmates and 78% of prison inmates had used marijuana, cocaine, amphetamines, barbiturates, or heroin, compared to 37% of the general population, and that one-third of all inmates drank alcoholic beverages daily during the year before the crime for which they were incarcerated. Approximately half of the offenders incarcerated for violent crimes and 40% of those imprisoned for crimes against property had used alcohol just before the crime for which they had been incarcerated.[5]

Although substance abuse, particularly alcohol abuse, is prevalent among offenders, it may receive insufficient attention in the correctional treatment process. In the fifth selection, "Substance Abusers: Identification and Treatment," Atmore and Bauchiero offer many practical suggestions for identifying and treating these offenders. The authors note that obtaining factual data should always be the initial focus of client interviews, and that a good deal of information about a client's substance abuse history can be gathered through indirect questions related to family history and educational and employment experiences. Judgmental or self-perception questions regarding the problems the client has experienced because of substance abuse and the relation of the abuse to his or her present difficulties can then be posed. The authors also stress the importance of the use of urine tests in the management of casework with substance abusers. They regard regular testing as an objective measure of a client's behavioral improvement and a deterrent to recurrent abuse.

Notes

1. C. Michael Nelson, Robert B. Rutherford, Jr., and Bruce I. Wolford, "Handicapped Offenders Meeting Education Needs," *Corrections Today*, 47 (5) (August 1985), 32.

2. *Ibid.*, 32, 34.

3. *Ibid.*, 34.

4. Harold T. Werner, "Cognitive Theory," in Francis J. Turner, ed., *Social Work Treatment* (New York: Free Press, 1974), 246.

5. U.S. Department of Justice, *Report to the Nation on Crime and Justice*, 2nd edition (Washington, D.C.: Bureau of Justice Statistics, 1988), 50-51.

Group Counseling with Retarded Offenders

Joseph Steiner

Retarded adults are increasingly being identified in prison and county jail populations. They constitute about 4.1 percent of the total inmate community according to a 1973 study.[1] Thus, rehabilitative approaches must become more relevant to the needs of this group. Providing services in a jail environment would seem an ambitious undertaking. As Rappaport describes prison, there exists "no less fertile ground for the growth of the human ego, for the betterment of man's condition, and for the resurrection of human character."[2] Yet an effort sponsored by the social work staff of the Case Western Reserve University Mental Development Center to provide group counseling to retarded offenders has existed for four years in a county jail in northeastern Ohio.

The opportunity to attend to the special needs of retarded offenders arose when the county jail began a procedure of identifying and placing such inmates on a special ward or "pod" (holding area). A simple questionnaire on educational history, institutional experience, and previous psychological evaluations helps to assess inmates after they are bound over to the county. Those identified as having borderline to moderate retardation (scoring 80 to 55 on the Wechsler Adult Intelligence Scale) are sent to a pod of ten cells set aside for retarded inmates on the psychiatric floor. One reason for this separation, even on the psychiatric floor, is that retarded offenders, because of their limited judgment, competence, and cognitive skills, can be abused by the general jail population. This procedure usually succeeds in filling the special pod with the intended population.

Transitions in Jail

As an inmate, particularly a retarded inmate, enters jail, he or she experiences the problem of coping with sudden life transitions. The

Reprinted by permission of the National Association of Social Workers, Inc., from *Social Work*, March-April 1984, pp. 181-185.

most significant is the loss of freedom—for example, to move about freely and to make decisions (except as deemed appropriate in relation to his or her legal case). The inmate suddenly has fewer material belongings, a symbol of status on the outside. Heterosexual relationships are interrupted, while feelings are still present. The social peer group, which is usually of great influence, is suddenly composed of criminals.

To retarded offenders who seem to have difficulty understanding and being aware of their feelings, all this can amount to an overwhelmingly stressful situation. They are confused about the legal procedures they are experiencing, such as booking, preliminary hearings, indictments, bond setting, and arraignment. For impoverished offenders, in particular, few people are available to spend time with them and explain the judicial process.

In planning the group program for retarded offenders, this unique period in their legal journey was viewed in terms of the two main life transitions involved: entering the jail, and placement (probation or sentencing to prison). It was felt that relevant intervention could help these inmates to make a more constructive adjustment during both stressful events. Intensive role play or practice of actual situations the retarded inmate would probably encounter could enable them to react more adaptively to these transitions. Pankratz and Buchan describe the value of using psychodrama with retarded populations as a concrete way of bringing them into more intense involvement with specific problems.[3] The skills, especially the verbal ones, needed to cope with stressful situations, as well as practice in using institutional supportive resources, make up the basic content of the group.

Although the Mental Development Center already provided individual services at the jail, it was felt that a group structure would allow optimal development of skills. The other participants could provide the opportunity for role playing, feedback, and support. The group members' perception that their problems were unique could be altered by working with common concerns. It was hoped that feelings might be shared through the practice of language skills and that impulsive behavior might decrease through the use of group pressure, thus allowing the retarded offenders to adapt more effectively to the jail environment.

In thinking through the theory behind the practical approach, the term "cognitive casework" seems appropriate. This may be defined as a "limited helping process dealing specifically with clients [whose] ... low-level cognitive deficits deprive [them] of the basic tools or skills necessary for thinking."[4] Translating Sunley's concept to the jail group, the goals included practicing labeling of feelings, using feeling language, and using these language gains for problem-solving practice.

Finally, it was hoped that the newly practiced skills could be generalized, at least at some limited level, to problem situations outside the group.

Describing the Group

One hundred seventy-five male inmates attended the group sessions in the four-year period since the sessions began. (This total of 175 inmates attended one or more group sessions, whether or not the inmates became fully registered clients of the Mental Development Center with a case number and a file. Not all inmates were fully registered because of administrative costs in registering clients who were seen only once or twice. Furthermore, only 6.6 percent of the inmates in the jail are female; there were no females in the original sample of 175). No more than 10 and no less than 5 inmates attended group sessions at one time. Of these inmates, 61 percent were black, 37 percent were white, and 2 percent were of other ethnicity. This closely parallels the general jail population, which is 65 percent black, 33 percent white, and 2 percent other. The group members included 53 percent with cognitive levels in the borderline range, 41 percent in the mildly retarded range, and 6 percent in the moderately retarded range. Their alleged crimes included serious offenses such as aggravated murder or arson as well as less serious probation violations and breaking and entering. About 63 percent of this population were charged with crimes against property (robbery, possession of criminal tools, burglary, and so forth), 23 percent with crimes against person (murder and assault), and 14 percent with sexual offenses (rape and gross sexual imposition). The inmates ranged in age from 16 years old to 60 years old, with 23 percent below age 20, 43 percent between 21 and 25, 21 percent between 26 and 30, and 13 percent age 31 or over. At least 30 percent had psychiatric diagnoses in addition to their cognitive deficit or were on psychotropic medication. Little information was available about past employment. In general, this description seems consistent with that of MacEachron, who found this population as being nonwhite, being in their mid twenties to thirties, having a sixth-to-eighth grade reading ability, being low-skilled or having no employment history, and being on public assistance.[5]

The setting for the group is the hall in the center of the ten cells of the pod. An unarmed guard or corrections officer (CO) is included in the group. This is done because inmates must deal with the CO's personality and interpretation of jail rules on a daily basis. He can also be a valuable ally to the group leader by making sure outside interruptions are held to a minimum. If conflict develops, such as competition between the group leader and CO for his "flock," the group can be virtually destroyed by scheduling interruptions, such as laundry duty and recreation. Bell found that prison guards are quite powerful and become involved in complex relationships with inmates, subject to a number of corrupting influences.[6] The CO on this pod was at times instrumental during sessions, especially in role modeling how he had "made it," despite his impoverished background.

An open-ended structure is required because of the group's constantly changing membership. Rappaport found this structure to be a strength in working with inmates. As other inmates receive probation or are sentenced, members can actually see movement out of the group and so can feel more hope (or despair).[7] An open-ended group is a hindrance to significant group development, however, because cohesiveness is limited to the number of sessions shared by a particular core group of inmates. Such a core group of five or six inmates will attend up to four months of sessions, and then a new core will form. The average number of sessions attended by the group members in the first four years was 4.8, with 28 percent of the total membership attending only 1 session, and 22 percent attending 8 or more. One member attended 30 meetings. There was an average of two new members per week, sometimes none, and, on rare occasions, as many as four. New members' anxieties about adjusting to the jail environment and about old members' acceptance of them, were constantly dynamic issues demanding immediate attention.

Exclusions from the group were made when an inmate who was clearly functioning at a high level was placed on the pod for a brief stay or when a retarded inmate chose not to participate. Membership was presented as voluntary, but some inmates probably perceived the group, like other activities in the jail, to be mandatory.

Issues Discussed

The retarded inmate who is new on the pod has to deal with many adjustment problems that can be subsumed under the common theme of confusion. He may be wondering why he is incarcerated, what the exact criminal charge is, or, more simply, "When can I be released?" An individual functioning at a higher level may ask about his rights, while the retarded offender may not be aware that he has any and assume a passive role. Being passive in jail can be taken as a sign of weakness, which can be an invitation to physical, sexual, and personal abuse. Other confusing questions include, "Who can help me?" (which usually refers to the legal case and not to counseling), "What are the procedures of the system?" and "How long must I stay here?" Suddenly intensified feelings, such as helplessness, anger, defiance, frustration, martyrdom, and apathy, can confuse the inmate further, particularly because the retarded offender is often unaware of what he is feeling at any one moment.

Trust is an issue that both new and experienced inmates constantly have to deal with. In a county jail atmosphere, there are many more reasons to be constantly alert than to share oneself freely. Showing trust may be interpreted as another sign of weakness. Information and rumors spread quickly in this population. Inmates fear that the disclosure of any information may be used against them in court; they are told as much when they are arrested. They are focused, then, on narcissistic concerns of self-preservation, which impairs their ability to trust others. The retarded offender, in addition, has a tremendous need for acceptance, having in many cases experienced a life of rejection and lack of achievement. He may be fearful of further rejection as a result of his limited verbal ability, social incompetence, and inadequate development of skills for independent living, which are self-perceived handicaps he tries to conceal.

The group begins with these and other existing issues. Nine inmates, the CO, and the social worker-group leader participate in the first meeting; other supportive service staff occasionally attend. (The CO has usually had special training or supervision concerning issues of mental retardation. All the COs assigned to the special pods are under the supervision of the director of supportive services, a clinical psychologist.) The worker announces that these sessions are for the purpose of helping to ease adjustment on the pod and to learn about and practice sharing feelings more freely. It is further explained that the sessions are confidential and that the group leaders are not legal advisors or involved with the court procedure. This introduction usually meets with an air of apathy.

Participants are then greeted individually and asked about their well-being. This usually leads to some discussion of the current legal status of those willing to comment. At this point, the group usually moves back to challenge the introduction. Questions that arise in this portion of the session include, "Will what we say be told to anyone or used in our case?" "How do we know you are not part of the prosecution staff?" and "Why would you want to help us?" There are also many requests for different privileges, telephone calls, activities, and so forth. This opportunity is used to begin addressing the issue of trust by saying simply that "trust will only be proven in time, but meanwhile you do not have to say anything that you feel is too personal for the group to hear." This seems to help by stressing again the inmates' right to privacy and giving them a sense of control over at least one issue—their verbal participation in the group. It is also common for new inmates to check with more experienced ones about how safe it is to participate in the group format.

Group Process and Content

The bulk of the verbal content in the first few sessions covers three main areas: (1) complaints about lack of activity and the inefficient justice system, (2) questions about inmates' confusing legal status, and (3) discussion of depression and suicidal feelings. Other subjects include sexual frustration, religion, future plans, and separation from family.

The lack of time-filling activities in the jail is a benign subject because inmates consider it acceptable to talk about in public, and it is for the most part reality-oriented. Activity in the county jail consists of television, crafts, and irregular recreation sessions. Most retarded offenders cannot read well and do not feel comfortable with their degree of skill in games. They describe time on the pod as seeming to never change; at times they do not know if it is day or night. The boredom causes them either to be isolated with their anxieties or to look to each other for entertainment. This entertainment can include anything from commissary trading deals to mutual sexual relationships.

Isolation leads the retarded inmates not quite to introspection, but to some thought about where they are and what they have lost. They rarely think about what they would have done. Depression is the most commonly ventilated feeling in the group. Offenders feel that their case is hopeless and that their family has abandoned them. Perhaps most difficult for the inmates is the anxiety-filled wait for legal action. Resource people exist for keeping inmates aware of legal progress, including attorneys, social workers, probation officers, other supportive service staff, and family. Yet the retarded inmates seem to be unaware of resources available to them individually or how to make constructive use of the services. It is common for an inmate to discuss feeling restless because of boredom, depressed because of his pending case, and anxious as he awaits the next, unknown step in the judicial system.

The issue of suicide frequently arises, perhaps as a result of the inmates' depressions continuing over an extended period of time. One inmate who had threatened suicide finally "copped" to a lower charge to stop the day-to-day, dreaded waiting. He was able to have some control over his life by "copping," just as someone who committed suicide would. The retarded inmate traditionally "breaks" under the pressure, is quick to heed the advice of an attorney because of his needs for acceptance, and "cops out" (cops a plea). In almost every other area of jail life, the inmate has no decision-making power or control.

A description of the inmate's alleged offense, a detailed denial of the charge, or a refusal to mention the crime at all are some of the topics discussed by the inmates. The retarded offenders seem to be similar to the general jail population in almost admiring crimes against the person, with the exception of sexual offenses. Inmates, even retarded offenders, quickly learn that it can be dangerous to discuss a sexual offense because it is looked down on by peers. Sexual offenses also occur in jail, and the fear of being sexually abused is ever present. However, the retarded offender may construe sexual behavior as acceptance and caring.

An interesting dynamic is the argument over what outsiders would consider insignificant issues. It is common, for example, for inmates to quarrel about who owes whom a cigarette or candy bar, while serious charges are pending against them. These exchanges are significant as negotiations in the power structure of the pod, as a release of frustration, and as an escape from the more serious business at hand.

As mentioned earlier, the major portion of the group is devoted to practice in problem solving. The inmates can confront each other in a very tightly structured social situation. For example, one young inmate who was the current leader on the pod attacked, along with several others, another inmate for preaching and making noise at night. The "target" inmate complained about their constant harassment. With intervention by the leader, the group established guidelines and limits for the inmates on each side of the conflict, which were to be enforced by the CO. There could be little complaint about the guidelines later because there were twelve witnesses to the "deal." Another instance of problem solving took place when a white inmate did a poor job of cutting a black inmate's hair. The black inmate was angry, even though he had allowed the other to cut his hair, because he felt the white inmate did a poor job on purpose. In the group session, members pointed out how both were at fault and made some recommendations, such as, "Ignore it because it will grow back." and "Talk to a counselor when your feelings seem overwhelming to you." The problem-solving process takes practice and has to be repeated as group membership changes.

Role playing must be based on a careful assessment of the group and can be started only after the leader has helped create an atmosphere that is conducive to taking the personal risk involved. The retarded offenders must have gained some increased level of verbal participation, such as labeling of thoughts and feelings. Inmates must feel accepted and safe enough to take on the many different and demanding roles that the group practices (such as authority figures or victim of crimes) and to accept the group's critique and feedback.

The group ends at lunchtime, which is variable, but the leader remains on the pod to get to know the participants better and to discuss personal issues with individuals. This has proved helpful in determining what is acceptable to discuss in the group, preparing new inmates for the next session, and demonstrating how the staff can be used as a resource. Staff members who are present can listen to requests and respond to troubling personal concerns such as "Why does my family ignore me?" "I fear abuse on this pod," and "I don't know how to communicate to my lawyer effectively." Not all questions and requests can yield the exact response inmates desire, but at least the inmates can feel that there are staff resources available who have some answers to their concerns.

Outcome Research

One of the aims of this project was to help the retarded offender begin to become aware of and utilize appropriate resources that exist in his environment. To measure the effect of the group on inmates' continuing utilization of resources, a study was made of a group of 100 fully registered inmates, some of whom received individual services and some of whom experienced the group as well. Both types of services were rendered in jail and in the community after probation by staff from the Case Western Reserve Mental Development Center.

In this study, an inmate was considered to have discontinued service if he had had the opportunity to continue service and wilfully decided to terminate or if he did not show up for numerous appointments, either in jail or at the Mental Development Center. Since 51 percent of the 100 fully registered participants were sentenced to prison at another facility, those 51 inmates did not have the opportunity to continue service, which ruled them out of the statistical study. Three inmates had group service only, which excluded them also. The remaining 46 inmates, who either had both group and individual services or individual services only, constituted the study population.

Of the 15 inmates who had individual services only in jail, 5 (33 percent) chose not to continue or did not attend appointments. Of the 10 who had individual services only at the center, 3 (30 percent) did not continue service. Thus, for the total group of 25 inmates who had individual services only, the failure rate for continuing service was 32 percent. In contrast, of the 21 inmates who experienced both group and individual service, 3, or 14 percent, discontinued further service. This would seem to indicate that those inmates who experienced group as well as individual services continued to attend appointments and participate in a treatment plan more than twice as often as those in individual counseling only. The sample is insufficient in number at this time for tests of significance.

Future Study

Of the 175 inmates who attended one or more group sessions (whether or not the inmates became fully registered clients of the Mental Development Center), 53 percent were sentenced to prison, 39 percent were either released on probation or acquitted, and 8 percent were sent to a mental health institution. The relationship between these figures and the existence of the group has not been statistically measured, because no similar county jail population was available to serve as a comparison group. Such a study still needs to be initiated.

According to subjective observations about the effects of the group, the inmates' verbal ability seemed increased and comparable to that of psychiatric or prison populations without developmental deficits. This particularly stressful period in the legal process—awaiting trial—rather than the inmates' retardation, seems to cause them to express a much greater range of emotions than they ordinarily would. Confusion and anxiety seem to be at a very intense level, which makes this a strategic time for intervention. The group interaction and the problem-solving skills inmates used as a result of experience in the group seem to dilute inmates' tension and conflict. The occurrence of incidents in the pod has decreased during the group's existence, at least according to the CO's reports, as the retarded offenders learn to express anger more appropriately. Perhaps, as the inmates experience some degree of acceptance and successful problem solving, they are making the first gains toward a more generalized sense of competence.

Another idea under consideration for future study is a comparison of the number of violent incidents on the pod during a period of weeks while the group is functioning and during another period without the group. Other questions for study may include, How would increasing the number of meetings affect the outcome of the group? What effect if any does the group have on the general support system in the jail? Is education or ventilation a more useful method with the group? How can the group techniques be used with retarded people in other settings, such as community group homes or developmental centers?

Group Development

Group development among the retarded offenders is limited because of the changing membership in an open-ended situation. There still seemed to be some movement, however, at least in the core of four or five members who experienced four months of sessions. Hartford's model of phase development in groups—which includes pregroup phases, group formation, integration-disintegration, group functioning, and termination—is helpful in understanding the limited development that does take place in the group.[8]

The initial group formation phase seems to cover a range of behaviors that helps members define their role in such a structured situation. In this phase, members express concerns such as "Is it safe for me to participate in this activity?" "What is this group about?" "Will I appear incompetent?" and similar ambivalent feelings. In the integration phase, the participants are more relaxed and confident in testing the structure after their expectations of what will happen in the group are verified by their experience in the first few sessions. At this phase, for example, it is common for the inmates to question the legal efficacy and amount of help that they perceive to be present. Others find it difficult to give up power or status roles on the pod, which is necessary to some extent for them to become active, constructive participants on a genuine sharing level. There is confusion at times about clarification of goals and how a group can help them move toward a constructive end. The development of the group rarely proceeds beyond these early phases, although there are many experiences of problem solving and some level of cohesion that are characteristic of the later phases.

Members of the retarded offenders group have moved on to probation, employment, and reintegration into the community. The continuing hope is that within the group, inmates can practice using language and problem-solving skills and learn to use the support systems necessary for the transitions from community to jail and back to the community. With more effective use of such resources, perhaps the retarded offender can develop a more constructive, adaptive, and socially acceptable repertoire of behavior that may endure in the face of the pressures in society.

Notes

1. G. Tarjan et al., "Natural History of Mental Retardation: Some Aspects of Epidemiology." *American Journal of Mental Deficiency*, 77 (1973), pp. 369-379, as cited in Ann E. MacEachron, "Mentally Retarded Offenders," *American Journal of Mental Deficiency*, 84 (September 1979), p. 165.

2. Richard G. Rappaport, "Group Therapy in Prison," in Milton Seligman, ed., *Group Counseling and Group Psychotherapy with Rehabilitation Clients,* (Springfield, Ill.: Charles C. Thomas, Publisher, 1977), p. 116.

3. Loren D. Pankratz and L. Gerald Buchan, "Techniques of Warm Up in Psychodrama with the Retarded," *Mental Retardation,* 4 (October 1966), pp. 12-15.

4. Harold T. Werner "Cognitive Theory," in Francis J. Turner, ed., *Social Work Treatment* (New York: Free Press, 1974), p. 246. See also Robert Sunley, "New Dimensions in Reaching-out Casework," *Social Work,* (April 1968), p. 71ff.

5. MacEachron, "Mentally Retarded Offenders," p. 171.

6. Robert R. Bell, *Social Deviance* (Homewood, Ill.: Dorsey Press, 1971), p. 333.

7. Rappaport, "Group Therapy in Prison," p. 127.

8. Margaret E. Hartford, *Groups in Social Work* (New York: Columbia University Press, 1971), pp. 67-93.

Halfway Houses:
Meeting Special Needs

Robert A. Lippold

In September 1984, a group of people gathered for a pizza party in Tacoma, Washington. This meeting was unremarkable, except for the fact that most of the participants were mentally retarded and mentally ill felons, still serving sentences for crimes ranging from burglary to arson. The occasion celebrated four years of Washington state's Department of Corrections' (DOC) community programming for special offenders. In contrast to professional eulogies for innovative programs, speakers at this function included the residents of two state-sponsored halfway houses who chronicled their successes and ratified the program's purpose and function.

Incarceration of the mentally ill and developmentally disabled offender can present exasperating problems for correctional systems. Special needs inmates experience poorer institutional adjustment than the general population. In addition, these offenders serve longer periods of incarceration than nondisabled offenders for similar crimes. Reasons for longer incarceration include poor family and community support, and fewer parole placement options as a result of the dual stigma of offender and disabled person. Group homes and congregate care facilities are reluctant to accept disabled or mentally ill offenders.

In 1977, Washington DOC began identifying the retarded population residing in adult correctional facilities. As a result, the DOC provided institutional placement as well as community residential placement programs that recognize the special needs of these offenders. The programs offer a transitional placement where, after a period of successful adjustment to specialized work release, offenders can move to less restrictive settings in the community.

Reprinted by permission of the American Correctional Association from *Corrections Today,* 47 (6) (October 1985), pp. 46, 82, 112.

Rap House

When Rap House opened in 1980, its target population was offenders with developmental disabilities. During the first months of operation, it became evident that, in addition to developmentally disabled offenders, the mentally ill offender required a similar facility. As a result, Lincoln Park House was opened a year later. The facilities are located next to each other in two large, older homes in a residential area of Tacoma, across from a city park.

The DOC contracted a Tacoma-based corporation to provide the houses, correctional staff, and support services, including therapists and cooks. A state supervisor and three parole officers provide on-going program supervision. In addition, a developmental disabilities specialist functions as a community liaison for both programs and develops community resources. A consulting psychiatrist and nurse provide medication.

A small caseload size (1 to 10 and 1 to 15) allows supervising parole officers to use intensive program planning with residents. Goal setting, skills training, and individual program planning are essential to work with offenders with limited developmental disabilities and mental illness.

Referrals to either program come from institution staff, field probation and parole officers, and other agencies that deal with the developmentally disabled or mentally ill. Cases are assigned to one of the supervising parole officers who then completes an investigation, including a personal interview. Following the investigation, the case is presented to the Community Screening Committee composed of participants from the neighborhood and professional community.

To prevent inappropriate referrals, program criteria have been made clear to all components of the correctional system. Candidates for Rap House are usually limited to those having a developmental disability prior to adulthood that is expected to continue. Mental retardation, indicated by a 69 IQ or below, would qualify for placement at Rap House. Also individuals suffering from cerebral palsy, epilepsy, dyslexia, autism, auditory impairment, or visual impairments may be referred. Additionally, inmates who are identified as somewhat less disabled may be considered as bed space allows.

Criteria for placement at Lincoln Park House include an evaluation and diagnosis completed by a psychiatrist or clinical psychologist. This diagnosis should fall under the categories of a major thought or affective disorder, such as schizophrenia, or bipolar disorders. Also, a disorder that would cause a substantial adverse effect on the individual's cognitive or volitional function, requiring specialized care, may be considered. The program does rule out individuals whose primary diagnosis is a personality or behavioral disorder. The mental illness should have reached partial remission prior to placement at Lincoln Park. Residents are also required to be medication compliant, at all times.

Program Phases

On entering the program, the offender is placed in the first of five phases. The first phase is a "black out" or stabilization phase, to establish relationships with correctional officers, residents, and supervising parole officers. It gives program staff the opportunity to observe the person's behavior and ability to be allowed safely out of the facility for specific lengths of time for specific tasks.

The resident moves gradually through the remaining four program phases, earning expanded privileges and responsibility toward the eventual goal of placement in the community. Residents are required to obtain a food-handler's card and current identification and to demonstrate progress in working with their parole officer in developing a work release plan and, eventually, a parole plan.

Weekly classification meetings determine movement through the phases and deal with any disciplinary matters that may occur. Appropriate socialization skills and use of leisure time are encouraged through weekly recreational outings with staff and residents. This may involve going to the local gymnasium, picnics, swimming, movies, or other community functions.

Inappropriate behavior can result in termination from the program and return to a state institution or county jail. Rules are tight; expectations, very clear. There have been a minimum of criminal activities by residents, although they travel daily through the neighborhood.

Program staff often witness significant improvements in behavior as a result of specialized programming. One inmate, who has now successfully reentered the community, had been placed on sedatives while in an institution because of what was referred to as "transitional stress syndrome." As a result of being teased by other inmates, the resident was eating feces and drinking his own urine. Once placed into Rap House, the resident became involved in vocational training and individual counseling. The sedating medication was discontinued. As a parolee, he still returns weekly to therapy sessions at Rap House.

Staff Creativity

The staff exhibits a high degree of creativity in dealing with resident problems. In the case of one resident enrolled in a vocational training program, attendance had become a problem. The parole officer began a contract in which the resident would receive $5 as incentive pay each Friday, if he had attended the five days of his training program. Attendance went from 14 of 19 days to 20 of 20 days in a single month. Sometimes remarkable development is demonstrated. One person, who was practically nonverbal in the institution, became much more social and communicative as a result of placement in this work release setting, which provides a home-like environment.

Developmentally disabled and mentally ill offenders remain a difficult population to work with, in both institution and community programs. Staff must constantly remind themselves that success is not measured according to ordinary standards. Success for this population may be in identifying appropriate and needed community supports that the person requires to refrain from reoffending and then working with professionals or social service agencies to ensure community resources are developed and appropriately used.

While both programs are more expensive to operate than traditional work release programs, there is less recidivism. A significant factor in the lower return rate is that both Rap House and Lincoln Park programs will consider reaccepting a former resident should a significant problem develop in a community placement. If a mentally ill parolee stops taking medications, and begins to decompensate, there is a chance for readmittance to the work release facility. If a developmentally disabled parolee loses a job and experiences difficulty in a living situation, a short period of stabilization may be granted.

Program Successes

This support has prevented reincarceration. In the last three years at Rap House, 22 residents have successfully completed the program and been released to the community. In the same period of time, there have been 35 terminations from the program resulting in return to the institution or a county jail. It is significant to note that of those 35, 18 have been readmitted to the program and either have completed the program or remain in residence at the present time. In the last two years of operation, the Lincoln Park program has seen 34 successful completions. Twenty-seven residents have been terminated for either disciplinary or psychological (decompensation) reasons. Of those, five have been processed through both programs, or are currently in residence. The average length of stay at Rap House is six months, and the average length of stay at Lincoln Park is four months.

The Rap House and Lincoln Park experiences clearly have demonstrated their value in dealing with this population. They also have clearly identified the necessity of program flexibility, specialized staff training, systemwide cooperation, and the interagency support needed for successful management of the mentally and developmentally disabled offender.

Treatment of the Sex Offender

Ernest M. DeZolt
and Peter C. Kratcoski

The concept of "sex offender" creates some difficulty in definition, because of the wide diversity of opinion and moral conviction as to what constitutes normal or acceptable sexual behavior. Researchers at the Kinsey Institute defined a sex offense as "an overt act committed by a person for his own immediate gratification which is contrary to the prevailing sexual mores of the society in which he lives, and/or is legally punishable; and results in his being legally convicted" (Gebhard, et al., 1965:8). In the past two decades, many activities which were defined as improper sexual behavior and subjected to criminal penalties became commonplace occurrences. Although premarital sexual activity, homosexual contacts, and dissemination of birth control information and devices to unmarried persons remained forbidden by statute in many jurisdictions, they were practiced with little fear of prosecution. However, in a recent decision the U.S. Supreme Court upheld a Georgia law which prohibits oral or anal sexual contacts between persons (*Bowers v. Hardwick*, 1986).

In the past ten years, notable increases have occurred in the number of reported and prosecuted cases of rape and of sexual abuse of children. These increases have forced mental health professionals to reevaluate the skills and techniques applied when dealing with offenders involved in these and other sex related offenses. State criminal codes have been revised to specifically define sexual offenses and the penalties attendant to their commission. For example, the Ohio Revised Code (1983) classifies sexual offenses as sexual assaults and displays, prostitution offenses, and offenses related to the dissemination of obscenity and matter harmful to juveniles (§2907.02-2907.37). Prostitution and offenses related to the dissemination of obscenity and matter harmful to juveniles are generally penalized through the imposition of fines or short jail terms, and treatment is not a factor in the disposition of such cases. In contrast, the dispositions of cases involving sexual assaults and displays frequently include treatment. Such treatment may be mandated by the courts or offered as an option for the offender.

Offenses defined as sexual assaults and displays include:

Rape, broadly defined as sexual intercourse with females by force, including anal intercourse, cunnilingus, and fellatio. Included are homosexual and lesbian assaults, rape by drugging the victim, and rape as sexual conduct with a pre-puberty victim.

Sexual battery, defined as including sexual conduct by coercion, impaired judgment, or incestuous conduct between parent and child, stepparent and stepchild, a guardian and a ward, or a custodian or person "in loco parentis" with his or her charge. This category includes sexual conduct with a prisoner or hospital patient within an institution by a person with supervisory authority.

Corruption of a minor, defined as sexual conduct by an offender who is age eighteen or over who knows his or her partner is between the ages of 13 through 15.

Gross sexual imposition is analogous to rape, but involves less serious "sexual contact," including any touching of the erogenous zone of another for the purpose of sexually arousing or gratifying either person.

Sexual imposition includes sexual touching when the offender knows or has reasonable cause to believe the touching is offensive. This section of the code further forbids sexual contact when the victim is in early adolescence and the offender is age eighteen or over and four or more years older than the victim.

Importuning prohibits the soliciting of a person under thirteen years of age to engage in sexual activity, or when the solicitor is age eighteen or over and four or more years older than the person solicited.

Voyeurism prohibitions make it illegal to be involved in trespassing, invasion of privacy, and spying for the purpose of obtaining vicarious sexual thrill.

Felonious sexual penetration is the insertion of any instrument, apparatus or other object into the vaginal or anal cavity of another through compelling force, threat of force, or after impairing the other person's judgment through intoxicant, force or deception. (Ohio Criminal Code, as amended through June 30, 1983 § 2907.2 through 2907.12).

While this list is not exhaustive, it represents the types of behavior which fall within the range of sexual assault and display offenses.

We noted earlier that the less serious types of sexual offenses may be ignored or punished with fines or short jail terms. However, when serious felonies of a sexual nature occur, several states have formulated laws which specifically designate the type and nature (determinate or indeterminate) of sentence which should be imposed, and even the type of facility where the offender should be housed.

While the vast majority of sexual offenders, if prosecuted and convicted, would be subject to the same types of sanctions and afforded the same treatment options as other offenders, in approximately half of the states statutes have been enacted that focus on the psychopathic sexual offender. Generally, these statutes are based on the assumption that such an offender lacks the willpower to control his actions or impulses, is dangerous, and is likely to commit the same offense again if the opportunity arises. The laws are applied to offenders who are considered a serious threat to the community, notably rapists and child molesters. Although they vary in specifics, these statutes allow for commitment of the offender to a mental hospital or an institution for the criminally insane if a psychiatrist has ruled that the individual has the characteristics of a sexual psychopath. Once hospitalized or institutionalized, treatment is mandated for such an offender. The commitment can be for life, if the offender does not respond to treatment.

Washington's Sexual Psychopath Act (1975) provides for treatment in a state mental hospital for sex offenders who have been defined as sexual psychopaths. In such cases, the prosecutor files a petition alleging that the offender is a sexual psychopath who is predisposed to commit sexual offenses in a degree which constitutes a menace to the health and safety of others. After the offender is convicted, sentence is suspended while the offender undergoes a 90-day period of observation in a state mental hospital. If the diagnosis of sexual psychopathy is confirmed, the offender is committed to the hospital until the treatment staff decides that he or she should be released and the court accepts this judgment. The offender may be unconditionally discharged or placed under probation supervision for up to five years.

Sexual psychopath statutes and habitual offender statutes (which frequently are applied to sexual offenders) are grounded in the assumption that there are viable treatment programs which can change the behavior of these persons. In *Allen v. Illinois* (1986), the U.S. Supreme Court upheld an Illinois law providing for commitment to prison psychiatric wards of persons who had demonstrated propensities toward acts of sexual assault, and declared that the state is serving its purpose of treating rather than punishing such persons by committing them to institutions designed to provide psychiatric care and treatment. The fact that the prison psychiatric wards house convicted criminals as well as persons who have not been convicted of sexual offenses does not alter the fact that the state is sending them there with the intention to treat them, not to punish them (*Allen v. Illinois*, 1986).

Treatment is frequently mandated for rapists and offenders who have sexually abused children. Because such offenders present unique problems, their treatment will be the focus of this chapter. The characteristics and motivations of these offenders will be examined, and programs which have been developed to treat them will be described.

Rapists—Typologies

Various typologies have been developed to examine the motivations and emotional processes of rapists. One classification, set by Groth Burgess and Holmstrom, describes rapists in terms of four basic types:

> *The power assertive rapist* regards rape as an expression of his virility and mastery and dominance. He feels entitled to "take it" or sees sexual domination as a way of keeping women in line. The rape is a reflection of the inadequacy he experiences in terms of his sense of identity and effectiveness . . . .

> *The power reassurance rapist* commits the offense in an effort to resolve disturbing doubts about his sexual adequacy and masculinity. He wants to place a woman in a helpless, controlled position in which she cannot refuse or reject him, thereby shoring up his failing sense of worth and adequacy . . . .

> *The anger-retaliation rapist* commits rape as an expression of his hostility and rage toward women. His motive is revenge and his aim is degradation and humiliation . . . .

> *The anger-excitation rapist* finds pleasure, thrills, and excitation in the suffering of his victim. He is sadistic and his aim is to punish, hurt, and torture his victim. His aggression is eroticized. (Groth, Burgess, and Holmstrom: 1977:1242-1242)

In their study of 146 rape victims, these researchers concluded that approximately two-thirds of the offenses were power rape situations, and the remaining third were anger rape situations (1242).

Although a good deal of theory and research related to rapists has been developed, there is considerable confusion about the personality characteristics of the individuals who commit rapes. Some psychologists and sociologists view rape as essentially an act of violence. As a form of violent behavior, rape may be instrumental, that is, used as a means of gaining the rewards of prestige with peers, control over others, and mastery of situations. Many researchers' typologies of rapists support the notion that rape is widely used to make victims helpless, fearful, and totally under the rapists' control (Menachem, 1971; Macdonald, 1971). Such rapists may feel that their behavior will go unreported or unpunished, and this supposition is given some weight by research. In *The Crime and the Consequences of Rape* (1982), Dean and deBruyn-Kops report, on the basis of governmental and research sources, that many incidents of rape continue to be unreported and, of those reported to police, only 25% lead to arrest, while many charges are dropped or reduced to misdemeanors. They reported that only 20% of the offenders who go to trial for rape receive actual prison sentences.

Rape may also be interpreted as pathological behavior which reflects a morally defective personality. There may not be any meaning attributed to the act beyond attempting to satisfy the rapist's sexual needs. The degree of psychological abnormality attributed to the offender would determine whether treatment or punishment is in order.

For example, the *Diagnostic and Statistical Manual of Mental Disorders*, (3rd ed.) lists compulsive rape under the sexual deviation category of paraphilia, and notes that sex offenses can be classified under various psychiatric conditions such as schizophrenia and manic depressive psychosis (1978:1-33). Treatment for a compulsive rapist, then, should be grounded in the assumption that this person is mentally ill.

Sex Abusers of Children—Typologies

Sexual abuse of children is regarded as a greatly underreported offense, and actual incidence may be as much as ten times the official reports (Elwell, 1979:227). Children may be abused through rape, sexual battery, gross sexual imposition, sexual imposition, or felonious sexual penetration. The female-to-male ratio of victims of sexual abuse is estimated to be 10 to 12 abused females for every male child abused, but there are indications that sexual abuse of male children is greatly underreported (Roth, 1978:3). Sexual offenses which involve family members (incest) are the least likely to be reported or fully prosecuted. There is evidence that a notable percentage of those involved in this activity were sexually abused themselves as children. Such persons tend to have been part of a disorganized lifestyle which also involved other forms of deviance and drug and/or alcohol abuse (Elwell, 1979:227-235).

The profile of an adult who sexually abuses a child is that of a young, heterosexual male, who is concerned with controlling, not injuring the young child. According to Krasner, et al., (1977:108) no force is used in 54% of all such incidents. Rosenfeld (1979) characterized the adult abuser as an individual who has experienced feelings of rejection or inadequacy and is emotionally estranged from his wife. The mother is often a key figure in the sexual abuse of female children. She may be aware that the child has assumed her sexual role and either does not protest this or even feels relieved about it. An American Humane Association study (1977:6-8) found that more than 10% of the mothers of sexually abused children had themselves been sexually abused as children. The assumption of the abused child of her mother's role may extend to taking over a good deal of the housework and care of the other children, as well as sexual contact with her father.

Gebhard and his associates at the Kinsey Institute, in a study of sexual offenders against children (1965) classified them as pedophiles (offenders who preferred sexual contact with children), sociosexually underdeveloped males (those who suffered from feelings of shyness and inferiority toward women), amoral delinquents (offenders who, when aroused, were apt to employ any convenient human or animal for gratification), mental defectives (who seek petting with children as much for attention and affection as for sexual gratification), psychotics, drunks, and senile deteriorates (characterized by deprivation, loneliness, and impotence) (216).

Issues in Treatment of Sex Offenders

Treatment modalities for rapists and other serious sexual offenders may involve three broad categories: psychosurgery-castration, drug therapy which produces "chemical castration," and counseling therapies. The use of psychosurgery-castration or drug therapy cannot be mandated without the offender's consent. An offender might agree to an operation or to use of a drug such as Depo-Provera, which reduces sexual drive and helps the offender control his sexual impulses, if a guaranteed reduction in sentence were offered as a trade-off. If an offender is diagnosed as suffering from a mental disorder, and if the offender is sentenced under a special section of the criminal code which mandates treatment, it is most likely that counseling therapies will be applied. However, even these cannot be undertaken without the offender's cooperation and consent.

Regardless of whether an offender's behavior is defined in a legal manner (by the type of act committed) or through psychological definition (emphasis placed on learned sexual deviation), once committed to an institution or hospital, the offender has the right to voluntary consent to treatment. Bohmer (1983) notes that: "Without consent from a subject, training professionals—and in some cases institutions, are technically liable for the charge of battery. At a minimum, the person to be treated should be given information about the basic nature of the treatment and the 'material risks' involved" (6). Material risks are defined by Schwitzgebel (1979) as information regarding a patient's position which a reasonable person would view as critical. He believes that information consists of six key elements: the diagnosis or purpose of the treatment, the nature and duration of the treatment, the risks involved, the prospects for success or benefits, possible disadvantages if the treatment is not undertaken, and alternative methods of treatment (6).

Mentally competent persons who have been involuntarily committed to hospitals or institutions have a right to refuse treatment. Their consent, or approval from the court, must be gained prior to beginning treatment. Although such patients have a right to treatment, they are not obliged to accept it. In contrast, mentally competent persons convicted of offenses generally do not have a legal right to refuse standard forms of treatment. However, there has been a trend toward establishing set procedures for obtaining consent from inmates prior to beginning treatment which might be termed "hazardous or exceptionally intrusive." Court decisions which have upheld a prisoner's right to refuse treatment have involved treatment which was considered "unreasonable or experimental" rather than treatment which met professionally recognized standards (Schwitzgebel, 1979:83).

Under Illinois state law, individuals may be committed to the psychiatric ward of a prison if they are proved to have a mental disorder for more than one year and had demonstrated propensities toward acts of sexual assault. Persons accused of being sexually dangerous must, under law, talk with state psychiatrists, who would evaluate their condition and make a determination whether these persons are mentally ill. If the determination is positive, they are housed in the psychiatric ward. In upholding the constitutionality of this law, the Supreme Court noted: "The state serves its purpose of treating rather than punishing sexually dangerous persons by committing them to an institution expressly designed to provide psychiatric care and treatment." (*Allen v. Illinois*, 54 U.S. Law Week: 4966).

Another issue in the treatment of sex offenders is the return of the offender to the community. Although treatment is initiated in a hospital or institutional setting, decisions are made in many instances to gradually return sex offenders who show evidence of responding positively to treatment to the community through placement in group homes of furlough from the hospital or institution while treatment continues. Public concern about the effectiveness of treatment is sometimes coupled with a perception that offenders who have been hospitalized rather than institutionalized have escaped punishment for their misdeeds.

Avery-Clark described the trend for mental health practitioners to lobby for the placement of offenders who are suffering from psychiatric disorders directly related to their crimes in hospitals rather than in institutions. She noted that offenders who served time in hospitals usually had shorter stays than those with comparable offenses who had been institutionalized (1983: 69). The concern of the local citizenry that serious sexual offenders who may still be "dangerous" are being released back into the community after a short stay in a mental hospital has resulted in movements to have legislatures establish new regulations which would require that the committing judge approve each release from a psychiatric facility. The judge's decision would be based on an evaluation of the sex offender by a psychiatrist appointed by the court.

Group Therapy for Sex Offenders in the Institutional Setting

Group therapy has been utilized as a treatment modality for rapists and sex offenders against children who have been committed to institutions. Theorists (Groth, et al., 1982; Alford, et al., 1985) have suggested that these offenders commit their offenses because of personality adjustment problems. Their sexual offenses are manifestations of hostilities and anger resulting from unsolved life issues. The group therapy approach stresses the personal involvement of each offender in improving his or her interpersonal and social skills.

An institution based program which used group therapy was applied at the United States Disciplinary Barracks in Fort Leavenworth, Kansas. Twenty male inmates were divided into two groups: those who had committed sexual offenses against children, and those who had raped adults. The "sexual offenses against children" group met for one hour, once a week, for a year. The entrance guidelines for this group were based on the offender acknowledging his responsibility for the offense, understanding the inappropriate nature of the offense, having concern for the victim's response, and feeling distressed over his behavior (Groth, 1982: 94).

The overall objectives of this group were reintegration of the offender's personality through the fostering of self-worth and development of interpersonal and social skills and impulse management. The actual treatment goals consisted of: keeping a written log of the issues and responses discussed in the group setting, writing an autobiography after three months in the program, developing better interpersonal skills in relating to women and forming expectation regarding women, dealing with the possibility that the offender had been a victim of sexual abuse as a child, and detecting impulses toward approaching a child with the need for sexual contact (Alford, et al., 1985).

The entrance guidelines for the rapist group were the same as those for the group of child sexual abusers. The rapist group was serviced by a male/female treatment team who "role modeled competency and self-confidence without putting each other down" (Alford, et al., 1985:84). The purpose of using the male/female team was to help break down the stereotypes of women internalized by the offenders. Therapy goals were developed through personal drawings with disclosure. Offenders were asked to draw pictures of themselves, parents, women, wives, and girlfriends, if applicable. Discussions following in which the concepts of preference, self-image, expectations, power, control, and competition were evaluated. The offenders were asked to draw a picture of the woman they raped and compare her to the "ideal woman, wife, or mother" (Alford, 1985:84).

Both the child sex abusers and the rapists were pre- and post-tested on the Tennessee Self-Concept Scale (TSCS), which measured identity, self-satisfaction, behavior, physical self, moral-ethical self, personal self, family self, and social self (Alford: 1985). It was found that the rapists had shallow relationships with women, were possessive, lacked commitment, and had a fear of being rejected. The child molesters had a lower self-esteem of and a worse opinion of the act they committed than did the rapists. However, these opinions changed after the group therapy. Molesters were also more prone to become dependent on the therapist. Both groups relied heavily on sexual sterotypes in their relationships (Alford: 1985).

Group therapy has also been used successfully with mentally disordered sex offenders, who had been found guilty of felony sexual offenses. Not all types of mentally disordered offenders are candidates for such treatment. Excluded from participation are "psychotics, mentally retarded, legally insane, and otherwise incompetent offenders, such as those judged to stand trial by reason of insanity" (Annis, et al., 1984: 428).

A program for treatment of mentally disordered sex offenders was operated at Florida State Hospital. It involved the treatment of twenty-five offenders ranging in age from 25 to 46. The group treatment involved offenders, therapists, and "victim workers," who had themselves been victims of sexual aggression. Each therapy session lasted 90 minutes, and the offenders were divided into groups of five to eight. Each "victim worker," along with one or two therapists, met with each group one to five times. The sessions involved exchange of information, culminating with the offenders detailing their sexual aggression against the victim. The group process often evolved into highly personal, often very intense, interactions with considerable disclosure by offenders and the "victim workers." (Annis, et al., 1984:430).

Approximately half of the offenders involved in this program were returned to court or prison for failure to gain from therapy, while the remaining half returned to the court or prison with a good report. The successful offenders usually received probation, reduced sentences, or assignment to a less restrictive correctional setting (Annis, et al.:428).

Evaluation of this program was accomplished through self-reports of offenders, therapists, and the "victim workers." These self-reports were administered before, during, and after the sessions, and by follow-up questionnaires. The offenders reported after completing the program that they believed they had helped educate the "victim workers" as to their human quality. They also reported that the program made them better able to share their feelings with women, improved their communication skills, gave them new perceptions of women as more than "objects," personalized their victims, and gave them a more accurate perception of society's perception of them (Annis, et al.:430-31).

The use of the "victim workers" in therapy for offenders was fairly unique. It was found that among forty-four rehabilitation programs serving incarcerated rapists, only four employed rape victims or those who work with survivors of sexual victimization in treatment roles (Annis, et al.:434). The use of victims in counseling other victims is widely applied through rape crisis centers and sexual abuse hotlines, and the possibility of their wider use in treating sexual offenders should be explored.

Behavior modification through group therapy was applied in the Missouri Sexual Offender Program. The philosophical foundation of this program was the belief that sexual offending is a learned behavior and therefore can be modified through a conscious awareness of personal behavior. The theoretical basis of the program is the supposition that when an offender assumes responsibility for his behavior and is given alternate social skills as reinforcement, socially acceptable behavior will result (Clark, 1986: 89).

The Missouri Sexual Offender Program involves two phases. During Phase I, the orientation, weekly two-hour classes were conducted to discuss the concept and the treatment with the offenders. The major possible consequence of failure to participate would be a delay in obtaining parole. After interviews, the offenders were classified as manipulative or aggressive, socially inadequate, or more average individuals who had exercised poor judgment and committed offenses as a result. A wide variety of testing instruments was also used, including the Minnesota Multiphasic Personality Inventory, the Norwicki-Strickland Personal Opinion Survey, the Rathus Assertiveness Scale, and the Anger Self-report Scale. Cognitive, affective, and behavioral disturbances specifically related to sexual concerns were evaluated with the Derogatis Sexual Functioning Inventory and the Thorne Sex Inventory (Avery-Clark, 1983). During Phase II, group therapy, based on confrontative techniques, was used to heighten offender awareness regarding learned behavior. Phase II lasted 9 to 12 months, with meetings held four hours each week. Evaluation of the program indicated statistically successful results.

Community Group Treatment for Sex Offenders

Community treatment of sex offenders raises the question of whether punishment or treatment should be the major purpose in dealing with sex offenders. One often overlooked benefit of community treatment of sex offenders is the possibility of educating the public regarding the existence of inappropriate sexual activity, its motivations, and the availability of treatment. State legislation in the late 1970s mandated community treatment for sex offenders. Atascadero State Hospital in California and Western State Hospital in Washington are the sites of innovative community treatment programs for sex offenders. At Atascadero State Hospital, the program begins with an orientation to educate offenders in the areas of sexual anatomy and physiology. Small group sessions are then employed to raise the offenders' level of awareness of the needs of others. Role playing is used, and college student volunteers, both heterosexual and homosexual, are brought in to assist offenders in learning to model behavior and gain assertiveness skills.

The therapy at Western State Hospital, in Washington, centers on group processing. MacDonald and Williams (1971) state the group treatment goals as awareness of problem behavior, understanding of treatment goals and expectations, acceptance of responsibility to change problem behavior, and the development of social skills to adopt new behavior patterns. In the first phase of the program, offenders' progress is measured in group living, work assignments, psychotherapy, family and sexual relationships, social and recreational activities, and leadership ability. Once offenders successfully complete Phase I, they are granted work furloughs, but return to the hospital at night.

Unlike the community programs described above, which are housed in state hospitals, the Child Sexual Abuse Treatment Program (CSATP) operates in the community, funded by Santa Clara County, California. County probation officers intervene in crisis situations involving child sexual abuse, and provide individual and family counseling. The therapy process emphasizes treatment of the involved family members separately, then as a family unit with a child, and, if necessary, marital therapy.

A group known as Parents United and a related group, Daughters United, share the counseling responsibilities with the probation officers by attending weekly meetings with the offenders similar to those held by Alcoholics Anonymous. Parents are forced to take responsibility for mistakes or oversights that led to incestuous patterns. Fathers must confront other mothers and fathers at the meetings regarding the abuse of their children. Offenders are not placed into the program until they admit and understand the seriousness of their actions. Those allowed to enter are given suspended sentences and then ordered by the judge to participate in this therapy as a condition of release to the community (Kiersh, 1980: 33).

Characteristics of Effective Therapy for Sex Offenders

The counseling programs developed to treat sexual offenders, whether used in an institution, psychiatric hospital, or the community, all seem to have a common theme. There is an assumption that the cause of the offense cannot totally be defined as a personality abnormality of the offender. If the offender is to change his behavior, the treatment must call for open, uninhibited communication with others who are affected by this person's behavior, including parents, spouse, other family members, or the victim. Group treatment seems to yield more positive results than individual counseling. If the group consists of offenders and counselors, the interaction may be initially characterized by dislike, distrust, aggressive behavior, insults, refusal to participate, or failure to identify with the other group members, but during the group process insights are gained. The topics and discussions during the meetings may vary tremendously, depending on the members and their needs.

VanNess, who supervised group therapy with violent sexual offenders over a number of years, lists the following matters as frequent topics of group discussions:

1. Being honest with yourself about the offense
2. Taking personal responsibility for your actions without blaming others
3. Understanding the laws and why you were sent to the institution
4. Understanding what happened to your victim
5. Dealing with your reputation in your community
6. Being honest with your family
7. Learning what makes you angry
8. Learning how to handle your anger
9. Learning to solve problems without using force
10. Chemical abuse and your offense
11. Building good relationships with people. (VanNess, 1983: 14)

During the sessions, various techniques were used to illustrate situations which might arise with family members or institution staff. Role playing, discussions of films, and various exercises and games provided offenders opportunities for communication and learning.

VanNess identified certain patterns of behavior in the rapists' lives which have also been noted by other researchers. These included a lack of close personal relationships with other persons, particularly women, distrust of other males, a view of the world as a hostile and "dog eat dog" place, and conceptions of parents as givers or withholders rather than emotionally bonded persons. In their dealings with others, the rapists viewed power or force as the important element in relating to other persons, and had great difficulty in recognizing that men and women could treat each other as equals. In describing events which immediately preceded the rapes they committed, they invariably described some type of highly emotional incident which aroused their anger (VanNess: 1983: 16).

Robinson A. Williams, who served as Assistant Director of the Treatment Center for Sexual Offenders at Western State Hospital, regarded abnormal sexual behavior as a learned method of relieving emotional stress. He maintained that sexual attacks or contacts become habitual ways of finding emotional release for offenders who feel inadequate and insecure in their relationships with women. He noted that sex offenders frequently have experienced troubled childhoods and may themselves have been victims of sexual abuse as children (Denenberg, 1974: 58).

Group therapy is beneficial for sex offenders because it provides a setting in which they can relate to fellow sex offenders and feel that they will understand their problems. As the group encourages the offender to reveal his inner conflicts and fears, he becomes aware of the motivations for his offenses and begins to recognize that he must change his behavior. The group provides constant support during this awareness experience. Various steps are established, which give the offender opportunities to take more responsibility for his actions. The steps usually involve increasing degrees of physical freedom to move about the institution or the grounds and acceptance of responsibility for the activities of the group.

Most of the group therapy programs which have some demonstrated success with sex offenders appear to follow the general outlines of the technique known as rational-emotive therapy. This therapy, developed by Ellis in the 1950s, identifies irrational thinking and erroneous belief systems as the roots of problems, and involves a process of reeducation by which the person being treated acquires a more rational and tolerant view of life. The therapist functions as a teacher who leads the offender to understand how his outlook has contributed to his self-defeating behavior and how to begin to behave rationally. The group plays a key role in leading the offender to critically examine his beliefs and behavior and work to change them. The eclectic approach involved may include probing, confrontation, challenging, behavior contracts, role playing, hypnotherapy, assertiveness training, and many other techniques. Encounter groups, marriage and family therapy, and sex therapy may be used. Rational-emotive therapy is most effective with persons who are not seriously emotionally disturbed, and, because of its emphasis on the thinking process, it is unlikely to be successful for persons of limited intelligence (Corey, 1982: 96-97).

References

Alford, Jane M., Gary E. Brown and James C. Kasper, 1985. "Group Treatment for Sex Offenders," *Corrective and Social Psychiatry and Journal of Behavioral Technology Methods and Treatment,* 31 (3): 83-86.

Allen V. Illinois, 1986. *U.S. Law Week:* 4966

Annis, Lawrence V., Leigh G. Mathers and Christy A. Baker, 1984. "Victim Workers As Therapists for Incarcerated Sex Offenders," *Victimology: An International Journal,* 9 (3-4): 426-435.

Avery-Clark, Constance A., 1983. "Sexual Offenders: Special Programatic Needs," *Corrections Today,* 45 (5): 68-70.

Bohmer, Carol, 1983. "Legal and Ethical Issues in Mandatory Treatment: The Patient's Rights versus Society's Rights," In *The Sexual Aggressor,* Joanne Green and Irving R. Stuart (Eds.). New York: Van Nostrand Reinhold Company.

Bowers v. Hardwick, 1986. 54 *U.S. Law Week:* 4919.

Clark, Marie, 1986. "Missouri's Sexual Offender Program, *Corrections Today,* 48 (3): 84-86.

Corey, Gerald, 1982. *Manual for Theory and Practice of Counseling and Psychotherapy,* 2nd ed., Monterey, Calif.: Brooks/Cole Publishing Company, 1982.

Dean, Charles and Mary deBruyn-Kops, 1982. *The Crime and the Consequences of Rape.* Springfield, Ill.: Charles C. Thomas.

DeFrancis, Vincent, 1977. "American Humane Association Publishes Highlights of National Study of Child Neglect and Abuse Reporting for 1975," Washington, D.C.: U.S. Department of Health, Education and Welfare, National Center on Child Abuse and Neglect, Publication OHD 77-20086: 6-8.

Denenberg, R.V., 1974. "Profile/Washington State, Sex Offenders Treat Themselves," *Corrections Magazine,* 1 (2): 53-64.

Diagnostic and Statistical Manual of Mental Disorders, 3rd ed., 1978. Washington, D.C.: Task Force on Nomenclature and Statistics of the American Psychiatric Association: L1-L33.

Elwell, M. E., 1979. "Sexually Assaulted Children and Their Families," *Social Casework,* 60 (4): 227-235.

Gebhard, Paul H., John H. Garnon, Wardell B. Pomeroy, and Cornelia V. Christenson, 1965. *Sex Offenders: An Analysis of Types.* New York: Harper & Row.

Groth, A. N., A. W. Burgess and L. L. Holmstrom, 1977. "Rape: Power, Anger, and Sexuality," *American Journal of Psychiatry,* 134: 1239-43.

Groth, A. N., W. F. Hobson and T. Gary, 1982. "The Child Molester: Clinical Observations," *In Social Work and Child Sexual Abuse.* New York: Haworth Press.

Kiersh, Edward, 1980. "Can Families Survive Incest?" *Corrections Magazine,* 6 (2): 31-38.

Krasner, W., Linda C. Meyer and Nancy E. Carroll, 1977. *Victims of Rape.* Washington, D.C.: U.S. Government Printing Office, 1977.

MacDonald, G. J. and R. T. Williams, 1971. "A Guided Self-help Approach to Treatment of the Habitual Sex Offender," Fort Steilacoom, Washington: Western State Hospital.

Macdonald, John M., 1971. *Rape Offenders and Their Victims.* Springfield, Ill.: Charles C. Thomas.

Menachem, Amir, 1971. *Patterns in Forcible Rape.* Chicago: University of Chicago Press.

Ohio Criminal Law Handbook, 3rd ed., 1983. Cincinnati: Anderson Publishing Company.

Rosenfeld, Alvin A., 1979. "Endogamic Incest and the Victim-Perpetrator Model," *American Journal of Diseases of Children,* 133: 406-410.

Roth, R. A., 1978. *Child Sexual Abuse—Incest, Assault, and Sexual Exploitation.* A Special Report from the National Center on Child Abuse and Neglect. Washington, D.C.: U.S. Department of Health and Human Services.

Schwitzgebel, R. Kirkland, 1979. *Legal Aspects of the Enforced Treatment of Offenders.* Washington: U.S. Department of Health, Education and Welfare.

Smith, Alexander B. and Louis Berlin, 1981. *Treating the Criminal Offender*, 2nd ed. Englewood Cliffs, N.J.: Prentice-Hall.

VanNess, Shela R., 1983. "Rape as Instrumental Violence: A Perspective for Theory, Research and Corrections," paper presented at the annual meeting of the Academy of Criminal Justice Sciences, San Antonio, Texas.

Vetter, Harold J. and Ira J. Silverman, 1986. *Criminology and Crime*. New York: Harper & Row.

Washington Sexual Psychopath Act, 1975. Wash. Rev. Code Ann. 71.06.010 Seq. (1975).

Northwest Treatment Associates

A Comprehensive, Community-Based Evaluation and Treatment Program for Adult Sex Offenders

Fay Honey Knopp

Northwest Treatment Associates (NWTA) is a partnership of five practitioners[1] who collectively have 50 years of full-time experience in the treatment of sex offenders. Since 1977, in their attractive, three-story converted house, Steven Silver, Timothy A. Smith, Steven C. Wolf, Roger W. Wolfe, and Florence A. Wolfe have provided what is believed to be one of the largest and most comprehensive outpatient sex-offender evaluation and treatment programs in the United States. At any given time, approximately 200 men (and a few women) are involved actively in weekly or twice-weekly treatment in two locations.[2] Nonoffending spouses and other family members also participate in the treatment program.

More than 85 percent of NWTA's clients are attached to the criminal justice system through either court-ordered evaluations or sentences of probation with conditions of treatment[3] Since probation provides very few treatment subsidies, NWTA's clients are mainly white and middle class[4] "Probation views treatment as a privilege," says Roger Wolfe (1981b). "If they want community treatment, they have to work for it." The average period of time spent in treatment is 18 months, though a few stay longer. Most felony offenders are on five years' probation.

Fee schedules are on a sliding scale. They range from $40 to $70 for individual treatment and $13 to $23 for two-hour sessions. On each therapist's caseload, NWTA usually subsidizes at least three particularly hard-working and well-motivated clients who do not have adequate funds to purchase treatment.

Reprinted by permission of Safer Society Press from: *Retraining Adult Sex Offenders: Methods and Models* by Fay Honey Knopp (Orwell, Vt.: Safer Society Press, 1989), pp. 85-101.

Evaluation and Assessment

The majority of the people accepted into the program "graduate" or complete treatment. The reason for this comparatively low dropout rate is the selection of clients prior to treatment. Like most community-based programs, NWTA excludes individuals from treatment if they show patterns of overt physical violence, if they show an extensive history of nonsexual crimes, if they are assessed as being psychotic or suffering from severe mental illness, if they have serious substance abuse problems, if they are identified as "grossly inadequate," or if they have poor motivational levels and counterproductive attitudes that prevail despite modeling, education, and confrontation during the assessment process (R. Wolfe, 1981a, 1984).

Roger Wolfe and his colleagues, like other experienced sex-offender treatment specialists, are justifiably skeptical and often distrustful of their clients' historical perceptions of the sexually aggressive behavior that led them to their present situation. To test a client's perceptions of the behavior for which he was convicted, staff use a polygraphist with an extensive history of working with sex offenders. Staff recount, not without humor, some standard staff responses to the traditional amnesia and shadowy memories of their clients during evaluation and assessment, particularly when the polygraph has indicated that the client was involved in defensive lying:

> I have this kind of standard approach I take and it is usually effective. When a sex offender comes in and I question him about the allegations against him and his perception of them, he may say: "Well, I really don't remember if I did—but it really happened all at once and I've never thought about it before, it never entered my mind before—it was just totally spontaneous"—etcetera. I then go into my old philosopher stance, lean back in my chair, and kind of squint my eyes and say, "Y'know—I guess I believe you. If you really are the way you are representing yourself—a person who just spontaneously with no forethought raped this kid—it says to me that you are so incredibly dangerous, you should not be on the street even this afternoon. In fact, I'm going to call the cops right now . . ." Then there's a quick turn around. "Well . . . I suddenly remember very clearly . . ." [S. Wolf, 1981]

> Another client said he remembered his offense but "just had these brief flashes. I'm there with this kid—she's a nameless, faceless figure, and I remember trying to insert my penis, but she is only a five year old . . ." We worked on that for three or four sessions, to no avail, and then I told him we could not continue to treat him. The primary criterion for working with anybody in the community is you have to have honesty. A good client—a really honest client—

is going to give us, at most, *maybe* 75 percent honesty. [R. Wolfe, 1981b]

Evaluation and assessment include psychological testing,[5] physiological monitoring via the plethysmograph (also used for monitoring treatment progress), and a period spent in one of the ongoing, guided sex-offender groups. A person under evaluation must obtain unanimous group and treatment-team sanction on four basic issues: (1) that he believes he is a sexual offender; (2) that he strongly desires specialized intervention; (3) that he will be helpful to others in their process of accomplishing similar goals; and (4) that he has demonstrated change in and outside the treatment setting.

Treatment Modalities

The NWTA treatment program consists of two major components: a confrontive, guided-group model modified for community use, and a range of behavioral treatment approaches.[6] Roger Wolfe is a strong advocate for treatment eclecticity:

> Behavioral treatment is very important, but not sufficient by itself. We need both group and individual counseling to deal with the offender's characterological problems. I think a great many treatment programs exaggerate the importance of one or the other approach. I am firmly convinced you have to have both. Above all, you need individual assessment and careful, individual treatment planning for each person. It is a great deal of work. [R. Wolfe, 1981b]

Staff at NWTA are aware that one of their most important tasks is to help their clients to develop appropriate sexuality. Sexual reorientation is provided for those men who have no appropriate sexual arousal system or history. Marital counseling, sexual enhancement, and treatment for sexual dysfunction also are provided where appropriate. Says Florence Wolfe (1981), "Many of our clients have poor social skills[7] and no orientation to appropriate sexuality. We help them go through all the steps to establish their own relationships."

Guided Sex-Offender Group

The guided sex-offender group at NWTA is a modified version of the one developed in Western State Hospital's Sex Offender Program.[8] Honesty is a program requirement, so the model is extremely confrontive. The men are expected to challenge directly any rationalization and character traits that make offending easier. The group also provides an arena for education, support for prosocial behavior, and positive role modeling.

Steven Silver, who facilitates the majority of the groups at NWTA, perceives his role as both teacher and therapist. He structures specific written and experiential situations for the men to explore. Silver, a nontraditional group therapist, is a powerful, conscious model of a nondeviant male. Though a highly skilled veteran of group process and therapy with traditional mental health patients, none of these experiences prepared him adequately for running a sex-offender group. He developed his expertise by working with offenders for 12 years and through studying the relevant literature. In describing his NWTA stance, he says,

> It is confrontive and challenging. It is insisting that behavior be totally honest and responsible. I tell our clients, "I may act like a teacher, but this is not a class. It is group therapy and every one of you has a very serious disorder." It is emphasized that the behavior has been seriously abusive and that there is certainly the potential for subsequent dangerous behavior.
>
> If you tolerate one guy minimizing what he did, four weeks later he will come back and he will have minimized it, accepted it, and be sliding backward. It is important, however, to allow the offender room to blame, rationalize, and in other ways misrepresent people and circumstances; otherwise a therapist will obtain lip service— compliance without behavioral or characterological change. The offender needs to believe that his side has at least been heard.
>
> This is the hardest group therapy that has ever been structured, because the sex-offenders' therapist has to take the responsibility for ensuring that, when these men walk out of the door, they are not going to reoffend. [Silver, 1981]

In group therapy at NWTA, the offender's character pathology that facilitates sexual offending and other destructive behaviors is brought into awareness, challenged, and gradually replaced with prosocial attitudes, traits, and behaviors. Traits such as impulsivity, manipulation, dishonesty, sexual preoccupation, low frustration tolerance, denial, and deviousness are among those focused upon. The offender must take full responsibility for the harmfulness and severity of the offense. He learns preoffense warning signs (emotional, cognitive, physical, and environmental antecedents) and internal and external controls over impulses and behaviors, and he structures his life to minimize the possibility of reoffense. Learning in group occurs through confrontation, modeling of appropriate behavior, discussion, assignments, experiential exercises and lectures given by people in the field, for example, a counselor for sexually abused children. The client must complete a long series of assignments including assigned texts and pass a comprehensive written examination and a polygraph test prior to any consideration for program completion. All assignments and exercises are offender focused; the client must understand thoroughly his offending cycle and demonstrate by living a positive, prosocial lifestyle that he is willing and able to make the necessary changes (Wolfe & Wolfe, 1984).

If a person reoffends while in the group (almost always these reoffenses are misdemeanors such as exhibitionism and voyeurism), he may be taken back on a provisional basis, depending on the combined decision of probation and NWTA staff. If he does come back, Silver explains,

> I think reaccepting him depends on the level of the offense, how it came to light, and the client's attitude about it and treatment. If an exhibitionist reoffends against an adult, you are going to be considerably more tolerant than if a child molester reoffends. It also depends on how long a person has been in the program. If he has been in the group a significant length of time and reoffends, it means there is a great deal of information regarding offense-related patterns and controls that he is keeping a secret. And there must be lots of things he has not been doing, a lot of cons and scams he has been running and getting away with. It speaks to a continued pattern of deviance and to trying to "beat" treatment. [Silver, 1981]

The average length of stay in treatment groups is 18 months, during which certain tasks must be accomplished. Individuals are evaluated periodically by both their fellow group members and the treatment team. The therapist is present at all group sessions to guide, monitor, and assist the offenders in their process.

Following graduation, a client is encouraged to return to the group at any time, for any reason at no charge. If a client begins to feel himself returning to his deviant pattern or if his family notices some slipping, there is no excuse for not returning and seeking further help.

Behavioral Treatment

Sex-offender clients are given an introductory explanation of the basic principles of behavioral treatment and assigned readings to familiarize them further with the approaches. The men go to their local library, find the readings, do the prescribed work, and bring it back to NWTA.

The behavioral treatment is geared toward reducing and/or eliminating the deviant sexual arousal, which staff believe provides a major motivation for the offender's behavioral pattern. The initial step in treatment is bringing the overt behavior under control:

> Sex-offender behavior is conditioned on a very basic level—sexual arousal. The individual has a long history of carrying out that particular behavior, paired with immediate gratification. A large chunk of that is sexual gratification, but a great many other things go along with that, too. Adrenalin rush, getting away with something, escaping from discomfort or boredom—these often are overlooked. The sex offense gives the offender something to focus on as an escape from tedium, problems, anxiety, and frustration. We are talking about the immediate application of a strong, powerful package of rewards. Our theory is, if you are going to deal with the compulsive nature of that behavior, you are going to have to do some counterconditioning. [R. Wolfe, 1981b]

This procedure involves pairing the deviant behavior and its antecedents with ungratifying, negative results. It also means encouraging nondeviant behavior and pairing it with positive reinforcers.

In the case involving an incest offender, for example, Roger Wolfe might use the following scenario to pair negative imagery with the offender's deviant behavior:

> Imagine you are walking into your daughter's room. You are pulling back the covers, feeling very excited, very aroused. You are reaching down, picking up her nightie. You've touched her, your hand is covered with pus, you can smell the overwhelming stench, you brush your hand against your clothes, the pus is smeared against your clothes, the stench is really making you nauseous, you feel like you have to throw up, you taste the sweet, sickly bile in the back of your throat . . . . (and so forth).

There are many other procedures commonly used by NWTA staff. First we will describe briefly six approaches to teaching impulse control. Next we describe, in greater detail, behavioral methods aimed at reducing deviant arousal and/or increasing appropriate arousal. These include covert sensitization, covert positive reinforcement, masturbatory reconditioning, boredom aversion, and the modified aversive behavioral rehearsal technique. Last, we examine a variety of techniques used in teaching victim empathy.

Simple Impulse-Control Techniques. The methods described here are among the simplest, most concise, and least intrusive interventions taught to the offender to assist him in controlling ongoing impulses. They are considered "bandaids" in that they are short-term pragmatic attempts to preclude reoffense until more long-term modalities can have an impact.

1. *Thought-stopping*[9] is used to disrupt a deviant thinking pattern. An example is given of a heterosexual pedophile walking down the street and noticing a little girl. His eyes may wander to her buttocks. He begins to think how beautiful and little they are. "We want him to stop those thoughts, to block them out," explains Roger Wolfe. "Thought-stopping, simply stated, is to have the offender scream at the top of his lungs — 'STOP' — *inside* his head. It disrupts that thought" (R. Wolfe, 1981b).

2. *Thought-shifting* to aversive imagery is equally simple. The pedophile, for example, sees a little girl and finds himself starting to dwell on her. Immediately he must try to think of something aversive. For instance, he imagines a police officer walking up behind him, tapping him on the shoulder, and saying, "I know what you are up to," then kneeing him in the groin and calling in the neighbors to deal with "the local pervert." Realistic aversive imagery disrupts arousal and deviant thought processes and applies a punishment to those behaviors. The probability of reoffense is diminished.

3. *Impulse-charting* is a method used to help the offender to focus on what is going on in his thinking and acting patterns. NWTA gives the client little cards that list the days of the week. After the offender controls an impulse, he records a number from one to 10 that indicates the intensity of that impulse and the difficulty he had in controlling it.[10] "It gives them something to do that takes them one step further away from offending," says Roger Wolfe. "It also gives us an ongoing measure that we can quantify in terms of the strength and frequency of his impulses. We get some idea of how well the person is doing, how good our techniques are, and how well they are working. If his impulses are not decreasing, we had better go back to the drawing board and come up with a new approach" (R. Wolfe, 1981b).

For people having greater difficulty controlling their impulses, or for someone who raises suspicion that he might be on the brink of reoffending, the program utilizes stronger, more intrusive types of controls. These are most appropriate for chronic child molesters or exhibitionists, the clients who usually are the most out of control.

1. *Scheduled overmasturbation* simply places the client on an escalating masturbation schedule, timed by the clock. The frequency of masturbation is increased steadily, to reduce sexual drive and thus make it easier to control. "This exercise also gives him a measure of control over his sexuality," says Roger Wolfe (1981b),

"since he is used to masturbating willy-nilly. Care is taken that he is utilizing appropriate imagery."

2. *Spouse monitoring* involves asking the spouse or significant other to give the program feedback in terms of how the offender is doing,[11] by signing the checklist of tasks and homework to be completed by the client and by monitoring his behavior. Spouse monitoring is used with nearly all clients.

3. *Environmental manipulation* helps to get the offender out of situations that are high risk for him and his potential victims. For instance, with an incest or pedophile offender, one of the standard procedures is to have him move himself right out of the house, as opposed to taking the victim out of the house and doubly victimizing him/her. Other examples provided by Roger Wolfe (1981b) are practical and creative:

> These are all basic, common-sense approaches that work. Here are some examples we have used with exposers. One person had a great many impulses to expose while he was aimlessly cruising around town. We told him he can no longer cruise, but he must have a specific destination, he must call his friend and tell him to meet him at a designated place at a specific time. In group we changed the time a guy jogged, where he jogged, the way he drove to work, the way he drove home from work, and what he does on Sunday afternoons in football season. These were all situations where he had flashed. One of the most creative kinds of things we do with flashers who exhibit in their cars is to have them put their names on the front, back, and sides of the car. Also, we had one fellow who was a jogger and who flashed while he was jogging. We had him get a T-shirt with his name on it.

If these impulse-control measures are not effective, Depo-Provera may be prescribed.

Covert Sensitization.[12] Approximately 10 weeks of treatment are devoted to covert sensitization. Conditioning sessions are audiotaped, and the 40-minute tape is sent home with the client, who is instructed to listen to it daily. Monitoring by spouses or significant others and quizzing for content make compliance more likely. Tapes also typically include covert positive reinforcement of alternatives to deviant behaviors (such as not responding to deviant stimulus situations, assertiveness, appropriate sexual behavior, and so forth). In the early sessions, the therapist constructs the tape; later, the client takes over this task, with the therapist serving as a consultant. After 10 weeks, additional elements are included in conditioning tapes.

Staff describe graphically how covert sensitization is used. First, the therapist induces a relaxed phase for about five to fifteen minutes, depending on how well trained and adept the client is in being able to drift down into a relaxed state where he can get good imagery.[13] Next he is given instructions that he is going to focus on the upcoming scenes and they are going to seem very real. The therapist then begins a description of a scene, tailor-made for the client, constructed from a fear inventory of about 175 items, from which the client has chosen those that are most fearful to him.

> We first start with a written checklist and then explore other things they are very afraid of—a bad experience where they nearly drowned, an automobile accident, a particular horror movie that really scared them—all their most relevant and immediate fears. Usually these men are fresh from their court experience, so we do all sorts of marvelous scenes about being taken down to the police station and what the judge said to them. The more impact the better, is the general rule. What you are after is finding the images that produce a strong reaction. [R. Wolfe, 1981b]

Roger Wolfe describes how one person's fear of snakes was paired with a scene reflective of his deviant pattern:

> You are restless. It is about three o'clock in the morning and you cannot sleep. You tell yourself you are going to go to the bathroom. You get up, you go to the bathroom, you urinate, and you continue to stand there. You are thinking, "Little Sally is sleeping in the room next door." You tell yourself. "Maybe I'd better check on her just to see if she kicked her covers off or something." As you are thinking that, you kind of put your hand down on your penis and you feel your excitment. You tell yourself, "She is sound asleep—she won't know if I was in there or not." You go up to her door, telling yourself she is sound asleep and you are just going to check on her, feeling sexual excitment, thinking about touching her, thinking you will just slip up her nightgown a little bit and maybe just look at her, and getting more excited. You are thinking about doing that, with your hand on the doorknob, getting really excited now, really turned on, and you gently, carefully, being really quiet, open that door, you open that door thinking about touching her . . . and you suddenly realize there is something on the floor. There is something moving on the floor in the bedroom. My God, my God, you say—it is a snake! There is more than one. There are creepy, crawly snakes all over and you can see their little forked tongues, see their beady eyes. They are moving toward you. You are just terrified standing there, you want to run, but you are just scared. A cold chill runs up and down your body. Your body gets tight. They are moving toward you. God, these cold slimy snakes are moving toward you. One of them is on your toe now . . . [R. Wolfe. 1981b]

The client, in an induced state, hears the scene for the first time at NWTA. Then he writes the scene down in his own words, monitored by his spouse or friend. A week later the client returns and guides the therapist through the scene. The therapist will check the client's memory at various points and ask for a self-report on what the impact of the tape has been.

"For instance," says Roger Wolfe, "I may ask him, at the place where his hand is on the doorknob, to tell me what he is feeling when he is home listening to the tape. Can he feel the coldness and hardness of the knob? Can he see the shadows of his own hallway? I'm trying to pick up how clear the imagery is" (R. Wolfe, 1981b). Wolfe also asks for bodily reactions to the scene. "When he says, 'That snake really scares me,' I say, 'What is your body doing?' I should hear things like 'My throat is dry, I am swallowing, my stomach flutters, and I have increased heart beat.' "

Some other measures of treatment impact are self-report of deviant impulses, plethysmograph assessment, and polygraph examination.

Covert Positive Reinforcement. The last two scenes on the tape will pair appropriate behavior with cognitive and material rewards. There are many approaches that can be used. One scene involves the offender just leaving a situation that is typical of his deviant pattern, where he would have had high impulses and temptations and could have reoffended. The scene would place him safely away from such temptations, and he would realize, "I didn't even think about it. By God, that feels really good. Hey, I'm more normal; all that work I am putting in—it is paying off." The tape would provide a material reward by having him drive home and find a letter telling him he had just been granted a job promotion.

A second approach involves an element of cognitive restructuring.[14] In this scenario, the sex offender starts repeating some of the excuses he typically has used himself. For instance, he might say, "Well it won't hurt, she's asleep, she likes it anyway, this is a good way for her to learn about sex." Then, instead of continuing this pattern, suddenly he thinks, "That's a bunch of bullshit! In fact, the reality is, it is harmful, it does hurt people, it is not okay. I don't care if she is asleep or not asleep— that is invading her privacy and that's being damaging and harmful."

Another approach, Roger Wolfe explains, is to take a range of the client's most positive behaviors and reinforce them by loading the end with rewards.

> For instance, you can walk a client through a scene where he is behaving assertively and pair that up with having him sit down in a restaurant where the waiter brings him some marvelous beefsteak.

You can smell the aroma, you can see the juices kind of flowing from the steak, and there are mushrooms on top, and french fries, and forth. The rationale for loading the end with rewards is that we want him to take the whole tape and come out of the experience feeling pretty good about himself. If he comes out of the tape feeling pretty good, it is that much easier for him to go back and do the tape again. If you do just total punishment, the client gets phobic about doing the tape. Scenes are changed with each tape to minimize adaptation and maximize generalization. [R. Wolfe, 1981b]

As mentioned earlier, the therapist makes the first few conditioning tapes and then encourages the client to construct his own. This process of gradually shifting responsibility is an integral part of NWTA's therapeutic plan:

I think this kind of self-help approach is reflective of our total treatment philosophy. We want to train the individual to change his own behavior. We want him to become his own behavioral therapist. By the time he leaves here he should be as good as we are, if not better, in terms of dealing with his own specific problem. We learn a great deal from the types of tapes he makes. He gets into much more when he is sitting on his own with that tape recorder. The clients do an amazingly good job. We could work with them for years and years, but they know more about their patterns than we do, they know more about what turns them off than we do, and they know more about what turns them on than we do. [R. Wolfe, 1981b]

Masturbatory Reconditioning[15] *and Boredom Aversion.*[16] Staff have combined and adapted the technique of masturbatory reconditioning and boredom aversion to function within outpatient, part-time treatment. The positive masturbatory reconditioning involves having the client masturbate to an appropriate fantasy, until he has an ejaculation. Roger Wolfe points out the need for therapist monitoring:

Their perceptions of what is an appropriate fantasy are incredible. We have had clients come in with their initial tapes and say, "I had a wonderful appropriate fantasy," and it turns out to be a tape describing what is essentially a rape! Many men in our male culture wouldn't graduate from our groups.

We have the clients focus on the antithesis of offending, that is, on warmth, caring, affectional, close, intimate human aspects of sexuality. We stress the sensual and erotic as well. When they are making their tapes, we want them to throw in lots of adjectives about warm and close, and a lot of respect for the female, what she is wanting, doing, and feeling. They focus on her feelings and responses and on their own feelings and responses. The woman should come across as a person and not a blow-up rubber doll. [R. Wolfe, 1981b]

Staff help the men develop appropriate fantasies. Their assignment at home is to verbalize the fantasy into a tape recorder while masturbating to ejaculation four to seven times a week. "The point is we want to reinforce—through the powerful mechanism of masturbatory conditioning—appropriate sexuality, and not only appropriate sexuality, but the antithesis of sexual offending where you have to make your victim a piece of meat," says Roger Wolfe (1981b).

The boredom-aversion technique is used by the offender after ejaculating to appropriate fantasies. Then he turns the tape cassette over and verbalizes 45 continual minutes of a series of his deviant sexual fantasies.[17] He must continue his fantasies for 45 minutes and cannot turn off the tape recorder until he fills up the whole side with no pauses and no blanks.

> We try to have the individual repeat the full fantasy, including antecedent conditions (emotional, environmental, physiological, and mental precursors). The actual sexual behavior and the immediate consequences, such as transitory feelings and his methods of resolving them (the false promise), are included. When he completes one fantasy, he begins another. [R. Wolfe, 1981b]

The Modified Aversive Behavioral Rehearsal Technique (MABRT). The MABRT, using mannequins and videotape, is a technique developed for systematically controlling deviant sexual expression in pedophiles and exhibitionists. It was adopted by NWTA's Timothy Smith and borrows many of the components of Aversive Behavioral Rehearsal (Wickramasekera, 1980). Mannequins have been used previously for assessment of sex offenders, where it was found that interacting with a "humanlike" figure elicited behavior not previously reported by the offender (Forgione, 1974).

This technique involves a client in re-enacting his sexual assault on a mannequin that is representative of the age and sex of his victims. This scene is videotaped[18] and viewed by the client, his significant other, and his treatment group. This very close simulation, including even the actual motor behaviors, is paired with powerful negative emotions that the client experiences in this situation. On a cognitive level, the client is confronted with the harmfulness, outrageousness, and absurdity of his rationalizations, feelings, and behaviors. "Sharing with others the impactful, visual depiction of his deviance is a greatly magnified mode of self-disclosure," says Roger Wolfe (Wolfe & Wolfe, 1984). "It forcefully breaks through most remnants of rationalization, justification, and minimization residual in the client."

Negative side-effects reported in the literature are almost precluded by utilizing this technique only after the client has been in treatment a minimum of six months. One unexpected side-effect of this procedure is that the emotional responses of a significant percentage of clients seem focused on the trauma they created for their victims; thus this procedure, in addition to its conditioning and cognitive impact, serves as an influential empathy training procedure (Wolfe & Wolfe, 1984).

Empathy Training. Staff use several techniques, including behavioral ones, to help the offender to come to grips with the reality of his offense and its effects on the victim. Efforts to correct the cognitive distortions in the offender's perception of the victim's feelings about sexual assault include making contact with victim counselors or advocates, as well as the techniques of cognitive restructuring, role playing, and bibliotherapy.

1. *Victim counselors* are invited to attend the group meeting, or the offender is sent to a victim advocate center, where, at his own expense, he must ask a victim counselor to tell him about victims' feelings. Wherever possible, NWTA staff try to arrange to have the counselor of his actual victim be the person to tell him of the victim's perception of the hurt and damage s/he experienced. With many clients, this process seems to have the desired level of emotional and intellectual impact.

2. *Cognitive restructuring.* The offender constructs scenes, casting himself or significant others in the role of the victim. Research such as reading and consultation with victim specialists or their spouses is assigned, to assure a thorough and accurate job. Cognitive restructuring is utilized at this point. The client focuses on his typical rationalizations; for example, an exhibitionist will say, "This will really turn her on." Scenes are constructed where he utilizes and buys the rationalizations. These scenes then are paired with aversive imagery. Finally, alternate scenes are constructed where he catches himself in the distortion and counters with the reality message; for example, the exhibitionist will say, "That is nonsense! I have done this hundreds of times and the only responses I have ever gotten are derision, disgust, and fear." The scene continues with the client performing some operant behavior to terminate the possibility of deviant behavior. Then the client shifts to a positively reinforcing scene, a "warm pink fuzzy" (Maletsky, 1980; R. Wolfe, 1981a).

3. *Roleplaying.* The group therapist tells the client, "Okay we talked about your view of the sexual assault scene, we talked about your thoughts about what was going on in the victim's head—that she really liked what you were doing. Now we are going to give you

the opportunity to do the scene and be your victim." This approach might occur on a variety of levels with the same client. He may begin with a 500-word essay on the effects of the abuse on the victim. The next step might be for him to become that victim in a role play. The offender may protest and start out by saying, "Well, I couldn't do that, because it creates all sorts of psychological trauma for me." Nevertheless, he is asked to become the victim, lying on the floor and simulating getting molested in front of 14 other group members.

Tapes also are used. A scene is reconstructed from his victim's perspective, telling the offender, "You are 11 years old. You lie in your bed at night. You hear your dad get up. You stiffen up. You are just hoping and praying he won't come in your room tonight like he did last night." The therapist then will describe what that particular offender actually did to the victim, while the offender is imagining he is that victim. Roger Wolfe explains, "Part of the offender's rationalization in his self-defense is that the victim never resisted, so we put that into focus. One of the ways we do that is to say to the offender, 'Your victim was three feet tall and weighed about 100 pounds. You are six feet tall and weigh 200 pounds. Imagine a man who was 12 feet tall and weighed 600 pounds coming into your bedroom and saying, 'Hi, you and I are going to do it'" (R. Wolfe, 1981b).

4. *Bibliotherapy.* Clients are asked to read books written by sexual assault victims (e.g., Brady, 1981; Morris, 1982). A report form developed by staff therapist Nancy Nissen asks clients to record arousal points, victim traits, and offender traits as they are reading. With most clients, this enhances perceptions of their victim's pain.

Reoffense Rate

The reoffense rate by graduates of NWTA's sex-offender treatment program is approximately 10 percent, according to Roger Wolfe (1981b). "Since most of the men are on probation for five years, we usually hear of any reoffense through that division. When the offender commits a new offense, it is usually the same or a lesser type for which we treated him." Rarely, the person will progress to a more serious offense.

NWTA also reports a high rate of success where the Modified Aversive Behavior Rehearsal Technique was used as a treatment component. These data show an overall success rate of 95 percent with 92 sex offenders who had engaged in a variety of, and often multiple, paraphilias. Length of follow-up ranged from one to 28 months, with a mean follow-up of 13.5 months.[19]

Northwest Treatment Associates'
Success Rates Where the MABRT is a Treatment Component

Offense Type	Number*	Reoffend	% Success	Type Reoffense
Molests female children	64	2	97	Expose, Child Molest, F. Rape
Exhibitionism	27	4	85	Expose, F. Child Molest
Voyeurism	6	1	83	Expose
Molests male children	17	0	100	_____
Rapes female children	3	1	66	Child Rape
Rapes female adults	3	0	100	_____
Grabs breasts	2	1	50	Expose
Molests boys & girls	8	0	100	_____
Cross-dresses/steals clothing	1	0	100	_____
Total Offenders & Reoffenses:				
Mean Success Rate	92	5	95%	

* Many of the sex offenders had multiple deviancies, so total offenses are greater then number of offenders. Sources NWTA

Wolfe reiterates the importance of continual evaluation and assessment while the offender is in treatment. He recounts the case of a person who came in as an exhibitionist and was in treatment for three or four weeks and doing very poorly. He suddenly disappeared from treatment because he was caught in a vicious rape.

> Whatever your relationship to a sex offender, you should keep foremost in mind, he is an *addict*. The individual verbalization, promises, assurances, and contentions should be regarded in the same light as those of alcoholics regarding alcohol or heroin addicts regarding their drug. An approach of healthy skepticism is advised, and behavior should speak to you much louder than words. [R. Wolfe, 1981b]

Notes

1. Six additional people have an associate status, and a secretary serves as a support staff person.

2. In 1982 a branch treatment program was established in Bellingham, Washington.

3. NWTA prefers not to handle paroled sex offenders. They consider perhaps one in 20 is treatable.

4. NWTA's clientele include a small percentage of ethnic groups. Such groups are underrepresented in almost all community-based adult sex-offender treatment programs.

5. Psychological tests include the MMPI, the Abel Card-Sort of Sexual Preferences, the Clarke Sexual History Questionnaire, and a general substance abuse overview checklist.

6. As a last resort, Depo-Provera may be used to reduce sexual arousal and sexual drive.

7. See Appendix C for description of social skills training used by NWTA.

8. For a description of this program, see Chapter 9 of this book.

9. See Cautela (1969).

10. Staff report that it is not an uncommon experience for clients to falsify these records and advise programs to be cautious and to look for a plausible learning curve. Additional confusion may be caused by the fact that some clients experience a lengthy period of suppression due to the trauma of discovery.

11. See Appendix D for a sample "Partner Alert List."

12. See Cautela (1967, 1970).

13. To train the client in stress-reducing and imagery-enhancing muscle relaxation methods, Roger Wolfe spends about 20 minutes with each client explaining NWTA's systematic format for inducing deep-muscle relaxation, followed by one hour in a taped session guiding the offender through the system. The client then can play the tape at home and do the exercises on his own for one or two weeks. Hypnosis also may be used when an offender is not successful with traditional methods.

14. See Meichenbaum (1977).

15. See Abel & Blanchard (1974); Marquis (1970).

16. See Laws & O'Neil (1979); Marshall & Lippens (1977).

17. See Appendix E for sample of "Protocol for Boredom Tapes." On occasion, when boredom tapes are being reviewed in the NWTA office, the therapist will ask the client to punish any deviant arousal while listening, by inhaling the noxious odor of placenta culture.

18. See Appendix F for two release forms for clients involved in MABRT; one is for client consent and the other provides permission for NWTA to use the tapes for the purpose of training professionals in the technique.

19. Wickramasekera (1980, p. 123) reports a high MABRI success rate also, especially with 23 exhibitionists (95 percent success) followed for 22 months to nine years.

References

Abel, G., & Blanchard, E. B. "The Role of Fantasy in the Treatment of Sexual Deviancy." *Archives of General Psychiatry, 30:* 4, 1974, 467-475.

Brady, K. *Father's Days.* New York: Dell, 1981.

Cautela, J. R. "Covert Sensitization." *Psychological Record, 20,* 1967, 459-468.

Cautela, J. R. "Behavioral Therapy and Self-Control Techniques and Implications." In C. M. Franks (ed.), *Behavioral Therapy: Appraisal and Status.* New York: McGraw-Hill, 1969.

Cautela, J. R. "Covert Reinforcement." *Behavior Therapy, 1,* 1970, 35-50.

Forgione, A. G. "The Use of Mannequins in the Behavioral Assessment of Child Molesters: Two Case Reports." *Behavior Therapy, 7,* 1974, 678-685.

Laws, D. R., & O'Neil, J. A. "Variations on Masturbatory Reconditioning." Paper presented at the Second National Conference on the Evaluation and Treatment of Sexual Aggressives, New York City, May 12, 1979.

Maletsky, B. M. "Assisted Covert Sensitization." In D. J. Cox & R. J. Daitzman (eds.), *Exhibitionism: Description, Assessment & Treatment.* New York: Garland Press, 1980.

Merquis, J. "Orgasmic Reconditioning: Changing Sexual Object Choice through Controlling Masturbation Fantasies." *Journal of Behavior Therapy and Experimental Psychiatry, 1,* 1970, 263-271.

Marshall, W. L., & Lippens, K. "Clinical Value of Boredom, A Procedure for Reducing Inappropriate Sexual Interest." *Journal of Nervous & Mental Disease, 165,* 1977, 283-287.

Meichenbaum, D. *Cognitive-Behavioral Modification.* New York: Plenum Press, 1977.

Morris, M. *If I Should Die Before I Wake,* Los Angeles: Tarcher, 1982.

Silver, S. Taped site-interview by F. H. Knopp, September 30, 1981.

Wickramasekera, I. "Aversive Behavioral Rehearsal." In D. J. Cox & R. J. Daitzman (eds.), *Exhibitionism: Description, Assessment & Treatment.* New York: Garland Press, 1980.

Wolf, S. Taped site-interview by F. H. Knopp, September 30, 1981.

Wolfe, F. Taped site-interview by F. H. Knopp, September 30, 1981.

Wolfe, F., & Wolfe, R. Letter and notes to F. H. Knopp, May 17, 1984.

Wolfe R. "Northwest Treatment Associates: An Outpatient Approach to the Treatment of Sex Offenders." *TSA News,* August 19, 1981. (a)

Wolfe R. Taped site-interview by F. H. Knopp, September 30, 1981.(b)

Substance Abusers:
Identification and Treatment

Toni Atmore
Edward J. Bauchiero

The focus of this article is a simple, practical assessment of substance abuse problems. A parole or probation officer need not administer a test or conduct a sophisticated interview in order to gain a clear idea of a person's drug/alcohol issues.

Our job at the Hampden County Pre-Release Center is to reintegrate a resident into the community, so that he or she does not commit future crimes. We demonstrate an 85 percent success rate in achieving this. Luckily, we also have Hampden County Sheriff Michael J. Ashe, who provides excellent leadership and support in working with the problem of massive substance abuse among our inmate population. We would fall short of our high professional standards if we put people back into the community without addressing their drug and/or alcohol problems. Substance abusers who are actively using pose a threat to public safety.

Part of our success lies in our ability to identify (assess) the problem of substance abuse and to plan programming and monitoring to address this problem. (Yes, we do believe in urine testing!)

When we started to assess our residents for substance abuse, we discovered that 87 percent of the residents in our Pre-Release Center had significant drug/alcohol problems. Tracing their incarceration histories, we found that the large majority of them committed their crimes while under the influence of a substance. These crimes ranged from property offenses to violent offenses. We do not feel that our facility is an exception, and we believe that these statistics would hold true for any probation or parole caseload.

Please do not buy into the myth that abusers have to be motivated and accept their substance abuse problems before they can receive

Reprinted by permission of the American Correctional Association from *Corrections Today,* 39 (7) (Dec. 1987), pp. 22, 24, 26, 110.

assistance. There are many stages of denial; many recovering drug or alcohol abusers get help only after being pressured by family, spouse, the job, the criminal justice system, and so forth.

This assessment process is simple to undertake, as it only requires the parole or probation officer to organize interview questions. As we point out below, an inmate, probationer, or parolee may not see himself or herself as having a substance abuse problem. We do not even inquire about a problem at the beginning of the interview. We begin by focusing on simple and practical data. If we ask the questions in an ordinary, low key, nonjudgmental, nonthreatening tone of voice, we tend to get straight answers.

The first step in identifying a drug/alcohol problem is to focus the assessment interview strictly on the "facts" of the individual's substance involvement. Such facts include the following:

- names of substances used
- date of first use
- date of most recent use
- usual pattern of use (amount and frequency)
- route of administration
- number of overdoses/blackouts.

The above items limit the interview to exploring only the facts surrounding an individual's substance use, such as the amount of cocaine inhaled on a daily basis. By concentrating strictly on factual data, the problems of defensiveness and denial that accompany "judgmental" questions can be avoided. For example, a judgmental question such as "Do you have a drug problem?" forces the inmate to make a judgment on his/her own behavior. This direct question would threaten most substance abusers, and the end result would be reduced interviewee cooperation and truthful answers. By limiting the beginning of the interview to factual questioning, many individuals feel less inhibited in divulging more accurate information. This also allows the probation or parole officer to assess the degree of substance abuse with greater accuracy.

Judgmental Questions

After exploring the factual data, the second step is to focus on judgmental questions, also known as self-perception questions. Such judgmental questions include:

- Have drugs or alcohol ever gotten you into trouble?

- Do you feel that drugs or alcohol have contributed to your being here (in jail, on probation, on parole)?
- Have you ever had a problem with drugs or alcohol?
- Have you ever been involved in a drug or alcohol counseling or treatment program in the past?

All of the questions above should be explored in detail. Responses to these items indicate the degree of any alcohol/drug abuse denial. Furthermore, because the interviewer already knows the extent of substance involvement (via the factual items previously explored), the interviewer can observe any denial behaviors first-hand within the context of the interview.

In addition to direct inquiry pertaining to substance use, the assessment may gather substance abuse information by examining other areas of the interviewee's personal history. In particular, family history and educational/employment history may provide clues to substance abuse. Because it is estimated that one-half of all substance abusers emerge from a family where another family member, usually a parental figure is a substance abuser, familial history provides vital information. Similar information concerning significant relationships (i.e., spouse, girlfriend) may also be indicative of substance involvement.

A sporadic or non-existent job history may also suggest substance abuse. Also indicative is a history of tardiness, absenteeism, interpersonal conflicts on the job, and losing jobs. Teenagers with substance abuse problems parallel this process in school. Therefore, obtaining educational/employment information is important when attempting to assess a suspected substance abuse problem.

The process of obtaining family history and educational/employment history is similar to the process of obtaining a substance abuse history. Factual questions are first (who, what, when, where), and judgmental questions are asked after the facts have been obtained. As mentioned earlier, this process circumvents the problems of heightened defensiveness and overt denial on behalf of the interviewee, because the anxiety-producing questions are posed at the end of the session.

It is interesting to note that approximately one-half of the interviewees who deny having a substance abuse problem (a self-perception answer) but who admit to a history of substance abuse will unwittingly divulge information confirming existence of a substance abuse problem when questioned about their family relationships. This information is obtained by posing perceptual questions about family members. For example, when asked, "If your mother were sitting with us today, what would she say if I asked her what she is most concerned about when it comes to you?" These individuals would respond "my drug use" or "my alcohol use." The individual has unwittingly informed the interviewer that he/she has a substance abuse problem, that this problem has affected their family life, and that the individual is denying the problem. This is more information than the individual could have given, or would have given, if simply asked to discuss his/her substance abuse.

We emphasize programming for substance abusers as well as urine testing. This programming includes individual and/or group addiction counseling, educational programming on addiction and recovery, couples or family counseling, and participation in Alcoholics Anonymous or Narcotics Anonymous.

This kind of programming is also used in our Day Reporting Center, which is one of the first alternative incarceration programs of its kind in the nation. Day Reporting was initiated under the dynamic leadership of the Crime and Justice Foundation in Boston, in collaboration with our Sheriff's Department. Our Deputy Superintendent of Human Services, J. John Ashe, was the facility leader in planning this program. The Day Reporting Center is unlike Pre-Release in that selected inmates are allowed to live at home. As Day Reporting Coordinator Kevin Warwick stated, "During the first nine months of operation, 51 inmates lived at home and 81 percent successfully completed the program.

Our experience has overwhelmingly proven the effectiveness of urine testing with a criminal population. Even a trained eye can miss a person who is abusing a substance. The urine test is an objective, scientific measurement that will answer questions a probation or parole officer may have about possible substance abuse.

We have noted significant behavioral improvements when we test regularly, because it serves as a deterrent. Therefore, we are returning less people to higher security for positive urines because they know they are taking a huge risk by substance use. In other words, test regularly! You need to have a consistent policy for testing and sanctions for positive results, or else word will get around quickly that one should not take this seriously.

There are some easy to use and very reliable machines for urine testing now available. Do not stick with your old machine if it is cumbersome. Shop around! Any probation or parole officer could be trained to use basic urinalysis equipment in a short period of time—and it is not messy.

Intensive Programming

One more step that we see as important for our substance abuse programming is to initiate an intensive 21-day substance abuse program within Pre-Release, which focuses entirely on the addiction process and recovery. Drug users with heavy chronic histories need to understand more about drug abstinence and the addiction process before they face the pressures of job hunting and reintegration into the community.

We commonly see chronic abusers who think all they need is a job and some money and all will be fine. Additionally, most chronic abusers have sporadic job histories. They fail to see that the reason they have never been able to hold a job is because of their abuse of drugs and alcohol. We do not wish to have our programming support this unrealistic thinking.

This 21-day program is our plan to add a fuller dimension to our addiction programming. Similar programs to this are usually offered throughout most major cities in the nation by various human service organizations.

In this article we have pointed out the high rate of substance abuse in the criminal population and how we address this population. We see identification of the problem by a probation or parole officer as the key to increasing the chances for a successful probation and parole. We offer an easy and practical assessment model to assess this problem. By using this model, we realize a low recidivism rate of 15 percent.

Addiction programming that encompasses a spectrum of available resources is essential in addressing the abuse issue, as is regular urine testing. Urine testing can be a key deterrent if there is a consistent policy for regular testing and sanctions for positive results.

10 Correctional Treatment: Past, Present and Future

Introduction

Does correctional treatment have a future? The corrections field does not operate in a vacuum, and the various social, economic and political factors that are of importance for the entire country eventually will be manifested in the correctional sphere. Thus the increasing crime rates of the 1970s, which may have resulted from a wide variety of factors, were interpreted by many to be a direct outcome of the failure of correctional treatment, coddling of offenders, and too little emphasis on punishment. Politicians and correctional administrators were quick to realize that they were on safe ground with the general public if they took a "hard line" approach. They could back up their position with studies which seemed to prove that rehabilitative programs, in particular those operated in institutional settings, had not achieved the expected results. Consequently, the 1980s witnessed a greatly reduced commitment to rehabilitation and correctional treatment and an increased emphasis on punishment as a deterrent.

A careful examination of correctional treatment programs geared toward rehabilitation reveals that it is not possible to definitively state whether most of the programs were failures, successes, or neutral aspects of the correctional process. Most of the earlier treatment programs did not have a research or evaluation component built into them. Programs of an experimental nature were initiated, completed, and discontinued without any evidence being gathered as to their effectiveness. As the various federal and state agencies funding these programs began to require evaluation reports, the evaluation was generally conducted by the agency directing the program or contracted with a research consulting firm. The findings were frequently open to question.

Inter-agency research on the effectiveness of programs seemed at first glance to be appropriate, since staff members had access to records and information it might be difficult for outside researchers to obtain. However, those given the responsibility of evaluating programs within agencies were usually not well versed in research methodology or program design techniques, and not well qualified to make recommendations for further development or program changes. Administrators who had committed themselves to a certain treatment philosophy could successfully ignore findings contrary to their expectations about the success of the programs being conducted under their direction. Evaluations conducted by outside consulting firms also had their limitations. Consulting agency staff usually did not have direct experience or expertise in correctional treatment and were oversensitive to the direction given to them. The incentive to make the programs "look good" to please the agencies and therefore receive more contracts also came to bear in this evaluation approach.

Even considering the questionable nature of some of the evaluative research and although a few programs have been demonstrated to reduce recidivism after release from institutional correctional treatment, there is overwhelming evidence that institutional treatment *does not* make those treated more law abiding after their release. The goal of rehabilitation through institutional treatment has proven to be an unattainable one in spite of the efforts of administrators to develop programs to attack every facet of the offenders' problems and the dedicated efforts of workers from many helping areas.

Bartollas and Miller advanced several explanations for the failure of the "rehabilitation model," including disillusionment and rapid turnover of the treatment staff, the fact that the size of the prison population made it impossible to put treatment ahead of security, the gap between the motivations and values of the middle-class treatment staff and the predominantly lower-class prison populations, insincerity and lack of desire for rehabilitation on the part of the inmates, and the inappropriateness of a dehumanizing institutional setting for the application of any type of effective treatment.[1]

In the 1970s, correctional planners and administrators began to turn to community-based treatment as an alternative to institutionalization. Economic considerations played an important part in this emerging trend. Prison overcrowding, lack of funds, and lack of public enthusiasm for the building of new facilities made placement of many offenders in the community a practical necessity. The halfway house movement, which began in the 1860s under the sponsorship of religious or public service groups and initially involved providing for the basic physical needs of homeless or alcoholic individuals, enjoyed a renaissance in the 1950s. Courts began to place offenders in halfway houses as a last resort before incarceration (halfway in); parole authorities allowed certain offenders to live in such settings before they were returned to the community and independent living (halfway out). As government agencies and private foundations offered grants for the development of such facilities to local communities, residential treatment began to emerge as the new hope for correctional treatment. The small-group setting characteristic of most residential treatment centers seemed to be ideally suited to use of the group treatment techniques being developed during the 1960s, and new hope emerged for rehabilitative treatment in community settings. The lower cost of placing offenders in community treatment also had an appeal, and the possibilities for job placement or educational opportunities for offenders provided an added dimension. By the early 1970s, populations of adult and juvenile correctional institutions were at all-time lows.[2]

Also in the early 1970s, the concept of "normalization" of the correctional experience for juveniles and adults gained wide acceptance. This idea involves providing those who have been placed under the supervision of the justice system with experiences that approximate as nearly as possible the experiences of normal community life.[3] For those who are not hardcore, dangerous, or severely emotionally disturbed and thus do not require institutionalization, the situation most closely approximating "normal" would obviously be supervision in their own homes or in small groups in community residential treatment. Massachusetts pioneered normalization and deinstitutionalization by closing its juvenile correctional institutions in 1972 and developing a completely community-centered program. This program, developed by Dr. Jerome Miller, included an admission, diagnostic, and classification procedure; detention placement for most juveniles in group homes or with foster parents; group homes used for treatment, with placement of youths according to age, sex, and behavioral characteristics; institutional treatment for dangerous or disturbed juveniles; use of counselors to work with juveniles in aftercare who had been placed in foster homes; and special placements for retarded youths or those with other special problems.[4]

Findings that recidivism rates for those juveniles under the new system did not differ significantly from those for the period when much more extensive institutionalization of juveniles took place[5] caused other states to copy the efforts of Massachusetts on a smaller scale.

Thus, in the mid-1970s, it seemed that those who favored rehabilitation as the goal of corrections finally had found the way to bring it about—community-based treatment for juveniles and adults and use of individual and small-group treatment techniques in a "normalized" atmosphere. Then, unexpectedly, there were sharp increases in violent crimes and crimes against persons, which gave rise to public outrage and demands for "get tough" policies applied to both juveniles and adults. Prisons that had fallen into disuse were reopened, and the downward trend in institutional placements quickly reversed itself.

Now, at the close of the 1980s, institutional populations are at an all time high, and, although community treatment continues to be used, it is often seen as the only alternative to overcrowded jails and prisons rather than as a desirable choice. Those placed in the community are frequently surveyed through electronic monitoring to insure compliance with restrictions on their activities. The first selection in this chapter, "Electronic Monitors," by Annesley K. Schmidt, explores the acceptability, legality, and cost of monitoring programs.

Given the current and likely to continue emphasis on incarceration and its deterrent effects, the prison population will continue to increase, and correctional services will also grow. Privatization of correctional services has been advanced as one way of dealing with this reality.

Privatization in corrections involves the use of the private sector to perform functions and services which formerly were handled by the correctional agencies themselves. Saxton noted four ways in which privatization has occurred in recent years. These include operation or management of prison industries by private firms, private financing of correctional construction, including lease-purchase arrangements, total private sector operation of correctional facilities, or contracting for services such as medical treatment, food preparation or specialized treatment for offenders.[6]

Total institutional privatization is still a new and untested concept. In the 1980s, thirteen private jails and prisons were opened in nine states, with seven of these contracted for by the U.S. Immigration and Naturalization Service. The total capacity of these institutions is less than 1% of the total incarcerated adult population.[7]

In the second selection in this chapter, "Privatization in Corrections," Donald B. Walker traces the development of this trend in the United States. He notes that contracting for medical services and psychological counseling has generally been an integral part of correctional management, and that the major controversies and issues regarding privatization center on the private ownership and operation of correctional facilities. He presents the advantages and disadvantages of privatization in general.

While privatization of institutional operations may increase in the future, it is not likely to lead to a solution to the problems of overcrowding and lack of funds. However, privatization through community based service offerings and residential center management is likely to increase in significance. In the third selection in this chapter, "Privatization in Juvenile Services: Competition Promotes Quality," Loughran shows how the State of Massachusetts, through privatization, was able to decrease its juvenile institution population drastically while increasing the counseling and services offered to juveniles who were brought into the system.

For offenders who are allowed to remain in the community under supervision, it is likely that the use of electronic monitoring devices will expand dramatically. These monitors have been promoted as a means for reducing the cost of supervising non-violent probationers or parolees and providing accurate information on their daily activities. Although use of the monitors has been criticized because their use places the emphasis of correctional activity on controlling the behavior of the offender rather than changing his or her attitudes and values or developing educational or job skills which would produce long range solutions to the offender's problems, their continued and expanded use is likely.

Current Emphases in Correctional Treatment

We noted in Chapter 1 that the pedulum of correctional thinking has swung back to reemphasis on punishment. Treatment is coming to be viewed as a privilege, which an offender may receive, but to which he is not entitled. Because of this trend, less attention is given to the emotional adjustment of offenders and more emphasis is placed on making the offender into a productive member of society. Career planning and guidance counseling—which could include achievement, interest, and aptitude testing; vocational rehabilitation; and enrollment in educational or job-preparation programs—assume top priority in the counseling hierarchy. Types of counseling or treatment aimed at resolving specific problems, such as substance abuse, are also given priority over treatment geared toward improving the offender's emotional well-being. Certain other "practical" types of therapy, such as peer counseling or assertiveness training, which are seen as more direct approaches toward making the offender into a functioning member of society, are also emphasized.

Role of the Correctional Counselor

Although correctional treatment personnel continue to serve many of their functions in institutional and community treatment settings, they have been called upon to assume new roles. One role is that of "client advocate," not in terms of taking an offender's part in struggles against those in authority, but in terms of helping the client locate needed services and finding the means to obtain such services. As Shulman stated:

> . . .the very institutions set up to solve problems became so complex themselves that new problems were generated. Social, medical, and educational systems are difficult to negotiate, even for individuals who are well equipped to deal with them, never mind those with limited education and resources. The services established for people are often so complex that it is difficult for individuals to make use of them.[8]

The treatment counselor, in addition to having training in various treatment techniques, is called upon to act as a "service broker," that is, the person who discovers and links those in need of specific services with the exact agency in the community that can provide those services most efficiently and effectively. Such activity presupposes a great deal of knowledge and well-developed contacts on the treatment counselor's part. The types of services in which the "service broker" must have connections would include psychological testing and treatment, social welfare, vocational rehabilitation, and educational testing and placement. Telling offenders *where* to seek help at the exact time when they are ready or willing to accept it may be the key activity a correctional treatment counselor performs. In all this coordination, the offender's contribution and efforts toward self-help and self-motivated change cannot be overlooked. Now that the emphasis appears to be on "justice," an offender who has received and accepted a just punishment for his or her misdeeds should also be able to expect a just and compassionate response to his efforts to secure treatment or assistance which, although no longer *required* or even regarded as a *right* of an adult offender, is available when sought in a sincere manner.

Notes

1. Clemens Bartollas and Stuart J. Miller, *Correctional Administration* (New York: McGraw-Hill, 1978), 30-2.

2. John P. Conrad, "We Should Never Have Promised a Hospital," *Federal Probation* 39 (1974): 4.

3. Daniel Katkin, Drew Hyman, and John Kramer, *Juvenile Delinquency and the Juvenile Justice System* (North Scituate, Mass.: Duxbury Press, 1976), 458.

4. E. Eugene Miller and M. Robert Montilla, *Corrections in the Community* (Reston, Va.: Reston Publishing, 1977), p. 117.

5. Lloyd E. Ohlin, Robert B. Coates, and Alden D. Miller, "Radical Correctional Reform: A Case Study of the Massachusetts Youth Correctional System," in *Juvenile Correctional Reform in Massachusetts* (Washington, D.C.: U.S. Government Printing Office, 1977), 117.

6. Samuel F. Saxton, "Contracting for Services: Different Facilities, Different Needs," *Corrections Today,* 50 (6) (Oct. 1988): 16-17.

7. U.S. Department of Justice, *Report to the Nation on Crime and Justice,* 2d ed. (Washington, D.C.: Bureau of Justice Statistics, 1988), p. 119.

8. Lawrence Shulman, *The Skills of Helping* (Itasca, Ill.,: F.E. Peacock, 1979), 296.

Electronic Monitors

Annesley K. Schmidt

Electronic monitors are a new telemetry device designed to verify that an offender is at a specified location during specified times. This technological option is stimulating a great deal of interest from jurisdictions considering the approach and from manufacturers entering the market. While the concept of electronic monitoring has been discussed in the literature and small experimental efforts have been undertaken since the sixties, the earliest of the currently operating programs only started in December 1984.[1]

In the short time since that first program began in Palm Beach County, Florida, many jurisdictions have considered whether to develop monitoring programs and some have ordered equipment. Programs have been established in locations as diverse as Kenton County, Kentucky and Clackamus County, Oregon and by organizations as diverse as the Administrative Office of the Courts in New Jersey and the Utah Department of Corrections.

As the National Institute of Justice (NIJ) has monitored these developments, we have found that the growth of programs has coincided with the entry of manufacturers into this field. The accompanying table provides a list of the manufacturers who are known to us. They have come to our attention through responses to a solicitation in the *Commerce Business Daily* for manufacturers willing to participate in the NIJ-sponsored equipment testing program at the Law Enforcement Standards Laboratory of the National Bureau of Standards. We also learned of manufacturers when they responded to requests for bids made by jurisdictions seeking to purchase equipment, when they requested information from us, and by word of mouth. The list reflects information current as of the date it was prepared. However, given the rate of development thus far, additional manufacturers may have entered the field before this article is printed.

Reprinted by permission from *Federal Probation,* 50 (2) (June 1986), pp. 56-59.

As shown on the table, there are four basic technologies presently available; two use the telephone at the monitored location and two do not. Each of the technologies reflects a different approach to the problem of monitoring offenders in the community. In fact, even products within the same general technological group have important differences. These differences, and the cost and desirability of particular features, are a small part of the decisions that must be made when establishing a monitoring program.

The technology is so new and the research is, thus far, so limited that there are many questions about monitors of all kinds, on all levels. Some of these questions are: Should equipment be purchased? Can it be used legally? On whom should it be used? Will the community

Electronic Monitoring Equipment

(Purpose: To monitor an offender's presence in a given environment where the offender is required to remain)

Devices that use a telephone at the monitored location		Devices that do not use a telephone	
Continuously signaling	Programmed contact	Continuously signaling	Radio signaling
A miniaturized *transmitter* is strapped to the offender and it broadcasts an encoded signal at regular intervals over a range.	A *computer* is programmed to call the offender during the hours being monitored either randomly or at specifically selected times. It prepares reports on the results of the calls.	A *transmitter* is strapped to the offender which sends out a constant signal.	The *link* is a small transmitter worn by the offender.
A *receiver-dialer*, located in the offender's home, detects signals from the transmitter and reports to a central computer when it stops receiving the signal form the transmitter and when it starts receiving the signal again; it also provides periodic checks.	Strapped on the offender's arm is a *wristlet*, a black plastic module.	A *portable receiver*, in the car of the officer who is monitoring the offender, is tuned to receive the signal from the specific transmitter when the officer drives within one block of the offender's house.	The *locator unit*, placed in the offender's home or other approved location, receives the signal from the link, records it and relays the information by radio signals to the local area monitor.
A central *computer* or *receiver* accepts reports from the receiver-dialer over the telephone lines, compares them with the offender's curfew schedule, and alerts correctional officials to unauthorized absences.	When the computer calls, the wristlet is inserted into a *verifier box* connected to the telephone to verify that the call is being answered by the offender being monitored.	Manufacturer/Distributor: *Cost-Effective Monitoring System.* Dr. Walter W. McMahon, 2207 Grange Circle, Urbana, IL 61801. Telephone Day 217—333-4579 or Evening 217—367-3990.	The *local area monitor* is a microcomputer and information management system. This equipment is placed with the network manager (the leader of a small group of people who supervise the offender and encourage him to succeed). It receives information from the offender and coordinates communications among the network members. Each local network can handle 15 to 25 people.
Manufacturers/Distributors: *CSD Home Escort.* Corrections Systems, Control Data Corporation, 7600 France Avenue, Edina, MN 55435. Telephone 612—921-6835.	Manufacturer/Distributor: *On Guard System.* Digital Products Corporation, 4021 Northeast 5th Terrace, Ft. Lauderdale, FL 33334. Telephone 305—564-0521.		If required, a *central base station* can be added to provide increased security and back-up functions.
Supervisor. CONTRAC. Controlled Activities Corp., 93351 Overseas Highway, Tavernier, FL 33070. Telephone 305—852-9507.	The computer functions similarly to that described above, calling the offender and preparing reports on the results of the call.		Manufacturer/Distributor: *LENS System.* Life Sciences Research Group, 515 Fargo Street, Thousand Oaks, CA 91360. Telephone 805—492-4406.
In-House Arrest System. Correctional Services Inc., P.O. Box 2941, West Palm Beach, FL 33402. Telephone 305—683-7166.	However, *voice verification* technology assures that the telephone is answered by the offender being monitored.		
Contac. Computrac Systems, Inc., 420 East South Temple, Suite 340, Salt Lake City, UT 84111. Telephone 801—531-0500.	Manufacturer/Distributor: *Provotron.* VoxTron Systems Inc., 190 Seguin St., New Braunfels, TX 78130. Telephone 512—629-4807.		
Prisoner Monitoring System. Controlec. Inc., Box 48132. Niles, IL 60648. Telephone 312—966-8435.			
ASC II b.* Advanced Signal Concepts, P.O. Box 1856. Clewiston, FL 33440. Telephone 813—983-2073.			
Home Incarceration Unit* American Security Communications. P.O. Box 5238. Norman, OK 73070. Telephone 405—360-6605.	*This device can transmit to the central unit over either telephone lines or long range wireless repeater system.		Annesley K. Schmidt U.S. Department of Justice National Institute of Justice April 22, 1986.

accept it? Will monitors provide the community with additional protection? The National Institute of Justice, through its Fiscal Year 1986 Solicited Research Programs, is seeking to support experimental projects that will provide some answers to some of these and other important questions. In the meantime, programmatic and technological questions remain.

Programmatic Questions

Monitors, at least in theory, could be used on any number of offender groups. They could be used on sentenced or unsentenced offenders. They could be used before sentencing, immediately after sentencing, or at a later point in the sentence when problems appear. They could be used to monitor house arrest, as an alternative to jail, as part of an intensive supervision program, or in the context of a work release program. All of these program possibilities have been discussed, and most of them are presently operational. However, we do not yet know if monitors are effective in these program applications much less where they are most effective.

We also do not know which offenders should be the focus of the program. There are clearly some offenders that nobody wants in the community, such as those who are violent. These offenders should go to prison. However, there are other offenders who are not so clearly dangerous and are not so obviously candidates for confinement. Can they be punished or deterred by other means? Can they be monitored in the community? Should they be monitored in the community? We do not know.

Whether particular types or groups of offenders can be monitored in a given community will depend, in part, on what that community, its judges, and its elected and political officials consider acceptable and appropriate punishment. For example, in some communities there may be strong pressure to jail drunk drivers; other communities may be satisfied if drunk drivers are required to stay home during their non-working hours with monitors used to assure that they do so.

Another consideration related to who can and should be monitored in the community may depend on the type of equipment selected and the structure of the program in which it is used. Some equipment monitors the offender continually while others do so only intermittently. Some devices send a signal if tampered with and some do not, so that removal of or damage to the equipment is only detected with visual inspection. And, if the equipment indicates that the offender is not where he is supposed to be or that some other problem has occurred, has the program been designed so that there will be an immediate response or does the program staff review these indicators on weekdays during the day? A few present programs have the base computer located in a facility that is staffed 24-hours a day, 7 days a week. They then know immediately that a problem has occurred and can send staff to the offender's house to check and, if necessary, attempt to locate him. In other programs, the print-out is reviewed in the morning, and offenders are contacted to explain abnormalities found the previous night.

Next, how long *will* the offenders be monitored by the equipment? Here again the equipment is too new and the experience too limited to provide an answer. Officials at Pride, Inc. in West Palm Beach, Florida believe that offenders can tolerate the monitors for about 90 to 120 days. After that, they feel, offenders begin to chafe under the restriction. And, how long *should* they be kept on the equipment? This question must be answered in the context of why the program is being operated. The answer would be quite different if the goal is retribution as opposed to fulfilling the requirement of the law. In Palm Beach County, it has been decided that 3 days on the monitor is the equivalent of 1 day in jail to fulfill the required mandatory sentence for a second conviction for driving while intoxicated. For other offenses, the proscribed sentence is a range, and, therefore, the appropriate time on the monitor is not so clear.

Can electronic monitors solve or alleviate prison and jail crowding? The answer to this question is probably "no" for a variety of reasons. First, in addition to issues related to what a community can, will, and should be expected to tolerate, it should be reiterated that monitors are technological devices potentially useful in a variety of program contexts. The population selected as the focus of monitoring programs may or may not be one that might otherwise be sent to jail or prison if monitors were not available. Second, consideration needs to be given to the likely impact on the total problem. In a thousand-man jail, the release of 20 monitored inmates would reduce the population by only 2 percent. One hundred monitored inmates would have to be released before the population would be affected by 10 percent. In a smaller jail, more impact would be achieved by a system with a capacity for monitoring 20 inmates, the typical size of the initial equipment purchase being made. In the prison systems of many states with much larger populations, more monitored inmates would have to be released before a significant reduction in population could occur. Furthermore, the cost of a monitoring program cannot be directly compared to per diem costs of incarceration. The largest component of per diem costs is staff salaries. Therefore, until the number of released inmates is large enough to affect staffing of the facility, the only savings achieved are in marginal categories such as food.

The inverse to the question about jail crowding is the question of net-widening. Will offenders be sanctioned who otherwise would not be? Will offenders be more severely sanctioned? These issues deserve attention. If offenders are being monitored who would not otherwise have been incarcerated, the cost benefit equation on the use of the equipment is changed. If, on the other hand, offenders are monitored who might otherwise receive probation with little direct supervision, the question becomes "Is the community being better protected?" At present, the answer to that question is also unknown.

Taken together, the questions of reducing prison population and net-widening lead to the more basic question: Why is a monitoring program being established? Any jurisdiction establishing a program should be able to answer this. Clearly here are a wide variety of possible reasons. Reduction of prison or jail population is only one. Net-widening is a possibility but is more likely an unintended byproduct. Another possible answer is to better protect citizens from those offenders already in the community on some form of release. If the question cannot be answered, then the situation is equipment in search of a program, perhaps the most inappropriate way for program development to proceed.

Whatever the rationale for the monitoring program, another issue that must be considered is the legality of the use of monitors, the subject of another article in this issue. However, it should be noted that there are no known test cases. Furthermore, the question of legality obviously would differ in each jurisdiction depending on statute and appellate decisions.

Another question is: "How much will it cost?" The answer, of course, depends on the type of equipment, the number of units, and whether the equipment is purchased or leased. In addition, there may be telephone charges and personnel costs. The In-House Arrest Work Release Program of the Sheriff's Stockade in Palm Beach County Florida charges participants in the voluntary program $9 per day.[2] Within the first 14 months of program operation, the program's investment in equipment had been returned by offender fees. However, if the initial amount invested is more or less, if fees are charged at a lower or higher rate or not at all, or if the equipment is in use a greater or lesser proportion of the time, then the pay-back period will change.

Existing programs using monitors in the community function as part of the criminal justice system. Therefore, they require the cooperation of the courts and probation and parole, at a minimum. Additionally, many times, they also may involve the sheriff, other law enforcement agencies, and others. As with any multi-agency effort, the lines of responsibility must be clear and the cooperation between them developed. For example, if the results of the monitoring are to be reviewed around the clock, then the base is optimally located where 24-hour staffing is already present. This facility might be a jail operated by the sheriff. The program, on the other hand, is being operated by the probation office. In this case, the division of responsibilities and expectations should be specified, preferably in writing.

Technological Questions

The questions above can be viewed at a theoretical, philosophical, or program planning level. However, there are also questions or potential problems that should be considered related to the functioning of the equipment itself. These questions emanate from the preliminary results of a study conducted at the Law Enforcement Standards Laboratory of the National Bureau of Standards supported by the National Institute of Justice. Information also has been gained from the experience of some of the monitoring programs. It should be noted that the comments are preliminary and often reflect results of testing of what is now the *previous* generation of equipment, since the technology itself is developing so rapidly.

One problem found was telephone line compatibility. Telephone lines carry electric current, and the characteristics of the current can vary with different telephone systems. Additionally, some telephone exchanges use very modern switching equipment and can handle pulses such as those from touchtone phones. Others use older equipment that may have trouble handling the electronic signals transmitted by some of the monitoring systems. Whether this is a problem can only be determined specifically through a test of the local system and local exchanges and/or consultation with the local telephone company.

Another problem that appears remediable and has been addressed by some manufacturers is the effects of weather conditions. During wind storms and thunderstorms, both electric lines and telephone lines are whipped around and may come into contact with other lines. This may lead to arcing of the power and power surges. In the same way that most users of home computers have surge protectors on the incoming power lines, these monitoring devices may have surge protectors placed on the incoming electrical and telephone lines. It appears that most manufacturers have installed surge protectors on their current equipment. In addition, uninterruptable power supplies are also provided by some manufacturers to guarantee power to the system even during power outages.

Many devices use radio frequency signals for communication between components of the system. In some locations, radio landing beacons from airports and radio station broadcasts can interfere with the functioning of the device. Whether this is a problem is dependent on the other radio transmissions in the area where the equipment is being used and the radio frequency that the device uses.

Another potential problem noted is the effect of iron and steel which may block signal transmission or create an electromagnetic field. This can occur in steel trailers or in stucco houses. It can also occur in houses which have large appliances such as refrigerators and cast iron bathroom fixtures. In some places, the problems can often be dealt with by moving the receiving equipment. In other settings, it may limit the offender's mobility to less than had been expected. At least one manufacturer provides repeater stations within the house to forward and amplify the signal.

These are some of the technological problems that have come to light and many of them have been solved. In other cases, ways to avoid them and minimize their effects have been noted. It is not surprising that they have developed, given the newness of the technologies. It would also not be surprising if additional problems come to light as broader experience with these devices is gained. It seems reasonable to assume that manufacturers will seek to solve any future problems as they have in the past.

In summary, monitors are new technological devices that offer exciting possibilities for controlling offenders in the community. However, there are still many unknowns, many issues which should be considered by those establishing programs and many questions yet to be asked and answered.

Notes

1. Ralph K. Switzgebel, "Electronic Alternatives to Imprisonment," *Lex et Scientia,* 5 (3), July-September 1968, 99-104.

Daniel Ford and A. K. Schmidt, "Electronically Monitored Home Confinement" *NIJ Reports,* SNI 194, November 1985, 2-6.

2. Lt. Eugene D. Garcia, personal communication and "In-House Arrest work Release Program," report of the Sheriff's Stockade, Palm Beach County, Florida, February 15, 1986. 6 pp.

Privatization in Corrections

Donald B. Walker

Proposals to increase private sector involvement in the delivery of services in the correctional field is a topic creating considerable controversy among correctional professionals. As noted by Levinson, "Correctional agencies have shown an increasing interest in the use of the private sector as a service provider" (Levinson, 1984:42). However, the reliance on the private sector or "the privatization of corrections" as this process has come to be labelled presents different strengths and weaknesses depending on the definition of the concept.

In its broader sense, *privatization* involves "turning to the private sector for new ideas and possibly untapped expertise" (Travis, et al., 1985:11). In a narrower sense it is used to mean "a process where government relies on private corporations to construct and manage prisons and jails for an agreed fee" (Allen and Simonsen, 1986:479). Obviously, the private sector has been providing resources for both adult and juvenile corrections for several decades.

Examples of this type of involvement range from foster care of adjudicated delinquents to the private operation of food services in adult correctional facilities. On the other hand, contracting with the private sector for the construction and operation of primary facilities is a relatively recent development. While the use of the private sector for the provision of selective services is not without its problems, it is the suggestion made by some correctional professionals that government turn to private enterprise for institutional operation which had created the most controversy.

The Problem: The recommendation that corrections should become more closely dependent on private enterprise is a consequence of a number of factors effecting contemporary corrections. First, the shift in correctional philosophy from the "medical model of individualized treatment" to the "just desserts model of equality of punishment" has produced higher rates of commitment coupled with longer institutional sentences.

Second, the overall conservative political climate has resulted in calls for the harsher treatment of offenders. The combined consequences of these factors has been a tremendous increase in the demand for prison and jail space coupled with escalating costs for services. For example, in 1982, the Ohio General Assembly authorized the expenditure of $600 million for new prison construction. Since that time, the state has constructed 14 new prisons adding 9,000 additional bed spaces to the prison system. Despite this increase in capacity, the system is 5,800 inmates over capacity. Even though new construction will continue, the gap between capacity and actual inmate population is projected to remain at the 5,800 figure at least through the mid-1990s. Unfortunately, Ohio is not unique as most states continue to experience serious problems of overcrowding despite ambitious prison construction programs.

A third factor, increasing reluctance of the taxpayer to pay for the increased need for correctional services has created a serious dilemma for government officials—how to support an increasing correctional clientele with dwindling public resources. Finally, one might argue that the overall political climate in recent years which has favored private enterprise generally makes the private sector a logical arena for hard pressed government officials to seek out as a resource for the solution to their problems. In short, "where demand for a service outstrips supply and where prices seem unreasonably high, conditions are ripe for competition and for the emergence of new sources of supply" (Logan and Rausch, 1985:303).

Private Enterprise and Corrections: As noted previously, private sector involvement in the correctional field is not a new phenomena. Even the private control of correctional facilities has its traditional counterpart in the private operation of early jails which were operated by publicly appointed jailers on a fee for service basis. "The managers of early detention facilities charged their inmates for food and clothing, provided substandard service, and were all too often open to bribery and graft" (Travis, et al., 1985:12). Private enterprise and prison industry also has its historical antecedents in the convict lease system, Southern chain gangs, and the contract labor system. For a partial understanding of the heated debate created by the current call for increasing *privatization*, one need only be reminded that correctional reforms which led to placing institutional corrections wholly within the public sector rested in part on the appalling conditions and the corruption created by these early examples of private enterprise.

Both adult and juvenile corrections have historically and are currently contracting with the private sector for the provision of services. Examples of these services include medical, mental health, and food services for both adults and juveniles; private foster care and privately operated non-profit institutions such as Boystown, George Jr. Republic, and Boys Village for juveniles; and community halfway houses and work release programs for adult offenders. According to a recently completed study (Camp and Camp, 1984), on the average states have 82 contracts for services with the private sector and spend approximately $200 million annually for contracted services (Levinson, 1984:42). Privately run facilities for juveniles do operate in Florida and Pennsylvania while the Federal government has private contracts for the operation of facilities for illegal aliens in Texas, California, Arizona and Colorado.

Contracting for Service: Reliance on the private sector to provide goods or resources for correctional clientele rests on two basic assumptions. First, that these resources already exist outside of the correctional field and secondly, that contacting for these resources is more economical and advantageous than is duplicating the services and providing them by correctional agencies. As Dell'Apa, et al., point out:

> Services needed by the offender to *make it* in society are available in the community service network rather than in the criminal justice system.
>
> (Dell'Apa, et al., 1976:38)

Further, "to be sure, there is ample evidence that certain government services can be provided in a more effective and efficient fashion by private companies" (Travis, et al., 1985:11).

One might analyze service brokerage into three levels of service delivery: community field service, community residential service, and institutional service. The first type refers to those services which might be provided totally within the community by already existing private agencies. In this instance, correctional clientele are referred to private agencies for mental health, job training, substance abuse counseling or educational services. The referring agency (e.g., adult probation department, juvenile court, state parole agency or state department of corrections) enters into a contractual arrangement with the private service provider to accept a certain number of referrals per contract term and to provide specified services. The clients in this type of arrangement would be primarily adult and juvenile probationers and parolees. Community residential services would involve contracting with private corporations for the complete operation of a residential facility for correctional clientele. Examples of this type of *privatization* would include the operation of halfway houses, group homes, pre-release centers, or jails within the community. Finally, contracting for institutional services is something quite different. *Privatization* in this sense means the complete operation of a correctional facility by a private corporation. In this approach, the total responsibility for care and custody of inmates on a long-term basis would be in the hands of a private corporation whose primary goal would be the profit motive. It is this latter proposal which has created the most heated controversy in contemporary corrections. As Mullen notes "Few proposals in the field of corrections have stimulated as sharply divided opinions as the prospect of contracting with the private sector for the management of prison and jail facilities" (Mullen, 1984:1). The reliance on the private sector for the provision of resources at any level presents both advantages and disadvantages for correctional professionals. The remainder of the paper will focus on these issues in each of the three forms of *privatization* previously proposed.

Community Field Service: The provision of specific services to correctional agencies on a contracted for basis is the form of *privatization* which has the longest history, is the most widespread, and which causes the least concern. The agencies responding to the Camp survey referred to previously reported an average of 63 contracts per agency. Typically, vendors provide health care, mental health service, counseling, or educational programs on a fee per client basis.

There are a number of advantages cited in this approach. First, is cost-effectiveness. Already existing agencies with specialized personnel whose total operation is designed to provide a specific service (e.g., health care provider, psychiatric clinic) can provide this service at a lower cost than can a public agency which must necessarily hire its own specialized personnel. A second advantage is the provision of specialized services. Typically, entry level positions in community corrections are staffed by persons having only a baccalaureate degree. As a consequence, they are not prepared by either experience or education to provide more specialized services required by clients. Further, the typical approach to service delivery is casework in which the caseworker attempts to be all things to his/her clients. Allen, et al., describes this method as follows:

> Casework is so extensively used in probation and parole supervision that it is considered the "norm" as a service provision strategy. It basically follows the medical model of corrections in which the

supervising officer, through a one-to-one relationship, diagnoses the offender, formulates a treatment strategy, implements that strategy, and, finally, evaluates the offender in light of the treatment.

(Allen, et al., 1985:174).

Given the educational level of most correctional caseworkers, the heavy caseloads, and limited resources, service delivery to clients is usually of the most elementary variety. Dell'Apa, et al., comment:

> . . . corrections programs insisting upon therapeutic intervention generally hire staff having a bachelor's degree or less . . . The bachelor level of study, however, is a long way from the training required of a "qualified therapist."

(Dell'Apa, et al., 1976:37).

The utilization of community resources through contracting with the private sector presents a very different service delivery strategy— brokerage. Allen, et al., point out that:

> almost diametrically opposed to the casework approach is the brokerage approach, in which the supervising officer is not concerned primarily with understanding or changing the behavior of the offender, but rather with assessing the concrete needs of the individual and arranging for the probation or parolee to receive services that directly address those needs.

(Allen, et al., 1985:175).

The brokerage approach, therefore, has the advantage of providing the correctional client with specialized services while at the same time making use of the skills which entry level practitioners have or can develop within a shorter period of time. The brokerage approach also has the advantage of more efficient delivery of services. Within the brokerage approach, the supervising officer becomes a manager of existing resources, assessing the needs of offenders and then arranging appropriate referrals for services from contracted agencies.

For example, the Summit County Juvenile Court maintains a contract with Phoenix Program which is an alternative school program for students who have had serious behavior problems in the Akron City schools. To illustrate the brokerage approach, assume that a youngster is referred to the Juvenile Court on a delinquency charge. Following a finding of delinquency, the youngster is placed on probation. At some point during the period of probation, the youngster is expelled from the Akron City schools for school misconduct. In a situation such as this the supervising officer would assess the needs of the youngster to continue his/her education and the ability of the youth to benefit from an alternative school program such as Phoenix. If both conditions were positive, i.e., the child must continue schooling and could benefit from Phoenix Program, then the supervising officer would contact Phoenix Program and make arrangements for the youngster to be enrolled.

On their part, Phoenix Program has contracted with the Summit County Juvenile Court to provide an 18-week program consisting of educational, vocational, and counseling components including remedial reading and math skills to a certain number of probationers at a cost per student basis. If the court has not exceeded the yearly quota of students, (Phoenix Program has similar contracts with other agencies—most notably Department of Youth Services), the student would be accepted. The court would be billed on a per diem basis for each day the student attended to a maximum of 18 weeks. The child would continue to live at home, be under the supervision of the probation officer, and attend Phoenix Program as an alternative to the regular school system. If the student successfully completes the program, he/she is then eligible to re-enroll in the Akron City School system.

Even though this form of *privatization* is the least controversial, it is not entirely without its problems. Three general areas of concern can be identified: contract performance, employee relations, and cost-benefit. The provision of services under the contract implies obligations on the part of both parties—the referring agency and the service provider. Since the referring agency is ultimately responsible for the quality of service provided to the client, the agency must develop plans for monitoring and evaluating the service. Prior to this phase, the obligations of each party must be carefully outlined in the contract and some agreed upon definition of quality must be developed. The formulation of a clear and well-defined contract coupled with a sound plan for monitoring and evaluating the vendor is no easy task.

Making the plans operational may be even more difficult. Presumably, the tasks of monitoring and evaluating the services provided to the correctional clientele will fall on the personnel of the correctional agency. If the original assumption is correct, that these personnel are not equipped by education or training to provide specialized services, are they any better prepared to evaluate the quality of services provided by others? Further, one must assume that these personnel will continue to have some responsibility for monitoring the correctional clients even though referrals will have been made to outside vendors for the provision of specific services. In short, brokerage seems to add an additional dimension to the role of the correctional professional—the need to monitor contract performance by private vendors. We have merely substituted the monitoring function for the direct service delivery function. While the quality of provided services *may* be enhanced, this benefit cannot be taken for granted. Given continuing heavy caseloads, will correctional personnel be able to provide more than a perfunctory monitoring of vendor services just as at present the heavy burdens of probation and parole officers too often lead to the perfunctory provision of services? This problem is one of more than academic interest since it relates to the issue of accountability. Who do we hold accountable if a client fails to receive contracted for services and consequently commits further serious criminal acts—the private vendor for failing to provide the service or the public agency for failing to properly monitor the contract?

A second problem that the brokerage approach creates lies in the arena of the professional correctional personnel. Dell'Apa, et al., who strongly favor an expanding brokerage model for community corrections (although not necessarily through private vendors) point out that staff resistance is a significant problem which must be overcome because

> the notion of the probation or parole agent acting as a broker of services was a complete reversal of traditional roles; the idea of a probation or parole officer assuming change agent responsibility in the area of community development was considered a major issue regarding job enlargement.
>
> (Dell'Apa, et al., 1976:40).

In short, the traditional professional role concept of the probation or parole agent is that of a caseworker rather than service broker. At the heart of the caseworker approach is the relationship between the supervising officer and the client. The correctional professional is viewed as the primary change agent in the casework approach. In the brokerage approach, however, the correctional professional becomes a resource manager rather than change agent. One can identify a basic dichotomy in the self-images of community corrections professionals, i.e. a treatment/surveillance role conception. To the extent that the correctional professional identifies his/her role as that of change agent, one would anticipate increased staff resistance to the brokerage model. While those professionals who identify their roles as primarily that of surveillance and enforcement may be less resistant to brokerage, it cannot be assumed that they are more capable of monitoring and evaluating services provided by others. As Dell'Apa, notes:

> Whether the worker's self-image is that of a control agent, advocate, or counselor, the CRMT (Community Resources Management Team) will have to assume an additional role—that of manager of community services.
>
> (Dell'Apa, et al., 1976:41).

From all of this emerges an interesting dilemma, namely, that the professional with a casework self-image may be professionally best prepared to monitor and evaluate brokerage services but will be most resistant to change while the professional with a control agent self-image may be least prepared to evaluate brokered services but most open to change. While staff resistance to a brokerage model continues to be a potential problem, one might argue that as caseloads continue to escalate and resources lag behind, correctional professionals regardless of their self-image will be increasingly open to a shift to a brokerage model. In any event, an agency moving into increased service contracting is likely to face significant staff retraining needs.

These first two problems—contract performance and staff resistance lead to the third problem—cost-benefit analysis. When the need for clearcut contract development, close monitoring of contract performance, and the evaluation of service quality is coupled with staff retraining, it may well be that service delivery cost will be greater not less. Agencies which realize cost savings may in fact do so by eliminating staff and/or engaging in superficial monitoring of service delivery.

Community Residential Service: A second form of private sector involvement is community residential service. Some examples of this type of contracting are pre-release centers, halfway houses and group homes for both adult and juvenile offenders. Contracting for community residential services by correctional agencies also has a long history and is still widely practiced. According to Mullen, twenty-eight states use pre-release, work-release, or halfway house facilities contracted with the private sector. California, Massachusetts, Michigan, New York, Ohio, Texas, and Washington have the most contracts for adult secondary facilities. Contracts with juvenile corrections is even more widely utilized (Mullen, 1984:4). Since this approach to privatization involves secondary placements in non-secure facilities, it has been successful and uncontroversial. The level of service provided is basically custodial rather than treatment oriented.

The principle rational for private contracting of community residential services is cost effectiveness. The argument is that the "free market" provides incentives to reduce costs below that of publicly funded bureaucracies which are then translated into savings for the taxpayer. Support for this contention exists since public corrections agencies generally report that private contracting does result in lower costs. Seventy-four percent of the agencies reporting in the Camp survey did indicate a savings over public cost (Camp and Camp, 1984).

Another advantage which the private sector offers is flexibility.

Flexibility becomes significant at the local level because it implies that private contractors are not constrained by jurisdictional boundaries. A privately operated group home, halfway house, or restitution center could service multiple juvenile or adult courts, again translating into staff savings while still providing community based sentencing alternatives for each of the courts involved.

Even though the history of private involvement in community residential services is generally a positive one, certain problems cannot be overlooked. Correctional agencies must face the problem of monitoring contracts and measuring the quality of services provided. These problems become particularly salient when one is reminded of the difficulties which have plagued the fields of mental health and gerontology following the deinstitutional movement. Scandalous conditions effecting the health and safety of residents in private nursing facilities for the aged and in privately operated group homes for the mentally retarded and mentally ill have been uncovered from coast to coast. These conditions are created by private entrepreneurs seeking to maximize profit by minimizing cost. Although one might argue that mentally ill, mentally retarded, and aged clients are far more vulnerable given their lack of autonomy than is the typical correctional client, the profit motive giving rise to these conditions is still present. Although the risk for poor quality of care in the correctional field may be less, the need for close monitoring of private vendors, especially in juvenile corrections, is still present.

Institutional Service: The provision of total institutional service by private contractors is the most recent form of *privatization*. Since the brokerage of specified community services and the provision of secondary community facilities by the private sector has proven generally successful, the suggestion is now being made by some correctional professionals that the management of secure primary correctional facilities be relegated to the private sector. Although the prospect of better quality institutions at a lower cost is an attractive argument, it is proving to be the most controversial form of *privatization*.

Presently, the market for primary facility management is only in the beginning stages. Illegal aliens are being detained in privately operated facilities under contracts from the Immigration and Naturalization Service in Arizona, California, Colorado, Nevada and Texas. Serious juvenile offenders are also being held in secure facilities by private vendors in California, Florida, and Pennsylvania. In addition, adults are being held in a number of privately operated jail facilities in several states. The nation's only private prison was opened in 1986 in Marion,

Kentucky. This institution is a 300-bed minimum security facility operated by the U.S. Corrections Corporation. Although the Corrections Corporation of America made an unsuccessful bid to take over the entire operation of Tennessee's prison system, further proposals for privately operated facilities at the local level are under consideration. Since interest in further expansion of private contracting is being given serious consideration at all levels—federal, state, and local—a careful examination of the issues is crucial.

Certainly, the cost factor is the primary impetus for further private expansion. Logan and Rausch comment:

> it is the overcrowding problem, and the vast sums of money presumably required for its solution, that have recently and rather suddenly caught the attention of the private sector.
> (Logan and Rausch, 1985:306)

Private entrepreneurs are of the opinion that they can operate prison facilities as effectively as the public sector but with greater efficiency. Increased efficiency means lower cost for the public but still allows a margin of profit for themselves. These same authors, utilizing a number of arguments conclude:

> initial empirical data, reports of correctional administrators, and *a priori* arguments derived from general considerations of public versus private services can all be used to support the proposition that commercial prisons could save taxpayers money.
> (Logan and Rausch, 1985:313).

On the other hand, Travis, et al., call for caution regarding the conclusion that private contracting for private facility operation will necessarily prove cheaper. They point out that the cost-benefit factor will be related to the type of contract utilized:

> a public utilities or "pentagon" model reimbursement where a contractor receives cost plus a profit percentage would not necessarily provide an incentive to contain cost of service.—a per client charge may result in cost-overruns or even bankruptcy should the initial estimate prove wrong.
> (Travis, et al., 1985:14)

Further, the cost analysis is beyond the direct control of the contracting agency. In monitoring cost, the contracting agency is dependent on reports provided by the vendor. Continuing "horror stories" from the Government Accounting Office of widespread abuses in government contracting in other areas of the private sector does not provide a sound basis for assuming that correctional contracting will be free of such abuses. The cost per inmate form of contract raises additional questions to be discussed later.

Another argument which is advanced for private contracting is flexibility. According to *privatization* advocates, flexibility in the private sector provides a number of advantages. First, the private vendor is not bound by bureaucratic "red tape" and hence is able to respond faster to changing demands. Concrete evidence of quick response by private contractors does exist to support this contention. The RCA Corporation set up and began operating the Weaversville Intensive Treatment Unit in Pennsylvania for hard core delinquents in ten days time. A facility under contract with INS for housing illegal aliens was built and operating in seven months. Other contractors claim to be able to place secure facilities "on-line" in six months time (Logan and Rausch, 1985:314).

These examples compare to the estimated three- to five-year time frame within the public sector. Most of the time savings is related to public financing (budget approval, funding appropriations, and bond issues) and site acquisition which is less burdensome for private entrepreneurs. Rapid response is especially attractive in times of severe prison overcrowding and continued population expansion. Mullen notes:

> Most observers would agree that contracting offers public agencies the ability to respond to immediate needs with greater flexibility and speed than is typically possible under government operation.
> (Mullen, 1984:6)

Thus one area of flexibility is rapid response. A second area of flexibility is geographic. Private contractors are not constrained by jurisdictional boundaries hence regional facilities shared by several public agencies become much more feasible. Regionalization and shared facilities is a salient argument at the local level. A third advantage of flexibility is in programming. Program flexibility could provide both experimentation within private facilities and the development of specialized facilities. A private contractor might experiment with new and unique programs within a facility without being forced into long-term commitment to staff and material as public institutions generally would be. Since staff in public institutions are, for the most part, hired under civil service protection or long range contracts, public institutions must proceed slowly in implementing innovative programs which may not prove worthwhile.

On the other hand, since private vendors would presumably hire personnel in the same manner as private corporations, they could more easily institute innovative programs and adapt personnel needs to the success or failure of these programs. The concept of flexibility, therefore, applies to both programming and staffing. Flexibility also provides the opportunity for private vendors to respond to the needs of special offender populations. The development of specialized facilities would then provide alternative placements for current public institutions housing offenders with special needs within a general population. Flexibility in the private sector, presumably, would allow private contractors to expand or contract space in specialized facilities according to market demand. If market demand for specialized housing should decrease, for example, a private facility operated by a private corporation might be more quickly converted to some other use or even closed than could a public facility controlled by a government bureaucracy.

In summary, the element of flexibility in private contracting provides additional features which may prove attractive to governmental units considering moving towards private facility management. Flexibility implies more rapid response to changing population needs, the option for shared facilities through regionalization, experimentation in programming and specialization in facility development to meet the needs of special offender populations.

However, just as the cost-benefit factor contains problems which must be considered, so does the element of flexibility. While rapid response to increasing offender populations means increasing the ability of government units to meet current needs, it also implies the reduction of public facilities and staff which may prove detrimental in the future. As Mullen notes:

> The possible cost may, however, be constraints on the government's ability to change course over the long term. . . . Contracting also means reducing the public sector's own facility management capabilities making it more difficult to revert to public management or limiting the personnel pool available to meet future corrections management needs.
>
> (Mullen, 1984:6)

The same objection could be raised with regard to specialized institutions within the private sector. If public sector staff and institutions are reduced or eliminated in favor of private contracting, what happens if these private facilities for special needs offenders prove unprofitable or if there is a shift in demand for specialized facilities? Should that occur, it may be very costly and time consuming for government units to "get back in business."

Flexibility in programming which might lead to experimentation in innovative correctional approaches is really nothing more than a theoretical possibility. It rests on the assumption that the private sector can attract and retain quality professional staff. At the same time, flexibility implies some degree of employee insecurity thus the two concepts may be incompatible and even self-defeating.

Finally, the idea of regionalization and shared facilities is likely to meet with staff resistance and management disputes over control. At this point, the issue of "turf consciousness" arises. Will local correctional managers relinquish control over budget and staff? Will employees in local public facilities step aside as they see their jobs threatened by private contracting? While cost benefits might be real and efficiency increased, local governments are likely to face serious opposition from staff and management in the form of political manipulation and lobbying. To underscore this issue, the National Sheriff's Association has already gone on record as formally opposing private jail operations. While this opposition may well be based on real concern for inmate welfare, the political element cannot be ignored.

Further Issues and Concerns: Thus far, we have set forth those issues and concerns which seem to arise from the apparent advantages of flexibility and cost benefits of total institutional management of correctional facilities by private entrepreneurs. There are a number of other issues, however, which are more generally related to this concept of *privatization*.

One fundamental issue is that of public responsibility for social defense. We take it for granted that the apprehension and conviction of offenders is a public responsibility, hence, the notion that convicted offenders should be the responsibility of private entrepreneurs motivated by profit seems contradictory and to some, even repugnant. Ultimately, the care, protection, and welfare of convicted offenders remains a public responsibility which cannot be delegated to private vendors. As Travis, et al., notes:

> Social defense is a legitimate concern of government, that the rights of individual offenders must be protected, and that the government is ultimately accountable for crime control, among others, are no less important today.

> (Travis, et al., 1985:12)

Historically, the care of offenders was placed in the private sector with privately operated jails and convict labor. The profit motive produced such abominable conditions and exploitation that public agencies assumed responsibility. The present day movement to "re-privatize" primary facility management appears to assume that modern entrepreneurs are somehow more benevolent and humanistic so that the exploitation of the past will not reoccur. Travis, et al., commenting on this issue note "when we consider privatizing institutional corrections today, the danger is that we may ignore the lessons of history" (Travis, et al., 1985:12).

A second issue of primary facility management is created by the form of contract utilized. If the private vendor enters into a per client charge basis (the most likely contract form), then the profit margin and even the continued operation of the private facility is related to population size. The profit motive may then become a substitute for individual inmate welfare leading to the retention of inmates beyond the point necessary either for their own well-being or public protection. As Travis, et al., point out "the profit motive could serve as an inhibitor to release of inmates and as an incentive to institutionalization" (Travis, et al., 1985:14). Not only does this create a risk for individual inmates but it could have a powerful effect on future correctional philosophy. Widespread development of private corporations dependant on "the prison business" has the potential for the development of a powerful lobby with a heavy stake in maintaining high prison populations, increasing utilization of institutional commitments as opposed to alternative dispositions, and continuing pressures for a conservative correctional philosophy on public officials. Who will ultimately be responsible for determining the release date for convicted offenders?

A third issue surrounds that of authority. In order to enter into contracts for primary facility operation by private vendors, most governmental units will need to pass enabling legislation. The key issue here is the extent to which previously assumed public responsibility can be delegated to the private sector. The delegation of authority to the private vendor involves the welfare of the inmate, the security of other inmates, and ultimately the public safety. Intimately involved in these problems are questions of the quality of medical care, food, housing, individual rights, population management, security, and even the use of deadly force. While the question of the right of public agencies to contract for services from private vendors is certainly clear, the legal obligations and ultimate accountability for the actions of private corporations in managing primary facilities appears to be beyond the authority of government to delegate. In short, do governmental units really wish to be held accountable for the actions of employees over which they have little or no direct control?

Summary and Conclusion: This paper has addressed many of the positive and negative features of the present movement towards increasing the involvement of the private sector in the field of corrections. It was pointed out that corrections has long relied on private vendors to provide specific correctional services and even to provide secondary community care facilities. However, the new meaning given to the concept *privatization* creates additional issues of far-reaching consequences requiring careful deliberation.

The primary impetus for any form of *privatization* still revolves around arguments of cost benefit and efficiency. However, even this approach referred to as community field service is not without problems. Public agencies are still left with the task of clearly defining contractual obligations and then monitoring contract performance. Any concerted effort toward a shift from the traditional casework model toward a more fully developed brokerage model is likely to increase the problems of contract monitoring and, at the same time, to encounter problems of staff resistance.

The continued utilization of community residential services as secondary care facilities also appears assured. However, increased involvement with the private sector brings with it further issues. The need for careful and continued monitoring of the quality of care provided is obvious. As private sector involvement increases, this problem simply becomes larger and more crucial. Additionally, private expansion in community residential services will encounter problems of "turf consciousness" by correctional administrators and staff resistance by public employees.

The expansion of *privatization* to include the provision of primary care facilities by private vendors presents even more critical issues requiring careful thought and deliberation. Philosophically, one might raise serious questions relative to the propriety of delegating the care and control of convicted offenders to profit seeking corporations. Since social defense is considered a fundamental role of government, this objection requires serious debate. On the more practical level, the promises of cost savings and flexibility remain unproven. While privately run institutions may prove cheaper, they may become so only at the expense of the offenders being housed. Profits may be realized only at the sacrifice of decent conditions of incarceration. While the private sector may provide greater flexibility in programming or in institutional specialization, they may create conditions such as loss of skilled personnel or the closing of specialized public facilities which will prove detrimental to the public sector of the corrections field in the long run. Finally, questions regarding accountability for quality care, security, and control must be resolved. Even though the private sector seems to be an easy and attractive solution to current problems of overcrowding and financing when the complexity of issues involved are clearly outlined this form of *privatization* may not prove to be the panacea which it now seems to be for some advocates.

References

Allen, Harry E., Eskridge, Chris W., Latessa, Edward J., and Vito, Gennaro (1985). *Probàtion and Parole in America.* New York: The Free Press

Allen, Harry E. and Simonsen, Clifford E. (1986). *Corrections in America,* 4th. ed. New York: The Macmillan Publishing Co.

Camp, George and Camp, Camille, (1984). *Private Sector Involvement in Prison Services and Operations.* South Salem, New York: National Institute of Corrections.

Dell'Apa, Frank, Adams, W. Tom, Jorgensen, James D., and Sigurdson, Herbert R. (1976). Advocacy, Brokerage, Community: The ABC's of Probation and Parole." *Federal Probation* (December) 37-44.

Levinson, Robert B. (1984). "The Private Sector and Corrections." *Corrections Today* (August) 42-46.

Logan, Charles H. and Rausch, Sharla P. (1985). "Punish and Profit: The Emergence of Private Enterprise Prisons". *Justice Quarterly* 2(3) (September) 303-318.

Mullen, Joan (1984). "Corrections and the Private Sector". *National Institute of Justice Research in Brief* (October) 1-7.

Travis, Lawrence F., Latessa, Edward J. Jr., and Vito, Gennaro F. (1985). "Private Enterprise and Institutional Corrections: A Call for Caution" *Federal Probation* (December) 11-16.

Privatization in Juvenile Services:
Competition Promotes Quality

Edward J. Loughran

The Massachusetts Department of Youth Services (DYS), the state's juvenile correctional agency, is notorious for being the first state agency to close all its large juvenile institutions and attempt a deinstitutionalized approach to reform. DYS Commissioner Jerome Miller took the quantum leap in 1970 when he emptied the Institute of Juvenile Guidance—a fortress-like building that had been opened in 1954 to house young people diagnosed as psychoneurotics, pre-psychotics, sexual deviants, habitual delinquents, custodial problems, and suffering from character disorders.

Encountering virtually no reprisals for this dramatic step, Miller dismantled the remaining "training schools" (as the institutions were called) during the next two years, leaving hundreds of delinquent youths free. The abrupt abandoning of this 125-year-old system of institutionalization signaled reform in the administration of justice for juveniles throughout the United States.

One observer who witnessed the closing of the Lyman School in 1973 described the scene like this:

> Jerome Miller hops off the first of several school buses that have just pulled through the gate. Like a commissar bent on dismantling one of the dreaded symbols of the "ancien régime," Miller strides into the administration building unannounced, determined to create history. "You can have the buildings," he tells the motley collection of political hangers-on who pass for the staff of the school, "but I'm taking the kids."

What followed in Massachusetts was the beginning of a balanced system of juvenile facilities, one in which privatization has played and

Reprinted by permission of the American Correctional Association from *Corrections Today,* 50 (6) (Oct. 1988), pp. 78-87.

continues to play a major role. As soon as the decision was made to replace reform schools with smaller, treatment-oriented programs, the state went in search of professional help from private providers to house and care for the recently liberated youths.

Initially, DYS turned to traditional child welfare agencies, such as the New England Home for Little Wanderers and Catholic Charities, since the majority of the programs needed did not exist prior to closing the institutions.

At that time, existing legislation permitted the department to purchase services and programs from nonprofit agencies. Before long, new alternatives to incarceration sprang up everywhere, albeit in a haphazard and uneven way. Still, they were considered far better than the institutions they had replaced. DYS was open to any ideas that would replace "bricks and mortar" with real people interested in caring for troubled kids.

The RFK Action Corps

The department found such a group in 1969 when it encountered a handful of young professionals who had cut their political teeth in the civil rights and anti-war movements and had labored in the field operations of the short-lived presidential campaign of Robert F. Kennedy. Still grieving over his loss, the group often gathered in the watering holes on historic Beacon Hill to comfort one another and speak of past glories. The sad talk gave way to ideas about how best to memorialize their slain leader.

They transformed their anger and sadness into political action and created a living memorial to their friend and mentor—an organization made up of people who would take care of children in trouble. The nonprofit Robert F. Kennedy Action Corps (RFK) was thus born.

RFK began contracting with various state agencies to care for neglected and abused children in Massachusetts. Today, as it begins its 20th year, the RFK Action Corps runs five DYS secure treatment units and four additional programs for the commonwealth's social service agency. It has more than 300 employees and an operating budget of $5 million.

Around the time that the RFK Action Corps was born, the Community Aftercare Program Inc., (CAP) entered the market. Now called the KEY program, CAP consisted of two brothers, Scott and Bill Wolfe. The Wolfes, one at Harvard, the other at Clark University, formed CAP with a vital idea and Harvard Business School methods to implement it.

Both had volunteered at institutions soon after Jerome Miller became

DYS commissioner. Aware that DYS facilities were soon to be closed, the Wolfes believed they could supervise many of the youths at home and do it more cheaply and effectively than the state. Only juveniles whose crimes were not considered a threat to public safety were allowed to remain at home, albeit under intense supervision.

The concept was simple enough: Hire young college graduates, give them an opportunity to make a difference, and don't overwhelm them with unmanageable caseloads. CAP workers oversaw seven youths at a time, supervising, tutoring, and assisting in job placement. The worker was responsible for making personal contact with each youth and his family at least three times a week, as well as phoning school officials and employers to ensure attendance.

The intensive supervision came to be known as Outreach and Tracking and represents the most successful model of diversity and innovation in Massachusetts' era of deinstitutionalization. Eligible youths are managed in a less restrictive and more productive environment than the training schools. Today, DYA spends $2 million on private agencies to supervise 280 youths in Outreach and Tracking programs.

Decentralization

Shortly before the state institutions closed, DYS decentralized its service-delivery system and created seven (now five) regional offices. This enabled local administrators to work with providers to develop small residential group homes (10-15 beds), foster care, and alternative schools that would care for the youths.

The market response for community-based services produced a vast array of entrepreneurs offering more than 200 kinds of programs. Rather than using the same approach to reform with all youths (as was the case in the training schools), these new private providers offered services tailored to the individual needs of each teenager.

The introduction of the private sector into all aspects of juvenile justice nurtured experimentation. Privatization's survival depended on transforming a movement into a system.

Typically, contracts with new providers were based on trust, and handshakes rather than formal contractual agreements were the order of the day. After deinstitutionalization the emphasis of juvenile justice in Massachusetts shifted from territorial issues to finding the right programs to meet the needs of the kids. Little thought was given to bureaucratic requirements or expectations on either side of the bargaining table. Once a youth entered a vendor's program it wasn't clear who had ultimate decision-making responsibility—the department or the vendor.

Soon, DYS realized that such an informal purchase of service systems involving millions of dollars invited fiscal and programmatic mischief. New programs were springing up overnight, and the department felt pressure to place as many youths as possible in them.

By the mid-70s, DYS managers turned their energies toward the development of uniform contracting procedures and monitoring protocols that would guarantee a reasonable return on their investment. A contract unit was established within DYS' Central Administrative Office. Today, this unit executes each contract under general purchasing guidelines established by the state.

Program monitoring consists of a number of informal reviews at the regional and central office levels. DYS staff from the commissioner to caseworkers frequently visit programs during business and nonbusiness hours. Total access to contracted programs by the department prevents what otherwise might become an isolated and autonomous program. Fiscal oversight, monthly and quarterly reports, and in-depth program reviews are essential to ensuring mutual satisfaction. Periodic audits of private agencies are conducted by the state auditor and the Executive Office of Human Services, the umbrella agency for DYS.

Needs assessments of the youths to be served are conducted annually and determine both the retention of existing programs and the development of new ones. The department routinely disseminates Requests for Proposals (RFP), inviting responses from interested vendors. A contract review committee, composed of a contract officer and field staff, is assembled for each review. Their task is to evaluate written proposals, hear oral presentations, negotiate mutual obligations and cost agreements, and finally to make a recommendation. Contracts are rebid on a three-year basis, subject to the department's annual budget allocation.

Today, DYS allocates 60.7 percent of its $51.6 million annual budget to Purchase of Service programs. Forty-five private agencies account for 70 individual contracts, including secure treatment facilities, group homes, alternative schools, outreach and tracking programs, psychological assessments, and health services.

Eighteen years have passed since DYS pioneered privatization within human services in Massachusetts. In the budget for fiscal year 1988, human service agencies such as the departments of Mental Health, Mental Retardation, Public Health, Correction, Social Services, and Welfare spent $500 million for contracted services.

Privatization Today

Privatization in Massachusetts is characterized by four factors: diversity, flexibilty, cost-effectiveness, and competition.

Diversity. Opening the rehabilitative process to competitive market forces has yielded an abundance of approaches to treating juveniles. Experimentation allowed program models such as Outreach and Tracking, Tracking Plus (a short-term residential backup to Outreach and Tracking), and residential programs to take root and become integral parts of the reintegration process.

The private sector has developed expertise in both outreach and service delivery. Unlike the state bureaucracy, the private provider is better positioned to involve the community as full partners in youth rehabilitation. Their boards of directors—chosen from among business, religious, academic, and political leaders—have a stake in the program's performance.

Flexibility. Tenured staff, complex organizational subsystems, and sheer size made modifying or replacing large institutions a difficult effort. Today, DYS enjoys a high degree of flexibility in meeting both its legal responsibilities and the ever-changing needs of youths in the state's juvenile justice system.

If a provider is not performing up to acceptable standards, the state can serve notice and rebid the contract. In fact, either party can end the contractual arrangement for any reason with appropriate notification.

The problems and needs presented by today's young offenders are substantially different from those presented by delinquents of 20 years ago. Increases in the numbers of juvenile sex offenders, emotionally disturbed delinquents, violent offenders, and drug- and alcohol-dependent youths all require specialized responses. Purchase of service accounts permit the state to redirect funding to new programs rather than trying to alter already existing programs in the state bureaucracy.

Cost-Effectiveness. The programs that have replaced the institutions in Massachusetts are not necessarily less costly than their counterparts elsewhere. It is dangerous to view deinstitutionalization and privatization solely in terms of money spent. Quality programs, whether they exist in institutions or in the community, will be expensive if they are adequately staffed and resourced. However, the move away from large state-operated institutions to small, privately managed programs has produced efficiencies that were not possible when all the youths committed to DYS were sent to five large training schools.

By their nature, institutions create specialized maintenance subsystems in order to remain operational. They become increasingly costly and inefficient because most of the daily business in institutions beomes control and population management.

Today, the department uses a variety of programs that provide appropiate levels of security and programming as determined by the risks and needs presented by the youths in each program.

Competition. For 125 years, Massachusetts committed itself to a single system of intervention with young offenders. This state-operated approach was virtually assured of funding from year to year and had little if any incentive to be creative or innovative. Privatization introduced an essential element. By regularly rebidding contracts, a competitive spirit is maintained that ensures the development of new and varied approaches to combating juvenile crime.

Adolescence is a state of "incompleteness" in the development of a life. Teenagers are still evolving emotionally, sexually, and psychologically. The juvenile court and its separate justice system was created in recognition of a youth's ability to change.

Having abandoned large training schools in favor of a community-based, contract-for-services approach, DYS committed itself to a policy that takes reasonable risks with the majority of young offenders, but yields a greater return. The state-run training schools took a low-risk approach and received equally low returns on their investment.

Experimentation with alternatives to institutions permitted DYS to discover what works best for whom and under what conditions. Today, it continues to take risks because tangible, positive outcomes result. The risks are appropiately managed by having more than 50 private programs to choose from, each with its own charateristics and strengths. Unlike the training school systems, DYS can now opt for another program at any point.

As our experience in community-based care increases and we incorporate new changes to better address the true needs of today's youth, privatization plays a key role in enabling us to combine order and stability with progress and change.